The Emotional Rollercoaster of Language Teaching

PSYCHOLOGY OF LANGUAGE LEARNING AND TEACHING
Series Editors: **Sarah Mercer**, *Universität Graz, Austria* and
Stephen Ryan, *Waseda University, Japan*

This international, interdisciplinary book series explores the exciting, emerging field of Psychology of Language Learning and Teaching. It is a series that aims to bring together works which address a diverse range of psychological constructs from a multitude of empirical and theoretical perspectives, but always with a clear focus on their applications within the domain of language learning and teaching. The field is one that integrates various areas of research that have been traditionally discussed as distinct entities, such as motivation, identity, beliefs, strategies and self-regulation, and it also explores other less familiar concepts for a language education audience, such as emotions, the self and positive psychology approaches. In theoretical terms, the new field represents a dynamic interface between psychology and foreign language education and books in the series draw on work from diverse branches of psychology, while remaining determinedly focused on their pedagogic value. In methodological terms, sociocultural and complexity perspectives have drawn attention to the relationships between individuals and their social worlds, leading to a field now marked by methodological pluralism. In view of this, books encompassing quantitative, qualitative and mixed methods studies are all welcomed.

All books in this series are externally peer-reviewed.

Full details of all the books in this series and of all our other publications can be found on http://www.multilingual-matters.com, or by writing to Multilingual Matters, St Nicholas House, 31-34 High Street, Bristol BS1 2AW, UK.

PSYCHOLOGY OF LANGUAGE LEARNING AND TEACHING: 4

The Emotional Rollercoaster of Language Teaching

Edited by
Christina Gkonou, Jean-Marc Dewaele and Jim King

MULTILINGUAL MATTERS
Bristol • Blue Ridge Summit

DOI https://doi.org/10.21832/GKONOU8335
Library of Congress Cataloging in Publication Data
A catalog record for this book is available from the Library of Congress.
Names: Gkonou, Christina, editor. | Dewaele, Jean-Marc, 1962-editor. | King, Jim, 1974-editor.
Title: The Emotional Rollercoaster of Language Teaching/Edited by Christina Gkonou, Jean-Marc Dewaele and Jim King.
Description: Blue Ridge Summit: Multilingual Matters, 2020. | Series: Psychology of Language Learning and Teaching: 4 | Includes bibliographical references and index. | Summary: 'This book focuses on the emotional complexity of language teaching and how the diverse emotions that teachers experience are shaped and function. The book covers a range of emotion-related topics on both positive and negative emotions, including emotional labour, burnout, emotion regulation, resilience, emotional intelligence and wellbeing' – Provided by publisher.
Identifiers: LCCN 2019056106 (print) | LCCN 2019056107 (ebook) | ISBN 9781788928328 (paperback) | ISBN 9781788928335 (hardback) | ISBN 9781788928342 (pdf) | ISBN 9781788928359 (epub) | ISBN 9781788928366 (kindle edition)
Subjects: LCSH: Language acquisition – Psychological aspects. | Language and languages – Study and teaching – Psychological aspects. | Psycholinguistics.
Classification: LCC P53.7 .E465 2020 (print) | LCC P53.7 (ebook) | DDC 418.0071 – dc23 LC record available at https://lccn.loc.gov/2019056106
LC ebook record available at https://lccn.loc.gov/2019056107
British Library Cataloguing in Publication Data
A catalogue entry for this book is available from the British Library.

ISBN-13: 978-1-78892-833-5 (hbk)
ISBN-13: 978-1-78892-832-8 (pbk)

Multilingual Matters
UK: St Nicholas House, 31-34 High Street, Bristol BS1 2AW, UK.
USA: NBN, Blue Ridge Summit, PA, USA.

Website: www.multilingual-matters.com
Twitter: Multi_Ling_Mat
Facebook: https://www.facebook.com/multilingualmatters
Blog: www.channelviewpublications.wordpress.com

The policy of Multilingual Matters/Channel View Publications is to use papers that are natural, renewable and recyclable products, made from wood grown in sustainable forests. In the manufacturing process of our books, and to further support our policy, preference is given to printers that have FSC and PEFC Chain of Custody certification. The FSC and/or PEFC logos will appear on those books where full certification has been granted to the printer concerned.

Typeset by Riverside Publishing Solutions.

Contents

Tables, Figures and Images

Tables

Figures

Images

Acknowledgments

Our heartfelt thanks go to all the contributors who showed such great enthusiasm to be part of this collection. We would also like to thank the PLLT series editors, Sarah Mercer and Stephen Ryan, for supporting our idea for this book right from the start, the anonymous reviewer whose feedback and suggestions have significantly improved the book, and Kate Maher for compiling the index. A sincere thanks also goes to Multilingual Matters and in particular Laura Longworth, for being a supportive and professional publisher.

Contributors

Kris Acheson (PhD, 2008, Arizona State University) currently serves as Director of Purdue University's Center for Intercultural Learning, Mentorship, Assessment and Research (CILMAR) with a courtesy faculty appointment in the Lamb School of Communication. Previously, she has been a faculty member in Applied Linguistics at Georgia State University, a Fulbright Scholar, and a secondary foreign language teacher, and her publications on intercultural communication and language pedagogy can be found in *The Modern Language Journal*, the *Foreign Language Annals* and *Communication Theory*.

Jane Arnold retired in 2016 as Full Professor of Language Teaching Methodology at the University of Seville, Spain.

Sarah Benesch is Professor Emerita of English, College of Staten Island, the City University of New York. Her earlier work was on critical EAP. More recently she has focused on emotions in English language teaching. Her 2012 book *Considering Emotions in English Language Teaching: Theories and Praxis* explored ways to theorize emotions critically and offered examples of the relationship between emotions and power in ELT classrooms. Her 2017 book *Emotions and English Language Teaching: Exploring Teachers' Emotion Labor* further investigated that relationship by highlighting emotion labour as a tool of collaboration and reform.

Anne Burns is Professor of TESOL at the University of New South Wales, Sydney, Australia, Professor Emerita at Aston University, Birmingham, UK, and Honorary Professor at the University of Sydney and The Education University, Hong Kong. She has published extensively on action research, teacher education and teaching speaking. Publications include *Collaborative Action Research for English Language Teachers* (1999), *The Cambridge Guide to Second Language Teacher Education* (2009, edited with Jack Richards), *Researching Language Teacher Cognition and Practice: International Case Studies* (2012, edited with Roger Barnard), *International Perspectives on Teaching the Four Skills in ELT* (2017, edited with Joseph Siegel) and *The Cambridge Guide to Learning English as a*

Second Language (2018, edited with Jack Richards). She is series editor with Jill Hadfield for the Routledge Research and Resources series, a Senior Academic Consultant to Cengage-National Geographic Learning, and the Academic Adviser (with Diane Larsen-Freeman) for the Oxford University Press Applied Linguistics series. In 2017, Anne was recognised by TESOL International as one of the 50@50 who had 'made significant contributions to the TESOL profession within the past 50 years'.

Peter De Costa (PhD) is Associate Professor in the Department of Linguistics and Languages and the Department of Teacher Education at Michigan State University. His primary areas of research are identity and ideology in SLA. He is the author of *The Power of Identity and Ideology in Language Learning* (2016). He also recently edited *Ethics in Applied Linguistics Research* (2016). His work has appeared in *AILA Review*, *Applied Linguistics Review*, *International Journal of Applied Linguistics*, *Language Learning*, *Language Policy*, *Language Teaching*, *Linguistics and Education*, *Research in the Teaching of English*, *System*, *TESOL Quarterly* and *The Modern Language Journal*. He recently guest edited special journal issues on scalar approaches to language learning and teaching (*Linguistics and Education*, 2016; with Suresh Canagarajah), teacher identity (*The Modern Language Journal*, 2017; with Bonny Norton), study abroad research methodologies (*System*, 2017; with Hima Rawal and Irina Zaykovskaya), World Englishes and second language acquisition (*World Englishes*, 2018; with Kingsley Bolton) and teacher emotions (*Chinese Journal of Applied Linguistics*, 2018; with Wendy Li and Hima Rawal). He is the co-editor of *TESOL Quarterly*.

Jean-Marc Dewaele is Professor of Applied Linguistics and Multilingualism at Birkbeck, University of London. He is a keen teacher, walker, karate-ka and author of *Emotions in Multiple Languages* (2010). He is currently scholarships and awards officer on the Executive Committee of the International Association of the Psychology of Language Learning. He is former president of the International Association of Multilingualism and the European Second Language Association. He was general editor of the *International Journal of Bilingual Education and Bilingualism* and is the new general editor of the *Journal of Multilingual and Multicultural Development* (2019–). He won the Equality and Diversity Research Award from the British Association for Counselling and Psychotherapy (2013) and the Robert Gardner Award for Excellence in Second Language and Bilingualism Research (2016) from the International Association of Language and Social Psychology.

Emily Edwards is Lecturer in Academic and Professional Language and Learning at the University of Technology Sydney. She recently completed her PhD in Education (TESOL) at the University of New South Wales,

Sydney. Her research explores the roles of emotions, agency and identity in language teaching and learning, in particular in the contexts of teacher research and academic language and literacy learning.

Joseph Falout, Associate Professor at Nihon University (Japan), has authored or co-authored over 50 papers and book chapters about language learning psychology. He has received awards for publications and presentations from the Japan Association for Language Teaching (JALT). He edits for JALT's *OnCUE Journal* and *Asian EFL Journal*. Collaborations include creating the theoretical and applied foundations of critical participatory looping, present communities of imagining and ideal classmates. Joseph has taught rhetoric and composition, public speaking and ESL at colleges in the US.

Christina Gkonou is Associate Professor of TESOL and MA TESOL Programme Leader in the Department of Language and Linguistics at the University of Essex, UK. She is also Deputy Director of Education in the same department. She convenes postgraduate modules on teacher education and development, and on psychological aspects surrounding the foreign language learning and teaching experience. She is the co-editor of *New Directions in Language Learning Psychology* and *New Insights into Language Anxiety: Theory, Research and Educational Implications*, and co-author of *MYE: Managing Your Emotions Questionnaire*.

Tammy Gregersen, currently a professor of TESOL at the American University of Sharjah in the United Arab Emirates, received her MA in Education and PhD in Linguistics in Chile, where she also began her academic career. She is co-author, with Peter MacIntyre, of *Capitalizing on Language Learner Individuality* and *Optimizing Language Learners' Nonverbal Communication in the Language Classroom*. She is also a co-editor with Peter and Sarah Mercer of *Positive Psychology in SLA* and *Innovations in Language Teacher Education*. She has published extensively in peer-reviewed journals and contributed several chapters in applied linguistics anthologies on individual differences, teacher education, language teaching methodology and nonverbal communication in language classrooms.

Nicole Hofstadler teaches English, History and History through English at a secondary school in Austria. She also educates future primary and secondary school teachers at the Pädagogische Hochschule Graz, a teacher training college. Her main interests include teacher education, CLIL and teacher subjective well-being.

Simon Humphries is a professor in the Faculty of Foreign Language Studies at Kansai University in Osaka, where he teaches business communication. He holds a PhD from Macquarie University and MSc from Aston

University. His main research interest is the factors influencing students' capacity to speak. His recent publications include 'Silence in Japanese Classrooms: Activities and Factors in Capacities to Speak English' (with N. Akamatsu, T. Tanaka and A. Burns) in *East Asian Perspectives on Silence in English Language Education* (Multilingual Matters, 2020, edited by J. King and S. Harumi).

Maiko Ikeda, PhD, is Professor of Applied Linguistics in the Faculty of Foreign Language Studies, Kansai University, Japan. Her main research interests are L2 learner strategies, teacher education and collaborative learning. Her recent publications include 'Situated willingness to communicate in an L2: Interplay of individual characteristics and context' (2018), in *Language Teaching Research* 22 (with T. Yashima & P. MacIntyre).

Hiroyuki Imai is Professor of Applied Linguistics in the Faculty of Foreign Language Studies, Kansai University, Japan. His research interests are EFL speaking skill assessment, lesson studies and teacher education from the perspective of sociocultural theory. His recent publications include 'Comparison of syllable counting ability between second-graders and fifth-graders in elementary school' (2015), in *JASTEC Journal* 34 (co-authored).

Jim King is Programme Director of the MA Applied Linguistics and TESOL courses at the University of Leicester, UK. His research interests centre around situated psychological aspects of foreign language education, with current projects exploring the issues of silence and nonverbal communication in language learning from an affective perspective and the role emotion regulation plays in teachers' professional practice. His books include *Silence in the Second Language Classroom*, *The Dynamic Interplay Between Context and the Language Learner* and *East Asian Perspectives on Silence in English Language Education* (co-edited with Seiko Harumi, Multilingual Matters, 2020).

Achilleas Kostoulas has held academic appointments at the University of Graz (Austria), the University of Manchester (UK) and the Epirus Institute of Technology (Greece). He holds a PhD in Education (TESOL) and an MA TESOL from the University of Manchester. His academic interests encompass multiple aspects of language education, often viewed through a complex systems theory perspective. He is the author of *A Language School as a Complex System* (2018) and editor of the volumes *Challenging Boundaries in Language Education* (2019) and *Language Teacher Psychology* (2018, with Sarah Mercer).

Anita Lämmerer is an English and History teacher and PhD student. She teaches both at secondary and tertiary level, focusing on Content and

Language Integrated Learning (CLIL). Having worked as a research assistant at the University of Graz, she now pursues her PhD on CLIL teacher education. Her research interests include language teacher education, CLIL and teacher psychology.

Wendy Li is a PhD candidate in the Second Language Studies programme at Michigan State University. She joined the programme in fall 2015. Before coming to the United States, she taught English as a foreign language in different educational institutions in China for more than two years. Her research interests include language teacher identity, agency, emotions and language socialization. She recently guest edited a special issue on teacher emotions in the *Chinese Journal of Applied Linguistics* with Dr Peter De Costa and Hima Rawal.

Peter D. MacIntyre is Professor of Psychology at Cape Breton University. His research areas include the psychology of language and communication. He has published books, articles and chapters on language anxiety, willingness to communicate, motivation, positive psychology and other topics, including *Optimizing Language Learners' Nonverbal Behavior* (Multilingual Matters, 2017).

Nicole Macmillan (BA, Honours Psychology, Cape Breton University) is a graduate student at the University of Calgary, studying at the School of Applied Child Psychology. Her current research focuses on the emotional work of teachers, burnout and the connection to a lack of preparedness in the diverse classroom. Aside from educational psychology and burnout literature, Nicole's other research interests include positive psychology, emotion research, anxiety disorder research and eating disorder research, all primarily within child and adolescent populations.

Sarah Mercer is Professor of Foreign Language Teaching at the University of Graz, Austria, where she is Head of ELT Methodology and Deputy Head of the Centre for Teaching and Learning in Arts and Humanities. Her research interests include all aspects of the psychology surrounding the foreign language learning experience. She is the author, co-author and co-editor of several books in this area including *Exploring Psychology for Language Teachers* (Winner of the IH Ben Warren Prize).

Elizabeth R. Miller is Professor of Applied Linguistics in the Department of English at the University of North Carolina at Charlotte, where she is Associate Chair and Director of Undergraduate Programs. Her research has explored issues relating to identity and agency, power relations and language ideologies among adult immigrant learners of English. More recently, it has focused on language teacher identity, agency and emotions. She has a monograph and two co-edited volumes that address the topic of agency in language learning and teaching, all published by Multilingual Matters. Her research can also be found in *Applied Linguistics*, *Modern Language Journal*, *International Journal of Applied Linguistics*, *TESOL Quarterly* and *Language Teaching Research*, among other journals.

Sam Morris is a senior lecturer in the English Language Institute at Kanda University of International Studies (Japan), and a PhD candidate at the University of Leicester (UK). He is interested broadly in the role that emotions play in second language teaching and acquisition, as well as the affective dimension of teacher psychology. His principal focus is on the situated emotion regulation behaviours that teachers employ during their work.

Robert Nelson is Assistant Director of International Admissions at the Savannah College of Art and Design (SCAD). He earned his MA in Applied Linguistics at Georgia State University in 2017. He taught English and French as second languages in collegiate and non-profit settings for five years before joining SCAD, where he now works with students from the Middle East and Africa. His interests include multilingualism and the effects of study abroad on intercultural competencies.

Rebecca L. Oxford earned a BA and MA in Russian (Vanderbilt and Yale Universities) and an MEd and PhD in Educational Psychology (Boston University and the University of North Carolina). Among her interests are emotion theories from different fields, emotion regulation, peak experiences, emotional soul work, and transformative learning. Based on her learning strategies research she received a lifetime achievement award for 'changing the way the world teaches languages'. She taught foreign languages, developmental and counselling psychology, and language teacher education. She has published 14 books and 260 articles and chapters, co-edited three book series, and presented research in 43 countries.

Hima Rawal is a PhD candidate in the Second Language Studies programme at Michigan State University. Her research interests include language teacher professional development, teacher identity/ideologies, teacher/learner beliefs and emotions, study abroad, translanguaging in multilingual classrooms, linguistic landscape and South Asian languages in diaspora settings.

Osamu Takeuchi, PhD, is Professor of Applied Linguistics in the Faculty of Foreign Language Studies, Kansai University, Osaka, Japan. His main research interests are language learner strategies, self-regulated learning and L2 motivation. His recent publications include 'Situating metacognition in context: Importance of others and affect in metacognitive interventions' (2018), in M.C.W. Yip (ed.) *Cognition, Metacognition and Academic Performance: An East Asian Perspective*.

Kyle Talbot is a PhD candidate at the University of Graz in Austria. Before enrolling as a PhD student, he taught English as a Second Language at the University of Iowa in the United States. He is currently acting as communications officer on the Executive Committee of the International Association of the Psychology of Language Learning. His research interests include the psychology of language teaching and learning, language teacher well-being, student engagement, and emotions in second language teaching and learning.

Foreword

Jane Arnold

In *The Emotional Rollercoaster of Language Teaching* we see many reasons why it is necessary to consider affective factors in the language teaching/learning process. However, knowledge about the need to give attention to emotional aspects of learning is not new. Aristotle is credited with the affirmation that 'Educating the mind without educating the heart is no education at all', and Comenius insisted that 'it is the responsibility of the teacher both to create and preserve the pupil's eagerness to learn' (Kelly, 1976: 324). In the last decades of the 20th century the importance of affect was recognized in the field of language learning. Stern (1983: 386) stated that 'the affective component contributes at least as much and often more to language learning than the cognitive skills'. In a research-based book, Benesch (2017) discusses the importance for language teachers and teacher trainers of considering diverse aspects of emotions. Contemporary neuroscience strongly supports these ideas.

A basic understanding of what is meant by affect and of its importance was expressed years ago in Stevick's comment on how in the language learning process, 'Success depends less on materials, techniques and linguistic analyses and more on what goes on inside and between the people in the classroom' (Stevick, 1980: 4). In other words, success depends on individual factors such as motivation, self-esteem, etc. and on the relationships that are established in the classroom. This volume supports the ideas that if students are engaged, they will dedicate more effort to the long and often complex process of learning the language and that a good atmosphere created by the teacher will encourage learners to participate in the interaction necessary to learn to communicate in the language. As speaking in front of others in a language that they do not always control can be somewhat threatening for students, it is essential that the teacher creates conditions that protect students from negative emotional reactions. While teachers benefit from developing good teaching techniques, they also need training in how to deal with the different psychological aspects of classroom language learning.

Student motivation is strongly influenced by teacher motivation. Teachers who are highly motivated will work to find the best ways to teach the language and to relate to their students. When teachers show interest in their students, have empathy with them, reduce their anxiety and contribute to their feeling of confidence, they will have more positive results with their teaching. There is ample evidence that students participate more actively and learn better when they see that their teacher is truly concerned about their learning process and about any problems they have in learning, and when they can observe their teachers' own motivation and active participation in the classroom (Noels, 2001).

Due to the importance of these factors, there should be room in language teacher education for aspects dealing with the psychology of language learning and with topics related to teachers' emotional aspects. This book deals with many of these elements, recognizing teachers' need to be concerned not only with the affective side of students but also with their own emotional state. Pre-service and in-service teacher training should include affective concerns such as reflection, teacher autonomy, active listening, how to establish good relationships with others, etc. Given the frequency of reports on teacher burnout and tension in schools and the fact that at times there are many problems facing language teachers in our classrooms, we can be sure that solutions will not come just from knowing more teaching techniques. Although for other reasons technical knowledge is useful too, it is essential to also explore areas related to personal development and teachers' own emotional reactions to help them be able to handle diverse unexpected problems that may occur in their classes. When teachers develop their emotional intelligence, they will be able to reduce their own and their students' anxiety and to make the learning experience more enjoyable and productive for all concerned.

References

Benesch, S. (2017) *Emotions and English Language Teaching: Exploring Teachers' Emotion Labor.* New York: Routledge Taylor & Francis Group.

Kelly, L.G. (1976) *25 Centuries of Language Teaching*. Rowley, MA: Newbury House.

Noels, K. (2001) Learning Spanish as a second language: Learners' orientations and perceptions of their teachers' communicative style. *Language Learning* 51 (1), 107–144.

Stern, H.H. (1983) *Fundamental Concepts of Language Teaching.* Oxford: Oxford University Press.

Stevick, E. (1980) *Teaching Languages: A Way and Ways.* Rowley, MA: Newbury House.

1 Introduction to the Emotional Rollercoaster of Language Teaching

Christina Gkonou, Jean-Marc Dewaele and Jim King

Language Teacher Emotions and the Focus of This Anthology

Emotions are at the centre of all human behaviour. Sometimes we may feel excited, motivated, energetic and happy, but at times we may also experience frustration, anxiety, fear or sadness. Emotions are not static but can instead fluctuate over time and across settings; and talking about the latter, certain settings are likely to generate more intense emotions than others. Research has shown, for instance, that language classrooms are inherently stressful environments for some people (Horwitz, 2017) but also places where students can feel enjoyment (Dewaele & MacIntyre, 2016). The now large body of research into language learner emotions and in particular language anxiety has highlighted the detrimental effects of high anxiety levels on academic performance and success as well as future attempts to learn foreign languages (Dewaele & Thirtle, 2009; Gkonou *et al.*, 2017). Although second language researchers have long been interested in aspects surrounding language learner anxiety, research into language teacher emotions – and other aspects of language teacher psychology – has started gaining momentum only in the last decade (Mercer & Kostoulas, 2018). This was largely inspired by work in general education, which focused on an exploration of specific emotions among teachers, such as satisfaction or anger, the relationship between student and teacher emotions, and emotions generated in moments of educational reform and change (see e.g. Hargreaves, 2000; Schutz & Zembylas, 2010. These publications have demonstrated that teaching is an emotion-laden process, yet there is still much that we do not fully understand about how teacher emotions function in classrooms, how they influence the practice of teaching and how they shape teacher professional identities.

In this introductory chapter, and before we turn to the focus of this collection, it is important to clarify definitional issues surrounding the construct of 'emotions' and also briefly discuss the main approaches to theorising emotions. We start with emotions versus feelings and the fact that many people use these words interchangeably, to mean the same thing. Emotions and feelings should, however, be seen as two distinct but highly interrelated concepts. Emotions refer to physical manifestations or responses to an event, as opposed to feelings which depict mental associations and reactions to an emotion (Barrett, 2017). In this sense, emotions lead to feelings. The second aspect to which we would like to draw attention concerns how emotions have been previously theorised. Biological approaches to emotions have suggested that emotions are innate, produced in the brain and thus universally shared (see e.g. Ekman, 1993). Such an approach therefore implies that emotions are common among all people and that all people would experience the same emotion in the same way, without considering context-related specificities and individual cultures and histories of each person that are likely to determine how an emotion is experienced. Next, the cognitive approach to emotions assumes that emotions are appraisals and arise when individuals evaluate a situation or an event and its impact on them (Lazarus, 1991; Scherer, 2005). This cognitive approach has largely informed key frameworks on emotion regulation such as Gross's process model of emotion regulation, which proposed that the attention attached to a situation is appraised, thus leading to cognitive change and a subsequent response (Gross, 2014). The third approach is the theory of constructed emotion (Barrett, 2017). In this view emotions are seen as psychological constructions rather than biological entities. Emotions do not have dedicated neural regions or networks in the brain. They also do not have unique fingerprints since individuals can express them in unique ways depending on the situation and on their own previous experiences, which are shaped by the culture in which they grew up. Societies generate emotion category labels and children acquire them through socialisation and observation of the language used around them to identify emotion categories in themselves and in others. The fourth approach, the poststructuralist/discursive approach to emotions, fits seamlessly within the former. It takes into account an individual's history, social identities, cultural contexts and power in understanding and interpreting emotions (see e.g. Benesch, 2017; Zembylas, 2005) and has inspired research into teacher emotions within mainstream education and second language acquisition (SLA).

The present anthology aims at extending our understandings and conceptualisations of language teacher emotions across a range of second language contexts. In these contexts, 'negative' emotions often emerge as a result of unexpected changes, language-related concerns, less supportive leadership, excessive workload, others' and one's own expectations, and dysfunctional interpersonal relationships among members involved in the educational process. Such conditions are most likely to exacerbate stress, uncertainty and dissatisfaction among teachers, thus occasionally leading to burnout and posing a threat to their professional longevity. Nevertheless, the picture is not totally gloomy and language teachers can also experience emotional rewards and associated 'positive' emotions. These are often felt after one has employed emotional self-regulation strategies or consciously undertaken emotional labour, a notion that was originally proposed by Hochschild (1979) in her research with flight attendants. Hochschild explored how the 'feeling rules' of a workplace determine what emotions are appropriate and should be displayed by employees during their interactions with customers. In particular, the focus was on the emotional equanimity that flight attendants were expected to project during these interactions without necessarily expecting the customers to reciprocate. The situation in the classroom is similar as teachers manage and display their emotions in front of students in appropriate ways.

In this anthology, it is not our intention to show how language teachers should feel; nor do we aim to divide emotions into 'positive' and 'negative' and contend that the former should be maximised and the latter minimised. Poststructuralist researchers within SLA have in fact suggested that instead of focusing on what emotions *are*, we should look at what emotions *do* (Ahmed, 2004; Benesch, 2017). Additionally, in avoiding the binary opposition between 'positive' and 'negative' emotions, terms like 'pleasant' and 'painful' have also been proposed as possible adjectives to describe the nature and function of emotions (see e.g. Oxford, 2017). Thus, for the present volume we intended to bring together insights into the complexity and dynamism of language teacher emotions, suggest possible methods for researching emotions and reflect on implications for classroom practice, with a view to investigating the broader experience of emotions as lived by language teachers.

Why an Anthology about Language Teacher Emotions?

A significant body of research into language teacher psychology has focused on issues surrounding language teacher cognition (see e.g. Borg, 2015) and motivation (see e.g. Dörnyei & Kubanyiova, 2014), with research into language teacher emotions remaining disproportionately less prevalent. Although it is worth acknowledging that emotions are interrelated with cognition and motivation, only one bespoke volume on language teacher emotions has been published to date. The edited volume by Martínez Agudo (2018) entitled *Emotions in Second Language Teaching: Theory, Research and Teacher Education* offers a holistic overview of language teacher emotions with a special focus on the teaching of English as a foreign language. Subsequently in early 2019, the *Chinese Journal of Applied Linguistics* also devoted a special issue to the topic of second language teachers' emotions, co-edited by De Costa, Rawal and Li. These publications are indicative of the increased importance attached to language teacher emotions and the recognition that they should form an integral part of academic discussions, teacher education programmes and language pedagogy as a whole.

We see the current collection of chapters as an attempt to provide impetus for further research into language teacher emotions and for a new agenda on what we still need to understand about teacher emotions in order to help teachers themselves as well as their learners. Through the diverse voices of researchers represented in this book, we hope to reach fellow researchers, language teachers, teacher educators, and undergraduate and postgraduate students, and entice them to conduct their own research into this fascinating area of language teacher psychology. We also hope that the post-reading tasks accompanying each chapter will incentivise readers of the book to critically reflect on the content of each chapter and will open up fresh and fruitful discussions on language teacher emotions.

The Organisation of this Anthology[1]

Following this introductory chapter, Chapter 2 by Hofstadler, Talbot, Mercer and Lämmerer concentrates on the professional subjective well-being of secondary school teachers of CLIL in Austria. The authors draw on previous research into content and language integrated learning (CLIL; see Pappa *et al.*, 2019), which has unravelled factors that contribute to and detract from teachers experiencing positive well-being, and use in-depth, semi-structured interviews with teachers to identify positive, negative and ambiguous aspects of teaching CLIL: what they have called the 'thrills' and 'ills' of CLIL. The teacher participants in their study were found to have positive attitudes towards CLIL and confidence in their CLIL teaching skills. They also felt that teaching CLIL contributed significantly to their own continuous professional development. However, they seemed concerned about their workload and issues of compensation, work–life balance and appreciation with regard to the amount of work they were confronted with. Factors such as CLIL teaching materials, their students and contextual support led to both positive and negative well-being. The authors conclude the chapter by highlighting the importance of teacher autonomy in CLIL contexts and calling for more research into how teacher well-being within CLIL settings could be addressed in more meaningful ways, both at a personal and contextual level.

In their 2016 interview-based study into the emotional labour performed by language teachers working in a rural high school in the southern United States, Acheson and her colleagues provided a thoroughly depressing account of poorly supported staff engaged in excessive emotional labour in response to apathetic students not invested in foreign language learning. Over time, such excessive emotional labour can lead to burnout (see Näring *et al.*, 2006) and ultimately teacher attrition. Acheson and Nelson take this research forward, turning towards quantitative methods in Chapter 3 to investigate to what extent a sample of 83 public high school language teachers in the state of Georgia engage in emotional labour and how contextual factors mediate their emotional performances in the workplace. Findings from a modified version of Brotheridge and Lee's (2003) Emotional Labour Scale (ELS) questionnaire seem to suggest that teachers in the study's sample tended to engage in moderate to high levels of emotional labour in their daily professional lives. Interestingly, gender did not seem to play a role in whether the teachers pretended, hid or made an effort to generate particular emotions whilst teaching, with men being just as likely as women to perform emotional labour. The research presented here is food for thought for those interested in teacher well-being and has implications for the amount and type of support afforded to language teachers currently working in Georgia's public school system.

In Chapter 4, Benesch builds upon her previous work considering emotions in English language education from a critical perspective (e.g. Benesch, 2012) by exploring the emotionally charged experiences of teachers who provide feedback on students' written work. In contrast to biological or cognitive theories which locate emotions within the mind or body of the individual, Benesch argues that it is more productive for critically orientated researchers to view emotions as sociocultural constructs mediated by power relationships. Following Ahmed's (2004) ideas about a cultural politics of emotion, she discusses the notion of 'sticky objects' as a tool for theorising about emotions, arguing that social norms of emotion become 'sticky' with affect through repetition. Drawing on data collected from interviews with English language instructors working within the author's own faculty, the chapter illustrates, via instances of interviewees' emotional discourse, the conflicts and dilemmas they experienced when responding to student writing. These conflicts and dilemmas appear to assemble around two main themes: emotion labour associated with a lack of time to provide feedback and uncertainty about the type of feedback to give students. In light of these findings, Benesch discusses the quandary of how to give meaningful feedback to students without spending unreasonable amounts of time on marking and highlights the ongoing debate about whether providing detailed written corrective feedback is in both the student's and the instructor's best interests.

Edwards and Burns use the metaphor of Pandora's box in their chapter (Chapter 5) on the dynamic emotional experiences of five in-service novice and more experienced English language teachers engaged in action research (AR). They propose a sociocultural perspective on the study of language teacher emotions and identity and show how metaphor analysis could be extended to the study of emotions, acknowledging that to date it has been constrained to focused explorations of teacher identities only. Moving from a teacher role to a researcher role requires institutional support from the teacher education programme and the workplace. Insufficient support can cause negative emotional experiences while sufficient support, combined with voluntary participation, can strengthen teacher engagement, solidarity with fellow teacher researchers and a feeling of belonging in institutional, cross-institutional or even global communities of practice. The authors discuss the wide range of emotional experiences of their participants, by showing how participants felt overwhelmed and euphoric during AR, humble or energised at the end of AR and restricted or re-energised after AR. Edwards and Burns conclude that teacher engagement with action research comes with personal, professional and wider institutional benefits.

In the next chapter (Chapter 6), Kostoulas and Lämmerer explore the concepts of resilient adaptation, which helps towards facilitating the management of unpleasant emotional states and expanding the repertoire of emotion regulation strategies for teachers; and teacher resilience, referring to teachers' ability to function effectively in their professional roles despite hurdles and adversities. The authors construct a tentative, complexity-informed model of teacher resilience by drawing on interview data from two pre-service teachers, who have just completed their first assignments on teaching, for the purposes of testing the descriptive utility of the model. The chapter illustrates the participants' inner strengths, the role of external support and environmental determinants in the development of resilience, how resilience can exert both an adaptive and maladaptive influence on the teachers' professional performance and in particular their adjustment to the demands of teaching, and how the so-called negative emotions of teaching, which are likely to be experienced in stressful environments, help practising teachers to grow professionally. The authors stress that adversity could be viewed as a trigger for psychological growth and continuous professional development, and are hopeful that the dynamism of teacher resilience will be taken forward in future projects.

Over the last decade there has been a blossoming of applied linguistics research into the notion of the L2 self, primarily focusing on how the concept relates to language learner motivation. In Chapter 7, Falout extends the construct by exploring how learners' *past selves* relate to emotions and group dynamics within classrooms. Past selves involve thinking back to previous learning and teaching experiences, with the subjective interpretation of past events helping to dynamically construct one's present identity. Falout argues that the complex interplay of personal and shared autobiographical histories of past selves therefore helps to mediate both learners' and teachers' present emotions and behaviours in language learning settings. With memory being plastic and fallible (in-the-moment emotions in particular appear difficult to reliably recollect), Falout presents some innovative ideas for researching past selves, using example studies focusing on strategic comparison, such as interpersonal comparisons of in-class emotions over time and intrapersonal comparisons of the effectiveness of different L2 teaching methods across age groups. The plasticity of memory would suggest that there is a potentially fruitful opportunity for teachers to help learners subjectively manipulate their recall of learning incidents with an emotional element in order to facilitate future learning goals.

In Chapter 8, Gkonou and Miller adopt a multiple case study approach for their empirical investigation of critical incidents mentioned by 13 English language teachers working in tertiary education programmes in the US and the UK. Interviews allowed the authors to collect critical incident stories from their participants, which emerged spontaneously while they were discussing the role of emotions in their past and current teaching. These stories were classified as critical incidents because they referred to a past event, included emotionally charged discourse, indicated a significant turning point for the teachers' practice and identity, and were treated as formative. Participants recounted how they dealt with challenging students and how they learned not to take things personally; they also recollected their constant endeavours to understand their students' emotions and behaviours, and their journey from emotional turmoil to reaping emotional rewards in their workplace. The interviews had an almost therapeutic function, as they allowed teachers to retell the difficult experiences and reflect on them, and even draw lessons for the future on how to deal with difficult students and how to frame students' behaviours and emotions, as well as the teachers' own reactions.

Chapter 9 sees Humphries discuss how changes to the English language curriculum in a Japanese engineering college had emotional consequences for teachers, with one instructor in particular, Daiki (pseudonym), struggling to adapt to the demands of using a new communication-orientated textbook. Drawing data from a series of classroom observations and interviews with Daiki, Humphries paints a vivid picture of a teacher frustrated by his students' poor performances in class and their lack of enthusiasm for learning. Interestingly, whereas a previous study by King (2016) revealed that L2 teachers in a similar context in Japan tended to engage in emotional labour by regulating their in-class emotion displays to hide negative emotions in order to motivate unenthusiastic learners, Daiki was observed to openly display his irritation and feelings of apathy towards his class. Humphries ponders whether a freedom to express true emotions might in part be related to the values teachers hold about communicative versus transmission models of learning and their attitudes to power inequalities within classrooms. Another intriguing feature of the chapter is that it explores how the actual process of research had emotional consequences for both the participant and the researcher. The study provided Daiki with many opportunities for self-reflection and, as a result, he seems to have become increasingly discomforted by his lack of professional development, seeing the research interviews as an opportunity to learn more about English language teaching from a teacher-researcher who, in turn, felt the emotional strain of keeping his distance and remaining neutral in the face of Daiki's pleas for help.

In Chapter 10, Ikeda and her colleagues adopt an emotions perspective to investigate the dynamic nature of foreign language anxiety amongst a group of Japanese teachers of English working in elementary schools. Using a dynamic systems theory (DST) framework which emphasises the interplay between contextual factors and individuals' psychological attributes (see King, 2015), the study details an intervention programme implemented over two terms aimed at alleviating instructors' feelings of anxiety when teaching English and which sought to more generally improve their L2 pedagogical techniques. As policymakers in various countries respond to the rather simplistic notion of 'the younger, the better' when it comes to English language instruction (for a more nuanced discussion of age effects in SLA, see e.g. Pfenninger & Singleton, 2017; Singleton & Pfenninger, 2019), these types of professional development opportunities acknowledging the emotional aspects of L2 teaching are becoming more and more important as non-specialist teachers of English, particularly those working in elementary or primary schools, struggle to teach a language in which they may lack proficiency and have received little training in. Although Ikeda *et al.*, found little change in anxiety levels amongst their participants overall as a group during the course of the intervention, the story at an individual level was quite different for a number of participants, with the dreaded demonstration class (an observed lesson open to other teachers, school administrators and members of local boards of education) proving to be particularly influential in the rollercoaster of teachers' fluctuating anxiety levels.

The next chapter (Chapter 11) by Morris and King reports on an exploratory study on the emotion regulation behaviour of experienced teachers of English as a foreign language working at a Japanese university, adopting Gross's (2015) process model of emotion regulation. The authors combined the feedback of seven in-service teachers in semi-structured interviews about their emotion regulation in the classroom with classroom observations and stimulated recall sessions. The teachers were found to deploy a range of strategies to control their own and their students' emotions, especially the negative ones, in order to attain goals connected with their perceived responsibilities, their teaching and especially their psychological well-being. Teachers also made conscious use of attention deployment, cognitive change and response modulation, thus appreciating the social responsibilities of language teaching and reaching better understandings of emotional honesty and the temporal dimensions of emotional behaviour. Morris and King additionally highlight the importance of individual and surrounding contexts that shape the emotion regulation behaviour of teachers and its efficacy. The authors call for institutions to invest in emotional regulation training for teachers.

In the next chapter (Chapter 12), De Costa, Li and Rawal explore the emotional experiences of teachers working in a less widely investigated educational context, that of Nepal. They highlight the recent shift to English as medium of instruction in Nepalese public schools and the difficulty for English language teachers in adapting linguistically and professionally to this new trend. Using Benesch's (2017) conceptualisation of emotion labour, they navigate through the professional demands and realities faced by their teacher participants by looking at the factors that shape teachers' emotion labour at the macro- (societal) and meso- (school and community) levels. Their findings demonstrate that the mandate to use only English in the classroom (and Nepali in specific teaching contexts) made teachers feel pressure and experience frustration in their teaching. This in turn reduced their sense and exercise of agency, causing teachers to feel powerless and exhausted emotionally, physically and mentally. Emotion labour was also associated with the lack of mentoring for these participants. In light of these findings, De Costa *et al.*, stress the need for English language teacher education programmes to incorporate elements of affective training to better equip teachers for the emotional difficulties encountered in their professional roles.

Gregersen, MacIntyre and Macmillan (Chapter 13) borrow a positive psychology intervention called 'finding silver linings' and examine how this is employed on a daily basis and in a stressful context by their case study participant. The intervention is in fact a cognitive reappraisal strategy, which is intended to mitigate the negative effects of stress. The authors first used established measures to take the 'emotional pulse' of their participant before the start of the actual intervention. During the week-long intervention, the participant also recorded her thoughts about stressors in her daily life in a personal journal. The findings showed that the stressors experienced by the case study participant could only be alleviated temporarily and without leading to a long-lasting change. In their conclusion, Gregersen *et al.*, highlight the interaction between individual and contextual parameters, which influences the efficacy of this intervention. They also recommend some caution moving forward in research on positive psychology interventions within SLA, stressing that the effects of such interventions might be measured or interpreted across different timescales by taking into consideration both positive emotions and cognitive and emotional processes that help to manage stress and enhance teacher well-being.

Oxford goes all poetic in looking into the well of language teachers' emotional well-being in Chapter 14. She finds a kaleidoscope of different highly dynamic and interacting emotions as well as personality traits and strategies to cope with the emotions, including interventions which address teachers' empathy, emotional intelligence, emotion regulation and emotional labour. She presents theoretical frameworks associated with these emotion-related concepts and reflects – in a positive tone – on the paradoxical benefits of difficult emotions and specifically how teachers can gain wisdom from them and how they can let go of emotional pain. She then extracts themes from the stories of five teachers and teacher educators percolating in their own well of positive and negative emotions. Specifically, she discusses emotions in connection with attitudes regarding immigrants, emotions involved in clashes between caring teachers and uncaring administration, and how caring and love can continue throughout one's career. Finally, she argues that the 'compass of emotion', which comprises both pleasant and painful emotions, can be an important catalyst for teacher growth and could thus form part of teacher education and development.

Chapter 15 is the volume's final empirical chapter and comprises Dewaele's correlational study on the relationship between teachers' motivation dimensions of intrinsic motivation, identified regulation, introjected regulation, external regulation and amotivation (Fernet *et al.*, 2008), and age, gender, English as L1/LX, English proficiency, global trait emotional intelligence (Trait EI), well-being, emotionality, self-control and sociability (Petrides & Furnham, 2000, 2001). The study builds on existing work on the link between English language teacher emotions and their self-reported classroom behaviour (Dewaele *et al.*, 2018; Dewaele & Mercer, 2018). Through a sociobiographical questionnaire, the short version of the Trait EI questionnaire (TEIQ-short form; Petrides, 2009) and the English version of the LEXTALE, the author concludes that motivation is linked with a range of psychological, demographic and linguistic variables, and builds psychological and personality profiles of motivated teachers. He also contends that more research, also measuring actual teaching performance, will shed more light onto these relationships.

In the concluding chapter by the editors we begin by reflecting upon the collection's diversity of works in terms of both research contexts and methodologies. After pondering upon the inherent difficulties of investigating teacher emotions effectively, the discussion turns to the significant implications of the book in terms of language teacher training and continuing professional development. Intimately linked to teachers' emotional experiences are teacher stress, burnout and attrition, all of which stubbornly remain worrying problems for the language teaching profession. We put forward a strong argument that an increased focus on developing emotional competence in teachers would not only enhance their own personal psychological well-being, but would also contribute to better classroom practice and, ultimately, improved learning outcomes for students.

Note

(1) All of the book's empirical studies followed standard ethical principles for conducting research with human participants. They were based on voluntary participation, informed consent, confidentiality and participant anonymity.

References

Acheson, K., Taylor, J. and Luna, K. (2016) The burnout spiral: The emotion labor of five rural US foreign language teachers. *The Modern Language Journal* 100 (2), 522–537.

Ahmed, S. (2004) *The Cultural Politics of Emotion*. New York: Routledge.

Barrett, L.F. (2017) *How Emotions Are Made: The Secret Life of the Brain*. New York: Macmillan.

Benesch, S. (2012) *Considering Emotions in Critical English Language Teaching: Theories and Praxis*. London: Routledge.

Benesch, S. (2017) *Emotions and English Language Teaching: Exploring Teachers' Emotion Labor.* New York: Routledge.

Borg, S. (2015) *Teacher Cognition and Language Education: Research and Practice*. London: Bloomsbury.

Brotheridge, C.M. and Lee, R.T. (2003) Development and validation of the emotional labour scale. *Journal of Occupational and Organizational Psychology* 76 (3), 365–379.

Dewaele, J.-M. and Thirtle, H. (2009) Why do some young learners drop foreign languages? A focus on learner-internal variables. *International Journal of Bilingual Education and Bilingualism* 12 (6), 635–649.

Dewaele, J.-M. and MacIntyre, P.D. (2016) Foreign language enjoyment and foreign language classroom anxiety: The right and left feet of the language learner. In T. Gregersen, P.D. MacIntyre and S. Mercer (eds) *Positive Psychology in SLA* (pp. 215–236). Bristol: Multilingual Matters.

Dewaele, J.-M. and Mercer, S. (2018) Variation in ESL/EFL teachers' attitudes towards their students. In S. Mercer and A. Kostoulas (eds) *Language Teacher Psychology* (pp. 178–195). Bristol: Multilingual Matters.

Dewaele, J.-M., Witney, J., Saito, K. and Dewaele, L. (2018) Foreign language enjoyment and anxiety in the FL classroom: The effect of teacher and learner variables. *Language Teaching Research* 22 (6), 676–697.

Dörnyei, Z. and Kubanyiova, M. (2014) *Motivating Learners, Motivating Teachers*. Cambridge: Cambridge University Press.

Ekman, P. (1993) Facial expression and emotion. *American Psychologist* 48 (4), 384–392.

Fernet, C., Senécal, C., Guay, F., Marsh, H. and Dowson, M. (2008) The Work Tasks Motivation Scale for Teachers (WTMST). *Journal of Career Assessment* 16 (2), 256–279.

Gkonou, C., Daubney, M., and Dewaele, J.-M. (eds) (2017) *New Insights into Language Anxiety: Theory, Research and Educational Implications*. Bristol: Multilingual Matters.

Gross, J.J. (ed.) (2014) *Handbook of Emotion Regulation*. New York: The Guildford Press.
Gross, J.J. (2015) Emotion regulation: Current status and future prospects. *Psychological Inquiry* 26 (1), 1–26.
Hargreaves, A. (2000) Mixed emotions: Teachers' perceptions of their interactions with students. *Teaching and Teacher Education* 16 (8), 811–826.
Hochschild, A. (1979) Emotion work, feeling rules, and social structures. *American Journal of Sociology* 85 (3), 551–575.
Horwitz, E.K. (2017) On the misreading of Horwitz, Horwitz, and Cope (1986) and the need to balance anxiety research and the experiences of anxious language learners. In C. Gkonou, J.-M. Dewaele and M. Daubney (eds) *New Insights into Language Anxiety: Theory, Research and Educational Implications* (pp. 31–47). Bristol: Multilingual Matters.
King, J. (ed.) (2015) *The Dynamic Interplay between Context and the Language Learner*. Basingstoke: Palgrave Macmillan.
King, J. (2016) 'It's time, put on the smile, it's time!': The emotional labour of second language teaching within a Japanese university. In C. Gkonou, D. Tatzl and S. Mercer (eds) *New Directions in Language Learning Psychology* (pp. 97–112). Dordrecht: Springer.
Lazarus, R.S. (1991) *Emotion and Adaptation*. Oxford: Oxford University Press.
Martínez Agudo, J. de D. (ed.) (2018) *Emotions in Second Language Teaching*. Cham, Switzerland: Springer International.
Mercer, S. and Kostoulas, A. (eds) (2018) *Language Teacher Psychology*. Bristol: Multilingual Matters.
Näring, G., Briët, M. and Brouwers, A. (2006) Beyond demand–control: Emotional labour and symptoms of burnout in teachers. *Work & Stress* 20 (4), 303–315.
Oxford, R.L. (2017) *Teaching and Researching Language Learning Strategies: Self-Regulation in Context* (2nd edn). New York: Routledge.
Pappa, S., Moate, J., Ruohotie-Lyhty, M. and Eteläpelto, A. (2019) Teacher agency within the Finnish CLIL context: Tensions and resources. *International Journal of Bilingual Education and Bilingualism* 22 (5), 593–613.
Petrides, K.V. (2009) Psychometric properties of the Trait Emotional Intelligence Questionnaire. In C. Stough, D.H. Saklofske and J.D. Parker (eds) *Advances in the Assessment of Emotional Intelligence* (pp. 85–101). New York: Springer.
Petrides, K.V. and Furnham, A. (2000) On the dimensional structure of emotional intelligence. *Personality and Individual Differences* 29 (2), 313–320.
Petrides, K.V. and Furnham, A. (2001) Trait emotional intelligence: Psychometric investigation with reference to established trait taxonomies. *European Journal of Personality* 15 (6), 425–448.
Pfenninger, S.E. and Singleton, D. (2017) *Beyond Age Effects in Instructional L2 Learning: Revisiting the Age Factor*. Bristol: Multilingual Matters.
Scherer, K.R. (2005) What are emotions? And how can they be measured? *Social Science Information* 44 (4), 696–729.
Schutz, P.A. and Zembylas, M. (eds) (2010) *Advances in Teacher Emotion Research: The Impact on Teachers' Lives*. Dordrecht: Springer.
Singleton, D. and Pfenninger, S.E. (2019) Exploring a poorly understood variable: An agenda for classroom research on the age factor. *Language Teaching* 52 (1), 111–127.
Zembylas, M. (2005) *Teaching with Emotion: A Postmodern Enactment*. Greenwich, CT: Information Age Publishing.

2 The Thrills and Ills of Content and Language Integrated Learning

Nicole Hofstadler, Kyle Talbot, Sarah Mercer and Anita Lämmerer

Introduction

In this chapter, we will report on an exploratory, qualitative study investigating the professional subjective well-being (SWB) of secondary school content and language integrated learning (CLIL) teachers in Austria. The aim is to better understand the factors which appear to contribute to CLIL teachers either 'flourishing' or 'floundering' in their professional roles. It has been found that CLIL teachers can suffer from anxiety, low self-efficacy and identity ambiguity (e.g. Aiello *et al.*, 2017; Pappa *et al.*, 2019), all of which can threaten their professional well-being. However, other teachers thrive in the CLIL setting seeing it as an exciting opportunity for growth and positive teacher–learner relationships (Pappa *et al.*, 2019).

We begin the chapter with a discussion of the nature of teacher professional well-being and the factors typically affecting this. We discuss the nature of CLIL teacher psychology, drawing on the literature to outline what we know about the psychology of CLIL teachers specifically and what we still need to understand. Next, we describe the context of this study and report on the nature of CLIL teaching at secondary level in Austria. We then outline our study and discuss the findings. These are organised according to positive, negative and ambiguous aspects of teaching CLIL. In the discussion, we reflect on the implications of the findings for a further programme of research as well as for teacher training at both pre- and in-service levels. We conclude the paper with a set of questions for further research and challenges for policy makers.

Literature Review

Teacher professional well-being

In language education, much focus has been dedicated to concepts relating specifically to language learner psychology such as learner motivation, autonomy, beliefs and identities. While these learner factors certainly have a significant role to play in effective language learning, these same factors in the teacher also play a critical role. Teachers are the central figures in any language classroom. As such, their perceptions, emotions, choices and behaviours will significantly impact the classroom environment in all its complexity including learners and their psychologies (Reyes *et al.*, 2012). Yet, despite the centrality of teachers, comparatively little attention has been dedicated to their psychology and the factors that allow these teachers to thrive in their professional roles and be the best educators they can possibly be (Castle & Buckler, 2009; Mercer & Kostoulas, 2018).

Essentially, teachers teach better when they are happy, motivated and enjoying their work. Their well-being is a core contributory factor to the effectiveness of their teaching and ultimately the achievement of their learners (Barber & Mourshed, 2007; Caprara *et al.*, 2006). Naturally, teacher professional well-being is a worthy research goal in itself (Holmes, 2005), but evidence linking teachers' well-being and the performance of students and overall quality of instruction is a further reason why we should better understand the nature of language teacher well-being (Caprara *et al.*, 2006; Day & Gu, 2009; Hiver, 2017; Sammons *et al.*, 2007).

In this study, we seek to understand how CLIL teachers experience their own subjective well-being (SWB). SWB is comprised of 'levels of pleasant affect, lack of unpleasant affect, and life satisfaction' (Diener, 1994: 103), and includes 'emotional reactions to their events, moods, and judgements they form about their life satisfaction, fulfilment, and satisfaction with domains such as marriage and work' (Diener *et al.*, 2003). More specifically, in this chapter, we will be focusing on the emotional components of SWB, positive affect (PA) and negative affect (NA), henceforth emotional well-being, and the unique role that these factors play in relation to secondary CLIL teachers in Austria in their professional roles. As Larsen and Prizmic (2008: 259) explain, 'most subjective well-being measures correlate highly with the ratio of PA to NA assessed over time, suggesting an emotional core to global well-being'.

While this paper focuses on emotional well-being of CLIL teachers in the professional domain, research suggests that the relationship between happiness at work and at home is reciprocal (Judge & Watanabe, 1993). Spill-over from one domain to the other is common, given that a job is a significant part of one's life, the correlation between job and life satisfaction makes sense – one's job experiences spill over into nonwork life. However, it also seems possible that causality could go the other way – a happy nonwork life spills over into job experiences and evaluations (Judge & Klinger, 2008). With this in mind, we tried to maintain a holistic perspective in our approach to understanding the emotional well-being of our participants in their professional lives.

CLIL teacher psychology – what we know so far

In the last decade, several scholars have examined CLIL-specific aspects and their effect on teachers in order to better understand the specific challenges teachers face when given the dual responsibility of teaching content and language. A key to understanding teachers' actions and behaviour during teaching is to examine their beliefs, attitudes and identities. For example, Hüttner *et al.* (2013) examined the influence of teachers' lay theories on the implementation of CLIL programmes in Austrian secondary education. Their interviews with teachers demonstrate the potential mismatch between teachers' understanding of CLIL and their actual teaching practices. Similarly, McDougald (2015: 31) found that 'there are still many teachers who are not aware of the CLIL approach even though many of them are currently teaching content in English'. In teaching CLIL, teachers often find that they need to spend more time on preparation and are expected to demonstrate proficiency in both content and language. For some teachers, this can lead to feelings of linguistic insecurity, a perceived lack of time, and can challenge an individual's sense of professional integrity (Moate, 2011). Pappa *et al.* (2019: 11) found similar tensions (i.e. around temporal and material resources) that were limiting teacher agency, whereas 'autonomy, openness to change, teacher versatility, and collegial community' were said to support CLIL teacher agency. Doiz *et al.* (2014) investigated possible selves of EMI (English as a medium of instruction) teachers and showed that teaching in a foreign language is perceived as being 'more tiring and frustrating' (Doiz *et al.*, 2014: 154) than teaching in their mother tongue. There is therefore a concern that for some teachers, CLIL can represent a challenge to their professional well-being.

However, CLIL has also been found to have positive effects on teacher psychology. Lorenzo *et al.* (2010) revealed a high degree of motivation and positive attitudes towards CLIL among the teachers in his study and, informally, we were aware of many colleagues who found CLIL to be rewarding and an enrichment of their professional lives. For these reasons, we were keen to understand when CLIL teachers benefited psychologically from the experience and when it was perceived as a burden and a threat to their professional well-being.

CLIL teaching in Austria at secondary level

In the last two decades, CLIL has become a fixed feature in the Austrian educational system. With the implementation of 'Englisch als Arbeitssprache' (EAA, i.e. English as a medium of instruction) for secondary schools in 1992 by the ÖSZ (Austrian Centre for Language Competence), the country has seen a continuous development of the programme, leading to its nationwide integration across all educational sectors in Austria (cf. Wilding *et al.*, 2009).

In general, CLIL in Austria is used as an umbrella term that encompasses a variety of approaches to learning and teaching non-language subjects through a foreign language. The implementation of CLIL in Austria does not follow a uniform pattern and it depends on a number of different factors, such as school type, location, resources, administration and teachers available. A key difference in how or whether it is implemented concerns the school type. In the schools that lead to the school-leaving exam (Matura), a distinction can be made between the BMS schools, which tend to have a specific focus such as business, tourism or engineering, and the AHS schools, which follow a more general, traditional curriculum. In legal terms, the AHS enjoy a high degree of flexibility in how or whether to implement CLIL, whereas HTL schools (a form of BHS) must include a minimum of 72 hours of CLIL teaching per academic year from Year 3 onwards, although they can choose how to distribute hours across teachers and subjects. This has led to many diverse forms of CLIL as well as varying conditions across different schools, meaning that it becomes hard to define clearly what falls under the very broad umbrella of CLIL as enacted in the Austrian secondary school system. In this study, we only worked with AHS teachers, who tend to have a high degree of autonomy in how they interpret and implement CLIL.

Methodology

Interviews

This study reports on the pilot phase of a larger, mixed-methods research project on the well-being of CLIL teachers at the primary, secondary and tertiary levels in Austria. Data were collected through in-depth semi-structured interviews. Interviews were chosen as the medium for data collection due to the experiential and explorative nature of the study. The interviews allowed the researchers to explore the ways in which the teachers described their own professional lives and personal perceptions of it in their own voice (Kvale, 2007). The interviews were semi-structured and utilised primarily open-ended questions which enabled the researchers to explore a series of predefined themes across all participants, while at the same time also allowing for new and often unexpected phenomena to emerge naturally in the flow of the conversation. The interviews were conducted by three members of the research team following an interview protocol and took place between April and May 2017. Each interview lasted approximately 45 minutes (43 minutes to one hour). They generated a corpus of 48,208 words. The interviews were transcribed by the researchers for content analysis attending to silences, laughter and pauses where they conveyed meaning. Normal grammatical errors and speech markers were not transcribed.

Participants

Six secondary school teachers (four female and two male) participated in the study. All the teachers taught at the same type of secondary school (AHS Gymnasium) in the federal state of Styria in Austria. In Austria, teachers teach two subjects. Four participants had subject combinations that included English as a foreign language, while two did not teach any languages and therefore had never received any training as language teachers. Regarding age, the pilot group was diverse, ranging from 27 years to 54 years. Correspondingly, the amount of experience as both general and CLIL teachers varied greatly among participants, stretching between one and a half and 26 years. A summary of the information can be found in the table below (Table 2.1), which includes detailed anonymised data of all pilot participants and assigned pseudonyms.

Ethics

The teachers were contacted by the project team via email. They were given an information sheet and consent form which outlined the nature of the study, what was expected from them and how their data would be used, particularly regarding identity protection. Voice recordings, transcription and notes were created with the explicit permission of all participants. All names, places and other confidential information have been anonymised to protect the identity of the

Table 2.1 Participants' demographic data and CLIL experience

Participant	Gender	Age	Subjects	Teaching Experience (years)	CLIL Teaching Experience (years)	Motivation to teach CLIL
Gerald	Male	33	English, Geography	8	8	Volunteered
Ursula	Female	54	Biology, Chemistry, Physics	25	12	Volunteered
Marta	Female	54	English, Geography, ICT	26	6	Volunteered
Otto	Male	45	Chemistry, Geography	15	½	Volunteered
Magdalena	Female	27	English, Geography	3	1	Volunteered
Mathilda	Female	43	English, Geography	17	10	Volunteered

participants. Participants were given a small gift as a sign of thanks for their time and contribution. They will also receive a copy of this book chapter in due course.

Data collection tools

The data were collected in individual in-depth, semi-structured interviews of approximately one hour, which were scheduled at a time and place of the participants choosing. Participants chose whether to hold the interview predominantly in English or German with occasional instances of code-switching (if initiated by the interviewee). The interviews were based on an interview guide, which comprised two main sections of open-ended questions. The first section focused on personal experiences, beliefs and attitudes in relation to CLIL. The second examined issues related to the teachers' professional well-being, specifically in respect to CLIL but also more generally, including questions such as: 'Has teaching CLIL generally enriched your professional life or weakened it?', 'What aspects of your professional role cause you stress?', 'What do you find rewarding about being a teacher?' and 'What do you find especially motivating in your job?'.

Data analysis

The analysis of the data began with each member of the research team carefully reading through the participant transcripts and creating detailed memos. These were discussed together, and individual vignette profiles were constructed for each participant. The data were then analysed inductively line-by-line using Atlas.ti. The first round was exploratory and consisted of open coding done first by one researcher and then continued with a second researcher and then a third researcher. Multiple rounds of coding and recoding helped narrow and group the codes into manageable core themes and proceeded until a 'saturation' point was reached (Charmaz, 2006). Further creating of memos occurred simultaneously alongside coding to assist with later recall of patterns and trends. This allowed all the researchers to begin to examine specific patterns related to the emotional well-being of the participants specifically as it pertains to their CLIL teaching.

Findings

The thrills of CLIL

Belief in CLIL

CLIL was described positively by all the teachers and this implies they are satisfied with the approach they are engaged in. For example, it was described as '[...] a kind of service for the students' (Mathilda),

'[...] great fun' (Gerald), and 'much more diverse' and 'less strenuous', when compared to traditional language classes (Marta). Further, the teachers were positively convinced of the purpose and meaning in what they did, which appears to contribute positively to their overall well-being and job satisfaction. In terms of CLIL classes specifically, four teachers commented that they feel that CLIL classes are effective for their pupils' language learning. Gerald, for example, said, 'And their English, without studying much English as such, is really remarkable. And that's why I think, yes. It really helps.' Perhaps surprisingly, in one case, CLIL was believed to be better for their pupils' English language learning when contrasted with traditional English language classes. Mathilda explained:

Mathilda: Well I personally think that the English as Arbeitssprache class is definitely a better language class, that's what I can say about the 5 years.

Interviewer: Can you explain why, what is it that makes it so effective or?

Mathilda: Well, the children are quite open-minded I think. And like talking, it makes everything more lively. Well not all of them, but most of them, and they're not afraid you know, that's the point.

Self-confidence

Five teachers in our study, to varying degrees and for different reasons, felt confident about their CLIL teaching. Marta, for example, explained:

> I've become more confident, obviously, but I – if I don't know the English word for something, it happens of course, then I just use the German word and I don't care. And the students don't mind, actually. Sometimes the students help out (laughs). That's what I like about it. So, it's a two-way street, not just a one-way street.

Marta's confidence seemed to be based in part on a lack of language pressure in her classroom. Ursula was also confident in her teaching. She noted, 'I'm good in teaching, you know. Bilingual or not bilingual'. In fact, her language skills did not seem to inhibit her as she cited many years of experience as a teacher as being more important for her in maintaining her confidence than her linguistic skills.

Interestingly, confidence in one's own CLIL teaching ability was also cited by one of the teachers as a prerequisite for success as a CLIL teacher. Gerald noted, 'If you yourself don't feel confident, if you yourself don't like or love the English language, it's not for you'.

As this teacher was very confident in his own English language proficiency and is passionate about the English language, he fulfils two of his own self-generated prerequisites of what he considers necessary to be a successful CLIL teacher, which may in turn enhance his own confidence in his ability to teach CLIL effectively. Mathilda had a similar opinion and believed that only those who love CLIL should do it. When asked about what a person would need to know to be prepared to be a good CLIL teacher, she said, 'they should just do it if they really love it I think. If not, if they have any type of doubts, I think I'd not do that'.

One teacher, Magdalena, though confident as a teacher generally, had somewhat of an uncertain sense of confidence as a CLIL teacher. She explained, 'I'm not sure if I'm doing really, full CLIL. I'm trying but I'm just starting. [...] It's very time consuming yeah. If you really did CLIL the whole, all throughout the whole year'.

Magdalena seems to acknowledge that what she is doing may not be the same as what other teachers might be doing when it comes to CLIL teaching or even what CLIL is, and this uncertainty might have implications for her self-confidence. She did, however, say she enjoyed the fact that she could be more creative in her CLIL classes, which she attributed to a perceived greater freedom compared to regular subjects.

Continual professional development

Another element that affected the emotional well-being of all the CLIL teachers in our study was their perception of CLIL as being a way to grow or develop as a teacher, or as a way to continue learning. This perception of CLIL facilitating growth and change manifested itself in different ways for the teachers. Ursula, for example, was interested in CLIL because it was a new challenge. She stated:

Interviewer: Ok. Why did you want to do it? What appealed to you about it?

Ursula: Um, because, um, this would be a new experience. I'm always searching for new experiences. And, yeah – it was a new *Herausforderung*.

Interviewer: A new challenge...

Ursula: A new challenge, so that was the reason.

She also mentioned the importance for her of continual learning throughout the professional lifespan: 'Never come to the point where you're saying ... I know everything, you know? I think it's good. Also for the kids.'

Mathilda also said that it was important to continue to develop herself professionally, otherwise things would get boring. Magdalena mentioned that even though she was more or less forced to teach CLIL, that she was very pleased because it was challenging and added variety to her teaching:

Magdalena: So I got a contract for another year. And they said I can only stay if I would be willing to teach Geography in English.

Interviewer: [Laughter both]

Magdalena: It's kind of like that.

Interviewer: So you put volunteered but it's kind of like...

Magdalena: Yeah but I was really happy about that because I was always interested in teaching Geography in English because for me it's a bit more challenging and it's something different. It kind of combines my two subjects which I really like. So...

Framing CLIL as a challenge and opportunity for growth for our teacher participants helped the teachers in the study to feel as if they were growing professionally. Not surprisingly, aiming to improve, and then improving, was likely to positively affect the teachers and their emotional well-being.

The ills of CLIL

In contrast to the 'thrills' of teaching CLIL, most of the more prominent 'ills' in our data were not CLIL-specific, but rather concerned negative aspects of being a teacher more generally.

Workload and compensation

Throughout the data, participants talked about the considerable workload that teachers in general and specifically CLIL teachers are confronted with. While teaching itself and the often time-intensive lesson preparation were generally reported as being ambivalent in that they may be both positive and negative contributors to professional well-being (see 'Neither thrill nor ill' section), the amount of correction work as well as the additional administrative duties of Austrian teachers were mentioned as downsides throughout the data. One participant even described the strain of administrative responsibilities by saying that, 'especially in Austria, you feel like a secretary' (Gerald).

With regards to CLIL, the workload was perceived as being even larger by all the participants, especially when first starting as a CLIL teacher. However, primarily, teachers were bothered by their perception that this extra effort was not recognised in any way – not financially or otherwise. For three of the participants this was a notable downside of their professional roles:

Interviewer: Do you get any kind of recognition of any kind in the school for being a CLIL teacher?

Magdalena: Not really. And I think that's also the problem. That we don't have enough resources for that. Because you get paid the same amount of money if you teach in

> Geography in English or in German and of course it's less effort if you teach it in German because you have the book and everything, and of course if you still want to have a good lesson, of course you have to do other stuff than what is written in the book, but still it's less effort because everything is there and ready, yeah.

As the quote above illustrates, two teachers report that they believe Austrian schools lack the funds to compensate for the extra hours invested by CLIL teachers. This is felt to be especially demotivating considering that regular English language lessons systemically count for more 'units of value' and are, de facto, better paid, whereas CLIL subjects – regardless of the effort and workload they entail – are typically categorised according to the equivalent subject taught in German.

Work–life balance

Related to workload, many teachers also expressed difficulty in maintaining a healthy work–life balance due to the fact that they habitually take their work home, both physically and mentally. As one participant put it, 'there is almost no weekend I do not work during the school year' (Marta), which corresponds to the experiences of the majority of respondents. Indeed, with the exception of one teacher, all participants found it hard to establish clear boundaries between their work and private lives, stating that, as a teacher, 'you're never done' (Gerald).

The teachers also noted how difficult it is to leave school behind emotionally and mentally. For example, three of the teachers reported having been involved in situations that not only challenged them professionally but also on a personal level:

> So, that's something I never thought about before, before becoming a teacher, that you really have to cope with serious dramatic situations, like for example a student of mine has lost her mother last May, and it was really very hard for the whole class and for the girl herself and it was, you know ... We are very, we were close when we were talking to each other just the two of us and of course I cannot ... I have to think about that at home as well. I can't. (Mathilda)

As such, teachers may be confronted with unexpected and emotionally straining situations that make it not only hard, but impossible to switch off or walk away. Across our data, respondents expressed an awareness of the role they played in their students' lives, and four of the six teachers we interviewed explicitly stated that they felt responsible for their students' emotional and physical well-being, which naturally adds an additional burden to their professional roles. These strains and demands are likely to affect all teachers, and not just CLIL teachers specifically.

Appreciation

Another emotional low that came up in our data related to feelings generated by the negative image of teachers reflected in the national media, but also expressed within some of the participants' circle of family and friends. Being a teacher encompasses a considerable workload but – unlike in some other professions – a large portion of this workload happens outside the classroom and is, in effect, virtually invisible. This lack of insight and understanding about teachers' lives and responsibilities was a cause of frustration for three of the teachers:

> Appreciation. Yeah. That's – because, I feel the appreciation in my school but I don't feel it outside. The media, even our authority, even our ministry. So that's why I think – we – in our school everybody tries to do a good job and – and then you – you hear things from Mr. Häupl [note: the current Viennese mayor] 'If I was a teacher I'd be finished Tuesday at lunch', so that's – yeah. Obsolete, actually. (Marta)

Three respondents stated that they have at one point or another struggled with the negative perception of teachers in Austria, feeling the constant need to justify what they do. As one of the teachers explained: 'My brother and my sister they are both lawyers [and] they tend to call me to tell me to organise all the Christmas presents, because I have time anyway' (Mathilda).

Neither thrill nor ill

One of the interesting findings in this study is that many of the emotional aspects of being a CLIL teacher cannot easily be categorised as either positive or negative but, in fact, they often incorporate both dimensions. It appears from the data that what could be an 'ill' might also potentially be a 'thrill' and vice versa, depending on the context and perspective.

Material

This phenomenon is especially apparent in our data when it comes to the amount of time CLIL takes up. Across respondents, CLIL is described as generally more time-consuming than non-CLIL due largely to factors related to the collection and/or creation of teaching materials:

> [...] the material, this is [sighs] a lot of work. There is not so much material out there. There is a book in Geography which we don't use, because it's not good enough, and then you have to come up with everything yourself. And then this is a lot of work. A huge amount of work, yes. (Marta)

However, while all participants expressed similar notions to the one above, despite the extra effort, creating material can equally be viewed as being 'a rewarding component or great fun' (Gerald).

In particular, all the teachers reported a sense of accomplishment regarding the materials they have designed themselves. Traditionally, EFL and many content subjects are taught through standardised course books in Austria. The absence of suitable materials for CLIL classes appears to not only drive teachers to be more creative but also enables them to exert more control over the content as well as teaching methods they use:

Gerald: [...] And I have to come up with everything from scratch. I can do it the way I see it meaningful, sensible.

Interviewer: So actually there's sort of a flipside of having to prepare all your own materials, you can really tailor it to your group and what you want to be doing with them.

Gerald: And you can adapt it, change it, right after the lesson you sit down and you just make a note. What didn't work, or it was just too long. And you can do that.

While CLIL is perceived as entailing more work for teachers, especially with regards to lesson preparation and the creation of suitable material, it was also described as a positive, creative process that instils teachers with a sense of accomplishment and pride in their work.

CLIL students

Another ambiguous aspect of CLIL that became apparent in our data concerned the students. Across all interviews, participants expressed the belief that students in CLIL programmes were more academically oriented and generally better students also in terms of work behaviours, regardless of whether they had to go through an official admission process (e.g. an entry exam) or not. As one teacher explained, 'the better students mostly choose this branch because you need to be really focused and study more' (Marta). In fact, one of the teachers we interviewed even named the students in his CLIL classes as the best part of being a CLIL teacher:

Interviewer: So what are the things, because you just referred to teaching CLIL as kind of fun. What are the upsides of CLIL? What are the best parts of being the CLIL teacher?

Gerald: That the focus really shifts. It's not just like any other subject any more. The students are not you know period 6, and students aren't motivated. But now all of a sudden, they pay closer attention. And it's not just subject any more, it's CLIL ... yeah, it's different. Different dynamics. And I really appreciate that. Because for me it's easier in a way that once I'm prepared, and once I've done my homework ... it's easier for me than going in a regular class, and having to deal with, let's say a difficult class, unmotivated students ... So, for me it's easier.

Initially, it appears that students can be categorised as a definite positive feature of teaching CLIL as they are frequently described as more focused, more motivated and generally better academically, compared to students in non-CLIL programmes. However, in the course of our analysis, our data also revealed a number of drawbacks that mark this aspect as an ambiguous contributor to the emotional well-being of CLIL teachers.

Some of the teachers also explained that CLIL students habitually came from higher social backgrounds with more academically involved parents. While this does not necessarily constitute a negative factor, three out of six teachers explained that their CLIL students were more 'complicated' and demanding because of that parental involvement:

> They're also so complicated because they come from families more affluent families, so are also more demanding families, and more this sounds very negative now, more complicated in a way that's just, everything is more complex. They, they negotiate regarding grades and are really used to negotiating here, and so on and so forth. (Gerald)

Another issue reported by two participants is that they have experienced resentment or even anger over the distribution of students in connection to CLIL. As one teacher explained, many non-CLIL teachers seem to hold the view that CLIL students 'are the better students – it's easier for [the teachers] to work with the students' (Gerald). Similarly, another respondent pointed out that he and other CLIL teachers at his school have been 'accused of breeding elite classes' (Otto) by their colleagues. He went on to explain that his colleagues felt that, after losing the better students to the CLIL class, 'all the bad students were allocated to the remaining three classes' (Otto). This perception of a two-tier system through student selection processes (even when self-selected) appears to have created some discord among colleagues.

Contextual support

One of the most notable problems with CLIL seems to be of a structural nature, rooted in the ad hoc approach to implementing CLIL across the Austrian school system. All participants mentioned the lack of administrative support by Austrian school authorities as a drawback to teaching CLIL, covering issues ranging from programme funding, teacher training and legal frameworks, to access to proper resources and regulations concerning testing in the CLIL classroom and in the A-levels:

Gerald: Exactly, so there's no legal framework. The legal framework is that it doesn't exist. So there really is no legal framework that would take CLIL into account [...]

Interviewer: So I mean, if I can be so bold, how does that affect you as a teacher?

Gerald: It's been difficult, definitely. It's been difficult and you're always in this grey area that officially doesn't really exist. On the other hand, your principal wants it, and you yourself think it's a good idea, and it's also great fun. But there is no legal basis.

This lack of a general structure also manifests itself in the way CLIL is defined and practised throughout Austria, resulting in a vast variety of different approaches that differ across the country, across the states and even within schools.

On the other hand, the lack of control through authorities, both institutional and national, was also reported as providing greater autonomy for CLIL teachers by all participants. The loose regulation surrounding CLIL in Austria for these AHS secondary teachers allows them the freedom to interpret and implement the concept according to their own ideas and beliefs, even within the same school. Thus, while these CLIL teachers might often feel neglected by education authorities to some degree, it is also apparent that the absence of a clear structure or even terminological definition of CLIL allows them to have greater flexibility and maybe even experience less pressure in the classroom:

> I think I can be more creative. I feel like you know, I have more room, which might not really be true because even if you only teach English, you can do a lot of stuff. Yeah but it's kind of more fixed what you have to teach in second, third, fourth grade ... grammar wise, and stuff like that. So, I feel like I can be more creative in those lessons. Maybe because also it's not that strict if you finish that topic [...] (Magdalena)

CLIL is perceived by these teachers as somewhat detached from the rules and conventions that usually apply to Austrian classrooms, allowing the teacher to regulate content as well as pace without feeling the pressure of having to comply with the national curriculum.

Discussion

In this study, CLIL teachers were found to report a range of emotions affecting their well-being. There were some, albeit relatively few, aspects which were wholly positive. Interestingly, the negative aspects did not tend to concern CLIL exclusively but rather reflected issues of being a teacher in Austria more generally. Perhaps the most interesting thing to note was that these teachers experienced a complex blend and paradoxical mix of emotions with key aspects of their professional lives eliciting neither straightforwardly positive or negative emotions, but rather being more ambiguous. This is important to consider when discussing teacher emotions, which may often be ambiguous, complex and potentially conflicting (King & Ng, 2018). Any simplistic division into positive and negative is not likely to capture the lived realities and range of teachers' emotional experiences (Benesch, 2018; Day & Gu, 2010).

The second point concerns teacher well-being, which these data also show to be affected by a range of factors within the immediate classroom and the school, as well as beyond in the wider ecology of the education system and national society. As such, we have concluded that it is important to consider teacher well-being as embedded within multi-layered ecologies (see e.g. Young *et al.*, 2002). Well-being is not merely a mental state but is concerned with how the individuals appraise their contexts and experience their roles in their social worlds (Diener *et al.*, 2003). A key issue related to teacher perceptions of their ecologies concerns CLIL teacher autonomy. As all of these teachers worked in contexts in which their teaching was not prescribed or structurally restricted, they had considerable autonomy in how they interpreted and taught CLIL. From their descriptions of their practice, this led to considerable diversity across the teachers in terms of their approaches to CLIL. This study did not examine the effects of these diverse approaches on pupil learning, although that would clearly be an important aspect to investigate. Instead, from a well-being perspective, the high degree of autonomy appeared to contribute positively to teachers feeling satisfied, confident and happy about their professional roles, despite some paradoxical frustration in terms of lack of guidance and support structures. We conclude that the role of teacher autonomy in CLIL contexts could be a key area worthy of further study from both teacher and learner perspectives in respect to practices, effects on learning, and connections to teacher well-being and job satisfaction.

In addition, it is important to note that all of these teachers volunteered to take part in the study and were fundamentally very positively inclined towards CLIL, as can be seen in the 'thrills' section. It was an approach they were all committed to and felt positive about. As such, it can be expected that such teachers would report high well-being in their roles as CLIL teachers. Yet we also know from other research (Doiz & Lasagabaster, 2017), and anecdotally from this study, that there are other CLIL teachers who are forced to teach CLIL, who do not believe in it as an educational approach (Cammarata & Tedick, 2012) and who have grave concerns about their own didactic and linguistic competences in this regard (Moate, 2011). These are the teachers it would be crucial to engage with in order to find out how we can better support them. Unfortunately, as we found out when conducting this study, such teachers tend to be reluctant to meet and discuss their work as CLIL educators and it can be difficult to get them involved in the research.

Conclusion

This study showed that these CLIL teachers experience a variety of emotional highs and lows in relation to their professional roles. While there were some notable thrills as well as ills, the majority of affective factors were more ambiguous than that. These teachers' professional lives were highly complex and their emotional experiences and responses tended to be neither straightforwardly positive or negative. On the whole, they all reported positive well-being which can only properly be understood within the ecologies of their professional as well as personal lives. Teaching has consistently been found to be one of the most stressful careers (Borg, 1990; Johnson *et al.*, 2005; Kieschke & Schaarschmidt, 2008; Kyriacou, 2001; Travers & Cooper, 1993) and it is possible that for some teaching CLIL is even more stressful (Bruton, 2013; Moate, 2011). Yet, as we see with the teachers in this study, many CLIL educators enjoy overall positive well-being in their jobs and feel that there are clear positive benefits of teaching CLIL. More research is now needed to understand how to harness the positive thrills of CLIL effectively in contextually and personally meaningful ways so that *all* CLIL teachers not only survive but thrive in their professional roles (Aiello *et al.*, 2017; Pappa *et al.*, 2019).

Post-Reading Tasks

(1) To what extent do you feel that having a large amount of autonomy when teaching CLIL is a good or a bad thing?
(2) What factors related to your professional roles affect your well-being positively?
(3) What emotional thrills and/or ills do you experience in your professional life and how does this impact your emotional well-being?
(4) To what extent do you feel that CLIL and your work is appreciated and valued by others (school, colleagues, parents, students)?

Acknowledgments

Please note that this research was made possible by a generous grant from the Austrian National Bank (ÖNB; project number 17136) for which we are very grateful.

References

Aiello, J., Di Martino, E. and Di Sabato, B. (2017) Preparing teachers in Italy for CLIL: Reflections on assessment, language proficiency and willingness to communicate. *International Journal of Bilingual Education and Bilingualism* 20 (1), 69–83.

Barber, M. and Mourshed, M. (2007) *How the World's Best-Performing School Systems Come Out on Top*. London: McKinsey and Company.

Benesch, S. (2018) Emotions as agency: Feeling rules, emotion labor, and English language teachers' decision-making. *System* 79, 60–69.

Borg, M.G. (1990) Occupational stress in British educational settings: A review. *Educational Psychology* 10 (2), 103–126.
Bruton, A. (2013) CLIL: Some of the reasons why ... and why not. *System* 41 (3), 587–597.
Cammarata, L. and Tedick, D.J. (2012) Balancing content and language in instruction: The experience of immersion teachers. *The Modern Language Journal* 96 (2), 251–269.
Caprara, G.V., Barbaranelli, C., Steca, P. and Malone, P.S. (2006) Teachers' self-efficacy beliefs as determinants of job satisfaction and students' academic achievement: A study at the school level. *Journal of School Psychology* 44 (6), 473–490.
Castle, P. and Buckler, S. (2009) *How to Be a Successful Teacher: Strategies for Personal and Professional Development*. Thousand Oaks, CA: SAGE.
Charmaz, K. (2006) *Constructing Grounded Theory*. Thousand Oaks, CA: SAGE.
Day, C. and Gu, Q. (2009) Teacher emotions: Wellbeing and effectiveness. In P.A. Schultz and M. Zembylas (eds) *Advances in Teacher Emotion Research* (pp. 15–31). Boston, MA: Springer.
Day, C. and Gu, Q. (2010) *The New Lives of Teachers*. London: Routledge.
Diener, E. (1994) Assessing subjective well-being: Progress and opportunities. *Social Indicators Research* 31 (2), 103–157.
Diener, E., Oishi, S. and Lucas, R.E. (2003) Personality, culture, and subjective well-being: Emotional and cognitive evaluations of life. *Annual Review of Psychology* 54 (1), 403–425.
Doiz, A. and Lasagabaster, D. (2017) Management teams and teaching staff: Do they share the same beliefs about obligatory CLIL programmes and the use of the L1? *Language and Education* 31 (2), 93–109.
Doiz, A., Lasagabaster, D. and Sierra, J.M. (2014) CLIL and motivation: The effect of individual and contextual variables. *The Language Learning Journal* 42 (2), 209–224.
Hiver, P. (2017) Tracing the signature dynamics of language teacher immunity: A retrodictive qualitative modeling study. *The Modern Language Journal* 101 (4), 669–690.
Holmes, E. (2005) *Teacher Well-Being: Looking After Yourself and Your Career in the Classroom*. New York, NY: Routledge Falmer.
Hüttner, J., Dalton-Puffer, C. and Smit, U. (2013) The power of beliefs: Lay theories and their influence on the implementation of CLIL programmes. *International Journal of Bilingual Education and Bilingualism* 16 (3), 267–284.
Johnson, S., Cooper, C., Cartwright, S., Donald, I., Taylor, P. and Millet, C. (2005) The experience of work-related stress across occupations. *Journal of Managerial Psychology* 20 (2), 178–187.
Judge, T.A. and Klinger, R. (2008) Job satisfaction: Subjective well-being at work. In M. Eid and R.J. Larsen (eds) *The Science of Subjective Well-Being* (pp. 393–413). New York, NY: Guilford Press.
Judge, T.A. and Watanabe, S. (1993) Another look at the job satisfaction–life satisfaction relationship. *Journal of Applied Psychology* 78 (6), 939–948.
Kieschke, U. and Schaarschmidt, U. (2008) Professional commitment and health among teachers in Germany: A typological approach. *Learning and Instruction* 18 (5), 429–437.
King, J. and Ng, K.-Y.S. (2018) Teacher emotions and the emotional labour of second language teaching. In S. Mercer and A. Kostoulas (eds) *Language Teacher Psychology* (pp. 141–157). Bristol: Multilingual Matters.
Kvale, S. (2007) *Doing Interviews*. Thousand Oaks, CA: SAGE.
Kyriacou, C. (2001) Teacher stress: Directions for future research. *Educational Review* 53 (1), 27–35.
Larsen, R.J. and Prizmic, Z. (2008) Regulation of emotional well-being: Overcoming the hedonic treadmill. In M. Eid and R.J. Larsen (eds) *The Science of Subjective Well-Being* (pp. 258–289). New York: Guilford Press.
Lorenzo, F., Casal, S. and Moore, P. (2010) The effects of content and language integrated learning in European education: Key findings from the Andalusian bilingual sections evaluation project. *Applied Linguistics* 31 (3), 418–442.

McDougald, J.S. (2015) Teachers' attitudes, perceptions and experiences in CLIL: A look at content and language. *Colombian Applied Linguistics Journal* 17 (1), 25–41.

Mercer, S. and Kostoulas, A. (eds) (2018) *Language Teacher Psychology*. Bristol: Multilingual Matters.

Moate, J.M. (2011) The impact of foreign language mediated teaching on teachers' sense of professional integrity in the CLIL classroom. *European Journal of Teacher Education* 34 (3), 333–346.

Pappa, S., Moate, J., Ruohotie-Lyhty, M. and Eteläpelto, A. (2019) Teacher agency within the Finnish CLIL context: Tensions and resources. *International Journal of Bilingual Education and Bilingualism* 22 (5), 593–613.

Reyes, M.R., Brackett, M.A., Rivers, S.E., White, M. and Salovey, P. (2012) Classroom emotional climate, student engagement, and academic achievement. *Journal of Educational Psychology* 104 (3), 700–712.

Sammons, P., Day, C., Kington, A., Gu, Q., Stobart, G. and Smees, R. (2007) Exploring variations in teachers' work, lives and their effects on pupils: Key findings and implications from a longitudinal mixed-method study. *British Educational Research Journal* 33 (5), 681–701.

Travers, C.J. and Cooper, C.L. (1993) Mental health, job satisfaction and occupational stress among UK teachers. *Work and Stress* 7 (3), 203–219.

Wilding, G., Plösch, M. and Kupplent, W. (2009) *PEA – das Projekt Englisch als Arbeitssprache an der HTBLuVA (Bulme) Graz-Gösting*. Graz: ÖSZ. See http://www.oesz.at/download/themenreihe_3.pdf (accessed 22 October 2017).

Young, M.F., DePalma, A. and Garrett, S. (2002) Situations, interaction, process and affordances: An ecological psychology perspective. *Instructional Science* 30 (1), 47–63.

3 Utilising the Emotional Labour Scale to Analyse the Form and Extent of Emotional Labour among Foreign Language Teachers in the US Public School System

Kris Acheson and Robert Nelson

Introduction

Since the early days of its conceptualisation by Hochschild (1983), the construct of emotional labour, also known as emotion labour, has resonated with many scholars and practitioners, both within its home disciplines of sociology and gender studies and in a variety of contexts where it has been transported and applied effectively. Emotional labour refers to the (often gendered) concealment and/or display of emotion that is expected or even demanded of some professionals as part of their daily work life. The construct has proven relevant to the study of many types of careers, including service-oriented and female-dominated professions such as teaching and nursing (Gray, 2010; Truta, 2014).

Over the past two decades, emotional labour has been applied extensively in the discipline of education (Isenbarger & Zembylas, 2006; Näring *et al.*, 2006). Scholars have found it useful in research related to teacher identity, best practices in and out of the classroom, and teacher burnout and attrition. However, while emotional labour is a familiar concept in education literature in general, foreign language (FL) teaching in particular has only begun to explore the significance of emotional labour theory to its unique challenges. Some of these challenges, according to a recent qualitative study of FL teachers in the southern

United States by Acheson, Taylor and Luna (2016), are a seeming lack of student motivation to study foreign languages and a perceived lack of administrative and community support for FL education. This study found that teachers at a rural public school in the state of Georgia responded to their professional challenges by performing excessive emotional labour, and that these unsustainable performances contribute to inefficacy, emotional burnout and teacher attrition.

Acheson and colleagues' (2016) work provides an important foundation for the application of the emotional labour construct to foreign language teachers by advancing a model that helps us understand how and why emotional labour is performed, as well as the impacts of those performances. Many questions remain, however. First and foremost, we need documentation of the extent of emotional labour in this context. By employing the Brotheridge and Lee (2003) Emotional Labour Scale (ELS), which was developed and has been used to delineate how much and which types of emotional labour are taken on by professionals in other contexts, the current project aims to document the form and extent of emotional labour among US public school foreign language teachers. The research questions guiding this study included:

(1) To what extent do FL teachers in the state of Georgia public school system report engaging in emotional labour?
(2) How do the demographic factors of urban versus suburban and rural settings, income level of school, length of career, gender, language taught and native speaker status impact how often teachers in this context perform different kinds of emotional labour?
(3) What are the relationships between job satisfaction, feelings of teacher burnout and plans to continue teaching and the performance of emotional labour by FL teachers?

In the following sections, we will synthesise relevant literature, explain the research methodology, present the study findings, and discuss the implications of the results. Important contributions of this study include demonstrating the usefulness of the ELS for analysing the emotional labour of foreign language teachers, offering much-needed documentation of the scope of emotional labour in this context and suggesting relationships between contextual factors and problematic excessive emotional labour.

Literature Review

The history of emotional labour theory

Hochschild (1983) coined the term emotional labour and introduced its foundational concepts, which are the different acts associated with the original form of the construct.

(1) *Surface acting* involves verbally and nonverbally displaying emotions that are appropriate for one's job despite whatever emotions might be actually felt.
(2) *Deep acting* means deploying strategies to sympathise and eventually create within oneself appropriate emotions for the work situation.
(3) *Consonance* is responding naturally with appropriate emotions to a job's demands, that is, specific to job tasks or environment.

A key point from Hochschild's foundational work is that emotional labour is commoditized, or a form of human capital. Since Hochschild, feminist organisational scholars have elevated that dialogue to the level of emotional division of labour across the sexes. For example, Gray (2010) found in the healthcare profession that women tend to do more emotional labour than men. The construct is often more applicable in careers that are dominated by women, and different genders sometimes encounter distinct sets of display rules for emotional labour within the same career.

Emotional labour theory has come to be applied by researchers from the fields of communication, psychology and management to what might be the gamut of high-stress service professions, everything from flight attendants (Sheehan, 2012) and clergymen (Kinman *et al.*, 2011a) to emergency response operators (Tracy & Tracy, 1998) and activists (Rodgers, 2010). Important developments in emotional labour theory came from Näring, Briët and Brouwers (2006), who divided surface acting into both the display of emotion and also the lack thereof. They also noted inconsistencies within the positive correlation between deep acting and emotional exhaustion, documenting the individual differences that affect the relationship between sustained emotional labour and the potential for burnout and, in doing so, concluded that emotional labour does not seem to have the same effects on everyone. Brotheridge and Lee (2003) launched a quantitative measure called the Emotional Labour Scale that could capture the multi-dimensionality of emotional labour. They parsed the dimensions established by Hochschild (1983) and also studied 'role requirements', – that is, the frequency, intensity, variety and duration of emotional labour. This operationalisation of emotional labour theory has also been widely adapted for use, especially in studying call-centre workers (Goldberg & Grandey, 2007) and psychiatric nurses (Mann & Cowburn, 2005), and in organizational studies.

The discipline of educational studies was tardy in adopting the concept but has over the past decade come to recognise the applicability of emotional labour theory to teaching. According to Truta, 'the teaching profession is one with the highest requirements for emotion labor' (Truta, 2014: 794). In the same vein, Näring, Vlerick and Van de Ven (2012) found that the emotional demands of teaching impact teachers personally, leading to burnout; they also argued that emotional labour is becoming more and more expected of teachers and is intertwined with conceptualisations of good teaching and teacher identity.

Although research utilising the Emotional Labour Scale has uncovered that teachers are subject to burnout from emotional labour, the instrument has not been used in studies specifically with foreign language teachers. The inventory has been utilised with teachers in general, who use emotional labour to develop 'rewarding relationships' with their students much as workers in other parts of the public sector do (Martínez-Iñigo *et al.*, 2007: 42). Teachers must manipulate students' motivational factors, be aware of differing learning styles, and generally be social and caring (Swanson, 2012). Yin, Lee, Zhang and Jin (2013) demonstrated that along with extensive surface and deep acting come difficult job requirements such as long hours in the classroom and challenging home situations whose consequences students bring into the classroom. Teachers with poor emotional labour regulation strategies are thus often subject to burnout, emotional exhaustion and low motivation (Näring *et al.*, 2006; Zhang & Zhu, 2008).

Emotional labour of US foreign language teachers

Foreign language teachers in the United States face steep challenges that lead to high attrition despite the high demand both in urban and rural environments (Swanson & Huff, 2010). There has not been much consensus on why foreign language teachers are leaving the job, but we do know that there is a relationship between emotional labour performed, the strategies deployed by individual teachers for dealing with emotional labour, and burnout. Previous to the present study, some scholars have certainly studied the emotions of students in the classroom (Aragão, 2011; Dewaele, 2011; Imai, 2010), especially with regard to language learning anxiety (Awan *et al.*, 2010; Dewaele & MacIntyre, 2014; Horwitz, 2010; Liu & Huang, 2011; Shao *et al.*, 2013). Yet only recently have scholars begun to explore the emotional job requirements of FL teachers (Cowie, 2011; Gkonou & Miller, 2017; Miller & Gkonou, forthcoming; King, 2016). While these studies begin to address a gap in the literature, more research is needed to fully understand the complex relationships between context, emotional labour and potential consequences of that labour. The goal of this study is thus to discover if foreign language teachers are indeed performing emotional labour and potential relationships of emotional labour to FL teacher burnout and attrition.

In 2016, a ground-breaking study of the emotional labour of FL teachers was published in the *Modern Language Journal*. Basing their research on thematic analysis of interview data with an entire foreign language department at a rural school in Georgia, Acheson

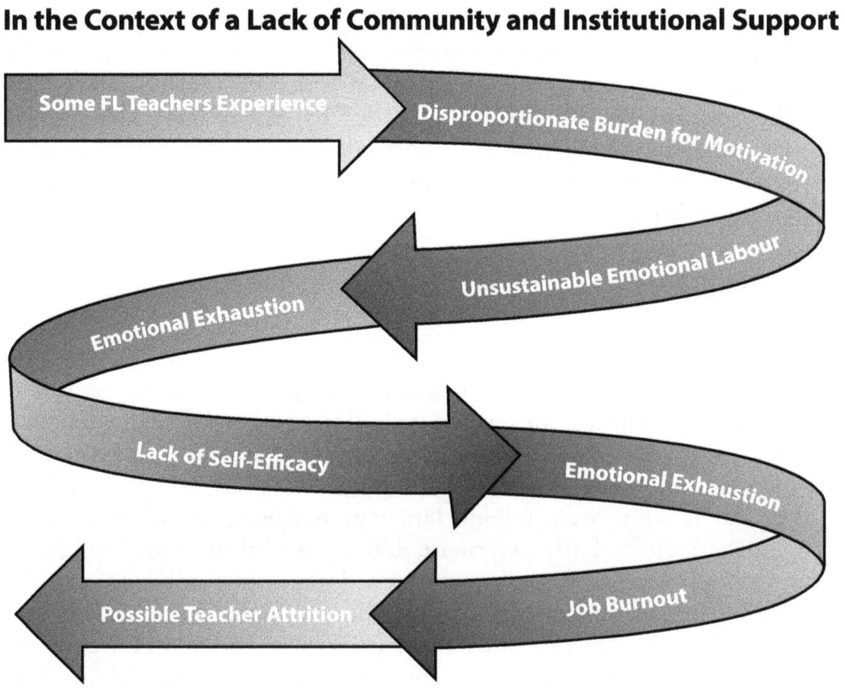

Figure 3.1 Burnout spiral of FL teacher emotional labour (Acheson *et al.*, 2016)

and colleagues developed a model that explains how, in this context, contextual factors stimulate excessive emotional labour that in turn can lead to emotional exhaustion, lack of self-efficacy, and teacher attrition in a burnout spiral (see Figure 3.1). This research and the model it generated lays important groundwork for the current study by recognising the salience of the emotional labour construct for US public foreign language teachers and identifying the need to document how generalisable these findings are to other teachers in this context.

The current study addresses the gap in literature on FL teacher emotions by documenting the extent of emotional labour in an unexplored context and, further, by investigating its relationships with contextual factors and individual characteristics. Based on previous research, we hypothesise that:

(1) FL teachers in the Georgia public school system will report frequently engaging in all types of emotional labour, resulting in ELS mean scores higher than 3, the midpoint of the five-point scale from *never* to *always*.
(2) Demographic factors such as urban versus suburban and rural settings, income level of school, length of career, gender, language

taught and native speaker status will impact how often teachers in this context perform different kinds of emotional labour, with statistically significant between-group differences revealed by analysis.

(3) The performance of emotional labour by FL teachers will predict job satisfaction (negative relationship), feelings of teacher burnout (positive relationship) and plans to continue teaching (negative relationship).

Methodology

Participants

The setting of the present study is the Georgia (in the southern United States) public school system, including rural, urban and suburban schools. It includes Title I (schools that have a significant percentage of low-income students) and non-Title I schools.

The participants were foreign language teachers, including teachers of Spanish, French, Latin, German, ESOL, American Sign Language, Japanese and Arabic. Initially, we opened the study to teachers in a variety of school levels (elementary, middle and high school), institution types (public and private) and states (beyond Georgia). However, all respondents with complete data indicated that they taught in high schools in the public school system in Georgia, making the sample more homogeneous in terms of teaching context. There were 102 respondents to the survey. However, 19 participants were excluded because their data was too incomplete for accurate analysis, leaving n = 83 for this study. See Table 3.1 for demographic information.

Instrument

The items for the questionnaire administered in this study comprise a modified version of the ELS. The original ELS (Brotheridge & Lee, 2003) evinced high internal consistency with Cronbach's α for subscales ranging from .74 to .91. However, the original ELS did not distinguish both forms of surface acting – that is, faking and hiding – from deep acting (Lee *et al.*, 2010). The modified version, which does make this distinction, is therefore better able to identify different types of emotion labour that may occur across different contexts. The confirmatory factor analysis for the revised scale yielded '$\chi^2(8) = 48.09$, $\rho < 0.001$; GFI = 0.94, AGFI = 0.83, TLI = 0.92, RMSEA = 0.15' (Lee & Brotheridge, 2011: 417). The instrument developers explained:

> Our three emotional labour dimensions … provide a broader assessment of emotional labour, without specifying discrete emotions. That the two surface acting dimensions were more strongly interrelated than either was with deep acting, and that all three were differentially

Table 3.1 Demographic information for participants

Independent Variables		N	Percent
Gender	Male	23	27.7
	Female	60	72.3
	Total	83	
Language Taught*	Spanish	50	60.2
	Other	35	42.2
	Total	83	
Native Language	Native Speaker (L1)	26	31.3
	Foreign Language User (LX)	57	68.7
	Total	83	
School Setting	Urban	29	34.9
	Rural	16	19.3
	Suburban	38	45.8
	Total	83	
School Title I Status	Low Income	46	55.4
	Not Low Income	37	44.6
	Total	83	
Teaching Experience	1–3 years	12	14.5
	4–8 years	9	10.8
	9–16 years	25	30.1
	17+ years	37	44.6
	Total	83	

(*Note: Some respondents teach more than one language, so counts exceed the N of 83.)

> associated with the work background variables, give evidence for the convergent and discriminant validities of the measure. (Lee & Brotheridge, 2011: 414)

The survey in this study consists of 30 questions: 17 five-point Likert scale type questions from the modified ELS (see Appendix), and 13 demographic questions dealing with school setting and teacher background, practices, goals and attitudes. Demographic questions were presented first in the survey, after which the ELS items were randomised for each participant.

Data collection

After human subjects ethics committee approval was obtained from the researchers' home institution, study recruitment was accomplished by emailing eligible participants (foreign language teachers currently employed in Georgia public schools). The teachers' emails were sourced from publicly available school website and county records. The survey was anonymous and entirely web-based, with responses collected through Qualtrics, a cloud-based survey software platform. The data collection period was three months, and potential participants who had not already done so were sent a reminder to respond to the survey after two months.

Data analysis

The analysis of the data gathered with the modified ELS was analysed in three stages. First, means and standard deviations for both full-scale and subscale scores were calculated. These descriptive statistics were examined in aggregate form in order to determine the extent and form of emotional labour in this context.

Second, independent samples t-tests between independent and dependent variables were used to parse out subgroup differences in emotional labour based on various two-level demographic variables such as gender (female vs male), language taught (Spanish vs other languages), poverty level of the school (Title I/low income vs not) and whether teachers were teaching their native language (native speaker vs not). Please note that language taught was not a two-level variable in the survey but was organised that way in the analysis because no language other than Spanish had an *n* large enough to calculate subgroup differences accurately. Likewise, in this second stage, ANOVAs were run for independent variables with more than two levels, including school setting (urban vs suburban vs rural), years of teaching experience and plans to continue teaching. Because group sizes were not equal, Waller-Duncan was utilized as a post hoc analysis method for ANOVAs that indicated significant subgroup differences. Due to the large number of comparisons made, the significance threshold was lowered for the set of analyses with a Bonferroni correction to avoid false positives.

In the third stage of analysis, correlations between the independent variables of job satisfaction and teacher burnout and the dependent variable of emotional labour (full-scale and subscale scores) were calculated with Pearson's r and Bonferroni's correction for multiple correlations. For the variables of job satisfaction, teacher burnout and plans to continue teaching, multiple regression was also conducted to control for the variance of other variables, providing stronger evidence of relationships and identifying which independent variables had the most predictive power. All statistical analyses were processed via SPSS software.

Findings

The results of the statistical analyses of the ELS data in this study are presented below in three sections that correspond to the three research

Table 3.2 Descriptive statistics for individual differences of respondents

		ELS Total	Generating Emotions	Pretending Emotions	Hiding Emotions
N	**Valid**	83	83	83	83
	Missing	0	0	0	0
Mean		3.2298	3.2170	3.0080	3.4776
Median		3.1800	3.0000	3.3300	3.6700
Std Deviation		.48324	.80243	.85541	.78970
Skewness		.113	.057	–.357	–.418

questions. In short, we present descriptive statistics, followed by analysis of subgroup differences and then correlations between variables.

Descriptive statistics

Table 3.2 presents descriptive statistics for the Emotional Labour Scale full-scale score (ELS Total) as well as three subscales: deep acting, or the deliberate generation of work-related emotions (Generating Emotions); positive surface acting or pretending to feel expected work-related emotions (Pretending Emotions); and negative surface acting or hiding stigmatised work-related emotions (Hiding Emotions). All mean and median scores are above 3 on a five-point Likert scale, indicating at least moderate engagement in emotional labour for this group.

The full-scale score for the instrument exhibited a normal distribution, with little difference between the mean and median and relatively small standard deviation and skewness. Subscale scores had much larger standard deviations, indicating greater diversity among respondents' behaviours. Distributions were slightly more skewed, with larger gaps between means and medians. Frequencies for demographic questions are reported in the methods section above in Table 3.1. Frequencies for questions that represent other individual differences, including plans to continue teaching, job satisfaction and emotional burnout, are presented in Table 3.3.

Note that the distributions for each of these independent variables is skewed. Plans to continue teaching is skewed towards more years, and job satisfaction and emotional burnout are both skewed towards higher levels (extremely and moderately).

Between-group differences

Independent samples t-tests and ANOVAs revealed no significant differences on the full scale and subscales of the Emotional Labour Scale among subgroups for most demographic variables, both for teachers (gender, language taught, native speaker status of the teacher and years

Table 3.3 Frequency of responses for independent variables

Independent Variables		N	Percent
Plans to Continue Teaching	Will not continue	7	8.4
	1 year more	7	8.4
	2–5 years more	21	25.3
	5–10 years more	17	20.5
	10+ years more	31	37.3
	Total	83	100.0
Job Satisfaction	Extremely satisfied	19	22.9
	Moderately satisfied	34	41.0
	Neither/both	12	14.5
	Moderately dissatisfied	12	14.5
	Extremely dissatisfied	6	7.2
	Total	83	100.0
Feels Emotionally Drained at/by Work	Extremely drained	12	14.5
	Very drained	26	31.3
	Moderately drained	34	41.0
	Slightly drained	10	12.0
	Not drained at all	1	1.2
	Total	83	100.0

of experience) and for schools (school income level). In fact, the only significant difference that surfaced in the between-groups comparison was for school setting. The item that exhibited group differences asked teachers to report how emotionally drained they felt by their work.

The *p* value for this difference (see Table 3.4) was low enough that it remains significant even after Bonferroni's correction was applied. The difference is only for urban settings; rural and suburban schools did not differ significantly from each other in terms of foreign language teacher emotional burnout, but urban schools were different from both other groups (see Table 3.5). This difference in burnout between teachers at urban and non-urban schools surfaced despite the fact that differences in the performance of emotional labour by setting were not significant. Note that for this item, which asked teachers about how emotionally

Table 3.4 One-way ANOVA: Emotional burnout by school setting

	Sum of Squares	df	Mean Square	F	Sig.
Between Groups	10.122	2	5.061	6.694	.002
Within Groups	60.480	80	.756		
Total	70.602	82			

Table 3.5 Pairwise comparisons: Emotional burnout by school setting

		Mean Difference	Std Error	Sig.	95% Confidence Interval	
					Lower Bound	Upper Bound
Urban	Rural	–.806*	.271	.004	–1.34	–.27
	Suburban	–.694*	.214	.002	–1.12	–.27
Rural	Urban	.806*	.271	.004	.27	1.34
	Suburban	.112	.259	.667	–.40	.63
Suburban	Urban	.694*	.214	.002	.27	1.12
	Rural	–.112	.259	.667	–.63	.40

drained they felt by their work, 1 referred to extremely drained and 5 represented not drained at all. Teachers at urban schools therefore reported the least emotional burnout.

Correlations between variables

In addition to the between-group differences explored in research question 2, we ran regression analyses in order to address research question 3 and find the predictors of emotional labour (see correlation matrix in Table 3.6). In our analyses, we controlled for the variables most

Table 3.6 Correlation matrix for independent variables

		Gender	Teaching Experience	Job Satisfaction	Plans to Teach	Emotional Burnout
Gender	Pearson *r*	1	.155	.061	.086	.160
	Sig. (2-tailed)		.163	.585	.441	.149
Teaching Experience	Pearson *r*	.155	1	–.045	–.087	.109
	Sig. (2-tailed)	.163		.690	.435	.329
Job Satisfaction	Pearson *r*	.061	–.045	1	–.430**	–.448**
	Sig. (2-tailed)	.585	.690		.000	.000
Plans to Teach	Pearson *r*	.086	–.087	–.430**	1	.169
	Sig. (2-tailed)	.441	.435	.000		.126
Emotional Burnout	Pearson *r*	.160	.109	–.448**	.169	1
	Sig. (2-tailed)	.149	.329	.000	.126	
Generating Emotions	Pearson *r*	–.023	–.045	–.138	.021	–.002
	Sig. (2-tailed)	.837	.683	.212	.852	.989
Pretending Emotions	Pearson *r*	.069	.004	.171	–.257	–.328**
	Sig. (2-tailed)	.534	.971	.123	.019	.002
Hiding Emotions	Pearson *r*	–.046	.083	.278*	–.173	–.347**
	Sig. (2-tailed)	.680	.455	.011	.118	.001

Table 3.7 ELS subscale coefficients for emotional burnout, controlled for gender and teaching experience

	B	Std Error	Beta	T	Sig.
(Constant)	3.441	.743		4.630	.000
Gender	.305	.215	.148	1.420	.160
TeachExp	.093	.090	.107	1.033	.305
Generating	.015	.120	.013	.125	.901
Pretending	–.251*	.126	–.232	–1.990	.050
Hiding	–.288*	.137	–.245	–2.106	.038

theoretically likely to influence emotional labour and its hypothesized outcomes: gender and years of teaching experience.

Emotional burnout was the dependent variable in the first multiple regression analysis. The analysis explained a fifth of variance ($R^2 = .196$, $F(5,77) = 3.762$, $p = .004$) with two significant predictors, namely two subscales of the Emotional Labour Scale – hiding and pretending (see Table 3.7). This corresponds to a small to medium effect (Plonsky & Ghanbar, 2018).The item is in effect reverse coded, with more emotional burnout reflected in lower scores on that item; therefore, according to this analysis, the more emotionally drained teachers felt at/by work, the more they hid their emotional state and the more they performed emotions they did not actually feel.

The multiple regression analysis revealed that a single variable, hiding, explained 10% of variance in job satisfaction ($R^2 = .107$, $F(5,77) = 1.839$, $p = .015$) (see Table 3.8). Therefore, the less satisfied teachers were with their jobs, the more likely they were to hide their emotional state at work. This corresponds to a small effect (Plonsky & Ghanbar, 2018). Again, the reverse coding of this item needed to be taken into account when interpreting these results.

The final multiple regression analysis revealed that the plans to continue teaching were not significantly predicted by the independent variables ($R^2 = .091$, $F(5,77) = 1.546$, $p = .185$).

Table 3.8 ELS subscale coefficients for job satisfaction, controlled for gender and teaching experience

	B	Std Error	Beta	t	Sig.
(Constant)	1.366	1.014		1.347	.182
Gender	.206	.293	.077	.702	.485
TeachExp	–.093	.123	–.083	–.757	.451
Generating	–.192	.164	–.128	–1.168	.247
Pretending	.100	.172	.071	.580	.563
Hiding	.374*	.186	.246	2.006	.048

Discussion

In the discussion below, which is divided into three sections corresponding to the three research questions for this study, we draw conclusions about the findings presented above, connect these findings to relevant literature and highlight some important implications of this project.

The extent of emotional labour among foreign language teachers in US public schools

Research question 1 in this study asked, 'To what extent do FL teachers in the state of Georgia public school system report engaging in emotional labour?' Based on the means in Table 3.2 for the full-scale score as well as all the subscale scores, foreign language teachers are engaging in a substantial amount of emotional labour, above 3 on a five-point scale between *never* and *always*. The standard deviation of the full-scale score is low at SD = .483 on a five-point Likert scale, meaning that 95% of respondents on the ELS fall within a range of less than 2 points on a five-point scale. Because the responses are clustered so tightly with a mean just above 3 points, we can conclude that, while of course some public high school FL teachers in Georgia perform more emotional labour than others, the vast majority of teachers in this context engage in moderate to high levels of emotional performances on the job.

The first hypothesis in this study was confirmed. These results are not surprising given the findings of other studies, including both those in other educational contexts (Näring *et al.*, 2006; Yin *et al.*, 2013; Zhang & Zhu, 2008) and for foreign language teachers specifically (Acheson *et al.*, 2016). None of these other studies used the ELS to document emotional labour; however, if studies are well designed to examine the same phenomenon, it stands to reason they would yield similar results across the literature even when different methodologies and instruments are used. While not unexpected, the finding that the participating teachers do engage in emotional labour frequently is vital to building a foundation of scholarly literature on emotional labour in the undocumented context of US foreign language teaching, providing clear evidence of the extent to which these public high school teachers are performing emotional work as part of their professional daily lives.

Also of note in the descriptive statistics are the frequencies for items meant to capture individual differences among respondents. On the surface, the frequencies might seem to indicate that teacher attrition is not an issue and that feeling emotionally drained does not negatively impact job satisfaction, since the skewed distributions suggest that many teachers plan to continue teaching for a number of years and are *more* rather than *less* satisfied with their jobs despite a tendency to feel emotionally drained. At the same time, 14 of the 83 teachers indicated that they will be leaving the profession this year or next. This anticipated turnover of 16.8% within a year reflects the actual data that we have on FL teacher attrition in Georgia:

> over half of teacher turnover costs are accrued by attrition as opposed to about a quarter for retirement (Nweke *et al.*, 2006). Strikingly, FL teacher attrition exceeds the rates for all other areas – that is, a higher percentage of Georgia FL teachers leave the profession each year than teachers of any other subject (Georgia Professional Standards Commission [GAPSC], 2006). In fact, according to the GAPSC report, Georgia loses more than one in ten FL teachers every year. (Acheson *et al.*, 2016: 2)

In short, the participants in this study seem to have realistic expectations about the sustainability of their own careers given attrition statistics in the area. Furthermore, the impact of their plans to not continue teaching or to continue teaching for only a short time will likely worsen what Swanson (2012) and other scholars have already documented as a problematic low supply of qualified instructors willing to teach foreign languages in Georgia public schools.

Nuances of FL teacher emotional labour in this setting

Research question 2 in this study asked, 'How do the demographic factors of urban versus suburban and rural settings, income level of school, length of career, gender, language taught and native speaker status impact how often teachers in this context perform different kinds of emotional labour?' No other emotional labour studies have explored the application of the ELS to foreign language teachers, so the data collection and analysis with demographic questions cast a wide net with regard to factors that may be related to the extent and form of emotional labour for FL teachers. Not knowing which independent variables might be salient in this context, we included a number of items about school setting and teacher individual differences. We were surprised to find very few significant subgroup differences with the independent samples t-tests and ANOVAs in this study.

Foundational studies argue that gender is a consistent predictor of emotional labour – a claim harkening back to the origins of emotional labour theory (Hochschild, 1983) and still salient in many applications of the construct since we have entered the new millennium (Payne, 2009). Historically emotional labour has been documented to be more of an issue for women, either in female-dominated careers such as nursing or childcare (Lee & Brotheridge, 2011; Vincent & Braun, 2013) or because the expectations of men's and women's emotional work vary even within the same career (Gray, 2010).

However, some more recent studies suggest emotional labour is not always gendered. As in the work of Torland (2011), the female and male teachers in this study are remarkably similar to each other in their performance of emotions on the job. In this case, male teachers report generating, pretending and hiding their emotions as much as females do. This is an important acknowledgment of gender role expectations that constrain men. Given power dynamics here in the US as well as many other places around the world, scholars tend to pay much more attention to the gendering of women and the implications of that gendering for self-actualisation, discrimination, oppression and violence (Brescoll, 2016; Glomb *et al.*, 2004; Yang & Guy, 2015). Yet it is important to acknowledge how gendered performances are also demanded of men in our society (Bauer & Murray, 2018; Bruhn, 2013; Scott & Myers, 2005). Although we cannot be sure without additional data that documents reasons for the lack of difference between males and females in this study, we may be seeing evidence of the primacy of teacher identities that subsume or mediate performances of gender. Another possibility is that men who are more willing to and more capable of performing emotional labour may be more prevalent in teaching roles than in other careers that have been examined in studies where differences were found.

The second hypothesis for this study was largely unconfirmed – in fact, few demographic variables surfaced as impactful for emotional labour in this context. The one significant demographic difference that did emerge in this project was between various school settings. There was no meaningful difference in teacher emotional labour between suburban and rural schools; however, urban foreign language teachers reported significantly less emotional burnout than either suburban or rural teachers. This data contradicts a common assumption in the US – that urban schools are demoralising places for teachers to work due to budget constraints, lack of parental support, high crime rates and many other social issues (Knoblauch & Chase, 2015).

Despite these well-documented issues in urban schools, though, another pertinent fact is the tendency of urban settings in the US to be more linguistically diverse. Historically, the terms urban, suburban and rural referred only to population density, yet contemporary use of the terms acknowledges complex demographic differences, including patterns of racial, ethnic and linguistic distribution (Newell & Looser, 2018; Miranda & Gutter, 2002). These distinctions are even more important than usual in the context of the state of Georgia, where the city of Atlanta houses large immigrant and refugee communities while the population of suburban and rural areas remains largely English-speaking with few racial/ethnic groups represented beyond Black and White (United States Census Bureau, 2010).

Diversity becomes relevant to emotional labour when we consider the model of FL teacher burnout presented by Acheson and colleagues

(2016), in which excessive emotional labour that led to burnout was performed by FL teachers in response to a perceived lack of community and school support for the study of languages (see Figure 3.1). In an urban social milieu where diverse languages are spoken and multilingualism is more common than in typically more homogenous and monolingual suburban and rural areas, it makes sense that the pressure to generate, pretend and hide emotions in unsustainable ways would be lessened. When teachers don't feel a need to compensate for a lack of value for FL study with their own emotional labour, it follows that burnout is less likely. In this case, teachers in urban settings did not indicate in their responses to the ELS that they perform significantly less emotional labour than those in suburban and rural settings. Even so, the impetus for those performances in urban versus other settings could very well impact the toll they take on teachers.

Relationships among variables

Research question 3 in this study asked, 'What are the relationships between job satisfaction, feelings of teacher burnout and plans to continue teaching and the performance of emotional labour by FL teachers?' The findings that help us to address this question, found in Tables 3.7 and 3.8, reveal that the predictor variables had a statistically significant effect on the dependent variables, albeit a relatively weak one. However, the predictor variables had no significant effect on the intention to remain in the teaching profession. Relationships between each of these variables and specific types of emotional labour move in the expected directions, thus partially confirming the third hypothesis.

With regard to emotional burnout, the regression provides evidence that at least some types of emotional labour predict emotional burnout. We can safely assume causality here, with emotional labour at times leading to or contributing to burnout; the reverse direction of impact is not logical, because feeling drained would likely result in an inability to perform emotional labour. Furthermore, this directionality is supported in recent literature: Cheng *et al.* (2013) found that hiding predicted burnout, leading to an increase in turnover retention with nurses. Moreover, Kinman and colleagues (2011a, 2011b) found that emotional labour negatively impacted emotional exhaustion, self-efficacy and job satisfaction. It is important to note that the current study offers supporting evidence for the draining effect of both types of surface acting (i.e. hiding and pretending) as well as for the ambiguity of the effects of deep acting. While both hiding and pretending predict emotional burnout, there is no relationship at all in this data between emotional burnout and generating emotions. Other research has suggested that, depending on individual differences, such as emotional resilience and environmental factors, for example team support, deep acting can exacerbate or mitigate the negative impacts of emotional labour, correlating to either more or less emotional burnout (Näring *et al.*, 2006).

The regression analysis also revealed that the surface acting subscale for hiding emotion predicted job satisfaction (see Table 3.7). As with the previous relationship, it was a significant but weak predictor. In other words, emotional hiding explains roughly 10% of the variation in job satisfaction. In addition to recognising the weakness of the relationship, we have to be careful not to assume causality in this statistical relationship. Most studies in this body of literature conclude that emotional labour is an antecedent in this relationship, leading to job dissatisfaction (Torland, 2011). While that may be the case here, the reverse directionality may also be true, with job dissatisfaction coming first, and teachers who feel dissatisfied more likely to hide those negative emotions at work until they are ready to leave.

The final regression indicates that the performance of emotional labour did not significantly predict plans to continue teaching. These results diverge from previous research. Kinman and colleagues (2011b) documented that very experienced teachers perform more emotional labour. Further research is needed to establish whether, in light of the downward spiral model introduced in Acheson and colleagues' study (2016), excessive emotional labour contributed to decisions to abandon teaching.

Conclusion

Our study found that public high school foreign language teachers in our sample consistently perform moderate to high levels of emotional labour on the job; our questionnaire also documented relatively high percentages of FL teachers with plans to leave the teaching profession and dissatisfaction with their jobs. Male FL teachers perform emotional labour much to the same degree as women, but urban settings proved quite different from suburban and rural in their reports of less teacher emotional labour. Importantly, we found that teachers who are dissatisfied with their jobs tend to hide their emotions more at work. In addition, this study corroborates other research findings that surface acting can lead to emotional burnout, while deep acting has ambiguous impacts. The hypotheses in this study were largely borne out, with the exception of plans to abandon teaching and a general lack of impact from demographic factors (other than school setting). The findings that align with previous research can be taken as evidence supporting the suitability of the ELS to this context.

One limitation of the study was the sample size: *n* was smaller and more homogeneous than expected, which could have been in part due to the email recruitment method. Teachers receive quite a lot of emails and are pressed for time during the day, and several respondents did not finish the survey; of 846 recruitment emails, 102 elicited responses, and 19 were incomplete for an incomplete rate of 18.6 %. Another limiting factor to the study is that only Georgia teachers were included in the population. Of course, Georgia has a unique FL teaching culture due to public attitudes towards foreign language learning as well as its own distinctive education system. Another key limitation is the quantitative nature of the study: while we see evidence of emotional labour and a relation to the challenges facing FL teachers, no possible solutions have arisen as might have been possible with a qualitative or mixed-methods approach.

Finally, using a previously validated instrument both provides benefits and presents challenges (Porter & McManus, 2019). On the one hand, using existing instruments, especially if they have strong demonstrated validity and reliability, saves researchers time and energy by not duplicating others' efforts unnecessarily. Perhaps even more importantly, when data is gathered by different researchers across a variety of contexts with the same instrument, the comparability of data makes meta-analysis and its resulting theoretical developments possible. Yet, at the same time, replications and extensions of an instrument into new domains can be problematic. One potential issue is the fit between instrument and the contexts in which it is applied. Brotheridge and Lee's (2003) revised ELS has proven useful in a number of related disciplines and settings, including with classroom teachers (though not language teachers in particular). Another challenge, however, is the tension between generality and specificity – that is, that items must be general enough to apply to multiple contexts but specific enough to be meaningful in any given one of these settings. In this case, it can be a challenge for respondents to think generally about their emotional labour when their performances and experiences likely vary day to day, or even moment by moment. Although these drawbacks in methodology must be acknowledged, all in all, the benefits of beginning to explore emotional labour among language teachers with the ELS justify its use in the current and other similar projects, in order to accomplish eventual wide-scale documentation.

Building on Acheson and colleagues' (2016) model of the burnout spiral of FL teachers, this study sought to use the Emotional Labour Scale to ascertain the extent, influencing factors, and ramifications of emotion labour for FL teachers. The findings and their implications suggest that emotion labour is indeed a key element to understanding and potentially resolving the challenge in foreign language teacher engagement. Because the ELS was successful in this study, we encourage its future use with FL teachers. However, future studies should seek a wider pool of participants through a nationwide survey of teachers from both public and private schools. Larger and more diverse samples could uncover potential regional differences rooted in varying social milieu, including attitudes towards FL learning and local immigration patterns (Lippi-Green, 2012); recruiting teachers from both public and private schools might also illuminate patterns of emotional labour across socioeconomic strata. An additional direction that could prove enlightening would be a mixed-methods approach wherein the ELS is used to identify potential interviewees. By focusing qualitative data collection on participants in extreme groups (for instance, those teachers who perform emotional labour at a high frequency), researchers may be able to better understand why some are in danger of attrition and others do not suffer emotional burnout or job dissatisfaction. Such a study might suggest best practices for regulating emotional labour in this context.

Post-Reading Tasks

(1) Reading through the Modified ELS in the Appendix, which items resonate with you most strongly, and why?
(2) If you have any experience teaching languages, what have been your own experiences with emotional labour? If you do not have language teaching experience, from a student's perspective, what emotional labour have you witnessed your teachers performing?
(3) What are potential differences (if any) between emotional labour in foreign language teachers in other contexts and social milieus within the United States (rural vs urban schools, coastal vs central states) or outside of the US (such as EFL)?
(4) Research on emotional labour suggests that the phenomenon has various potential consequences, both positive and negative. Do you have any suggestions for managing emotional labour in the context of language teaching to maximise its benefits while minimising its harm?

References

Acheson, K., Taylor, J. and Luna, K. (2016) The burnout spiral: The emotion labor of five rural U.S. foreign language teachers. *The Modern Language Journal* 100, 522–537.

Aragão, R. (2011) Beliefs and emotions in foreign language learning. *System* 39 (3), 302–313.

Awan, R., Azher, M., Anwar, M.N. and Nax, A. (2010) An investigation of foreign language classroom anxiety and its relationship with students' achievement. *Journal of College Teaching and Learning* 7 (11), 33–40.

Bauer, J.C. and Murray, M.A. (2018) 'Leave your emotions at home': Bereavement, organizational space, and professional identity. *Women's Studies in Communication* 41 (1), 60–81.

Brescoll, V.L. (2016) Leading with their hearts? How gender stereotypes of emotion lead to biased evaluations of female leaders. *The Leadership Quarterly* 27, 415–428.

Brotheridge, C.M. and Lee, R.T. (2003) Development and validation of the emotional labour scale. *Journal of Occupational and Organizational Psychology* 76, 365–379.

Bruhn, A. (2013) Gender relations and division of labour among prison officers in Swedish male prisons. *Journal of Scandinavian Studies in Criminology and Crime Prevention* 14 (2), 115–132.

Cheng, C., Bartram, T., Karimi, L. and Leggat, S.G. (2013) The role of team climate in the management of emotional labour: Implications for nurse retention. *Journal of Advanced Nursing* 69, 2812–2825.

Cowie, N. (2011) Emotions that experienced English as a Foreign Language (EFL) teachers feel about their students, their colleagues and their work. *Teaching and Teacher Education* 27 (1), 235–242.

Dewaele, J.-M. (2011) Reflections on the emotional and psychological aspects of foreign language learning and use. *Anglistik: International Journal of English Studies* 22 (1), 23–42.

Dewaele, J.-M. and MacIntyre, P.D. (2014) The two faces of Janus? Anxiety and enjoyment in the foreign language classroom. *Studies in Second Language Learning and Teaching* 4 (2), 237–274.

Georgia Professional Standards Commission (2006) *Status Report, 2006: The Georgia Educator Workforce: A Report of the Supply, Demand, and Utilization of Teachers, Administrative, and Student Services Personnel in Georgia Public Schools.* See http://www.gapsc.com/Commission/research_publication/downloads/2006%20Status%20Report.pdf (accessed 30 December 2015).

Gkonou, C. and Miller, E.R. (2017) Caring and emotional labour: Language teachers' engagement with anxious learners in private language school classrooms. *Language Teaching Research*. doi: 10.1177/1362168817728739.

Glomb, T.M., Kammeyer-Mueller, J.D. and Rotundo, M. (2004) Emotion labor demands and compensating wage differentials. *Journal of Applied Psychology* 89 (4), 700–714.

Goldberg, L.S. and Grandey, A.A. (2007) Display rules versus display autonomy: Emotion regulation, emotional exhaustion, and task performance in a call center simulation. *Journal of Occupational Health Psychology* 12 (3), 301–318.

Gray, B. (2010) Emotional labour, gender and professional stereotypes of emotional and physical contact, and personal perspectives on the emotional labour of nursing. *Journal of Gender Studies* 19, 349–360.

Hochschild, A.R. (1983) *The Managed Heart: Commercialization of Human Feeling.* Berkeley, CA: University of California Press.

Horwitz, E.K. (2010) Foreign and second language anxiety. *Language Teaching* 43 (2), 154–167.

Imai, Y. (2010) Emotions in SLA: New insights from collaborative learning for an EFL classroom. *Modern Language Journal* 94, 278–292.

Isenbarger, L. and Zembylas, M. (2006) The emotional labour of caring in teaching. *Teaching and Teacher Education* 22, 120–134.

King, J. (2016) 'It's time, put on the smile, it's time!': The emotional labour of second language teaching within a Japanese university. In C. Gkonou, D. Tatzl and S. Mercer (eds) *New Directions in Language Learning Psychology* (pp. 97–112). Dordrecht: Springer.

Kinman, G., McFall, O. and Rodriguez, J. (2011a) The cost of caring? Emotional labour, wellbeing and the clergy. *Pastoral Psychology* 60, 671–680.

Kinman, G., Wray, S. and Strange, C. (2011b) Emotional labour, burnout and job satisfaction in UK teachers: The role of workplace social support. *Educational Psychology* 31, 843–856.

Knoblauch, D. and Chase, M.A. (2015) Rural, suburban, and urban schools: The impact of school setting on the efficacy beliefs and attributions of student teachers. *Teaching and Teacher Education* 45, 104–114.

Lee, R.T. and Brotheridge, C.M. (2011) Words from the heart speak to the heart: A study of deep acting, faking, and hiding among child care workers. *Career Development International* 16, 401–420.

Lee, R.T., Lovall, B.L. and Brotheridge, C.M. (2010) Tenderness and steadiness: Relating job and interpersonal demands and resources with burnout and the physical symptoms of stress in Canadian physicians. *Journal of Applied Social Psychology* 40, 2319–2342.

Lippi-Green, R. (2012) *English with an Accent: Language, Ideology, and Discrimination in the United States* (2nd edn). New York: Routledge.
Liu, M. and Huang, W. (2011) An exploration of foreign language anxiety and English learning motivation. *Education Research International*, 1–8.
Mann, S. and Cowburn, J. (2005) Emotional labour and stress within mental health nursing. *Journal of Psychiatric and Mental Health Nursing* 12, 154–162.
Martínez–Iñigo, D., Totterdell, P., Alcover, C.M. and Holman, D. (2007) Emotional labour and emotional exhaustion: Interpersonal and intrapersonal mechanisms. *Work and Stress* 21 (1), 30–47.
Miller, E.R. and Gkonou, C. (forthcoming) Language teacher agency, emotion labor and emotional rewards in tertiary-level English language programs. *System*.
Miranda, A. and Gutter, P. (2002) Diversity research literature in school psychology: 1990–1999. *Psychology in the Schools* 39 (5), 597–604.
Näring, G., Briët, M. and Brouwers, A. (2006) Beyond demand–control: Emotional labour and symptoms of burnout in teachers. *Work and Stress* 20, 303–315.
Näring, G., Vlerick, P. and Van de Ven, B. (2012) Emotion work and emotional exhaustion in teachers: The job and individual perspective. *Educational Studies* 38 (1), 63–72.
Newell, M. and Looser, J. (2018) Does context matter? An analysis of training in multicultural assessment, consultation, and intervention between school psychologists in urban and rural contexts. *Psychology in the Schools* 55 (1), 85–92.
Nweke, W.C., Eads, G.M., Afolabi, C.Y., Stephens, C.E. and Toth, F.D. (2006, April) *The Impact of Teacher Workforce Retirement/Attrition on Personnel Replacement Cost*. Atlanta, GA: Georgia Professional Standards Commission. See http://www.gapsc.com/Commission/Research_Publication/downloads/Teacher_Workforce_Retirement_and_Turnover_Cost.pdf (accessed 30 December 2015).
Payne, J. (2009) Emotional labour and skill: A reappraisal. *Gender, Work and Organization* 16, 348–367.
Plonsky, L. and Ghanbar, H. (2018) Multiple regression in L2 research: A methodological synthesis and guide to interpreting R^2 values. *The Modern Language Journal*. doi: 10.1111/modl.12509.
Porter, G. and McManus, K. (2019) *Doing Replication Research in Applied Linguistics*. New York: Routledge.
Rodgers, K. (2010) 'Anger is why we're all here': Mobilizing and managing emotions in a professional activist organization. *Social Movement Studies* 9, 273–291.
Scott, C. and Myers, K.K. (2005) The socialization of emotion: Learning emotion management at the fire station. *Journal of Applied Communication Research* 33 (1), 67–92.
Shao, K., Yu, W. and Ji, Z. (2013) An exploration of Chinese EFL students' emotional intelligence and foreign language anxiety. *The Modern Language Journal* 97 (4), 917–929.
Sheehan, C. (2012) Hard labour at 35,000 feet: A reconsideration of emotional demands in airline service work. *Hospitality and Society* 2 (1), 99–116.
Swanson, P.B. (2012) The congruence of vocational interests and the workplace environment: Reducing the language teacher shortage. *Language Teaching Research* 16, 519–537.
Swanson, P. and Huff, R. (2010) The relationship of Georgia's rural foreign language teachers' sense of efficacy to teacher attrition. *Rural Educator* 31 (3), 16–29.
Torland, M. (2011) Emotional labour and job satisfaction of adventure tour leaders: Does gender matter? *Annals of Leisure Research* 14, 369–389.
Tracy, S.J. and Tracy, K. (1998) Emotion labor at 911: A case study and theoretical critique. *Journal of Applied Communication Research* 26, 390–411.
Truta, C. (2014) Emotional labor and motivation in teachers. *Procedia – Social and Behavioral Sciences* 127 (22), 791–795. See http://dx.doi.org/10.1016/j.sbspro.2014.03.356 (accessed 30 December 2015).
United States Census Bureau (2010) American fact finder. See https://factfinder.census.gov (accessed 30 December 2015).

Vincent, C. and Braun, A. (2013) Being 'fun' at work: Emotional labour, class, gender and childcare. *British Educational Research Journal* 39, 751–768.

Yang, S. and Guy, M.E. (2015) Gender effects on emotional labor in Seoul metropolitan area. *Public Personnel Management* 44 (1), 3–24.

Yin, H., Lee, J.C.K., Zhang, Z. and Jin, Y. (2013) Exploring the relationship among teachers' emotional intelligence, emotional labor strategies and teaching satisfaction. *Teaching and Teacher Education* 35, 137–145.

Zhang, Q. and Zhu, W. (2008) Exploring emotion in teaching: Emotional labor, burnout, and satisfaction in Chinese higher education. *Communication Education* 57, 105–122.

Appendix: Modified Emotional Labour Scale (Lee & Brotheridge, 2011)

On a typical day, how frequently do you perform each of the following?

1	2	3	4	5
Never				Always

(1) Display specific emotions required by your job.
(2) Adopt certain emotions required as part of your job.
(3) Express particular emotions needed for your job.
(4) Show some strong emotions.
(5) Express intense emotions.
(6) Display many different kinds of emotions.
(7) Express many different emotions.
(8) Display many different emotions when interacting with others.
(9) Make an effort to actually feel the emotions that you need to display.
(10) Try to actually experience the emotions that you must show.
(11) Really try to feel the emotions you have to show as part of your job.
(12) Show emotions that you don't feel.
(13) Pretend to have emotions that you don't really have.
(14) Show emotions that are expected rather than what you feel.
(15) Resist expressing your true feelings.
(16) Hide your true feelings about a situation.
(17) Conceal what you're feeling.

4 Theorising Emotions from a Critical Perspective: English Language Teachers' Emotion Labour when Responding to Student Writing

Sarah Benesch

> Who is allowed to feel and express enthusiasm (or contempt) for particular ideas or practices? Which display rules are dominant and why? To what extent can alternative discourses of emotivity co-exist in particular socio-historical settings?
> – Svasek & Skrbis, 2007: 378–379

Introduction

The questions that open this chapter reflect a critical approach to emotions. Posed by anthropologist Svasek and sociologist Skrbis, they challenge the dominant notions of emotions as genetically coded features of human minds or cognitive appraisals carried out by individuals. These authors, and others cited in this chapter, theorise emotions as sociocultural constructs mediated by power relations rather than cognitive or biological properties. By asking such questions as 'Who is allowed to feel?' they signal attention to social and institutional rules that regulate emotions in varying contexts. The relationship between power and emotions is central to their study of emotions, including resistance to power.

In keeping with these concerns, this chapter explores how power and emotions are interconnected in English language teaching. To address that relationship, I will first outline the theoretical assumptions of critical approaches to emotions, including the role of power. Along these lines, the literature review begins with a discussion of Ahmed's (2004) proposal for a *cultural politics of emotion*, focusing on her notion of sticky objects. Next, I will introduce emotion labour, a conceptual tool borrowed from sociologist Arlie Hochschild (1979, 1983) that can be used to study emotions from a critical perspective.

The discussion of sticky objects and emotion labour will be followed by examples of these concepts in the data analysis section. The data are drawn from interviews conducted with English language teachers at a US university about activities and conditions that might be considered emotionally charged in their teaching: high-stakes literacy testing, responding to student writing, plagiarism and attendance (Benesch, 2012, 2017). In this chapter I will focus on two of the findings about responding to student writing.

The data analysis is intended to demonstrate how emotion labour may come into play in ELT. Equally important though is that the data analysis highlights the role of power in teachers' emotional responses to the pedagogical demands they face. By focusing on power, I hope to encourage emotions as a lens that reveals unreasonable or unfair demands, thereby provoking resistance and reform toward better conditions for teachers and students. The purpose of examining the relationship between emotions and power is to support greater teacher agency in curricular and pedagogical matters, in order to move toward better teaching and learning conditions.

Related Literature

Sticky objects as a tool for theorising emotions critically

> Emotions are intentional in the sense that they are 'about' something: they involve a direction or orientation towards an object ... Emotions are both about objects, which they hence shape, and are also shaped by contact with other objects. (Ahmed, 2004: 7)

Ahmed's (2004) proposal for a cultural politics of emotions offers a striking alternative to biological and cognitive theories that locate emotions within individuals' bodies or minds. Not only did Ahmed challenge intrapersonal models of emotions but also social theories that locate emotions in society and posit the movement of emotions between individuals. Instead, Ahmed claimed that 'it is the objects of emotions that circulate rather than emotions as such' (2004: 11). The twin notions of movement and attachment are key to her political perspective where the focus is 'what sticks' and 'what connects us to this or that' (2004: 11). Her central question was: Why do we become so attached to certain ideas, activities, people or objects that it is difficult to live without them or away from them?

According to Ahmed, it is through repetition that objects become sticky with affect. That is, social norms are naturalised when they are repeatedly enacted. Repetition lends social norms, such as heterosexuality and marriage, the appearance of 'forms of life' (2004: 12). Studying emotions is a way to denaturalise social norms by revealing that they came into being through repetition, not because they are necessary or inevitable. The aim of Ahmed's cultural politics of emotion is to reveal 'how subjects become *invested* in particular structures' (2004: 12) so much so that they cling to them tenaciously.

Equally important, from a political perspective, is that a reckoning with stickiness is a means toward greater social justice. Coming to terms with which objects and signs are emotionally saturated can start the process toward transformation, or 'a reorientation of one's bodily relations' (2004: 171) away from sticky objects that are associated with inequality and injustice.

Above all, the notion of stickiness, or sticky objects, highlights the relationship between emotions and power. It reveals 'how power shapes the very surface of bodies as well as worlds' (2004: 12). Some questions regarding this relationship are: 'Why is social transformation so difficult to achieve? Why are relations of power so intractable and enduring, even in the face of collective forms of resistance?' (2004: 11–12).

In her exploration of these questions, Ahmed (2004, 2010) acknowledged the price that must be paid for reorientation away from social norms just as there are benefits for remaining oriented toward them. Those who embrace mainstream expectations are rewarded for holding sanctioned sticky objects close them, while those who turn their bodies away may find themselves ridiculed, shunned or punished. To illustrate these different possibilities, Ahmed (2010) offered a book-length treatment, *The Promise of Happiness*, on social norms that are held out as objects of acceptability and fulfilment. These include heterosexuality, marriage and procreation. Those who turn their bodies away from these objects of promised happiness run the risk of being identified as misfits and even troublemakers due to their refusal to join the majority in embracing sanctioned happy objects.

Whereas Ahmed (2004, 2010) examined discourses of feminism, immigration, nationalism and family in her study of emotions, in English language teaching, sticky objects might include literacy testing, classroom observations, textbooks, attendance, plagiarism and the topic of this chapter, responding to student writing. In the data analysis section, I will present teachers' answers to my questions about responding to their students' writing to explore their affective responses to this sticky object and related ones.

Emotion labour as a tool for studying teachers' emotions critically

Like Ahmed, sociologist Arlie Hochschild (1979, 1983) examined the relationship between emotions and power, though decades earlier. Her landmark study of the training of US flight attendants in the late 1970s exposed their struggle in attempting to manage their emotions to bring them in line with those they were expected to display in the workplace. They managed their emotions, according to Hochschild, through both surface and deep acting.

Surface acting involves changing one's demeanour to appear to have feelings that are expected to be displayed, such as smiling at customers. According to Hochschild (1983), people routinely pretend to share the mandated emotions of a context by displaying them outwardly while inwardly experiencing divergent ones.

Deep acting, on the other hand, involves not just changing one's outward display of feelings, but also one's internal feelings. It is not simply the display of feelings that changes, but also the feelings themselves. In her study, she found examples of both surface and deep acting among flight attendants who were explicitly trained to display particular feelings before, during and after flights. They reported emotion labour when the emotion rules they were mandated to follow clashed with their genuine feelings.

Hochschild's (1983) concern about surface and deep acting in the workplace was that they are commodified as 'forms of labor to be sold' (1983: 89). She warned that 'when private capacities for empathy and warmth are put to corporate use' (1983: 89), workers may no longer be able to experience genuine emotions. Furthermore, the mandate from management to display certain emotions was a clear illustration of unequal workplace power in the affective domain.

The use of emotion labour in this chapter is a homage to Hochschild's pioneering attention to the relationship between power and emotions in the workplace. However, it departs from her modernist notion of genuine feelings and an authentic self that are violated by surface and deep acting in the workplace. Rather than taking a modernist or psychological approach to emotions as internal and real, I take a poststructural approach whereby emotion labour is a lens for studying the responses of English language teachers to institutional power, including whether they obey or resist institutional norms. Furthermore, it should be noted that rather than adopt the more commonly used phrase *emotional labour*, I instead use *emotion labour*. The reason for this choice is that *emotional* can be negatively associated with someone, especially a woman, behaving in an overwrought and socially unacceptable way. To avoid that negative connotation and to highlight the relationship between emotions and power, I use *emotion labour*. Two examples of qualitative emotion labour research taking a poststructural approach are offered next.

Qualitative studies of teachers' emotion labour take into account the wider social context rather than focusing on the intrapsychic life of teachers (see Gkonou & Miller, 2017; King, 2016). For example, Zembylas's (2005) ethnography of a K-1 science teacher, Catherine, was grounded in poststructural understandings of emotions and emotion labour as discursively constructed. Using a Foucauldian framework, Zembylas (2005) described how the emotion rules of the school in which his participant taught were historically contingent and therefore subject to contestation rather than strict obedience.

For example, Zembylas (2005) found that Catherine's emotion labour was shaped in part by the emotion rules promulgated by the school and wider science-teaching discourses, ones that influenced which pedagogies were favoured and which were disfavoured. Catherine repeatedly ran up against a masculinist discourse promulgating science as objective, science teaching as fact- and test-driven, and colleagues' refusal to discuss affective dimensions of teaching or pedagogies that did not directly support standardised testing. In addition, Catherine was frequently dismissed or ridiculed when she tried to discuss her excitement or other emotions with her colleagues. However, though she experienced emotion labour, Catherine eventually resisted the prevailing discourses, generating greater excitement about learning among her students and greater professional satisfaction for herself.

Loh and Liew (2016) also took a discursive approach in their analysis of the emotion labour of secondary English language teachers in Singapore. Embedding their data analysis in a rich description of the social context, the authors discussed the government's demand for English language literacy as a way to promote economic competitiveness. Furthermore, the education ministry demanded the use of so-called standard English, despite the fact that 50% of secondary students come from non-English speaking homes.

Given these conditions, Loh and Liew (2016) found emotion labour in several areas. The first was a conflict between the mandate to teach English as if it were a neutral medium of economic gain and the teachers' desire to prepare students to think critically about language and the world. The second emotion labour theme was the culture of testing that evaluated teachers according to scores their students received on standardised tests. The third theme was the burden of grading writing. Here the emotion labour was twofold. First was just the sheer exhaustion of having to read so many papers. Second was the mandate to give grades despite the subjectivity of evaluating writing. Furthermore, when students wrote about personal topics, teachers were reluctant to grade their writing though they were required to do so. Finally, teachers reported conflict between their training in culturally responsive teaching and the schools' demand for one-size-fits-all pedagogy grounded in standardised testing.

Loh and Liew (2016) called for attention in English language teacher education to the affective dimension of teaching so that teachers might collaborate with each other rather than experiencing their emotion labour as personal and private. These issues are taken up in the data analysis and implications sections.

To sum up the use of emotion labour in this chapter, it is a clash between institutional demands or expectations and teachers' beliefs/preferences/expectations. As I will discuss next, emotion labour was manifested in teachers' talk as conflict between social or institutional demands and teachers' training/ethics. Dissonance among institutional requirements, student expectations and teachers' preferences was reported to produce emotion labour by interviewees, who expressed ongoing anxiety about how best to respond to student writing.

Data Collection and Analysis

Responding to student writing and emotion labour

> Responding to students' writing is one of the most controversial topics in second- and foreign-language (SL and FL) instruction and theory. Do students benefit from teachers' corrections and written comments on their writing? If so, what types of feedback are effective? (Diab, 2005: 28)

As Diab (2005) pointed out, responding to writing remains contentious. Enduring questions include whether teacher feedback is beneficial and, if it is, which types are most effective. Given these controversies, my goal in interviewing teachers about responding to student writing was to discover any emotion labour surrounding this ubiquitous yet fraught process. Ultimately I hoped that emotion labour might indicate a pathway to more satisfying outcomes for English language teachers and their students.

The interviews were conducted with 13 part- and full-time English language instructors at the City University of New York where I was also on the faculty. Two additional respondents filled out a questionnaire containing the interview questions.

The semi-structured interviews revolved around the process of responding to writing and any feelings associated with it, using the following questions: (1) Do you assign writing in your classes? (2) If so, describe how you go about reading student papers: Where do you read them? When do you read them? How many do you read at one sitting? (3) What are some of the feelings that emerge when reading them? (4) How do you feel about evaluating the writing?

I read the interview data repeatedly for evidence of emotion labour – that is, some type of conflict or dilemma embedded in the discourse, such as that which Loh and Liew (2016) uncovered. After many readings, themes revolving around a conflict began to emerge. I report on two of these themes: (1) the sense of spending too much time or not enough time commenting and (2) what type of feedback to offer, toward content or usage. Both of these are discussed next with supporting examples from the interview data. It should be noted that the responses are numbered consecutively (R1, R2, etc.) with no reference to the respondents' gender, age or other identifying characteristics because I was not attempting to correlate identity and emotion labour. Instead each response should be seen as an example of English language teachers' emotion discourse about a particular topic.

Results

Emotion labour theme one: Too much time responding to writing or not enough time?

Responses to the questions about the process of reading student papers (where, when and how many) revealed the sheer work of responding, including it being 'manageable but still the whole day' (R1), part of a long daily subway commute (R2), and a task that is put off 'as long as possible' (R3):

R1: I usually read them in the course of a limited number of days. So I read a lot on one or two or three days. A regular class is 28 students. In such a class I would read maybe half of them on one day and the other half on another day. So it's like 14 and 14, something like that. It's manageable, but it's still the whole day. It's an off day and it's the whole day.

R2: I read their papers on the subway mainly, during the two and a half hours I spend commuting to and from work every day. I read them until I read all of them. That will depend on how many I have at any given time.

R3: I read them all over the place. Not in my office because my office is too cramped. There's papers and books everywhere all out of order and it makes me crazy to be in there so I don't read them there. I read them in the subway. I read them at home at my desk. I put off reading them as long as possible. So I often read them all day Sunday.

Not only was the amount of time discussed, but also emotion labour centred on how much to write. For example, R4 highlights the difficulty a newly hired instructor faced in a highly regulated pre-freshman programme where the 'general consensus' was to spend no more than 10 minutes on each paper. This respondent reported feeling 'pressure' at the time to keep up with that speed, wondering whether quality was being sacrificed:

R4: They were very painful at first for me because I wasn't quite sure what to focus on and how to formulate my comments. So they would go very slow and over time I sort of figured out some approaches and strategies to make it better. So I would sit down and do three or four in an hour. No, like two or maybe three in an hour. They were taking me 30 minutes each. Eventually I got it down to like 15 or 20. But there was pressure to get it down lower. Most teachers were doing it a lot faster.

SB: Why was there pressure?

R4: There was just a lot to get through with the other work. So, there was sort of a general consensus that you were supposed to be getting them done or they were assuming that you could get them done in 10 minutes per paper. There were different approaches that I think some teachers used that probably weren't as … emphasizing speed over quality. One of the shifts I made, somebody pointed out a strategy: reading a bunch of them first before making a mark. I would get so anxious about it that I would start marking them right away.

R5, too, describes a struggle around the amount of time commenting takes, describing the process as 'torture' because 'it takes a lot of time'. Indeed, R5 reveals the sense that responding is a 'constant source of stress' that 'has taken over' the respondent's life. Included in this response is the expression of a desire to be more 'efficient' and avoid attending to 'every mistake because it's counterproductive':

R5: I'm always carrying essays around to check and I'm always putting off checking them. Because I think that it's gonna be this torture. It's just a procrastination technique but also because it takes a lot of time. I do it better when I'm waiting for something to happen like waiting for an appointment or if I'm on the train I can do it and I get it done. But at home I'm always putting it off. So lately I've been reading like four or five papers and I feel like I get something done. And then I'm like, 'Oh my God, I've only read four or five. I've got 20 more to read.' It's a constant source of stress for me and the sense of a burden, a sense of guilt that I haven't done it. So one of my goals is to read them more efficiently and to not check every mistake because it's counterproductive. We all learn not to do that and then we end up doing it … It's such a relief to get it done. It makes me think that checking writing has taken over my life and I need to have a sense of limit. Like some day when I just don't touch it. But I can't really do that unless I get it done first.

Like R4 and R5, R6 expresses the concern that writing too many comments limits the number of papers that can be read in one sitting:

R6: I can't do probably more than three or four at a time because it's just exhausting and I just run out of energy to make comments, right? Sometimes I just scribble way too much.

Finally, R7, a part-time teacher, demonstrates emotion labour related to marginalisation due to a lack of physical space allocated to part-time teachers, referred to as *adjuncts*, those who carry out the lion's share of ESL teaching in CUNY, and a lack of compensation for the work of responding to student writing:

> **R7:** I usually read them at home because, as an adjunct, I do not have an office. I read them on unpaid time, as an adjunct, evenings and weekends. How many I read will depend on how long they are. If it is a short essay, I may read 10 or more at a sitting. If they are term papers, I will read about three or four at a time.

R7 underscores the university's reliance on English language teachers, mainly adjuncts, to assign writing regularly as a way of preparing students for the high-stakes literacy test they need to pass before entering first-year writing courses. English language teachers are not only expected to help students pass that test, but also prepare students to write first-year composition level essays. Yet, the per-course salary adjuncts receive does not include hours for preparation or commenting on papers. Furthermore, as indicated in R1, there may be 28 students in a single class, making responding to writing the defining activity for many teachers.

This last point about the exploitation of part-time teachers is not a startling revelation nor a new discovery. Yet it is important when studying responding to writing to take these socioeconomic factors (time and money) into account. For the purpose of this chapter, I want to underscore the emotion labour of being unsure of how much time to spend reading and responding to student writing, particularly given the number of papers that must be read and the sense of responsibility to facilitate students' entry into mainstream college courses. This issue is discussed further in the next section. In the implications for pedagogy section I discuss possible ways to address the question of how much time to spend responding to each paper.

Emotion labour theme two: Type of feedback to offer – toward content or usage?

Given the ongoing debate in the responding-to-writing literature about which types of feedback are most effective, it is not surprising that respondents discussed conflict between responding to usage and to ideas. In some cases, the dilemma was reported to be resolved by offering a split grade (R8) or using a two-part rubric (R9):

> **R8:** I always give a double grade. I give a second grade for the grammar. And I know that … I think a lot of ESL teachers do that and I know at [name of college], we recommend to writing teachers often who will have some ESL students in their class that they do that, that they grade the papers like that. One grade for the ideas and another grade for the grammar.

R9: Based on a very specific set of instructions, I've created a two-part rubric. The first part deals with content issues; the second part deals with grammar/mechanics. And what I do is I end up reading their papers twice. I read them first for content things and I have my rubric at hand.

Though R8 and R9 indicate satisfaction with the two-grade solution, others reported a struggle around the issue of which type of feedback was most appropriate, especially given the tacit institutional expectation that ESL teachers were solely responsible for addressing usage errors. Added to that expectation are the other types of comments that English language teachers are trained to offer. The range of possible comments creates a dilemma, especially given how overwhelmed respondents reported feeling by the number of papers they had to read, discussed earlier in the chapter. Furthermore, as seen in R10, there may be an awareness that English language learners do not receive comments about usage from other faculty members.

R10 begins by discussing different types of feedback: toward correctness, development, focus and organisation. But there is also a reference to getting 'bogged down' in correcting language, given the responsibility of being perhaps the only teacher to comment on NNES students' language: '[I]f they're not getting feedback on their language from me, who are they gonna get it from?' Emotion labour, in this case, consists of juggling three types of response: to language (given that other teachers may not address it), to organisation and to ideas. R10 ends with the observation that responding to meaning requires the most energy and attention, both of which may be in short supply 'at the end of it'. This is an important point, given the number of papers ESL instructors are typically expected to respond to each week:

R10: …my idiosyncrasy is if it's filled with language issues I get bogged down in the … in correcting the language. I guess I'm kind of old school in that respect. I think if they're not seeing … if they're not getting feedback on their language from me, who are they gonna get it from? But I still try to step back after I've looked at it and ask questions about development, focus, organization. So I'm trying more to respond in the last four or five years, trying more to respond to content and ask questions about meaning and … but that also depends on how tired I am at the end of it. How much attention I can dedicate to that.

As in R10, the sense of responsibility seems strong in R11, compensating for what non-ESL teachers might not offer. However, in R11, the supplemental work is not just commenting about grammar, but also challenging students' assumption that their writing will improve if they gain more grammar and vocabulary and simply 'mush them together'. This teacher outlines a paradox: whereas grammar correction is the 'reward' offered for writing a well-developed and well-organised paper, the aim is also to make students aware that writing is not just 'words and grammar', but, instead, a more complex process:

R11: I mean I have an order in which I address issues. I start with development. I go on to organization and clarity and at the very end sort of treat grammar as a reward. Like if your essay is really well developed and organized perfectly, I will correct your grammar or at least I'll indicate where your errors are and ask you to figure out what's wrong and if you can't, we'll talk about it.

SB: Why do you say 'reward'?

R11: It's kind of all they want from me because they don't know what writing is about. And I think maybe all the feedback they've ever gotten is about grammar. They think that the problem is grammar and vocabulary ... If they just knew all the words and grammar, they could mush them together and make writing. So I try to teach them it's more complicated than that.

Related to R10 and R11 about English language teachers' sense of responsibility to give feedback about usage were responses that explicitly referenced how the teachers viewed their roles as responders, including conflicts among them. Embedded in these responses was the expression of varying degrees of confidence about choosing between the roles or how to reconcile them.

In R12 and R13, the underlying question seems to be: Am I a reader or evaluator? The answer in R12 is that the teacher is a reader who is able to see students as 'people who have something to say' rather than as 'error makers':

R12: So I don't say that I'm marking papers. I say I'm reading papers. It also changes my attitude toward the student. That's the idea here: what are you trying to say? And look at them as people who have something to say, not as little error makers.

While R12 communicates confidence about the respondent's role as a reader, R13 is less sanguine. The respondent expresses the intention of being a positive reader, open to the value of students' developing ideas. But this requires setting aside any negative experiences at work or at home that could impede openness to the text as one that 'has something to offer'. It is a goal, not easily attained, but aimed for and 'taken to heart':

R13: You come to papers, to texts, every time you come to the text you come to it with a different frame of mind. And something might have happened to you. You might have had a bad experience with the student. You might have a personal issue. You might have been too tired. Your children might have upset you at home. You know, something. So trying to bring yourself to that reading in an emotional state where you're kind of positive and ready to look at the work as student work that is developing, that is valuable, that has something to offer. Now this sounds lofty. It's a worthy cause. It's not always easy. But it's something that I've taken to heart.

R14 poses the question more explicitly: Am I a language teacher or a writing teacher? In this response, it can be seen that there was a change between beginner ESL teacher and the present. At the beginning, the answer was language teacher. However, as the years went by the teacher learned to 'sit on [their] hands' to avoid correcting grammar prematurely and to notice and respond to the ideas:

R14: I also feel like you know when I first started out as an ESL teacher no one really told me anything about how to teach writing. I did have a tendency and I think many teachers have this tendency to immediately start correcting the grammar. I felt like I was more of a language teacher than a writing teacher and over time … I think I've heard other people say this, I learned to sit on my hands and not immediately … I mean I think I'd sometimes go so quickly into correcting grammar that I wouldn't even notice the ideas so much.

This is not to say that this particular teacher eschews grammar correction, but instead reported using a split-grade system: one for ideas and the other for usage. The claim of a shift to writing teacher along with the split-grade technique signals that the relationship between teaching usage and development of ideas is a vexed one for this particular instructor, as it was reported to be for many of the respondents.

Another example of tension surrounding feedback toward usage, or one might say the stickiness of written corrective feedback (WCF), can be seen in R15 where the respondent goes so far as to dramatise grammar correction as an addiction: the ESL teacher makes corrections even after promising, or warning, never to do it again. In this extended metaphor, both teacher and students have their mutually dependent roles, with students not checking their errors before turning in their papers and the teacher continuing to correct them, despite the warning. The addiction is fed by entrenched habits, ones with questionable benefits:

R15: So I think I'm not helping myself and maybe not helping my students as much as I could or should be by checking it for them. By being the first one to mark their typed paper, right? They should mark it in some editing way first. And I have said that many times to students that I'm not gonna check your paper. If you want me to check your paper, you gotta mark something on it first. And then I go and take it. So they know they can … I don't know if they do it on purpose. We're like a bunch of alcoholics giving each other drinks, in a way. There's just certain dependence, you know, that they have to get past.

Similarly R16 describes the impulse to make corrections as a strong 'human urge', one that must be consciously curbed by 'reading a bunch of them first before making a mark':

R16: One of the shifts I made, somebody pointed out a strategy: reading a bunch of them first before making a mark. I would get so anxious about it that I would start marking them right away ... Still it's a very strong impulse to mark. And I always remember I wrote for my college newspaper and there was a sign in the editing room: 'The greatest human urge is not food or drink or even sex, but the urge to change what someone else has written.' And I always thought that was a really appropriate statement.

Overall, the responses about the types of comments made on student papers revealed emotion labor about the relationship between error correction and comments about meaning correction and comments about meaning, offering clear evidence that this split is in full force in the field of ELT. Finding this tension in the data was not surprising given the ongoing debate in the literature about WCF and its relationship to feedback about content. Whether participants characterised their responses as more readerly than evaluative, or more grammar-intensive, the data indicated a persistent lack of assuredness about the amount of feedback to offer and the most appropriate types of comments to write.

Discussion

The two findings reported in this chapter from my interviews with English language teachers about responding to writing indicate emotion labour around time and around the types of feedback to offer. As to time, respondents reported struggling with how much time to spend reading and responding to each paper, given the volume of papers they faced each week. There was the sense that were teachers to have fewer papers to read, they would be able to devote more time to each. In some cases, as in R4, there was institutional pressure to minimise the time spent on each paper, leaving the respondent with the sense that quality was being sacrificed for speed.

Concerning which types of feedback to offer, there was evidence of difficulty reconciling comments toward usage and comments toward the development of ideas. Solutions varied from not correcting to flagging errors to offering separate grades for usage and ideas. There was also evidence in the data of the additional burden of being students' sole instructor to attend to usage and therefore a sense of obligation to offer WCF. In addition, one respondent who described WCF as a 'reward' for well-written essays also reported a sense of obligation to teach students that writing is not simply a matter of acquiring grammatical knowledge and vocabulary that might then be 'mushed together'. Above all, there seemed to be a struggle around the relationship between comments toward revision and those toward correctness, with some using rubrics to address both.

In fact, a teacher who claimed early in the interview to have shifted from language teacher to writing teacher later discussed an elaborate process of signalling errors and a split-grade technique. In addition, one interviewee described WCF as an addiction and another as a strong human urge. These responses suggest the powerful draw of correcting, one that seduces both English language learners, who expect correction, and teachers, who feel compelled to provide it. Seen through the lenses of addiction, urge and seduction, WCF appears as a sticky object (Ahmed, 2004), one that is difficult to resist despite a lack of clear evidence in the literature of its short- or long-term benefits. Given the stickiness of WCF for students and teachers, considerable emotion labour is expended on a series of interconnected questions: Is the time taken to correct well spent? How, if at all, is it useful to students? Might it be harmful, as Truscott (2007) claimed? Does it end up engendering desire for and offering of more correction?

These questions indicate emotion labour which itself indicates that dialogues between teachers, between teachers and their students, and between teachers and administrators are needed to improve conditions for post-secondary teachers and their students around responding to writing.

Implications for Pedagogy: Debunking the Myth of Improvement

To address emotion labour related to concerns about how much time to spend commenting and/or what types of feedback to offer, it may be useful to debunk the *myth of improvement*, as Brannon and Knoblauch (2006) suggested. This is the belief that the comments a particular teacher makes on a student paper will lead to improved student writing, though research evidence to support this claim is ambiguous at best. Summarizing 50 years of research on responding to student writing, Brannon and Knoblauch (2006) found that the question about the effectiveness of this feedback 'remains unresolved' (1). To address the 'persistently unconvincing demonstration' (2) in composition research that teacher feedback leads to improved student writing, they challenged assumptions guiding the research. For one, they questioned the premise that only if 'prompt and steady improvement' (2) is documented can it be said that response works. Supporting the more rational assumption that 'human development is unpredictable, irregular, and time-consuming' (3), they called for research and practice honouring the complexity of composition teaching and learning and the indeterminate relationship between them.

In making these claims about the tenuous relationship between teaching writing and learning to write, Brannon and Knoblauch (2006) were taking a political position. The danger of the myth of improvement, they claimed, is that it leads to the type of measurement to which education has fallen prey in the neoliberal age of accountability. When it comes to composition, the myth of improvement, by propagating the notion of fast gains given the right kind of teaching, justifies high-stakes literacy testing. In this paradigm, the burden is exclusively on teachers, who are expected to provide appropriate feedback in the service of measurable results.

Rather than agonizing over which types of feedback are most effective, Brannon and Knoblauch (2006) suggested that the concern should be with 'the impact of commentary on the quality of the relationship between teacher and student' (2006: 12). To that end, they called for a shift in conceptualising feedback from an instrument of progress to a means of social engagement. This shift represents a rejection of 'behaviorist' goals, promoting, instead, 'the complicated intellectual, rhetorical, logical, emotional, stylistic, ethical, political, and other dimensions of language practice' (2006: 14).

Sommers (2006) came to similar conclusions about the centrality of the teacher/student relationship in responding to writing, based on her four-year study of teachers' comments on the writing of 400 undergraduate students and interviews with the students about the feedback. Overall, Sommers (2006) found that teachers' comments played a 'social role', helping students develop a sense of 'academic belonging' (Sommers, 2006: 251) and diminished anonymity, the affective dimension of response that Brannon and Knoblauch (2006) promoted.

The myth of improvement and the focus on responding to writing as an affective undertaking intersect with emotion labour in ways that suggest greater latitude and equanimity when it comes to responding to student writing. Brannon and Knoblauch's (2006) observation that any particular teacher is only one in a student's writing history may offer a reprieve from the emotion labour of how much time to spend and which types of comments to offer. If, as they claimed, students' literacy acquisition is 'always, already, underway' (2006: 15) and one teacher is therefore not solely responsible, might there be a more casual attitude toward responding to writing, particularly if instantaneous or obvious gains are not anticipated?

Given the lack of consensus over the last 50 years about the short-term and long-term impact of teacher comments on student writing and my findings about emotion labour (Benesch, 2012, 2017), English language teachers might aim to communicate interest in their students' writing without having to spent unreasonable amounts of time commenting on each paper or trying to address every concern. This might lead to minimising written feedback while still honouring relationships with students while also being aware that improvement, however that might be defined, does not fall to EL teachers, or any single teacher, alone.

Another strategy might be to engage students in a discussion of their expectations of teacher feedback through a questionnaire. Questions might include: What type(s) of feedback are you used to receiving on your writing? Have you found this feedback helpful or not? Why? What type(s) of feedback would you like to receive? How would that feedback help you?

Engaging students in a discussion of these issues is a way to dramatise writing and responding to writing as potentially satisfying activities through which teachers and students develop relationships that can enhance a sense of belonging and decrease the anonymity of academic life, as Sommers (2006) found.

At the institutional level, it might be beneficial to discuss the emotion labour of responding to writing with colleagues within one's department and across the curriculum. Intradepartmental and college-wide discussions about institutional expectations and teachers' emotion labour around responding to writing might lead to greater clarity and more satisfying experiences all around.

Implications for Research: Sticky Objects and Emotion Labour

The data presented in this chapter were meant to illustrate how sticky objects and emotion labour, as conceptual tools, can highlight the role of emotions in English language teaching from a sociopolitical perspective. By bringing power into the picture, these tools can provoke questions about teachers' emotions that are left out of cognitive research in which emotions are considered as intrapsychic phenomena. Instead, the notion of sticky objects allows for a focus on teaching activities, such as WCF, that are so saturated with affect, and therefore naturalised, that they may deter thoughtful implementation or meaningful reform.

Furthermore, emotion labour as a concept invites consideration of teachers' stress not as a private matter that can be eradicated through emotional literacy, but, rather, as a signal that current conditions, such as how English language teachers respond to student writing, may need to change. Along these lines I end with the following questions for future research:

(1) What are the sticky objects of English language teaching?
(2) What are institutional expectations that may make a particular object sticky with affect?
(3) How does teachers' training/ethics differ from those institutional expectations, leading to emotion labour?
(4) How do students' and teachers' expectations differ, producing emotion labour in both groups?

(5) How can emotion labour be reconceptualised as a social tool of educational transformation rather than individual teachers' personal emotional turmoil to be overcome privately?

Post-Reading Tasks

(1) What has been a sticky object in your teaching (or graduate studies if you are pre-service)? What makes it particularly sticky and how have you responded to it?
(2) How, if at all, does the concept of emotion labour pertain to your teaching (or studies)?
(3) What are some institutional feeling rules where you work or study?
(4) How do you see your role when responding to student writing? What are its emotional demands?

References

Ahmed, S. (2004) *The Cultural Politics of Emotion*. New York: Routledge.

Ahmed, S. (2010) *The Promise of Happiness*. Durham, NH: Duke University Press.

Benesch, S. (2012) *Considering Emotions in Critical English Language Teaching: Theories and Praxis*. New York: Routledge.

Benesch, S. (2017) *Emotions and English Language Teaching: Exploring Teachers' Emotion Labor*. New York: Routledge.

Brannon, L. and Knoblauch, C. (2006) Introduction: The emperor still has no clothes: Revisiting the myth of improvement. In R. Straub (ed.) *Keyworks on Teacher Response: An Anthology* (pp. 1–15). Portsmouth, NH: Boynton/Cook.

Diab, R.L. (2005) Teachers' and students' beliefs about responding to ESL writing: A case study. *TESL Canada Journal/Revue TESL du Canada* 23 (1), 28–43.

Gkonou, C. and Miller, E.R. (2017) Caring and emotional labour: Language teachers' engagement with anxious learners in private language school classrooms. *Language Teaching Research*. doi: 10.1177/1362168817728739.

Hochschild, A.R. (1979) Emotion work, feeling rules, and social structure. *American Journal of Sociology* 85 (3), 551–575.

Hochschild, A.R. (1983) *The Managed Heart: Commercialization of Human Feeling*. Berkeley: University of California Press.

King, J. (2016) 'It's time, put on the smile, it's time!': The emotional labour of second language teaching within a Japanese university. In C. Gkonou, D. Tatzl and S. Mercer (eds) *New Directions in Language Learning Psychology* (pp. 97–112). Dordrecht: Springer.

Loh, C.E. and Liew, W.M. (2016) Voices from the ground: The emotional labour of English teachers' work. *Teaching and Teacher Education* 55, 267–278.

Sommers, N. (2006) Across the drafts. *College Composition and Communication* 58 (2), 248–257.

Svasek, M. and Skrbis, Z. (2007) Passions and power: Emotions and globalisation. *Identities: Global Studies in Culture and Power* 14 (4), 367–383.

Truscott, J. (2007) The effect of error correction on learners' ability to write accurately. *Journal of Second Language Writing* 16 (4), 255–272.

Zembylas, M. (2005) *Teaching with Emotion: A Postmodern Enactment*. Greenwich, CT: Information Age Publishing.

5 'Opening Pandora's Box': Language Teachers' Dynamic Emotional Experiences of Conducting Action Research

Emily Edwards and Anne Burns

Introduction

The importance of emotions as a component of language teacher development and teacher identity is now well recognised, and the construct is currently being explored in more depth. In the field of second language teacher education, researchers now highlight the role that emotions play in shaping how teachers experience professional learning programmes (e.g. Golombek, 2015; Johnson & Golombek, 2016; Kubanyiova, 2012). In addition, teachers' emotions are considered to be dynamic, closely connected to teachers' cognitions (Yuan & Lee, 2015) and significantly influenced by a teacher's sociocultural environment and learning experience (Beauchamp & Thomas, 2009; Yuan & Lee, 2015). However, there is still little understanding in the field about the relationship between teachers' fluctuating emotions and their identity development over time. We define both emotions and identity from a sociocultural perspective, which is unpacked in the next section. In addition, very little research has explored the relationship between language teacher emotions and experiences of action research, which is pertinent since action research can unearth uncomfortable truths about teaching (Mockler & Groundwater-Smith, 2015) that are likely to trigger a range of emotions.

This chapter is structured as follows. First, we outline a sociocultural perspective on language teacher identity and emotions, and then connect this literature to the teacher education context of the current study: an action research programme. Next, we discuss recent studies that have used metaphor analysis to investigate teacher identity, but have rarely analysed emotions. We then explain the specific context and qualitative design of the study, before presenting the findings in terms of the metaphors used by some of the teachers, and explaining how these metaphors reveal both emotional experiences and identity transformations.

Identity and Emotions from a Sociocultural Perspective

The construct of language teacher identity has recently been defined by Varghese, Motha, Park, Reeves and Trent (2016: 548) as 'a process in which individuals negotiate external and internal expectations as they work to make sense of themselves and their work as educators'. Identity can also be conceptualised as a sense of 'self', which refers to how people perceive themselves, their roles and status, and how they think others perceive them: 'the self is [...] an on-going project of establishing one's place in the world' (van Lier, 2004: 115). Van Lier (2008) adds that identity can be viewed as a continuous process of aligning and re-aligning perceptions of self from different sources (yourself, and how others see you). We view identities as being constantly mediated and co- and re-constructed through a dynamic process involving ourselves (and our perceptions), and other people and tools within our cultural, social and institutional environments.

A small number of recent studies from various theoretical perspectives have investigated the relationship between language teacher identity and emotions. Research taking a postmodern or poststructuralist perspective has explored the emotional, embodied work of English language teachers (Benesch, 2012), while Song (2016) looks at teacher emotionality as constituted by social forces and ideologies within teaching institutions and considers how it shapes teachers' identities. While a sociocultural perspective is similar in recognising that language teacher emotions 'orient, underpin, and arise from' social contexts (Golombek, 2015: 472), it places more emphasis on the experience of the individual operating within their micro (classroom) and meso (schools and schooling) contexts. For example, Golombek conceptualised emotional identity-related struggles as *emotional dissonance*, a 'disharmony' (2015: 471) between the emotions experienced in a given situation and those that would be 'normative' or expected in that context. Some researchers claim emotional dissonance is necessary for development to occur (Hiver, 2013; Kubanyiova, 2012), and that negative emotions may be catalytic for teachers' continuing development:

> Emotional vulnerability outcomes are an inescapable part of teachers' ongoing professional development, but this should not be viewed as detrimental by any means as it leads to a commitment to the most effective and sustainable form of CTD [continuing teacher development]: the bottom-up, self-initiated kind. (Hiver, 2013: 221)

Another example of a socioculturally oriented study is Yuan and Lee (2015), in which pre-service EFL teachers in China experienced self-doubt, anxiety and frustration. Receiving emotional support from peers helped one of these EFL teachers sustain her evolving teacher identity; another overcame feelings of guilt by seeking help from her mentor, and subsequently improved her teaching practice. The current study adds to this emerging body of literature by exploring another potentially identity-challenging context, that of experienced teachers engaging in action research.

Action Research and Teacher Identity Development

Action research (AR) is growing in popularity as a sustainable model of second language teacher education, and as a context for researching teacher development (e.g. Edwards & Burns, 2016; Yuan & Lee, 2015). AR is a form of systematic, inquiry-based professional development that involves a dynamic combination of action and self-reflection focusing on a particular topic, puzzle, or issue of interest and importance to a teacher in their given classroom context. The processes of conducting AR are generally conceptualised as a cyclical framework that may involve the steps of planning (identifying a gap or dilemma in practice), action (implementing an intervention in the classroom), observation (collecting evidence regarding the intervention's impact) and reflection (deepening insights and personal theories about practice) (Kemmis & McTaggart, 1988). AR programmes may span several weeks, months or longer, and often involve teachers presenting and reporting on their research. This research engagement can sometimes be a very new experience for teachers, who may also find themselves challenged by confronting sometimes unwelcome truths about their teaching through AR (Mockler & Groundwater-Smith, 2015).

Previous studies on teacher identity development through AR have produced interesting findings. Trent's (2010) study of pre-service teachers showed that they experienced dissonance in terms of their images of self and prevailing educational discourses. The teachers expressed emotions of surprise, shock and disappointment in reflecting on their AR projects, prompting them to question their previous assumptions about teaching and what techniques would engage students. In the context of in-service teacher education, Yuan and Burns' (2017) study details how teachers experienced more positive emotions as a result of their AR collaborations. They shifted from feeling like *lonely fighters*, isolated in their own classrooms, to *collaborators* who worked together to observe and discuss each other's teaching. Therefore, the role of emotions in experiencing AR and in teachers' subsequent identity development is gradually being recognised. The present study makes a contribution by further exploring the relationships between identity, emotions and AR, using the lens of metaphor analysis.

Metaphor Analysis in Language Teacher Identity Research

In the existing research on teacher identity, metaphor analysis has been increasingly used as a tool to gain insight into how teachers perceive their roles (e.g. Nguyen, 2016; Yesilbursa, 2012). Metaphors can be useful ways of representing feelings or understandings about ourselves and our experiences. Indeed, Lakoff and Johnson (1980) explain that self-understanding involves the 'search for appropriate personal metaphors that make sense of our lives ... The process of self-understanding is the continual development of new life stories for yourself' (1980: 232–233). Teachers' use of metaphors to describe their work can help make the tacit more explicit, providing a helpful framework for understanding their experiences, beliefs, knowledge and feelings (Erickson & Pinnegar, 2017).

Studies exploring teacher identity have drawn on metaphor analysis to shed light on the complex ways in which teachers construct their identities during the process of learning to teach (e.g. Farrell, 2006; Thomas & Beauchamp, 2011) or as more experienced in-service teachers (e.g. Erickson & Pinnegar, 2017; Nguyen, 2016; Yesilbursa, 2012). Yesilbursa's (2012) study of university English language instructors in Turkey focused on metaphors which teachers used to describe their roles. The roles that emerged included guide, nurturer, authority figure, entertainer, challenger and novice, and other important themes included the need for flexibility, and also frequent frustration because teachers perceived their students as unmotivated.

Metaphors revealing insights into teachers' emotions are more frequently found in studies of pre-service teachers, whose focus is often on classroom survival and who may face daily challenges in learning to teach. For example, novice elementary and secondary school teachers in Canada described feeling like the captain of a ship in rocky waters, as well as feelings of uncertainty (Thomas & Beauchamp, 2011). However, there has been little exploration of what metaphors reveal about in-service teachers' emotions as they participate in professional development programmes that challenge their existing teacher identities.

Research Design

The study was framed by two research questions. The study initially sought to explore the first question, and the second question emerged once it was clear that some of the teachers were expressing their emotions about AR through metaphors.

(1) How do in-service ESL teachers' professional identities shift by participating in a national AR programme, both during and after the programme?

(2) What does metaphor analysis reveal about the in-service ESL teachers' emotional experiences of the AR programme and their identity shifts?

Research context and participants

The specific teacher education context for this qualitative, longitudinal study was a national, annually offered nine-month AR programme established in Australia in 2010 by peak body English Australia in collaboration with the second author and Cambridge Assessment English (see Burns & Khalifa, 2017). ESL teachers working in the English Language Intensive Courses for Overseas Students (ELICOS) sector in Australia, who teach international students coming from a wide range of countries, are eligible to submit a voluntary expression of interest for the programme, and each year six AR projects are selected and conducted by teachers working either individually or in pairs. Since 2012, a broad theme has been chosen for each annual programme (such as 'reading' or 'assessment') and teachers' proposals can address any issue within the theme that is relevant to their teaching context and current situation. The programme incorporates a series of three workshops held in Sydney in March, July/August and September, which set up, facilitate, and provide the space for discussion and peer feedback on the teachers' AR projects. Following the third workshop in September, teachers present their projects at the annual English Australia conference, and they then prepare 3000-word AR reports for submission in November, which are published in the freely accessible journal *Cambridge Research Notes* the following May (see http://www.cambridgeenglish.org/research-notes/).

Five teachers who participated in a recent iteration of the AR programme volunteered to participate in the current longitudinal study. Their pseudonyms and years of experience as EFL/ESL teachers are as follows: Alex (1 year), Quinn (5 years), Sarah (10 years), Katie (16 years) and Phoebe (25 years). Quinn is male, and the other teachers are all female. Three of the teachers are Australians who had taught EFL overseas as well as ESL in Australia for a number of years, whereas two of the teachers had recently moved to Australia from other countries. While Alex had only been teaching ESL for a year, she had previously taught a different language in high schools, so she had considerable overall teaching experience. Most of these teachers were working in ELICOS colleges affiliated with universities, teaching Academic English programmes that led to university admission for international students. The teachers' specific AR project topics are not mentioned here in order to protect their anonymity, since their AR reports are published online, but also because the focus is on their identities and emotions in relation to their experiences of AR more broadly.

Data collection and analysis

This study collected data during and after the AR programme in which the five teachers all participated. The first author conducted a series of five in-depth interviews with each of the five teachers over 12 months to align with different stages of the AR process: interview 1 in March (after the first workshop), interview 2 in June (during data collection), interview 3 in September (after their conference presentations), interview 4 in December (two months after the official end of the programme) and interview 5 in March (four months after the programme). Since the second author facilitated the programme, she was not involved in the process of data collection in order to ensure participant anonymity and avoid the potential of biasing the responses. The interviews were conducted face to face as far as possible, but sometimes Skype was more convenient due to the long distances between cities in Australia. The first author designed some general questions for each interview, asking teachers to describe their AR experience to date, how they felt as teachers and/or researchers, and whether they were experiencing any changes in their perceptions of themselves, and/or in terms of how others perceived them.

After each round of interviews, the first author transcribed the data and conducted one level of inductive in vivo or descriptive coding (following Saldaña, 2013) in order to determine important categories emerging from the teachers' experiences. These categories were used to form questions for each subsequent interview that were specific to each teacher. This process allowed us to develop detailed profiles of each teacher's experiences over the 12 months of data collection. At the end of the 12-month period, we then conducted a second round of coding, followed by metaphor analysis. In the findings section, the data extracts from the interviews are labelled with the teachers' pseudonyms and interview numbers (1–5).

Metaphor analysis

Metaphor analysis was not originally anticipated in the design of the study. However, because the use of metaphor by some of the teachers emerged naturally and powerfully from the first interviews, we realised that it would be a valuable analytical tool. In line with the flexibility enabled by qualitative interviewing, further descriptions were then prompted in the final interviews, for example:

- In our last interview, you mentioned that being a researcher is (like) [metaphor]. Do you still feel like this? Can you tell me more about it?
- One of the main themes from our four previous interviews was the metaphors you used to talk about AR: [examples].

- I understand these to mean [first author's interpretation]. Is that a correct interpretation or can you explain that in a bit more detail?

In adopting this more inductive approach to metaphor analysis, we aimed to avoid some of the validity issues associated with metaphor elicitation research, such as task difficulty, that are summarised by Wan (2011). We considered the use of metaphors in quite a broad sense, to include similes and idioms, in line with other metaphor analysis studies in education research (Nguyen, 2016; Wan, 2011). In analysing the metaphors used, we categorised them according to what they described, and then into themes according to what they revealed about teachers' emotional experiences at different stages of the AR programme.

Findings

First, we provide a brief overview of the dynamic process of identity development for each teacher, which was the initial focus of the study. The teachers all negotiated newly emerging professional identities after their participation in the AR programme. For Alex, her emerging identity was focused on teaching. She went from perceiving herself as a 'newbie' to English language teaching at the start of the programme, to feeling that she had gained 'maturity as a teacher': knowledge, teaching skills and curriculum development skills. She perceived herself as a more valued member of her college's staffroom, as other teachers frequently consulted her on the topic of her AR project. Sarah's identity was also teaching-related, but more negative. She commenced the AR programme as a competitive teacher who was thirsty for growth and development. By the end, she believed she was a 'more explicit teacher', but she also felt 'burnt-out' by the process for a range of reasons: a lack of support from her research partner, which led to her doing most of the project by herself, a lack of interest (in her project) from her colleagues, and a sense that she could not continue exploring any of the ideas from her project due to her heavy teaching workload.

Quinn, Katie and Phoebe developed identities that specifically involved becoming researchers; for Quinn and Phoebe this identity was quite new, while Katie already had a researcher identity that developed further. After the AR programme, Quinn described himself as a 'teacher AND researcher' who was able to 'contribute to colleagues within the industry', while Phoebe was 'kick-started' into conference presentations, supporting other teachers at conferences, and became a more community-minded teacher in her workplace as well. However, Katie went from feeling like an 'extra excited' teacher-researcher at the beginning, to describing herself as 'an extra-terrestrial researcher' after the programme, implying that she felt alienated from many of her colleagues who considered research to be going beyond a teacher's role.

Some of the teachers used metaphors to express emotions about their experiences of AR, or their perceptions of themselves, which were also emotionally charged. In the remainder of this analysis we focus on the insights that deeper exploration of these metaphors can offer. Table 5.1 lists the different metaphors that the teachers used to describe AR or to describe perceptions of themselves. All of the metaphors are 'in vivo' (direct quotes, the exact words used by the teachers in the interviews). We would point out that metaphors were used by some teachers only at some stages, and one teacher – Phoebe – used metaphors much more frequently than the others. Therefore, this analysis seeks to explore patterns from the insights offered by metaphor use, rather than patterns in general across all of the teachers' emotional experiences during the whole AR process.

The following section is structured around three key phases of the AR process – during AR, at the end of the AR programme, and after the programme – and the main emotional themes that emerged for each phase, as indicated by the teachers' use of metaphors. The analysis focuses on examining the metaphors used within each phase, what they reveal about teachers' shifting emotional experiences of AR, and how their emotions connect to their identity development.

During AR: Feeling overwhelmed or euphoric

In interviews 1 and 2, Phoebe was the main participant to use metaphors, and all of these metaphors indicate a sense of being overwhelmed. In the first interview, held shortly after the first AR workshop, Phoebe described having felt under-prepared for the workshop, and afterwards in 'a tailspin'. These feelings were in response to her perception that the other AR participants all had clearly organised project plans: 'we didn't seem to have a plan, and a lot [of the other participants] seemed to be finished (laughing) more than anything else, which really threw us into a tailspin, so that was a bit daunting' (Phoebe Interview 1). As an experienced reflective teacher and leader, who had previously completed master's level academic research, Phoebe's professional identity seemed to be in turmoil as she negotiated the challenges of conducting AR. She also described feeling 'like a blind person' as she struggled to find direction for her project:

> To me it [AR] is nothing like university research, so I know that, and yet to be really honest, I don't know, and [...] I feel like a blind person who's just feeling my way, it's not quite clear up here, I don't have a clear direction. (Phoebe Interview 1)

Phoebe's sense of being overwhelmed continued into the middle of the AR programme, and in the second interview she used another

Table 5.1 Metaphors used by the ESL teachers during each stage of the AR programme (Interviews 1–5)

	Interview 1: Start of AR programme (March)	**Interview 2: Middle of AR programme (June)**	**Interview 3: Presentation at end of AR programme (Sept)**	**Interview 4: Two months after AR (Dec/Jan)**	**Interview 5: Four months after AR (March)**
Metaphors used to describe AR	'Opening Pandora's box' (Phoebe)	'Opening Pandora's box' (Alex)	'A curse' (Alex)	'A blessing and a curse' (Quinn)	
		'A bushfire' (Phoebe)			
		'A dream coming true' (Katie)			
Metaphors used to describe perceptions of self (identity)	'In a tailspin' (Phoebe)		'Not the guru' (Alex)	'In a quagmire' (Sarah)	'Climbing a ladder' (Alex)
	'A blind person' (Phoebe)		'Not an all-knowing expert' (Quinn)		'In a tunnel' (Sarah)
			'A child in a lolly shop' (Phoebe)		'An extra-terrestrial' (Katie)

metaphor, this time culturally specific to Australia. She explained that her AR project was 'like a bushfire' that was burning out of control, which makes reference to the ferocious and rapidly spreading fires that can occur regularly during Australia's spring and summer:

> It can be also depressing, it's weighing heavily. It's opening too many doors at the moment for me, it's not giving me just one focus or one path to go down and then I'm focused on it [...] I'm now finding that it's like a bushfire, [...] where do I go, what do I incorporate? And I know my focus is on the [AR topic], but it's like the problem's over here, so what do you do? (Phoebe Interview 2)

The bushfire metaphor is a further insight into the strong overwhelming feelings that Phoebe was experiencing. She wanted to explore the many interrelated areas her initial investigation had revealed, but this desire reduced her ability to focus on one specific AR topic. The image of a bushfire spreading uncontrollably is similar to the kayak metaphor that a pre-service teacher in Thomas and Beauchamp's study used (when prompted) to describe their shifting teacher identity:

> A kayak in the river: it's in a river that gets bigger and bigger as we know more about the teaching profession, and it's like we end up going from the river to the sea where we're kind of lost. (Thomas & Beauchamp, 2011: 766)

This teacher's metaphor reveals their doubts at being able to keep up with the demands of the teacher education programme, just as Phoebe expressed doubt at being able to meet the daunting tasks ahead in her AR explorations.

Interestingly, both Phoebe and Alex used the metaphor of AR being like 'opening Pandora's box'. This metaphor refers to a Greek mythology story in which the god Zeus gives the first woman, Pandora, a box that should not be opened. Tempted by curiosity, Pandora opens the box and unleashes all the evils of the world. Phoebe used this metaphor to describe the way AR uncovers many issues in teaching and learning that she had not previously been aware of, but that suddenly seemed important to solve:

> When we talk about one thing and put something together it suddenly seems to open Pandora's box and we're suddenly re-writing the whole course (laughing). [...] I keep trying to come back to that focus. But it's so hard. (Phoebe Interview 1)

During the AR process, Phoebe seemed to have taken on a heavy emotional burden and sense of responsibility for addressing all the issues uncovered by her AR project.

Alex's use of the opening Pandora's box metaphor was similar to Phoebe's in terms of feeling overwhelmed by AR, but she felt empowered rather than burdened by the different avenues that had opened up. She recognised that her AR project was having a significant impact on her students, which led her to wonder what else she could achieve now that Pandora's box had been opened:

> **A:** So I think I've been quietly aware of the fact that I haven't changed the world, I haven't come up with a completely new idea, [...] but the impact it's had on individuals is quite mind-blowing at this point I think. And I've just become very aware of it [...].
>
> **I:** So it's quite powerful then?
>
> **A:** It is, [...] but it's powerful in a very subdued way I suppose [...] It's definitely made me more aware of the things that I COULD do, and the potential in it.
>
> **I:** Ok, and how does that make you feel?
>
> **A:** Excited, and maybe a little bit tired (laughing). Because you open Pandora's box, and it's always quite overwhelming I think, because there's also a feeling of, you can't have this power now and not do anything with it. (Alex Interview 2)

Perhaps one of the reasons why Alex was empowered but Phoebe felt burdened by the AR process was Alex's previous experience of conducting AR in her former high school teaching context. While Phoebe was more overwhelmed by the processes of AR, it being very different from her previous trial and error approach to teaching, Alex was overwhelmed by the positive impact of her project and opportunities arising from it. For both teachers, negotiating this daunting phase had positive influences on their identities: Phoebe became significantly re-energised in later phases, and Alex developed a strong sense of maturity as a teacher.

In contrast to the metaphors indicating a state of being overwhelmed, Katie felt fulfilled and even euphoric while conducting her AR project. She described her AR experience using the metaphor of 'like a dream coming true, definitely' (Katie Interview 2), and she felt validated in her professional identity as a researcher: 'by doing the AR right now, I'm absolutely sure that I was born to be a researcher' (Katie Interview 2). Her emotions about AR and her new perception of self can be attributed to her relative familiarity with the processes of AR, as she had previously conducted various types of research. However, despite her euphoria, she also felt conflicted by the lack of interest she received from her colleagues and manager, making her feel very 'alone' in her workplace. Katie's institutional context afforded few opportunities for continued mediation of her researcher identity, which eventually led her to feel quite alienated after the AR programme (see below).

Notably, the other two teachers (Quinn and Sarah) did not use any metaphors to describe their experiences or perceptions of self during the AR programme. AR was also a new approach to professional development for them both, and Quinn seemed to take it in his stride. Sarah, however, explicitly stated that she felt overwhelmed by her project ('It's overwhelming at the moment [...] so I'm quite stressed', Sarah Interview 1), but at the same time well supported by her manager.

The end of AR: Feeling humble or awakened/energised

The third interview with each teacher took place shortly after they presented their AR projects at the English Australia conference. Three of the teachers used metaphors to describe their emotional experiences or identities at this time – Alex, Quinn and Phoebe. In terms of professional identities, both Alex and Quinn expressed a strong sense of humility and learner-centredness through the metaphors they used. Quinn explained that he felt more confident about involving students in decision-making, and in collaborating with students rather than trying to appear as an 'expert':

> I'll be more confident to ask students what they think, and that's something about growing as a teacher generally. [...] I remember in early days of teaching feeling that I had to be this all-knowing expert. Whereas I think now, and probably the AR has helped, recognising that I don't have to be an all-knowing expert, that you're actually collaborating with these students to help them develop whatever they need to develop, and to listen to them and to ask them if they think things are working or not working in the classroom. (Quinn Interview 3)

Quinn's comments reflect a shift to engaging in more learner-centred teaching, and seeing himself as a guide and collaborator rather than an 'all-knowing expert' within a more traditional teacher-centred approach.

Alex, however, seemed to have adopted the role of a 'go-to' person in her college through an (unpaid) promotion which allowed her to extend her AR project findings within the college, a position she found bemusing and humbling. She reported that her colleagues continued to consult her for advice on her AR topic. Although her role and higher status were contributing to her maturing teacher identity, Alex also found it rather unreal, positioning herself in opposition to the metaphor of a 'guru':

> It's also a bit scary, because I'm not the guru at all (laughing), not even close, and I find it actually quite funny that they think they should

> ask me things. [...] In a sense I have gone from being the newbie and the one who's just finished her CELTA to the one who actually gets the questions. (Alex Interview 3)

For Phoebe, her experience of attending the English Australia conference 'kick-started' her into thinking about the possibilities of attending more conferences and the benefits she could gain both from watching other teachers give presentations and from feeling part of a community. She expressed her excitement and energy through the 'child in a lolly shop' metaphor:

> We did not leave the building [...] we were just going to everything (laughing), getting everything, I mean I came back on the plane loaded with sample bags, it was so exciting, like a child in a lolly shop. And then, because of that I decided I've got to get to [next conference], how do I get to [next conference]? (Phoebe Interview 4)

Phoebe's emotional experience had shifted remarkably from feeling overwhelmed and daunted to being rejuvenated by attending the conference, which contributed to a kind of awakening in her professional identity towards becoming a more collaborative and community-focused teacher.

Neither Sarah nor Katie used metaphors to describe their experience of AR or perceptions of self directly after the AR programme, but they expressed their emotions more directly. Sarah felt tired after the preparation for the conference presentation ('It [the AR presentation] was too exhausting for me', Sarah Interview 3), especially because she felt that her research partner had not contributed enough. However, Sarah also felt supported by her manager, which helped her to maintain a sense of achievement. Katie felt a similar mix of positive and negative emotions at this stage. She continued to feel euphoric about her project ('That's how I feel right now, accomplished, really accomplished', Katie Interview 3), but simultaneously frustrated that no one at her workplace seemed to show interest.

Finally, in terms of the experience of AR, Alex described it as a 'curse', a metaphor that was used again by Quinn in the fourth interview two months after the AR programme. Alex meant 'curse' in a humorous way that implied the reflective mindset she had developed from conducting AR was causing her extra work:

> Action research is almost like a curse, because from here on you can never just do something and not reflect on it (laughing), you're done now, you can never go back to being that teacher that just presents a lesson and goes home, it's over, that time is gone. (Alex Interview 3)

Alex explained that she highly valued reflection on teaching, and wanted to start another AR project with a colleague on a different topic, but the heavy demands of teaching a new Academic English course prevented her from commencing. Therefore, her institutional context and teaching duties at that time strongly influenced her perception of AR as a 'curse'.

After AR: Feeling restricted or re-energised

In the fourth and fifth interviews, two and four months after the official end of the AR programme (marked by the conference), all teachers apart from Phoebe used metaphors to describe their professional identities or experience of AR. Quinn described the reflective AR mindset he had developed as 'a blessing and a curse', with the same intended meaning as Alex ('It makes me think critically each day that I'm teaching, but it's always extra work as well to be doing that', Quinn Interview 4).

Two of the teachers, Sarah and Katie, reported feeling quite restricted after the AR programme: Sarah in the sense of being 'stuck' with her AR project and unsure how to move forward, and Katie in the sense of feeling isolated from her colleagues and even the English language teaching sector. Although Sarah was excited about her AR report being published the following year, she also used the metaphor of feeling stuck 'in a quagmire', with the AR process 'dragging on' (Sarah Interview 4) as she waited for the publication, and because she lacked time to reflect on the whole process and notice the benefits. She was unsure how she could build on her AR project for her own professional development. Using a similar metaphor to the 'quagmire' of the fourth interview, Sarah described still feeling that she was in a 'tunnel' four months after the AR programme:

> I probably haven't quite come out the other end yet of the tunnel to sort of go 'ok, well how can I implement it [her AR findings]?' I'm also not teaching the level [of students] any more, I've been totally taken off that level that I used for my AR. […] I'm just trying to get my head around teaching a whole new course, and therefore I don't have the time to work out how I am going to implement what I did in the AR. (Sarah Interview 5)

These two negative metaphors indicate emotions of anxiety, uncertainty and frustration, of waiting for the light at the end of the tunnel but being too exhausted to get there. As Sarah explained, she was teaching a new course and lacked time to sustain any aspect of her AR project or reflections, which Alex and Quinn also noted in terms of the 'curse' of AR. Sarah's institutional environment seemed to be restricting rather than mediating her development, and consequently her perception of herself as a 'burnt-out' teacher continued.

Katie was also restricted by her environment and continued to feel like an outsider – using the metaphor of an 'extra-terrestrial' – when she tried to engage in conversation with colleagues in her workplace:

> There's a certain tension when I talk about [my AR] to other professionals. I think they mean well actually, but I feel more like [...] an extra-terrestrial person, because they say 'oh wow, how can you do all these things?' and that's not [...] the kind of comment I'm looking for. I'm looking for 'oh that's interesting, tell me more!' (Katie Interview 4).

Her sense of alienation, she explained, was partly because her colleagues were surprised and slightly confused about why she wanted to do research, professional development and further study. As a result, Katie felt that she could not connect meaningfully with them and experienced a lack of belonging, contributing to her identity as an alienated teacher-researcher.

On a more positive note, Alex and Phoebe were both re-energised four months after the AR programme, which is interesting because they both explicitly described feeling overwhelmed during their research. Alex perceived herself as progressing and maturing in her profession and career as an ELICOS teacher:

> It's like a little ladder, or [...] it's climbing, it's going up in your own profession, in your own everything, your maturity as a teacher. [...] So all that hardship and energy got you up there, and now you're at a different level but now you can relax into it, you can just breathe now. (Alex Interview 5)

These comments reflect Alex's continuing professional development as a teacher who had also become a researcher. She portrayed a sense of having gone through a challenging process, but having successfully emerged as a teacher with more 'maturity', who felt valued within her college community. Phoebe also continued to feel re-energised, as she had after the English Australia conference, and she had numerous ideas for sustaining her AR approach by taking part in her college's new internal AR programme, presenting at conferences or starting a diploma:

> I'd like to do more, I mean I have the energy to do more, I was thinking even [...], I want to throw in an idea and go to the [college's internal] AR and think about whether I can do another one, [...] and at the same time I was thinking of doing a DELTA. (Phoebe Interview 5)

It is interesting that Phoebe did not use any metaphors to describe AR or her identity in the final two interviews. When prompted for a metaphor in the final interview, she could not think of one, showing that observing metaphors occurring naturally in discourse might be more meaningful than forcing them deliberately. Phoebe also appeared calmer and more confident in the final interview, whereas in the earlier stages metaphors had been a way for her to express her negative emotions and the difficulties she was experiencing. A final noteworthy point is that both Alex and Phoebe perceived there to be growing interest in AR in their colleges. In both workplaces, other teachers were starting to engage with AR through programmes the colleges had set up, and it is likely that this AR-friendly environment supported Alex and Phoebe in feeling more confident, mature and valued as teaching professionals.

Discussion

The analysis in this chapter provides theoretical insights for the fields of teacher education and language teacher identity research, as well as methodological insights for studies that incorporate metaphor analysis. First, this study contributes to the limited literature on language teacher researcher identity development (e.g. Trent, 2010; Yuan & Burns, 2017) by demonstrating how in-service teachers can experience emotional turmoil while conducting AR and directly afterwards. Such emotional turmoil can, for some teachers (such as Phoebe), be likened to being on an emotional rollercoaster. Indeed, Burns (2017: 135–136) also uses the rollercoaster metaphor to describe the process of language teacher identity development – 'the unpredictable terrain and variegated process of identity construction of a language teacher researcher'. Even where teachers' experiences are less turbulent, the current study shows that each stage of the AR process can be emotionally charged and closely connected to teachers' ongoing identity negotiation. Teachers' evolving identities, for example shifting from newbie to 'go-to' person (Alex), or from pursuing a research dream to becoming alienated (Katie), are also mediated or restricted by their sociocultural institutional contexts. Further studies exploring in-service teachers' emotions and use of metaphor to illuminate experiences of challenging professional development events such as AR would complement the existing literature on pre-service teachers' challenges when learning to teach (e.g. Farrell, 2006; Thomas & Beauchamp, 2011) and on in-service teachers' identity roles (e.g. Erickson & Pinnegar, 2017; Nguyen, 2016; Yesilbursa, 2012).

Secondly, the present study shows that feelings of being overwhelmed or 'cursed' by the AR reflective mindset can be catalysts for fruitful identity development if teachers' sociocultural environmental conditions are conducive to this development. Both Alex and Phoebe used the 'opening Pandora's box' metaphor to describe their sense of being overwhelmed by a barrage of possibilities for improving teaching and learning in their contexts, and feeling a strong sense of responsibility or empowerment as a result. Without these emotional experiences or critical incidents, these teachers may not have been able to re-negotiate the more mature, confident identities as experts and collaborators they developed and maintained several months after their AR engagement. The study supports Kubanyiova's (2012: 125) assertion that emotional dissonance is 'an essential but insufficient catalyst' for language teacher development, but provides an alternative perspective on another prerequisite for development. If teachers' work environments provide sufficient mediation (through support and opportunities) during and after the professional development event, emotional conflicts such as feeling overwhelmed or burdened can contribute to constructive identity development. However, without conducive conditions, teachers' identity shifts can be damaging and increase their sense of isolation and exhaustion. In particular, this study found that a school's culture of – or interest in – research can have a profound (positive or negative) influence on teachers' emotions and identity development following an AR programme. Those teachers who felt part of emerging research cultures in their workplaces (Alex and Phoebe) were re-energised after their AR experience, whereas those who noted a distinct lack of research culture (Katie and to some extent Sarah) felt restricted, alone and frustrated.

In terms of methodological contributions, the current study demonstrates that analysis of teachers' metaphor use offers meaningful insights into their emotional conflicts, since negative and unsettling emotions can perhaps be more easily expressed figuratively rather than directly. Metaphors used to describe present experiences and perceptions of self allow for multiple meanings, emotions and images to be conveyed simultaneously, and are therefore powerful sense-makers. Further metaphor analysis work might include not only verbal metaphors, but also visual, musical or multimodal metaphors to uncover deeper meanings about teachers' experiences and identities. In addition, this study offers one way of addressing the validity issues associated with metaphor elicitation techniques (see Wan, 2011). Future language teacher identity and emotions studies might consider, rather than explicitly eliciting metaphors, observing the natural or unconscious use of metaphor during the most potentially difficult or challenging moments of a professional development experience or curriculum, policy or workplace change.

Implications and Conclusions

While this study involved only a small group of five in-service English language teachers in one particular AR context, there are several implications which may apply to other contexts where teachers are conducting research. Our study suggests that the initial stages of a research project are likely to be overwhelming for both novice and more experienced teachers alike. In addition to being supported on the teacher education programme itself, teacher researchers require ongoing support from their workplaces to mediate productive outcomes and continuous development during and after their research project. Where support is inadequate, teacher research engagement can lead to exhaustion, frustration and burnout, which is in line with other studies such as Tran, Burns and Ollerhead (2017). Our research suggests that teacher engagement is likely to be richer when participation is voluntary, and teachers have opportunities for collaboration with and support from fellow teacher researchers and with teacher colleagues and managers within their own institution. Such conditions contribute towards building a positive research culture and opportunities for the research to be disseminated for wider institutional benefit. Those supporting teacher research should consider in particular the dynamic emotional experiences that are incurred as teachers move into researcher roles. Moreover, studies investigating teachers' emotional experiences and sense of belonging as they participate collaboratively over time in institutional, cross-institutional or even global communities of practice would greatly enrich the growing field of research on language teachers as researchers.

Post-Reading Tasks

(1) How could you apply metaphor analysis to your own research or teaching context to explore teacher or learner emotions?
(2) What has been your own emotional experience of conducting action research, or other forms of teacher research? In what ways can you identify with the emotional journeys of any of the teachers in this chapter (Alex, Katie, Phoebe, Quinn, Sarah)?
(3) The teachers' sociocultural institutional environments significantly affected their emotional experiences of action research. In your own teaching context or research, how do you think your environment (or the one you are studying) might influence teachers' emotions?
(4) What kinds of support for a positive research culture could be further developed in your own workplace or in one you are studying?

References

Beauchamp, C. and Thomas, L. (2009) Understanding teacher identity: An overview of issues in the literature and implications for teacher education. *Cambridge Journal of Education* 39 (2), 175–189.

Benesch, S. (2012) *Considering Emotions in Critical English Language Teaching*. Oxon and New York: Routledge.

Burns, A. (2017) 'This life-changing experience': Teachers be(com)ing action researchers. In G. Barkhuizen (ed.) *Reflections on Language Teacher Identity Research* (pp. 133–138). New York: Routledge.

Burns, A. and Khalifa, H. (eds) (2017) *Studies in Language Testing 48: Second Language Assessment and Action Research*. Cambridge: Cambridge University Press.

Edwards, E. and Burns, A. (2016) Language teacher-researcher identity negotiation: An ecological perspective. *TESOL Quarterly* 50 (3), 735–745.
Erickson, L.B. and Pinnegar, S. (2017) Consequences of personal teaching metaphors for teacher identity and practice. *Teachers and Teaching* 23 (1), 106–122.
Farrell, T.S.C. (2006) 'The teachers is an octopus': Uncovering preservice English language teachers' prior beliefs through metaphor analysis. *RELC Journal* 37, 236–248.
Golombek, P. (2015) Redrawing the boundaries of language teacher cognition: Language teacher educators' emotion, cognition and activity. *The Modern Language Journal* 99 (3), 470–484.
Hiver, P. (2013) The interplay of possible language teacher selves in professional development choices. *Language Teaching Research* 17 (2), 210–227.
Johnson, K.E. and Golombek, P.R. (2016) *Mindful L2 Teacher Education: A Sociocultural Perspective on Cultivating Teachers' Professional Development*. New York: Routledge.
Kemmis, S. and McTaggart, R. (eds) (1988) *The Action Research Planner* (3rd edn). Geelong, Victoria: Deakin University Press.
Kubanyiova, M. (2012) *Teacher Development in Action: Understanding Language Teachers' Conceptual Change*. Basingstoke: Palgrave Macmillan.
Lakoff, G. and Johnson, M. (1980) *Metaphors we Live by*. Chicago: University of Chicago Press.
Mockler, N. and Groundwater-Smith, S. (2015) Seeking for the unwelcome truths: Beyond celebration in inquiry-based teacher professional learning. *Teachers and Teaching* 21 (5), 603–614.
Nguyen, C.D. (2016) Metaphors as a window into identity: A study of teachers of English to young learners in Vietnam. *System* 60, 66–78.
Saldaña, J. (2013) *The Coding Manual for Qualitative Researchers*. Thousand Oaks, CA: SAGE.
Song, J. (2016) Emotions and language teacher identity: Conflicts, vulnerability, and transformation. *TESOL Quarterly* 50 (3), 631–654.
Thomas, L. and Beauchamp, C. (2011) Understanding new teachers' professional identities through metaphor. *Teaching and Teacher Education* 27, 762–769.
Tran, A., Burns, A. and Ollerhead, S. (2017) ELT lecturers' experiences of a new research policy: Exploring emotion and academic identity. *System* 67, 65–76.
Trent, J. (2010) Teacher education as identity construction: Insights from action research. *Journal of Education for Teaching: International Research and Pedagogy* 36 (2), 153–168.
van Lier, L. (2004) *The Ecology and Semiotics of Language Learning: A Sociocultural Perspective*. Norwell, MA: Kluwer Academic Publishers.
van Lier, L. (2008) The ecology of language learning and sociocultural theory. In A. Creese, P. Martin and N.H. Hornberger (eds) *Encyclopedia of Language and Education: Ecology of Language* (vol. 9, 2nd edn). New York: Springer.
Varghese, M.M., Motha, S., Park, G., Reeves, J. and Trent, J. (2016) In this issue. *TESOL Quarterly* 50 (3), 545–571.
Wan, W. (2011) An examination of the validity of metaphor analysis studies: Problems with metaphor elicitation techniques. *Metaphor and the Social World* 1 (2), 261–287.
Yesilbursa, A. (2012) Using metaphor to explore the professional role identities of higher education English language instructors. *Procedia – Social and Behavioural Sciences* 46, 468–472.
Yuan, R. and Burns, A. (2017) Teacher identity development through action research: A Chinese experience. *Teachers and Teaching* 23 (6), 729–749.
Yuan, R. and Lee, I. (2015) The cognitive, social and emotional processes of teacher identity construction in a pre-service teacher education programme. *Research Papers in Education* 30 (4), 469–491.

6 Resilience in Language Teaching: Adaptive and Maladaptive Outcomes in Pre-Service Teachers

Achilleas Kostoulas and Anita Lämmerer

We cannot have happiness without being prepared for unhappiness.
– Emmy van Deurzen (2009: 91)

As indexed by the title of this volume, language teaching is an emotionally intense experience. This constitutes a cause of concern both because of the inherent vulnerabilities of the teaching profession (Kelchtermans, 1996) and in view of the high attrition rates among teachers (Farrell, 2016; Johnson *et al.*, 2016). A common response, among language educators, to the existence of intense emotion that might compromise their ability to deliver effective teaching is what has been termed 'emotional labour', which involves suppression, distancing and the outward display of emotions that conform to societal expectations about teaching (King, 2016). Other ways in which teachers can regulate their emotions include modifying their teaching contexts so as to minimise the occurrence of negative emotion triggers, selectively focusing on positive aspects of their teaching experience, and cognitively reappraising any stress-inducing situations (King & Ng, 2018). While acknowledging the importance of regulating emotion in such ways, the perspective that we take in this chapter is that emotionally challenging experiences can trigger processes of growth and professional development. Specifically, we argue that processing negative emotion leads to restructuring of psychological resources, or *resilient adaptation*, which can result in an increased tolerance of unpleasant affective states, as well as a broadening of the repertoire of emotional regulation strategies available to teachers.

In the chapter, we take a focused look into how teachers cope with negativity, using the psychological construct of teacher resilience, which we provisionally define as the teachers' capacity to continue to function effectively in their professional roles in the face of adversity. In the mainstream psychological literature, resilience has been variously defined as a psychological trait or as a process of adaptation. We believe that these broad conceptualisations can be supplemented by a definition of resilience that is more particular to language education. Such a definition, firstly, can highlight how the characteristics and processes connected to resilience are manifested in a teaching context: there are important differences between the traumatic experiences encountered by counselling psychologists and the kinds of stressors with which teachers contend. Secondly, it takes into account that the outcomes of resilient adaptation do not always conform to professional expectations in language education. For instance, an enhanced ability to selectively ignore disruptive behaviour in class, or, alternatively, to downplay its effects, could be viewed as contributing to overall well-being, but would be difficult to reconcile with a teacher's role.

In the sections that follow, we begin by synthesising relevant literature into a tentative model of teacher resilience. We then use interview data from two pre-service teachers, who had just completed their first teaching assignments, as empirical touchstones to test the descriptive utility of the model. These examples illustrate how resilient adaptation could lead to positive (adaptive) or negative (maladaptive) professional outcomes (cf. Hiver, 2018).

What is Resilience?

The first attempts to understand resilience tended to focus on small numbers of individuals (the so-called 'super-survivors'), who maintained normal psychological functioning despite traumatic experiences that predisposed them towards psychopathology (Masten & Obradović, 2006). Examples of super-survivors included individuals who had grown up among mentally ill parents or siblings (e.g. Bleuler, 1972/1978; Rutter, 1976, 1979), or individuals made vulnerable by extreme socioeconomic deprivation (e.g. Werner & Smith, 1982). This strand of research, which often took a longitudinal perspective, aimed at identifying the protective or compensatory factors that made positive psychological outcomes possible (Richardson, 2002).

Although the multitude of inventories that have been put forward in the literature pose challenges to their theoretical integration, these factors can be grouped into two loose sets. The first of these sets includes intrapersonal constructs, such as self-concept (Zolkoski & Bullock, 2012), internal locus of control (Kuterovac-Jagodić, 2003), internal motivation (Masten, 2001), optimistic outlooks (Werner & Smith, 1982) and identity complexity (Mancini & Bonanno, 2009). Of particular interest to our perspective as language educators is the connection between resilience and emotional regulation. The ability to manage emotion has been shown to be a contributory factor to resilience (Troy & Mauss, 2011), but this relation could well be reciprocal. The second set of resilience-related constructs contains interpersonal characteristics, such as sociability (Werner & Smith, 1982), support from family and peers (Gonzales & Padilla, 1997) and connectedness to social environment (Denz-Penhey & Murdoch, 2008). Especially in early resilience research, there has been a tendency to view all these constructs as trait characteristics, which are relatively stable, although later research has highlighted their context-specificity (Fergus & Zimmerman, 2005) and their dynamism (Kostoulas & Lämmerer, 2018; Richardson, 2002).

More recently, there has been a trend towards viewing resilience as a process of psychological adaptation (Masten, 2001; Winfield, 1991). Seen from this perspective, resilience is understood not as an aggregate of static traits but rather as a 'dynamical capacity' to adapt to adversity (Day & Gu, 2015: xvii). A key difference that distinguishes this line of scholarship from previous research is that the resilience is viewed as universal potential. In other words:

> Resilience does not come from rare or special qualities, but from the operations of ordinary human systems [...] from their relationships in the family and community, and from schools, religions, cultures and other aspects of societies. (Masten *et al.*, 2009: 129)

The emphasis, in this strand of research, therefore shifts towards understanding how individuals draw on whatever psychological resources are available to them in order to create this 'ordinary magic' (Masten, 2001), and also on understanding what lasting effect is produced by the interplay between adversity and coping mechanisms.

Richardson's (2002) model of resilience (which he terms *resiliency*) is typical of this developmental approach. It proposes that individuals normally exist in a state of 'biopsychospiritual homeostasis' (i.e. a comfort zone), which may be disrupted due to adversity. The disruption leads to any of four possible outcomes: (a) dysfunctional re-integration, (b) re-integration with loss, (c) reintegration back to homeostasis, or (d) resilient reintegration. In Richardson's model, and similar ones, resilience is described as a process of adaptation, whereby some kind of perceived adversity causes individuals to adopt new patterns of cognition, affect or behaviour that make them less vulnerable to future adversity. The empirical challenge that this view poses involves comprehending why outcomes are not uniform and what processes lead to differentiated outcomes.

A similar model, which was developed with specific reference to teachers, has been put forward by Hiver and Dörnyei (2015), who draw an interesting analogy with the biological process of acquired immunity.

In their *immunity* model, teachers can react to adversity by becoming immunocompromised (i.e. lacking immunity), partially immunised or fully immunised in either a productive or a maladaptive way. Although there are parallels between Richardson's (2002) and Hiver and Dörnyei's (2015) conceptualisations, the latter model usefully highlights that resilient adaptation is not a unidimensional process, and that it could also potentially lead to professionally unhelpful outcomes, like resistance to change, apathy or cynicism. This resonates with remarks by Masten *et al.* (2009: 123), who point out that:

> models that focus on a single aspect of 'outcome' or one dimension of the criterion for good adaptation will not capture the overall pattern of resilience in a person's life, which is multifaceted and configural.

There is an important implication of Masten *et al.*'s observation for our purposes. If resilience is a multifaceted psychological construct, then the overall pattern, which is of interest to mainstream psychology, might be unhelpful in understanding outcomes in particular domains. Hence, a domain-specific model, which focuses on outcomes for language teaching, might be more appropriate to the needs of language education psychology.

One more thing to note about resilience is that, while the capacity for resilience is likely to be universal (Masten, 2001; Zolkoski & Bullock, 2012), it would be a bold claim to assert that everybody has equal capacity to overcome challenges. The role of context seems especially pertinent in explaining why individuals facing similar challenges attain different outcomes. Writing from the perspective of community psychology, Prilleltensky (2012) offers a useful taxonomy of societal determinants that provide scope for the development of psychological phenomena like resilience. Conditions of *persisting injustice* are most commonly associated with suffering, manifested in feelings of oppression, internalisation and helplessness. Conditions of *vulnerability to injustice* are likely associated with confrontational and critical outcomes. The development of resilience, adaptation and compensation is possible under conditions of *suboptimal justice*, whereas *optimal justice* leads to thriving, but not necessarily growth. These insights into the role of context have not yet been integrated well in resilience theory. However, they seem to hint at the limitations of the positive psychology paradigm that is increasingly taking hold in teaching and learning psychology, as this seems to have dispensed with the contextual lens (Lazarus, 2003), and privileges a rather too narrow focus on positive affect (Wong & Roy, 2018).

Although adversity constitutes an essential component of adaptation models of resilience, such adversity need not take the form of catastrophic risk, as described in early resilience research. Recent empirical work has shown that low-level but persistent stressors, such as the ones present in the everyday professional lives of teachers, can also sustain the development of resilient qualities (Davis *et al.*, 2009; Gu & Day, 2007). Fletcher and Sarkar (2013: 14) also intriguingly point out that even 'ostensibly positive life events', such as getting a job promotion, might be associated with stressors that can trigger resilient adaptation. The lack of linear correspondences between stressors, protective factors, resilience-related processes and ultimate outcomes suggests a need to look beyond linear causality models in order to understand how resilience emerges. Complex systems theory (Byrne, 1998) provides us with intriguing possibilities in this endeavour.

To synthesise the above: a theory of resilience for language teaching should fulfil four requirements. First, it should comprehensively account for the psychological resources that combine to produce resilience. Every individual teacher is likely to have different resources at their disposal, and a theoretical description should not simply aim to catalogue them; rather it should aspire to show how these combine into universal patterns. Secondly, a domain-specific theory of resilience should account for those outcomes of resilient adaptation that are most relevant professionally. Thirdly, a theory of resilience for language teaching must acknowledge that some aspects of human functioning are of universal nature, but it should foreground the situated way in which these are manifested in teaching and learning. Finally, a theory of language teacher resilience should adopt a broad definition of stress and adversity, in order to account for the cumulative impact of moderate stressors that are likely to be present in the teachers' professional lives.

A Complexity-Informed Model of Teacher Resilience

In an earlier publication (Kostoulas & Lämmerer, 2018), we put forward a model of resilience which synthesised 'trait' and 'process' conceptualisations, tapping on complex systems theory (Byrne, 1998) as an underlying epistemological frame. The main element of the model is the *resilience system*, a dense web of interacting psychological resources, on which individuals draw when facing adversity (Figure 6.1). We conceptualise resilience as an emergent phenomenon, which is created by the interaction of the resources in the resilience system. We further argue that the relationship between resilience and the system is reciprocal: resilience does not just emerge from the system, but also it recursively shapes it by reinforcing those resources that prove most beneficial.

Resilience systems are specific to individuals, but for descriptive convenience we propose that the resources that make up such systems up can be grouped into three universal clusters. The first cluster comprises what might be called *inner strengths*, and it corresponds loosely to the constructs identified by empirical investigations of 'trait' resilience.

Figure 6.1 A resilience system

These are relatively stable characteristics, which make up a teacher's personality. A non-exhaustive list of such resources that are potentially relevant to language education includes language teacher self-efficacy beliefs, strong teacher identity, a sense of purpose in professional activity, the ability to regulate emotion and more.

The second cluster includes the *external support* structures that a teacher perceives in their context. This set of resources brings together the interpersonal characteristics identified by earlier work on resilience and the contextual influences highlighted by community psychology. Some resources relevant to language education include personal and professional networks, and effective support from school leadership. Other resources, such as mentorship schemes, or the availability of counselling, could also be subsumed in this category. One should note that the mere availability of these resources is necessary but not sufficient for the development for resilience, as these also have to be perceived as being available and useful.

The third cluster of resources comprises the repertoire of *learned strategies* that are available to a teacher in order to cope with adversity. This broad category includes behavioural strategies, such as actively seeking support, distancing oneself from stressors, or investing time and effort in professional development. It also encompasses cognitive patterns, such as downplaying or rationalising setbacks. Sometimes these strategies are deployed through conscious decisions, but they are just as likely to be produced by subconscious psychological processes.

In our model, resilience is produced by the interaction between the system components, which constantly reinforces the resources that are most helpful in dealing with adversity. For instance, if a teacher perceives that a mentorship scheme is supportive, they might actively seek guidance from their mentor in order to deal with persistent challenges that threaten their confidence; a successful mentorship encounter could reinforce the guidance-seeking strategy, and repeated successful encounters could lead to the development of stronger self-efficacy beliefs. The density and complexity of the interconnections in the system means that such linear patterns should be treated as oversimplifications, but this example illustrates how interaction is generated and how resilience emerges from it.

The description of the resilience system might appear static, but teacher resilience systems are in constant flux, as their configuration constantly changes in response to stressors that perturb the system. A balance between the stressors typical in teaching and the resources at a teacher's disposal (*dynamical stability*) allows the system to absorb perturbations with gradual, possibly imperceptible change. A large perturbation, such as a professional crisis or a major transition, might lead to a radical restructuring of the system. A radical restructuring could also be produced by persistent low-level stressors if their cumulative effect is sustained for enough time to push the system beyond a tipping point. Both these processes of change, gradual or radical, are forms of resilient adjustment.

What interests us, from a complexity perspective, is not just the exact configuration of the system, or its *internal structure*, at any given moment, but rather its activity as an integrated whole (Kostoulas, 2018). Expanding on our previous conceptualisation of the model (Kostoulas & Lämmerer, 2018), and drawing on Hiver and Dörnyei (2015), we distinguish between two possible directions in which resilience might drive a system. We define *adaptive adjustment* as a process in which the reconfigured system enables the teacher to enact their professional role more effectively. On the other hand, *maladaptive adjustment* is a reconfiguration that is unhelpful in coping with the demands of teaching. Our conceptions of adaptive and maladaptive adjustment, we should note, connect resilient outcomes to the professional demands of teaching, and are distinct from the general outcomes of resilience for the person as a whole, which are by definition positive (Fletcher & Sarkar, 2013).

This Study

Our first attempt to empirically test our resilience model involved a case study, which documented the experiences of a veteran teacher who was transitioning into a new role as a teacher educator (Kostoulas & Lämmerer, 2018). That study underscored the dynamism and situatedness of resilience, but our observations could not capture the ongoing development of resilience because our participant would only report examples of adversity in her professional past. To shed further light on the way resilience emerges, we conducted a similar study with a cohort of pre-service teachers at the time of their first practicum. As teacher educators working in the same programme as the participants, we had extensive anecdotal experience that suggested that the first practicum was commonly perceived as an intensely stressful period, and we thus hypothesised that it would likely provide us with opportunities to observe the emergence of resilient phenomena in real time.

The setting of this study was an initial teacher education programme in an Austrian university. The ten-semester programme consisted of theoretical modules on language, linguistics, literature and foreign language education, interspersed with school-based practical components (practica). In the first practicum, which normally took place in the sixth semester of studies, future teachers were expected to conduct teaching observations and supervised teaching. For most participants, this constituted their first teaching experience.

Initial insights about resilience

As a preparatory step to the study, a questionnaire survey was used to estimate the participants' baseline resilience. The questionnaire consisted of three sections, of which the first two elicited demographic data and information about prior language learning and teaching experiences. The third section consisted of a 24-item Likert scale, based on the CD-RISC inventory (Connor & Davidson, 2003). Following piloting, minor linguistic simplifications were made to the wording of items, and one potentially confusing item was removed from the original 25-item inventory. The internal consistency of the revised scale was not compromised by these changes ($\alpha = 0.791$).

The questionnaire was completed by 94 pre-service teachers, shortly before their practicum. The participants' ages ranged from 19 to 47 years ($M = 22.23$, $SD = 3.98$). Most respondents were female ($n = 69$), males accounted for approximately one quarter of the sample ($n = 24$), and one participant did not specify their gender. The gender distribution of the sample was in line with the population of pre-service teachers enrolled in the programme. A statistically significant, if somewhat weak, link was found between the participants' reported resilience levels and teaching experience. Specifically, participants who reported having had some teaching experience, usually as informal tutors for schoolchildren, seemed to have slightly higher resilience levels ($t = 2.904$, $df = 92$, $p = 0.005$). No statistically significant links connected resilience to any of the other variables we examined, including age, gender, linguistic background, experience of living abroad, etc.

Two resilience scores were calculated for each participant: an *overall resilience* score, obtained by adding the Likert items scores, and an *adjusted resilience* score, which ranged from 0 to 100, and rendered our 24-item scale comparable to the 25-item CD-RISC. The mean value for the adjusted resilience score was 71.51, and the standard deviation (SD) was 11.49. Based on this information, we divided participants in three categories, namely 'low', 'average' and 'high' resilience. Students within

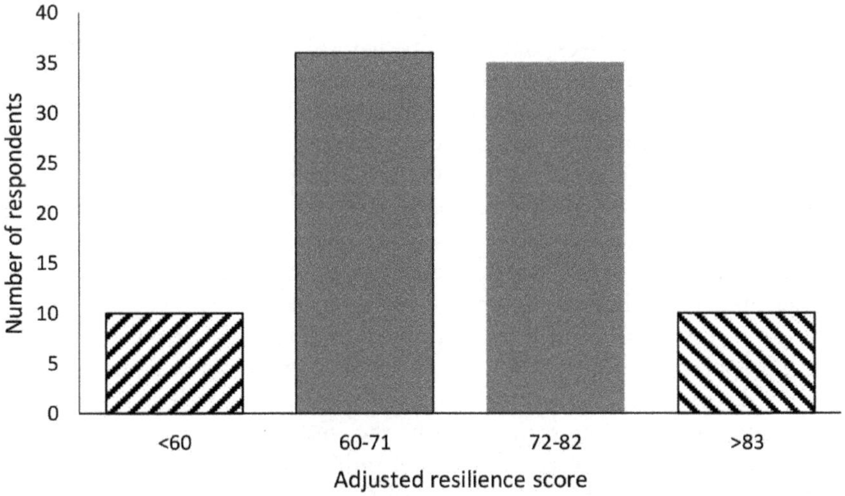

Figure 6.2 Distribution of adjusted resilience scores

one SD on either direction of the mean were placed in the 'average' resilience category ($n = 74$), and there were 10 participants in each of the 'low' and 'high' categories, which comprised respondents with adjusted resilience scores under 60 and over 83 respectively (Figure 6.2).

In-depth interviews

Immediately after the practicum, semi-structured interviews were conducted with seven pre-service teachers who volunteered to discuss their experience. Table 6.1 presents some information about this group of participants, who are identified by pseudonyms. Although the seven participants were not systematically selected, they were evenly spread as regards their adjusted resilience scores: five were in the 'average' resilience category, and there was one in either extremity of the scale. During the interviews, which lasted between 49 and 64 minutes, the seven volunteers were invited to talk about the practicum, as well as their teaching

Table 6.1 Interview participants' demographic and resilience data

Pseudonym	Age	Teaching experience	Adjusted resilience score
Peter	21	none	84 (high)
Sean	25	none	77 (average)
Sophie	19	tutoring	74 (average)
Michelle	22	tutoring	67 (average)
Lena	19	tutoring	66 (average)
Emilia	24	none	63 (average)
John	21	none	58 (low)

motivation, language learner history, self-beliefs, and any other aspects of their personality and lives that might be helpful in coping with challenges they faced. The interviews were conducted in English, the working language of the teacher education programme. The participants, who were all highly proficient in English (C1 level of the Common European Framework of Reference), did not seem hindered in expressing their views, and only resorted to very sporadic code-switching when referring to concepts and practices that were specific to the local school culture.

All interviews were transcribed in full by the authors. In the transcripts, the verbatim content of the interviews was recorded, along with any repetitions, false starts, pauses, variations in volume and rate of speech, and extra-linguistic or paralinguistic information (a simplified version of the transcription conventions we used is reproduced in the Appendix). After transcription, the interviews were subjected to two waves of coding. In the first wave, inductive methods were used to identify the components of each pre-service teacher's resilience system. The first interview was coded cooperatively by both authors, using Atlas.ti 7.0, in order to create a rough coding frame. The six remaining transcripts were coded separately by both authors and subsequently compared. During this stage, we did not draw explicitly on the resilience model described in the previous section. Rather, we flagged various types of stressors, psychological resources and phenomena associated with resilience, and used constant comparison methods to derive analytical categories from them. When the first wave of coding had been completed, the inductively generated categories were related to the three clusters in the model, namely inner strengths, external support and learned strategies. This resulted in snapshots of the participants' resilience systems (see Figures 6.3 and 6.4 for simplified versions).

Findings

Given space limitations, in this chapter we report on data from only two participants, Peter and John, whose adjusted resilience scores place them in the 'high' and 'low' resilience categories respectively (Table 6.1).

Inner strengths

Throughout the interview, Peter presented himself as a confident teacher, with a strong teacher identity. His sense of identity was evident in a vivid description of how he would like to be described by his students ten years in the future:

> Professor [surname], the fun guy who (.) who is nice to work with, erm, we don't like the way he is teaching us vocab because he wants us to: to know the prepositions as well ((both laugh)) <u>and an example sentence,</u>

> and we don't like that, but he really loves it ((laughs)) and, erm, yeah, he's fun to work with. Even tho:ugh he has to fail some people sometimes. He gives his, he he always wants wants everyone to pass, but some [students] just have some problems they need to work out. He's helpful, he's helpful with that because he tortures us with, extra: extra work, he hands out individually to: people who have some issues here and there ((chuckles)) a::nd, and that's how I want to– my students to describe me ((chuckles)).

Peter's well-worked out description of his future self suggested confidence in his ability to work even with challenging students, as well as some investment in his teacher identity.

When discussing unexpected and challenging situations in his practicum, Peter tended to talk with confidence about his coping ability. In a typical extract, he described an incident involving an uncooperative student, and discussed how he remained in control of the lesson by regulating his emotions and engaging in reflection-in-action:

> In this situation, you can't do anything. If he doesn't want to, he isn't going to start working with you in this lesson again, I would say. So that's why I remained calm and thought 'Well, it wouldn't do any good to get mad or angry at all'. I wasn't even mad or angry [...] I just thought, 'Well, that's something that went wrong. [It] can happen. Let's go on.'

He went on to relate his reaction to his innately calm disposition ('I guess, again, I think it is my naturally calm nature when working with younger ones'), which suggests that he perceived this as a stable trait of his character.

Elsewhere in the interview, Peter mentioned that his cheerful predisposition served him well as a pedagogical tool. This helped him to maintain classroom discipline as well as to establish classroom rapport:

> It helps me to diffuse whatever tension there might be, and, erm, that really was a quality at first because some students didn't know me at all, and given my physique, I might look intimidating to some small kids, but then I make them laugh.

Peter's use of humour was also evident in the light-hearted exaggerations evident in his description of his future self (above), which indicates that this may be a relatively stable part of his resilience system, on which he drew in any potentially intimidating situation, including the interview.

In contrast to Peter, John seemed much less confident about his ability to deal with the demands of his teaching role. In the following extract, John appears especially unprepared, or even unwilling, to reflect on his qualities as a language teacher, as indexed by his pauses and hesitations and the adjective he eventually chose in order to describe himself.

Interviewer: If I asked you to describe yourself as a language teacher in a short phrase, how would you describe yourself?

John: Hmm … ((chuckles)) as a language teacher? Erm … (.3) (.hh) Oh, I have to think about that. Ah.

Interviewer: Take your time.

John: Ok. Erm. (.6) (.h) (.7) Sometimes insecure maybe.

In fact, John's lack of confidence in his teaching ability was so strong that he seemed reluctant to even consider evidence to the contrary. Later in the interview, the interviewer deliberately challenged John's self-appraisal as an insecure teacher, by explicitly contrasting it with John's classroom behaviour:

Interviewer: … you say that you are not a spontaneous person and you walk into a class without any preparation and do very well.

John: Well, 'very well' might be an overstatement.

Interviewer: Ok (.3)

John: And you <u>cannot imagine</u> how nervous I was before the first lesson. So, really questioned everything. And that, yeah, so–

Interviewer: And you say that you are quite insecure, but when the students started chatting to each other you just raised your voice and stopped them.

John: Yeah, that's true. But, I mean, I couldn't just ignore it […] But, I just think that maybe I was able to fake it or something.

In this extract, what at first seems like a display behaviour of modesty develops into an active attempt, by John, to resist any discursive engagement with perceptions that were not in line with his self-image.

External support

In order to examine the role of external support structures, we asked participants to talk to us about their relationships with trusted people to whom they might turn for support if they felt overwhelmed.

When talking about the people he trusted to support him, Peter described a dense network of connections:

> I can always talk to my parents regarding teaching, especially to my mother [who is a teacher]. Regarding music, to my father, erm, I think I can– when I am thinking about my career as a musician, so mini-career, nothing big, I like to talk to my (.) piano teacher, a professor. And regarding other problems I can also, can always talk to my girlfriend. So, as long as she is by my side, I always have someone to talk to. And I also have two very or three very close friends, so I know that I can talk to them about everything.

What is interesting about Peter's support network is not only its density, but also its functional differentiation, in the sense that he seemed to seek support from different people depending on the nature of the difficulties he was facing. Although Peter did not explicitly mention asking for assistance during the practicum, his description suggests that he felt well supported to deal with a wide range of potential problems.

John, on the other hand, described himself as being socially isolated. He initially seemed reluctant to discuss the role of other people in his life, and only after some probing did he explain that 'I don't really get too close with other people'. When talking about other students in the teacher training programme, John acknowledged that 'we are all on the same boat and we can talk about these things [i.e. issues related to the practicum]', but he felt that the quality of their interactions was superficial:

> I mean they do ask 'How was it [i.e. the practicum]?' and things. 'How did it go?', and then I say: 'Yeah, it went pretty good. And some minor troubles.' But yeah, I mean that's it. And I don't think you can really call that support, because I think it's just, erm, well, small talk.

He went on to explain that he was cautious about seeking support from his peer network, because he did not perceive them as significant parts of his life.

> I guess, after my studies I wouldn't, won't see them ever again. So I am not really close friends with them and I think if something bad happens I wouldn't tell them or discuss it in detail.

Perhaps unsurprisingly, he seemed equally unwilling to engage with the problems of people in his peer network. His somewhat aloof attitude is well illustrated in the following extract, where John describes an incident when his roommate was experiencing high levels of stress:

> I remember one time, on Friday or something, she had an exam. And on Thursday, she started to clean the whole apartment, and she really stayed up to midnight and cleaned the bathroom and stuff. And I thought: 'OK, that's your way [of dealing with stress]'.

Tellingly, however, he did not seem to have considered it appropriate to help his roommate in any practical or affective way, which could suggest that he was either uninterested in fostering a more supportive relationship, or uncomfortable doing so.

Elsewhere in the interview, he also nervously suggested that he was wary of involving his parents in aspects of his student and teaching life, because he felt uncomfortable with the control he perceived they exercised over him:

> I do get money from my mother and father so I rely on them and they kind of (.) indirectly control me. And, erm, yeah, I mean, I (.) do not talk about these things [i.e. academic challenges]. I guess I avoid >I don't know< ((chuckles))

Overall, John appeared to be very protective of his privacy as he refused to form strong connections to other people in his social environment.

Learned strategies

The final cluster of factors we looked into were the strategies that Peter and John reportedly deployed during their practicum.

In Peter's case, there was little evidence of the conscious use of such strategies, possibly because his practicum was relatively unchallenging. However, he did make some general comments about how he actively managed his stress levels. He reported being very conscious of the debilitating effects of stress, having observed his mother, a teacher, suffer from burnout, and having personally experienced traumatic stress at school ('They [i.e. exams] made me quite sick ... I became ill'). Because of this, he explained, he proactively monitored his stress levels ('if I know my limits I will try to (.) not to overstep them again [...] because it is also better for my health'). He also mentioned that he was committed to maintaining a healthy work–life balance:

> I know that I have a lot of work, I know that I want to have spare time. I want to play video games. I want to meet with friends and all the other things. I have a girlfriend [...] There are a lot of things going on in my life and studying is the– one of the major things I do, so I try to concentrate and to finish my studies in time, but at the same time I want to have freedom.

The variety of activities in which Peter engaged, and the priority he attached to his studies, seemed to help him engage with the expectations of his role as a pre-service teacher in an effective way.

John's attitudes towards stress were markedly different. To begin with, he appeared to be in a state of denial towards his own stress. He made claims like:

> I mean before exams ((chuckles)) of course I, get a lot– get stressed easily. But generally I mean, I don't get too stressed. It's just when I have an exam or something.

This emphatic denial seemed to contradict multiple unguarded comments made *passim* in the interview (e.g. 'And you cannot imagine how nervous I was before the first lesson'). Elsewhere, he summarised his practicum experience as follows:

John: I think it was good. Erm, I mean– There are both sides. I think. I guess– I mean [it was a] negative [experience] because (.3) No, first of all positive things were that I [...] didn't have a nervous breakdown [...]

Interviewer: Were you actually afraid you might have a breakdown?

John: Yeah. No! ((chuckles))

It also seems telling that when John was asked about how he dealt with stress, he deflected the question by remarking that everyone has different coping strategies, and by narrating an example about his roommate (above).

In terms of actually dealing with stress, John tended to use avoidance strategies, including sleep or solitary recreational activities:

Interviewer: So, one of the stress management techniques you mentioned is (.) sleeping?

John: Sleeping, yes.

Interviewer: Are there any other things that you, that help you cope with this?

John: Ah yes, for example, I like to play video games.

Although rest and recreation are important components of a healthy work–life balance, in John's case they seemed to be getting in the way of effective professional functioning. With regard to the latter, John avoided any contact with his mentors until the day when he had to teach, which was highly unusual given the structure of the practicum. He also deliberately avoided any sort of cognitive engagement with his upcoming teaching assignments, such as lesson planning or even visualising the lesson:

> And before I went to school I just shut up my mind and said: 'Well, o. I am just gonna drive there and I won't think about it and we'll see what happens.' That was one way of not being too stressed. I don't know if it's a good idea, because you have to prepare. What I did basically was just to avoid it.

Although he eventually performed his teaching tasks with a degree of competence that was perhaps unexpected given his reported lack of preparation, John acknowledged that his avoidance strategy was professionally unhelpful ('I was less happy with the listening [task]. Because I simply wasn't prepared'). However, he hastened to add that he 'couldn't be prepared' for the challenges of the lesson anyway, which seemed to suggest that his avoidance strategy also provided him with a pretext for absolving himself from responsibility for disappointing teaching.

Adaptive and maladaptive adjustment

Peter and John's resilience systems are typical of the two directions towards which resilience might be oriented. When faced with challenges in his teaching, Peter seemed able to draw on a wide range of psychological resources (Figure 6.3). These included a strong set of teacher self-efficacy beliefs, a well-developed sense of teacher identity, and aspects of his personality that he perceived to be pedagogically useful, such as a calm and cheerful disposition. He carefully monitored his stress levels, maintained a healthy work–life balance and prioritised effectively. He could also count on a dense network of connections to support him in case of difficulties, which added to his confidence. In the absence of serious challenges in Peter's practicum, it is hard to discern the dynamism of the system, but if one takes a broader developmental perspective, it is interesting to note that Peter explicitly attributes his ability to deal with stress to past trauma. In all, the interaction of the components that make up Peter's resilience system seemed to help him

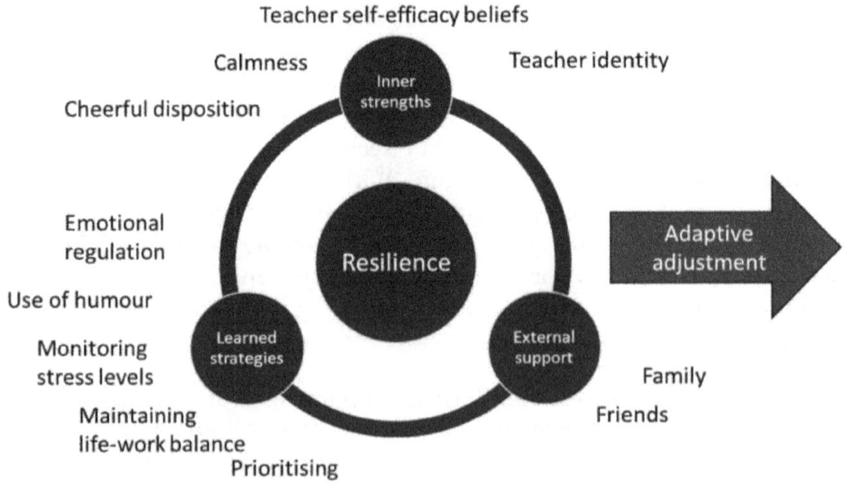

Figure 6.3 Peter's resilience system

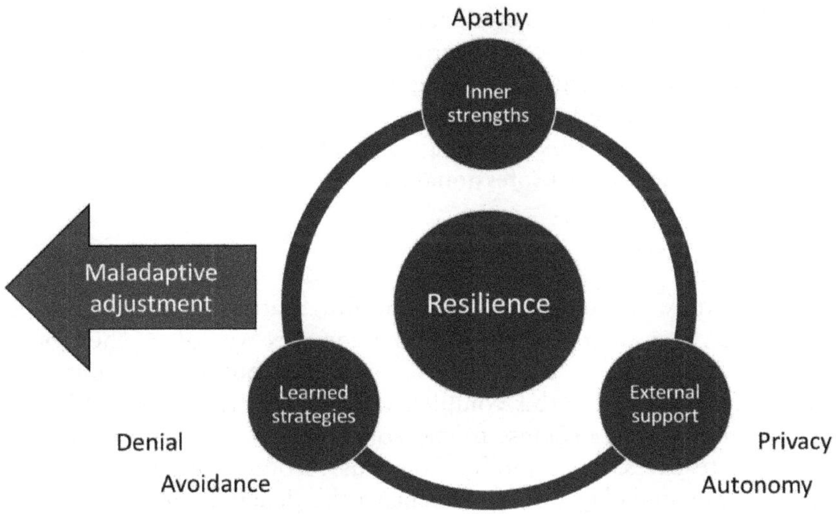

Figure 6.4 John's resilience system

deal effectively with his teaching tasks, and therefore exemplify adaptive adjustment.

In comparison, John's resilience system seemed relatively resource-impoverished (Figure 6.4). He reported a relatively apathetic attitude towards his teaching. This was manifested by avoiding lesson preparation and meetings with his mentor. His refusal to accept credit for those aspects of the lesson where he was successful is also indicative of this professed apathy. John had a relatively atomistic attitude that placed a premium on privacy and autonomy, and this made him unlikely to solicit assistance from external support structures, or to nurture supportive relationships. His repertoire of strategies for coping with stress consisted of denying the existence of stressors and refusing to engage with them. Such differences hint at a very different personality type from Peter, but more importantly, they reveal a very different potential for teacher effectiveness.

One way to describe this resilience system would be as indicative of a low resilience, and indeed John's low adjusted resilience score (Table 6.1) might privilege such an interpretation. A complementary perspective, however, might be that John's resources were combining to produce a different form of resilience. John's apathetic attitude served to protect him from possible frustration when faced with suboptimal teaching outcomes. His reluctance to draw on parental support seemed to connect with his need to assert autonomy, and his reserved attitude towards peers might be related to a desire to protect himself from eventual disillusionment and separation (cf. his comment that 'after my studies I [...] won't see them ever again'). Lastly, his denial and avoidance strategies, while arguably counterproductive in the long run, seemed to protect John from engaging with disconcerting thoughts and feelings. What is perhaps cause for concern, seen from the perspective of John's career choices, is that this emerging form of resilience did not appear conducive to enacting his professional role.

Discussion

In this study, we put forward a conceptualisation of resilience as a phenomenon that emerges from within a complex web of psychological resources. Building on our earlier work (Kostoulas & Lämmerer, 2018), we discussed how this complex web (the resilience system) keeps reconfiguring itself in response to stressors. We then used data from two pre-service teachers to exemplify how this reconfiguration could lead to adaptive or maladaptive adjustment to the demands of teaching. In doing so, we have shown how negative emotions, such as the ones which might be experienced in a stressful context, can trigger processes of growth.

It should be noted that, in this theory of teacher resilience, both outcomes are valourised in relation to professional roles, as our definition of adaptive and maladaptive adjustment explicitly connects psychological outcomes to the demands of teaching. The limited scope of this study has meant that we were unable to specify these outcomes in detail using empirical methods at this stage. One possibility for refining the model might involve developing and empirically validating insights put forward in Hiver and Dörnyei (2015) and connecting them to the teachers' professional roles. Moreover, in view of the connections between resilience and emotional regulation, and the importance of managing emotions in teaching, it may be possible to connect adaptive and maladaptive outcomes to measures of emotional regulation. Its limitations notwithstanding, the resilience model that is put forward here is perhaps easier to relate to the professional domain of language teaching, compared to models imported from developmental and counselling psychology.

Our model of resilience also highlights the role of adversity as a trigger or impetus for psychological growth and professional development. The dynamism of the resilience system, as conceptualised above, is fuelled by stressors that teachers perceive in their professional contexts, which then cause reconfigurations of the systems' internal structure. In our study, we were again unable to document the genesis of such phenomena in real time, possibly because this restructuring develops over longer time frames than what we had at our disposal. Connections between stress and resilient adaptation were easier to document when taking a longer-term perspective, such as when Peter reflected on how his stress management strategies related to traumatic experiences in his childhood. Additional work, possibly involving longitudinal or life history methods, might generate more insights about the development of resilience over time.

Finally, our study underscores the importance of environmental determinants in the development of resilience. Looking at the resilience system, many of the components connect the individuals to the environment in which they are embedded, as is the case with external support structures and the behavioural strategies that are available for deployment. Contextual considerations are also important, as the intensity and nature of stressors can have an impact on whether resilience will emerge. Prilleltensky's (2012) typology of contextual conditions seems relevant in this regard, because it reminds us that resilience can only develop in what are described as 'suboptimal conditions of justice', defined as a generally supportive but not adversity-free environment. Future work into resilience that brings professional context back into focus seems to be a high priority, and this might look into what teachers perceive as supportive or non-supportive conditions.

Concluding Remarks

The model of resilience that is at the core of our ongoing work advances our understanding of teacher resilience in multiple ways. The broad categories that constitute the resilience system highlight the universal aspects of resilience, and the relatively loose way in which these are specified provides theoretical scope to accommodate individual variation. By differentiating between adaptive and maladaptive trajectories of resilience development, the model relates explicitly to the particularities of teaching. In doing so, the model allows for connections to be made between a holistic psychological description of resilience and more focused descriptions that foreground the teachers' professional roles. Finally, our model of teacher resilience raises the salience of moderate stressors and shows how these can trigger resilient growth.

In developing our model of teacher resilience, we aimed to bring to centre stage a view of language teachers and language teaching that is holistic, situated and complex. It is also a view that goes beyond linear causal patterns, whereby negative experiences must be associated with negative outcomes. Our perspective describes aspects of teacher psychology in terms that are less predictable, and arguably more interesting. It is a developmental view, which brings to the forefront growth and potential, even in the face of adversity. It is, we hope, a view that might take broader hold in the field of language teacher psychology.

Post-Reading Tasks

(1) Figures 6.3 and 6.4 show the resilience systems of the two participants of this study. What does your own resilience system look like? Using those figures as examples, outline your resilience system.
(2) Can you think of any events that have been particularly relevant to shaping your own resilience system? Write a short narrative describing these events and the ways in which they helped you cope with later adversity.
(3) Draft a plan outlining aspects of your resilience system that you would like to improve. For each area of potential growth, describe your current state, your target and some practical steps that can help you reach this target.
(4) Thinking of your own experiences and the examples in this chapter, in what ways might teacher education and school administrations help foster resilience?

Acknowledgment

The authors express their gratitude to Prof Sarah Mercer for assistance with the adaptation of the questionnaire survey and participant recruitment.

References

Bleuler, M. (1972/1978) *The Schizophrenic Disorders: Long-Term Patient and Family Studies*. New Haven, CT: Yale University Press.
Byrne, D. (1998) *Complexity Theory and the Social Sciences: An Introduction*. London: Routledge.
Connor, K.M. and Davidson, J.R.T. (2003) Development of a new resilience scale: The Connor-Davidson resilience scale (CD-RISC). *Depression and Anxiety* 18 (2), 76–82.
Davis, M.C., Luecken, L. and Lemery-Chalfant, K. (2009) Resilience in common life: Introduction to the special issue. *Journal of Personality* 77 (6), 1637–1644.
Day, C. and Gu, Q. (2015) *Resilient Teachers, Resilient Schools: Building and Sustaining Quality in Testing Times*. New York: Routledge.
Denz-Penhey, H. and Murdoch, C. (2008) Personal resiliency: Serious diagnosis and prognosis with unexpected quality outcomes. *Qualitative Health Research* 18 (3), 391–404.
Farrell, T.S.C. (2016) Surviving the transition shock in the first year of teaching through reflective practice. *System* 61, 12–19.
Fergus, S. and Zimmerman, M.A. (2005) Adolescent resilience: A framework for understanding healthy development in the face of risk. *Annual Review of Public Health* 26, 399–419.
Fletcher, D. and Sarkar, M. (2013) A review of psychological resilience. *European Psychologist* 18 (1), 12–23.
Gonzalez, R. and Padilla, A.M. (1997) The academic resilience of Mexican American high school students. *Hispanic Journal of Behavioral Sciences* 19 (3), 301–317.
Gu, Q. and Day, C. (2007) Teachers' resilience: A necessary condition for effectiveness. *Teaching and Teacher Education* 23 (8), 1302–1316.
Hiver, P. (2018) Teachstrong: The power of teacher resilience for L2 practitioners. In S. Mercer and A. Kostoulas (eds) *Language Teacher Psychology* (pp. 231–246). Bristol: Multilingual Matters.

Hiver, P. and Dörnyei, Z. (2015) Language teacher immunity: A double-edged sword. *Applied Linguistics* 38 (3), 405–423.
Johnson, B., Down, B., Le Cornu, R., Peters, J., Sullivan, A., Pearce, J. and Hunter, J. (2016) *Promoting Early Career Teacher Resilience: A Socio-Cultural and Critical Guide to Action.* London: Routledge.
Kelchtermans, G. (1996) Teacher vulnerability: Understanding its moral and political roots. *Cambridge Journal of Education* 26 (3), 307–323.
King, J. (2016) 'It's time, put on the smile, it's time!': The emotional labour of second language teaching within a Japanese university. In C. Gkonou, D. Tatzl and S. Mercer (eds) *New Directions in Language Learning Psychology* (pp. 97–112). Cham: Springer.
King, J. and Ng, K.-Y.S. (2018) Teacher emotions and the emotional labour of second language teaching. In S. Mercer and A. Kostoulas (eds) *Language Teacher Psychology* (pp. 140–157). Bristol: Multilingual Matters.
Kostoulas, A. (2018) *A Language School as a Complex System: Complex Systems Theory in English Language Teaching.* Berlin: Peter Lang.
Kostoulas, A. and Lämmerer, A. (2018) Making the transition into teacher education: Resilience as a process of growth. In S. Mercer and A. Kostoulas (eds) *Language Teacher Psychology* (pp. 274–263). Bristol: Multilingual Matters.
Kuterovac-Jagodić, G. (2003) Posttraumatic stress symptoms in Croatian children exposed to war: A prospective study. *Journal of Clinical Psychology* 59 (1), 9–25.
Lazarus, R.S. (2003) The Lazarus manifesto for positive psychology and psychology in general. *Psychological Inquiry* 14 (2), 173–189.
Mancini, A.D. and Bonanno, G.A. (2009) Predictors and parameters of resilience to loss: Toward an individual differences model. *Journal of Personality* 77 (6), 1805–1832.
Masten, A.S. (2001) Ordinary magic: Resilience processes in development. *American Psychologist* 56 (3), 227–238.
Masten, A.S. and Obradović, J. (2006) Competence and resilience in development. *Annals of the New York Academy of Sciences* 1094, 13–27.
Masten, A.S., Cutuli, J.J., Herbers, J.E. and Reed, J.M.-G. (2009) Resilience in development. In S.J. Lopez and C.R. Snyder (eds) *The Oxford Handbook of Positive Psychology* (pp. 117–312). Oxford: Oxford University Press.
Prilleltensky, I. (2012) Wellness as fairness. *American Journal of Community Psychology* 49 (1–2), 1–21.
Richardson, G. (2002) The metatheory of resilience and resiliency. *Journal of Clinical Psychology* 58 (3), 307–321.
Rutter, M. (1976) Research report: Isle of Wight studies. *Psychological Medicine* 6 (2), 313–332.
Rutter, M. (1979) Protective factors in children's responses to stress and disadvantage. *Annals of the Academy of Medicine, Singapore* 8 (3), 324–338.
Troy, A.S. and Mauss, I.B. (2011) Resilience in the face of stress: Emotion regulation as a protective factor. In S.M. Southwick, B.T. Litz, D. Charney and M.J. Friedman (eds) *Resilience and Mental Health: Challenges across the Lifespan* (pp. 30–44). Cambridge: Cambridge University Press.
van Deurzen, E. (2009) *Psychotherapy and the Quest for Happiness.* Thousand Oaks, CA: SAGE.
Werner, E.E. and Smith, R.S. (1982) *Vulnerable but Invincible: A Study of Resilient Children and Youth.* New York: McGraw-Hill.
Winfield, L.F. (1991) Resilience, schooling, and development in African-American youth: A conceptual framework. *Education and Urban Society* 24 (1), 5–14.
Wong, P.T.P. and Roy, S. (2018) Critique of positive psychology and positive interventions. In N.J.L. Brown, T. Lomas and F.J. Eiroa-Orosa (eds) *The Routledge International Handbook of Critical Positive Psychology* (pp. 142–160). London: Routledge.
Zolkoski, S.M. and Bullock, L.M. (2012) Resilience in children and youth: A review. *Children and Youth Services Review* 34 (12), 2295–2303.

Appendix: Transcription Conventions

Symbol	**Denotes**
(.)	brief pause
(.3)	longer pause, in seconds
[	onset of overlapping speech
=	latched turns
emphasis	stress (marked by volume, pitch, rate of delivery, etc.)
:	prolonged vowel sound
.h	sharp inhaling sound (number of letters indicates length in seconds)
> <	onset and end of noticeably faster speech
(( ))	paralinguistic/extra-linguistic information
[information]	comment by the authors (e.g. clarifications)
[...]	redacted content

7 Past L2 Selves, Emotions and Classroom Group Dynamics: The Don't Ask, Can't Tell Policy

Joseph Falout

> Odd as it may seem, I am my remembering self, and the experiencing self, who does my living, is like a stranger to me.
> – Kahneman, 2011: 390

Benefits and Challenges in Researching Past L2 Selves

The professional identities and classroom behaviours of language teachers can be linked not simply to their past language learning experiences themselves, but more relevantly to what they make of those experiences in relation to who they believe they are, or their *history-in-person* views (Davin *et al.*, 2018). These self-representations are also known as *past selves*. Explicit links of past selves to the emotions and emotional well-being of teachers, however, have not yet surfaced prominently in the literature.

Past selves are the ripples of identities catching up to us from our own or others' pasts, continually recreated by storytelling or lived experiences. They are the narratives of our lives, woven and re-woven up through now, that help us interpret the meaning of life's circumstances and events. Our past experiences in learning and teaching also ripple into our distinctive weavings of present identities as learners and teachers. The fabric of our present identities can twist from and twist into the threads of our past emotions, which can robustly and distortedly twist back again into our present emotions when interacting with others. The past selves of students, teachers and even others outside of the classroom can mediate the formation of each other's present emotions, identities and behaviours in learning and teaching (Falout, 2016a, 2016b). In this way, hidden emotional structures play out in the classroom and can affect the emotional well-being of students and teachers together. Presuming that past selves relate to the teacher's temperament and contributions to the socioemotional atmosphere of the classroom, it would be vital to gain insight about past selves, plus their long-lasting influences upon the emotional self-regulation and other-regulation of potentially every member of the classroom, including the teacher.

The inherent difficulty in researching such invisible complexity is compounded further by the way past selves are psychologically reconstructed piecemeal and continually revised without our even knowing. These unconscious fabrications can lead us to false explanations of how we have behaved in the past, and false impressions of how our current thoughts and identities are formed. Since people cannot accurately perceive connections between their past and present selves, asking students and teachers to explain their present actions in light of how they remember their past experiences is not necessarily reliable – a caution expressed in the *don't ask, can't tell policy* (Wilson, 2011).

This chapter starts by explaining the basic concepts of past selves, how they form and their importance for healthy living. A background section will present selected studies involving past L2 selves to reveal their important relationship with emotions and group dynamics in the classroom. Then potential new research methods for SLA are introduced by short descriptions of example studies, with explanations given for how they might be used for researching student and teacher past L2 selves.

Past Selves, Emotions and Social Interactions

A personal narrative helps people to evaluate how they feel about themselves in the present moment via the story of from where they have come. This temporal self-comparison, in turn, helps people to see where the story for themselves may be going. The process of mental time travel to re-experience one's past is known as *retrospection*, while *prospection* is the mental simulation of experiencing – or *prefeeling* – the future (Gilbert & Wilson, 2007). These mental processes of imaginary temporal projection together share the same neural pathways with another imaginary projection – that of into the mind of another person, which is a process called *theory of mind*. The default mode network, the region of the brain that tunes into daydreaming, seems responsible for reliving one's past experiences, peering into one's future and stepping into other people's shoes to see life from their perspectives (Spreng & Grady, 2010). These neural processes correspond to key theoretical concepts of self-referential and socio-referential mind-time phenomena as researched in social psychology, behavioural economics, sociocultural theory, neuroscience and SLA (Figure 7.1).

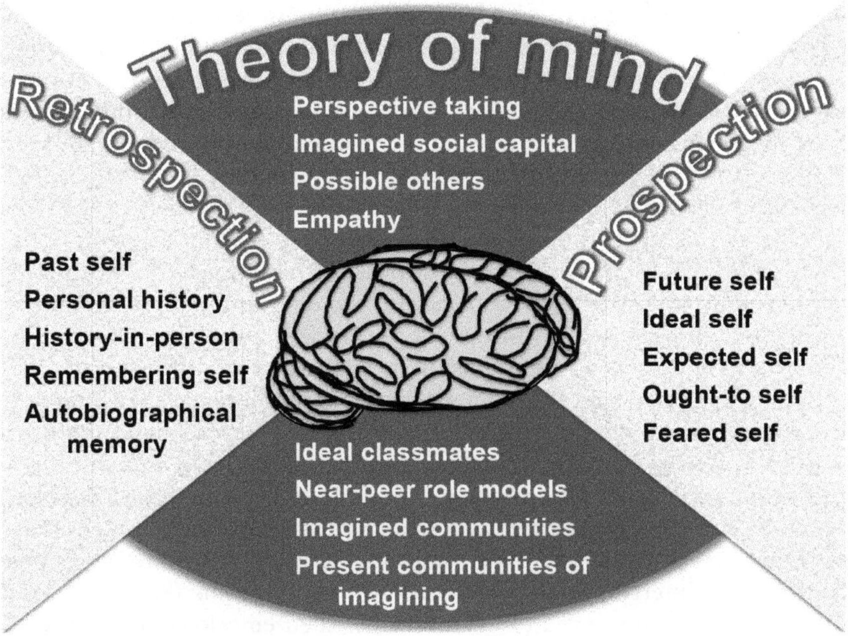

Figure 7.1 The default mode network processes self-referential and socio-referential mind-time phenomena

Sharing narratives has been shown to simultaneously activate the same neural circuits over many regions across individuals' brains, particularly in an area which is usually tuned out to outside stimulation, the default mode network (Nummenmaa *et al.*, 2012). From the prefrontal cortex to the limbic system, covering cognitive senses to emotional states, brain activity among groups of people can become synchronized when listening together to the same stories, especially when the content has high emotional input, whether positive or negative. Shared emotional states, or *emotional intersubjectivity*, may help people to understand each other's perspectives so that they might be able to predict behaviours and engage appropriately with others within their immediate social situations.

Autobiographical memory, one's own life narrative, starts early in infanthood but develops slowly into adulthood. Studies in natural and controlled settings found that mothers who reminisce with their children in frequent and elaborative ways, and who evaluate the emotional meanings of past experiences and encourage the child's own recall and involvement in co-constructing the experiences, provide their children with abilities later in life to better integrate episodes from their past into a coherent sense of self. Moreover, these children, as opposed to children whose mothers less often reminisced with them in these ways, were more likely to develop emotional coping strategies and achieve higher levels of well-being (Fivush, 2011). Similar comparisons were found for children whose families more often shared the autobiographical memories of other family members together – even creating intergenerational narratives of parents' past selves, those of grandparents, and further back – which helped them throughout adolescence via better abilities of perspective taking and of reframing past experiences for emotional regulation (Fivush *et al.*, 2011).

The stretching, bending and reconstructing of mind-time frames, memory and emotions are adaptive processes that regulate formation of self-explanatory frameworks and goal-oriented planning. For example, when the sense of self-improvement is needed, people tend to make *downward revisions* of their past self, making their present self and situation appear better in comparison, and improving their moods. Conversely, when self-consistency is desired, people can make *upward revisions* of their past self, thereby idealizing their present self-concepts and helping themselves to improve their moods (McFarland & Buehler, 2012). Emotions in the moment are mediated more by temperament than are emotions after-the-moment, which undergo retrospective revisions that become filtered through sociocultural expectations (Scollon *et al.*, 2009). People seem to need to misremember their emotions, misrepresent who they were and be mistaken in who they will become, all for the sake of helping themselves 'to live at the fulcrum of stark reality and comforting illusion' (Gilbert, 2006: 171).

Prospects in Researching Past L2 Selves: The 'Don't Ask, Can't Tell' Policy

Questionnaires, diary studies and autobiographies retain a long-established pedigree as research methodologies in SLA precisely because of their leverage and finesse at discriminating and untangling the complex relationships of human interactions and emotions within language learning development (Schumann, 1997). These methods are thus valuable and need to be continued within research in all areas of human development. However, for researching the effects of social policies and practices, such as pedagogical interventions, relying on self-reported data alone is not recommended because of the human limitations in accurately understanding and directly reporting back on what happened, what was felt and what was the cause of specific actions. Therefore, the *don't ask, can't tell policy* (Wilson, 2011) recommends research methods involving strategically designed comparisons, plus random assignments of participants and control groups. Including such methods in research designs helps to rigorously test whether interventions are actually effective and reliably establish how.

Since memory is plastic and can be fallible, this chapter proposes incorporating new research methods for furthering the understanding of past L2 selves, emotions and group dynamics in language learning. After covering a selected background in SLA research with fresh explications pertaining to past selves, this chapter proceeds to offer examples of new research methods for investigating various aspects of past selves that could relate to classroom interactions and the emotional lives of teachers and students. Brief rationales indicate why conducting such future investigations within the context of language learning could be useful. The purpose of past selves research is to inform teachers about ways of improving the emotional effects they could have on students while improving the emotional effects students could have on teachers.

Past L2 Selves, Emotions and Classroom Group Dynamics

Teacher–student and student–student interactions inside classrooms have been found to affect and be affected by classroom members' past selves regarding their L2 learning. Moreover, interactions with others outside the classroom, and past selves in other subject domains, have also been shown to enter the multiplex interconnections of emotions, psychologies and group dynamics within language classrooms. Portions of three studies are presented here to illustrate the interplay of past L2 selves, emotions and group dynamics. The roles of emotional exchanges teachers had with their students will be highlighted, to illustrate how they affected the autobiographical development and resulting long-term emotional self-regulation of the students. Any guess can be made about the emotional base from which the teachers in these studies were working from, or their actual intentions, but key to remember is that the teachers, in affecting the emotional lives of their students, were in certain ways reciprocally affecting their own emotional lives, as well as the emotional lives of teachers who in the future will be receiving these students in their classes. Also, given briefly are the research methods used to understand these emotional exchanges and their long-lasting emotional effects.

From the first study (Falout *et al.*, 2013), complex relationships were discovered to be interwoven among the past selves of L2 learners, their motivational changes over time, and their interpersonal interactions inside and outside the classroom. At the start of the academic school year, 265 university students in Japan wrote their personal language learning history. They were told that motivational levels to study English could fluctuate like a rollercoaster going up and down. Then each student charted out their personal motivational levels on a motivational timeline grid, starting back from junior high school (JHS, where many had begun their formal study of English), through high school (HS) and up to their present year in university. They drew a line to follow the dips, slumps, perks and peaks of the rollercoaster of their motivations, and then accounted for these changes by answering a series of open-ended questions relating to their past experiences of demotivation and remotivation. Students were encouraged to answer in English, and for cases in which they had opted to answer in Japanese, bilingual members of the research team translated the answers into English.

The students also completed a scaled questionnaire comprising a validated construct called the antecedent conditions of the learner, which can capture, in the moment of contemplation, a kind of retrospective, grainy snapshot or thumbnail sketch of an individual's EFL-related past self (Falout, 2016a). Through these data, the valence of these past selves could be reliably determined, meaning the past L2 self of each student could be indexed by a level of positivity or negativity. This allowed the data from the participants to be separated into three groupings of students whose past selves were negative, low-positive and high-positive. These demarcations recognized only very simplified qualities of past selves, the academic emotional baggage these students were currently carrying at university, but remarkable patterns between the groups emerged.

As positivity of past selves decreased from high-positive to low-positive, and on to negative past selves, the three groups overall reflected back across time with incrementally lower levels of motivation, displaying three concentric curves, with the lowest levels of motivation bottoming out during secondary education for all groups. Students with past negative selves had the lowest average dip, while students with low-positive past selves suffered from a lesser dip, and students with high-positive past selves showed barely a dip, and then a gradual but continual incline in their motivation up through to their present moment at university.

All three groups were about as frequent to report experiencing demotivation caused by personality differences and even conflicts between them and their teachers. However, the two positive past selves groups were more likely than the negative past selves group to have been remotivated by subsequent teachers, their classroom friends or members of their families. Most often, this help came unexpectedly and the students' motivations improved unintentionally. They had not sought it, but many students became remotivated when someone listened patiently and empathized about their struggles to learn English, or someone offered constructive advice about using coping strategies, or someone was just there to joke and play and reduce stress.

For comparison, here are self-reports (heretofore unreported) from students with different valences of past selves, taken from the data set of this study (Falout *et al.*, 2013). Minami and Shota (all names are pseudonyms) hold contrasting opinions in that Minami believes her friends can often unexpectedly give her motivational boosts by complimenting her on her English, whereas Shota believes that no one can motivate anyone other than oneself, adding that he had failed in his many past attempts to convince himself that he liked English. Consider the contrasts between these two university students in their past experiences and present perspectives regarding classroom social interactions:

> When I was JH student, I started to have an interest in English and watched the movies or listened to music in English a lot. However, HS's class was just translate a textbook into Japanese. No conversation, no listening made me lost my motivation … When I was a [university] freshman, I always compared my English with my friend, and I was depressed. Besides, I have wondered what I really want to do in my future. Anyway, I lost my confident completely. At the times, my teacher said to me 'Look how you have progressed. A year ago, you were so shy and afraid of everything. But now, you've changed and overcome a lot of things.' I was almost crying. I was so motivated by his word. (Minami, high-positive past self)

> I hated the teacher at JHS [and became demotivated]. I didn't hate him at first but he kept saying lots of things about my sickness I had at that time. At HS, English classes were only what is called 'Juken Eigo [test English]', and it was not fun … teachers started to nag me repeatedly 'you better study English harder' before I even recovered my motivation. This decreased my motivation even more. (Shota, negative past self)

Minami began learning English in a JHS classroom environment involving a connection of the language with unfolding human drama in movies and emotions from music. Then she went on to a classroom in HS in which she felt the form of language learning was depersonalizing as it was disconnected from dialogue and the human voice. Upon entering university, her past self seems to have developed negatively, causing her fear of interacting with others in the classroom. Her reserve might have furthered her own unfavourable social comparisons of herself to her classmates, reinforcing a poor psychological state and putting an ambivalent if not antipathetic sway on imagining her future self. A crucial moment came when a teacher's personal attention and positive words reconnected Minami to her confidence and perhaps her sense of belonging in class. Her past self is now high-positive, and she enjoys going to the self-access learning centre to study English together with her friends.

Shota, on the other hand, experienced personalized attacks from his JHS teacher, lost interest and became poor at English, and consequently experienced further depersonalization later on when interacting with his HS teachers. As well-intending as they may have been, from Shota's perspective the kind of attention they placed upon him deprived him of relief. Shota never regained his motivation nor improved the image of his past self. Now he currently shuns the notion that others could help him remotivate. This kind of academic emotional baggage encumbers Shota with a mindset that could impede his receptiveness to kinder teachers and peers, such as Minami's friends in need, and to other socio-motivational interventions he may encounter at university or beyond.

One teacher's display of empathy uplifted Minami in a way that has sustained her motivations and prosocial engagement with others she encounters in her academic pursuits. This could mean that the interactions among herself, her classmates, teachers and other educational staff would be promising in terms of emotional enrichments for all. Meanwhile, another teacher's apparent bullying had left emotional scars on Shota to the extent that years later he was unable to accept the (perhaps well-meaning) encouragement of other teachers, teachers who may themselves have become emotionally burdened in the wake of too many silent and disengaged students (King, 2013) such as Shota may now be.

Next from the unreported data of Falout *et al.* (2013) is a comparative set of student experiences depicting what can happen when teachers seem to their students as unapproachable, neglectful or unable to relate. At the point of entering JHS, Kimiko's and Yuto's past selves differed qualitatively: Kimiko's first encounter with English was playing cards at her friend's house with a foreigner, while Yuto's earliest impressions evolved from watching the children's programme *Sesame Street* on television. Their past selves at this point may have established expectations about their future situations and social interactions involving English, and consequently the help-seeking steps they took when they felt depersonalized by their JHS teachers:

> The English class started at the first year of JHS and I couldn't understand the concept of third person. I fell behind the class and my motivation decreased. Furthermore, at the second year of JHS, the teacher taught in a way of targeting his lessons to only certain students, ignoring the rest of the class. That made me hate English even more ... [To remotivate myself] If I could understand what's taught in the class, I would present my answers, so I asked my mother and older sister to teach me English so the teacher would turn his attention to me ... I could ask my family very basic English questions which I would be embarrassed to ask teachers and my classmates. I could also say to my family without reservation that I still didn't understand after their explanation. They were very important to me. (Kimiko, high-positive past self)

> When I started to study English right away, my motivation decreased because the teacher didn't teach well and the explanations were hard for me to understand ... Teachers wrote things on the blackboard and I copied them into my notebook. Except for the blackboard, my relationship with teachers was not necessary. Whenever I had something I couldn't understand, I asked my friends. Their explanations were much easier to understand, compared with the ones of the teachers, and they were very valuable. (Yuto, negative past self)

Kimiko felt excluded from the instructional dialogue of the teacher to the students in her JHS classroom. Instead of turning inward, she sought help from her family, who appear to have been able to offer her not only emotional support and understanding, but also appropriate subject knowledge. Most interestingly, Kimiko's initial purpose in seeking help from her family at home was to intentionally remotivate by becoming socially active and connected to her teacher in the classroom. However, her familial interactions fortified bonds of trust and support within the family, carrying much meaningfulness to her. About three years after this JHS experience, her world into English was thrown wide open when she visited her older sister overseas, who by that time was studying in New Zealand.

Yuto, on the other hand, turned to his classroom peers when he could not understand the teacher's lessons. Apparently, their subject knowledge or clarifications were not adequate, as his performance on tests continued to drop, which then caused his motivation to drop. Whereas Yuto considered his classmates as resources instrumental for his knowledge – expressing appreciation for their explanations rather than their personal relationships with him – Kimiko valued her family's help personally. Moreover, she looked up to her sister as a positive role model for using English.

Although Kimiko perceived her JHS teacher's favouritism with some students as social exclusion toward others – presenting perhaps a more emotionally hurtful interactional style than the impersonal stance displayed by Yuto's JHS teacher – Kimiko nevertheless held onto something that could carry her forward in learning. Her academic emotional baggage, repacked with the help and care of her family, could transport her from negative classroom experience in JHS to better experiences in HS classrooms and eventually out to overseas travel. Now at university, her past self remains high-positive. Yuto, in comparison, currently holds negative academic emotional baggage, and he specifically says that he has no plans to use English after graduating university. As students majoring in science and engineering, both Kimiko and Yuto will likely need good English skills for improving their chances of employment after graduation and career advancement thereafter. Unfortunately, the present negative valence of Yuto's past L2 self predisposes him with a similar valence in the future for his past L2 self and imagined future L2 self, with matching negative effects on his engagement with others.

Conversely, from another study (Norton, 2000), Katrina quite purposefully uses her past identity as a teacher in Poland with a master's degree in biology to strive as an immigrant in Canada toward engaging again within a high-status professional community – her *imagined community*, which presupposes an imagined future identity and stimulates investment in L2 learning (Norton & McKinney, 2011). Norton (2000) followed Katrina, among four others, for 18 months using interviews, diaries and diary meetings in which the participants were welcomed to share from their entries by reading out loud to each other.

As Katrina studied English at a community college, raised her daughter, worked menial jobs and all the while felt marginalized, she drew upon her past self-image as a teacher. She wanted her life to become 'normal again, which [meant] fellow professionals would validate her symbolic resources ... values and educated status' (Norton, 2000: 121). She had recognized learning English as fundamentally key to her access to the community and to the life in which she aspired to live, and she did well in her first English course. But she felt her English teacher in the second course had been viewing her as an immigrant rather than a former teacher, making her feel belittled. One day in class, the teacher said that her English was not good enough for entering a computer course she was planning to take – a course which Katrina valued as a step toward belonging to her imagined community – and she 'dropped out [of the English class] in anger and indignation ... and never returned to the class' (2000: 140). The teacher's rejection of her past self was too much for Katrina to bear. She wanted to hold on to her past self closely. She needed to protect the place from where she had come, for the purpose of keeping the path open to where she wanted to go:

> When Katrina felt that her teacher failed to acknowledge her professional identity, thereby positioning her as a newcomer, she was greatly distressed ... Katrina's act of non-participation helped her to preserve her integrity of her imagined community. (Norton & McKinney, 2011: 81)

It is worth noting that Katrina enrolled in the computer class in which her English teacher could not imagine her performing capably. Katrina herself, however, could imagine it and she did it, successfully completing the 18-month computer programme. It seems that by opposing her language teacher, Katrina had prospered in language learning.

Elsewhere, a group of three Japanese university students with respectable English proficiencies and international experiences, studying SLA theory in Japan, wanted to oppose the pedagogical theory that the teacher championed and the way he seemed to ignore or disvalue their opinions. The way they accomplished this was subtle, subversive, almost accidental and ultimately rewarding for them emotionally. They appropriated the past L2 self of one of their members, Nana, who had formal English education at HS in the US. They wanted to use her language learning history to anchor a critical view they were preparing to convey in their group presentation for class. In the course of their preparations, they reconfigured the meaning they placed on her past experiences, collaboratively reconstructing a possible past self for her. They also developed emotional intersubjectivity, took their negative emotions toward the teacher and his course, and converted them into positive emotions regarding their collaborative engagements and the statement they managed to put into their group presentation. In a three-month study on their out-of-class meetings, Imai (2010) videotaped their conversations, collected the emotion logs each had written during the meetings, took their emotional temperatures with questionnaires before and after the meetings, and used stimulated recall from the videos in follow-up interviews.

At the start of their project, this self-selected group felt bored, angry and frustrated with their teacher, a native speaker of English whose opinions about SLA theory, with which they disagreed, seemed to be shared among their classmates. The majority of the opinions among the class aligned with mainstream SLA theory in that the communicative approach takes precedence over more explicit L2 teaching approaches. Their minority opinion was that explicit teaching provides a base of knowledge upon which oral communication could develop. The proposal they wrote for their group presentation featured a dramatic re-enactment of Nana's former self gaining elucidation from a lecture in a HS English class in the US. They hoped it would be exciting for the class to watch while suggesting their provocative perspective on the nature of language learning.

Their teacher read the group's proposal and then assigned them additional reading, requiring them to incorporate the ideas from an article into their presentation. The article, however, primarily countered their ideas. The group felt confused as to whether the teacher had understood their point. But rather than ignoring the teacher's directions, as they had initially considered, they negotiated together further, and decided to include the article's main point at the start of their rhetorical argument by recognizing the value of a pedagogical aim that centred on teaching for oral communicative competence. They then worked backward, making a claim for the importance of vocabulary and grammar knowledge, the crux upon which they had placed their freshly reconstructed image of Nana's possible past self:

(35) Naomi: Her English skills were developed because she had an opportunity to formally study grammar and vocabulary, while practicing the skills in communication with her friends. ((Looking at Nana and making a V sign)).
(36) Nana: ((Holding a thumb up)) Cool!
(37) Tomoyo: If she hadn't had that class to learn things like vocabulary, I should say.
(38) Naomi: That's right, that's right. How do I put it?
(39) Tomoyo: How should I put it? She might have made the same mistake repeatedly all the time…
(40) Naomi: That's right. She wouldn't have been able to manage a conversation because of basic errors.
(41) Tomoyo: And I guess that might lead to, what was it called? Fossilization, fossilization of errors.

(Imai, 2010: 286)

Through discussion, the group had stumbled upon *downward counterfactual* thinking: how the situation for Nana might have gone wrong. By remaking Nana's past L2 self as a negative past self, or perhaps even a feared past self, the group found an appropriate and clever way to make their point without subverting the project requirements. They could please the teacher while staying true to their initial thesis. The challenge of reconciling the differences between their teacher's perspectives and their own brought them joy and interest from an otherwise meaningless class, about which they could empathetically share their common regret for having to go through with it.

The teachers in the above illustrations – whether callous or clever in their emotional management of the classroom – acted and reacted in the moments they spent with their students, moments that may have left enduring impressions upon the students and teachers themselves. But the emotions experienced during those moments and the emotions as remembered could be different. If so, how were they different and why? Tantalizing questions for past L2 selves research such as these, with suggestions for ways to research them, will be explored in the next section.

Introducing New Research Methods for SLA

Interpersonal comparisons across time trials

Emotions in the moment can be influenced by personality traits, but as the event moves into the past, memory of the then-emotions becomes increasingly susceptible to mediation by sociocultural norms (Scollon *et al.*, 2009). What did the teachers from the illustrated cases above sense about these students' in-class emotions and dispositions? Were these students truly displeased in the moment? Members of the classroom may actually be having a good time during class, but what will they think a day, a week or a year later? Their retrospective evaluations may be crucial for whether they continue or change their educational programmes or teaching practices: the *experiencing self* tends not to make decisions for the future; the *remembering self* does (Kahneman, 2011).

Dissatisfaction with specific moments of classroom interaction may not appear within a student's or teacher's immediate affective state, but later on within their emotional past self. In other words, sociocultural environments outside class could be changing their perspectives about the class in retrospect. Understanding such discrepancies between their experiencing selves and remembering selves could yield important implications regarding the receptivity or enculturation of the value of certain learning and teaching practices, particularly for methods in which students or teachers are not familiar. One method is to sample emotions of individuals across time trials, checking for differences between in-the-moment measurements of emotions during class and retrospective estimates or summaries afterward.

Consider a study that followed such interpersonal comparisons of emotions across time trials (Wirtz *et al.*, 2003). At intervals of about two weeks and a few days before going on their vacations, students answered questions that assessed their level of emotions on a scale of their predictions (i.e. pre-feelings) on their positive affect, negative affect and overall evaluation of their vacations. Then at seven random moments each day during their vacation, which lasted an average of eight days, the students were asked to respond on their personal devices to the same questions as in their predictions, but this time their affective assessments were made in the moment. At intervals of about a few days and two weeks following their vacations, the students answered the same questions in retrospect – their remembered emotions – with a last question added at the very end in which the students indicated on a scale as to whether or not they would repeat the same vacation.

From the results, positive, negative and summative in-the-moment emotions were not as strongly felt as those within the predicted or remembered emotions. Then from structural equation modelling, path results revealed that in-the-moment emotions were not likely to lead to repeat experience decisions, but that predicted emotions were the strongest and only predictor. This means that the students were likely to prefer repeating the same vacations that they actually did *not* like much, and to prefer *not* repeating the same vacations that they actually *did* like a lot. These would seem to be poor decisions for future enjoyment. What happened is they tended to remember their emotions during peak moments or at the end of their vacation. Although these emotions were not necessarily representative of the aggregated emotions they actually experienced over the duration of their vacation – their averaged in-the-moment emotions – it was their past-self emotions that guided decision-making for their future.

Questions can be raised about the differences between in-the-moment and retrospective student and teacher emotions and other perspectives in L2 education. For example, how do the in-the-moment emotions during classroom activities and classroom member interactions relate with retrospective emotions? How do in-the-moment motivations to teach or learn compare to long-term retrospective emotions? How do teachers deal with their own emotions while handling the emotional management of their students' emotions? Research methods using interpersonal comparisons across time trials may be pertinent in answering these and similar questions.

Intrapersonal comparisons across age groups

Do age and experience matter in how students emotionally react to teachers, and vice versa? Back in Nana's group, they seem to think they know more than their teacher about L2 education. If they are the traditional ages of Japanese students, they would probably be somewhere in their early twenties. Katrina also disagreed with her teacher's teaching methods, but she was over 35 years old, had spent 17 years studying at schools in Poland, and had been a teacher herself; so she had considerably more education-related experience than each member of Nana's group when she disagreed with her Canadian teacher's L2 classroom practices. Minami, Shota and Yuto were younger, respectively 19, 21 and 20. They each had at least several years of formal English education, and, like Katrina, they were also demotivated by teacher-centred lectures and grammar translation. Little is known about the teachers' ages or pedagogical perspectives in these cases, but a question can be raised about the influence of each teacher's past L2 self on their pedagogical decisions. Are retrospective perspectives about L2 teaching and learning developmental? If so, at what ages or at how many accumulative years of experience do they change?

A series of four related studies (Quoidbach *et al.*, 2013), conducted on volunteers recruited through the internet homepage of a popular American television programme, started out by asking similar questions. The first three studies used scaled questionnaires to measure, respectively, personality, values and preferences. The participants in each study were randomly placed into one of two conditions: the reporters, who looked back into their past at the level of changes in themselves over the last 10 years; or the predictors, who looked forward into their future at the level of changes in themselves over the coming 10 years.

Results from each of these three studies were repeated. Regardless of actual age, spanning from ages 18 through 68, those who looked back into their pasts saw much change in themselves, whereas those who looked forward saw almost zero foreseeable changes in their personalities, values or preferences. These data were drawn onto comparative sets, placing predictors against reporters in spans of 10-year differences in age, in which, for example, the level of expected self-change by predictors at 21 years old was juxtaposed against the level of retrospective self-change by reporters at 31 years old. Twenty-one-year-olds anticipated they would change little by the time they reached 31 years old, while 31-year-olds reported that since the time they were 21 years old, they had indeed changed much. This pattern remained consistent across the lifespan. Quoidbach *et al.* (2013) termed this phenomenon *the end of history illusion*. This means that no matter what age someone is, they probably look back and recognize their personal growth, but believe this growth is concluded by their present age and they have finally become the person they were born to be.

The fourth study compared two randomly selected groups, asking the first group how much they would pay now to see their favourite musical band from 10 years ago, and the second group how much they would pay to see their present favourite musical band in 10 years.

It turned out that people were ready to spend much more to see a performance in 10 years for a band they liked now, than to now see a band that they liked 10 years ago. The end of history illusion predicts that people can make poor evaluations, decisions and investments for their future selves. This is because by the time they become their future selves, they will have changed enough that their then-present personalities, values and preferences will be different from those of their self 10 years ago, who had not understood how much personal change for them was to come.

Do retrospective and prospective self-change perspectives of teachers and learners in L2 education likewise differ? Are students or teachers making evaluations, decisions and investments for themselves, or teachers for their students, that they will regret in 10 years? What is happening in contexts in which compulsory education obligates a significant portion of students' lives to L2 learning? Research methods in SLA could incorporate such intrapersonal comparisons across age groups when looking into changes in temporal self-perspectives.

Intrapersonal comparisons of sociocultural framing

Implicit biases can be inferred in the previously sampled studies. One JHS teacher in Japan negatively targeted Shota's affliction, demotivating Shota in L2 learning and possibly disconnecting him from the classroom community. Kimiko said her JHS teacher exposed favouritism for certain students by including them in the classroom dialogue while excluding others. In Canada, Katrina believed her teacher looked down upon her, positioning her as an outsider, an immigrant. She felt this stance alienated her from the community in which she was hoping to become socially integrated. Meanwhile, Nana and her two friends were studying L2 pedagogy at university in Japan under a foreign teacher, someone different from them. Since these friends favoured the grammar translation method prevalent in Japanese schooling, the question can be raised as to how much they consciously or unconsciously perceived their teacher's advocation of the communicative method as an attempt to import an outside pedagogy into the Japanese education system.

How much do other L2 students balk at their teacher's good instruction simply due to unconscious stereotyping? How much do L2 teachers inadvertently alienate students by subtle cues that reveal their implicit biases? What is the potential for hidden biases to affect the group dynamics in a classroom? The societies from which people come can colour perceptions and perpetuate exclusionary behaviours, in spite of egalitarian values that people may otherwise consciously uphold.

The matched-guise technique is only one of many validated, indirect tests used for uncovering implicit biases. Indirect measures are commonly used to detect the degree of implicit biases individuals may have, because direct measures, i.e. conscious self-reports, fail to capture concealed or unconscious stereotypes, as well as alterations or errors in summative evaluations of episodic memories that occur during retrospection (Long, 2006).

At a university in Tokyo, two separate classes of Japanese sophomores studying sociolinguistics through English mediated instruction by a foreign teacher participated in a matched-guise study (Long, 2008). They believed they were listening to two audio recordings made by bilingual foreigners, speaking only in Japanese, who had claimed in their recordings that they had grown up in Japan, and thus were fluent in Japanese. Both short self-introductions were actually fictional, i.e. guises, and in fact were made by two Japanese native speakers; one recording had a male voice, the other a female voice. Class A listened to these recordings and were told that the male voice was of an American and the female voice of a Chinese individual. For Class B, these guises were switched, meaning they were told that the male was Chinese and the female American. Then based on what they had listened to, the students rated each speaker on 12 characteristics relating to personality, speaking style and physical appearance. From the results, the supposed Americans were appraised overall more favourably, rated as better looking, easier to understand and more cheerful, among having other more positive traits. The speakers believed to be Chinese were perceived as thinner, calmer and more intelligent. Such implicit biases could be affecting these Japanese students' attitudes and behaviours toward their foreign teacher.

How might similar implicit biases influence the approaches L2 students take toward interacting with their teachers or each other? How do students' implicit biases around their teachers affect the teacher's emotions? How could implicit biases that L2 teachers may have affect the way they think about and interact with students? Intrapersonal comparisons of sociocultural framing offer one way to uncover the hidden imprints that societal norms and biases can weave into the personal narratives of individuals.

Intragroup comparisons of group framing

Regarding the reported experiences of Minami, Kimiko, Katrina, and Nana and her friends, the ways they engaged or were engaged by others helped them to overcome setbacks in their motivations. Moreover, these coping strategies improved the valences of their past L2 selves and fortified their resolve to continue engaging with others and take control of their future L2 learning. For Shota and Yuto, on the other hand, their past L2 selves seem to have developed in a way that shuts them off from future interactions with others pertaining to L2 learning. These predispositions can negatively affect classroom group dynamics and subsequently the teacher's emotions.

Intervention studies aimed at promoting and protecting the positive valences of student and teacher past L2 selves could address some of the following questions. How can teachers and students amend their personal narratives that involve presumptions about themselves or classroom members that inhibit interactions beneficial for everyone's learning and personal development? How might they reframe their past personal experiences and control for their built-in sociocultural biases to gain trust in each other and work more cooperatively? How can classroom members become less exclusionary and more inclusionary in intentions and behaviours toward each other?

When whole classes share the individual member's L2 self-images as part of L2 learning activities in which meaning is negotiated, a group-framing effect is potentiated, marked by emotional intersubjectivity and harmonized mind-time frames of motivation. This means students together experience similar positive changes in emotions and temporal-based motivations of past, present and future selves (Fukada *et al.*, 2017). A recent intervention study (Fukuda *et al.*, forthcoming) was conducted in EFL communication-oriented classes at universities in Japan. Whole-class groups were randomly placed into one of two treatments, ideal classmates or future selves, to test the efficacy of the ideal classmates treatment on motivation and engagement. According to the respective treatments, students individually described their ideal L2 classmates or future L2 selves. These descriptions were collected and shared anonymously among the whole-class groups, and communicative activities related to the treatments were performed occasionally over one semester. A comparative analysis of student responses helped to determine how much the treatments influenced: (a) degree of change in intrapersonal mind-time frames of motivation, (b) degree of interpersonal prosocial peer learning engagement, and (c) correlational sizes between motivational growth and interpersonal engagement. Although both treatments appeared to have similar positive effects on gains in motivation and engagement, only the ideal classmates treatment resulted in a statistically significant correlation between motivational growth and engagement. Randomized treatment studies such as this one can help test the efficacy of classroom interventions on motivations, emotions and group dynamics.

How might whole-class groups be helped to adjust to each member's expectations about classroom interaction? What interventions can be used to promote and protect the positive valences of student and teacher past L2 selves? How can teachers adopt interventions that make both students and teacher feel positive? Intragroup comparisons of group framing can help show the potential socioemotional changes of whole classrooms under different conditions.

Conclusions

The self-fictionalizations and sociocultural filters produced within the default mode network of the brain help individuals to interpret and predict each other's emotions and behaviours, as well as help make meaning of their own experiences, which informs them how to adaptively plan and act socially in their worlds. However, this can present a problem for researching past L2 selves in that self-reports may not reliably describe how individuals actually felt in the past or why they really acted in the ways they did. New methods, therefore, were introduced in this chapter for augmenting established SLA research methods. The research methods of the example studies employed strategically designed comparisons: interpersonal comparisons across time trials, intrapersonal comparisons across age groups, intrapersonal comparisons of sociocultural framing and intragroup comparisons of group framing. None of the example studies assigned random control samples, however, which does not satisfy the *don't ask, can't tell policy*; but similar research designs used in future research could readily incorporate randomized placement of individual participants and whole groups. These approaches could reveal hidden processes involving past and future L2 selves on the ways language learners and teachers form their present self-concepts and motivations, make decisions about learning and teaching, and interact with others inside and outside the classroom. Such new knowledge would help teachers better manage classroom emotions and ultimately emotions of their own.

Post-Reading Tasks

(1) How have your past language learning experiences shaped your view of yourself as a language learner, teacher and researcher?
(2) How do you think some of your students' behaviours or past teachers' behaviours changed your emotions in the long run? How have their behaviours changed what you think of yourself now as a teacher?
(3) How might implicit biases of students, colleagues and staff be affecting the ways they interact with you, and vice versa?
(4) How have your past experiences shaped or prepared you for the investments you are making for your professional development, career path and post-retirement life?

Acknowledgments

All my thanks to Yoshifumi Fukada, Tetsuya Fukuda and Tim Murphey for collaborations making this chapter possible. Special thanks also to Kristin Davin, Richard Donato and Richard F. Young for discussions involving history-in-person research.

References

Davin, K.J., Chavoshan, I. and Donato, R. (2018) Images of past teachers: Present when you teach. *System* 72, 139–150.

Falout, J. (2016a) Past selves: Emerging motivational guides across temporal contexts. In J. King (ed.) *The Dynamic Interplay Between Context and the Language Learner* (pp. 47–65). Basingstoke: Palgrave Macmillan.

Falout, J. (2016b) The dynamics of past selves in language learning and well-being. In P.D. MacIntyre, T. Gregersen and S. Mercer (eds) *Positive Psychology in SLA* (pp. 112–129). Bristol: Multilingual Matters.

Falout, J., Murphey, T., Fukuda, T. and Trovela, M. (2013) Japanese EFL learners' remotivation strategies. In M. Cortazzi and L. Jin (eds) *Researching Cultures of Learning: International Perspectives on Language Learning and Education* (pp. 328–349). Basingstoke, UK: Palgrave Macmillan.

Fivush, R. (2011) The development of autobiographical memory. *Annual Review of Psychology* 62, 559–582.

Fivush, R., Bohanek, J.G. and Zaman, W. (2011) Personal and intergenerational narratives in relation to adolescents' well-being. *New Directions for Child and Adolescent Development* 131, 45–57.

Fukada, Y., Murphey, T., Falout, J. and Fukuda, T. (2017) Essential motivational group dynamics: A 3-year panel study. In R. Breeze and C.S. Guinda (eds) *Essential Competencies for English-Medium University Teaching* (pp. 249–266). Switzerland: Springer.

Fukuda, T., Fukada, Y., Falout, J. and Murphey, T. (forthcoming) How ideal classmates priming (ICP) increases EFL prosocial engagement. In P. Hiver, S. Mercer and A. Al-Hoorie (eds) *Engagement in the Second Language Classroom*. Bristol: Multilingual Matters.

Gilbert, D. (2006) *Stumbling on Happiness*. London: Harper Perennial.

Gilbert, D.T. and Wilson, T.D. (2007) Prospection: Experiencing the future. *Science* 317 (5843), 1351–1354.

Imai, Y. (2010) Emotions in SLA: New insight from collaborative learning for an EFL classroom. *The Modern Language Journal* 94, 278–292.

Kahneman, D. (2011) *Thinking Fast and Slow*. London: Penguin Books.

King, J. (2013) *Silence in the Second Language Classroom*. Basingstoke: Palgrave Macmillan.

Long, C. (2006) Quantitative methods for investigating attitudes: The matched-guise technique. *OnCUE* 14 (1), 43–47.

Long, C. (2008) Japanese attitudes towards Chinese and American foreigners: A matched-guise study. *Kokusai Koudou Gakkai [Journal of International Behavioral Studies]* 3, 60–68.

McFarland, C. and Buehler, R. (2012) Negative moods and the motivated remembering of past selves: The role of implicit theories of personal stability. *Journal of Personality and Social Psychology* 102 (2), 242–263.

Norton, B. (2000) *Identity and Language Learning: Gender, Ethnicity and Educational Change*. Harlow: Pearson Education.

Norton, B. and McKinney, C. (2011) An identity approach to second language acquisition. In D. Atkinson (ed.) *Alternative Approaches to Second Language Learning* (pp. 73–94). Abingdon: Routledge.

Nummenmaa, L., Glerean, E., Viinikainen, M., Jääskeläinen, I.P., Hari, R. and Sams, M. (2012) Emotions promote social interaction by synchronizing brain activity across individuals. *Proceedings of the National Academy of Science of the United States of America* 24 (109), 9599–9604.

Quoidbach, J., Gilbert, D.T. and Wilson, T.D. (2013) The end of history illusion. *Science* 339 (6115), 96–98.

Schumann, J.H. (1997) *The Neurobiology of Affect in Language*. Malden, MA: Blackwell.

Scollon, C.N., Howard, A.H., Caldwell, A.E. and Ito, S. (2009) The role of ideal affect in the experience and memory of emotions. *Journal of Happiness Studies* 10, 257–269.

Spreng, R.N. and Grady, C.L. (2010) Patterns of brain activity supporting autobiographical memory, prospection, and theory of mind, and their relationship to the default mode network. *Journal of Cognitive Neuroscience* 22 (6), 1112–1123.

Wilson, T.D. (2011) *Redirect: Changing the Stories We Live By*. New York: Back Bay Books.

Wirtz, D., Kruger, J., Scollon, C.N. and Diener, E. (2003) What to do on spring break? The role of predicted, on-line, and remembered experiences in future choice. *Psychological Science* 14 (5), 520–542.

8 'Critical Incidents' in Language Teachers' Narratives of Emotional Experience

Christina Gkonou and Elizabeth R. Miller

Introduction

Emotion is enmeshed in all brain networks and thus interacts with cognition, reasoning, behaviour and decision-making processes (Damasio, 2006). This is mostly evinced in the fact that individuals can mentally evaluate a situation that causes an emotion and then also mentally decide how to respond to an emotion by choosing appropriate emotion-regulation strategies. Emotion is ubiquitous in all human activities, and teaching and learning are no exception. Factors both inside and outside of classrooms can influence teachers' emotions and, taken together, these factors can generate specific sets of emotions; even one day in teaching is an emotional and mental rollercoaster, with teachers oscillating between diverse emotions which impact on their personal and professional well-being in various ways.

In this chapter we draw on research interviews with teachers of English in six tertiary-level programmes in the US and the UK, and analyse their storytelling of critical incidents throughout their careers and how they interpreted the effects of 'what happened' in retrospective sense-making. We borrow Barkhuizen's (2016, 2017) definition of short stories as excerpts of larger sets of narrative data, which are reflective or evaluative of past experiences. We focus specifically on those stories which are classified as critical incidents, i.e. events that mark a significant turning point in one's professional life, are often highly emotionally charged, and are cast as having a continuing significance (Tripp, 2012). We begin our chapter by reviewing the theoretical background on language teacher emotions, stories of teacher self-reflection and critical incidents. We then outline our study on English language teachers' emotions as these unfold in their recounting of critical incidents from the past. In describing a complex array of emotional turmoil and ethical dilemmas from their past, the teachers nevertheless reflected on how much they had learned from them and how these critical incidents led to emotional victories, novel ways of understanding themselves and changes in their practice. We conclude the chapter by discussing implications for language teacher emotion research and applied linguistics research that draws on critical incidents.

Theoretical Background

Language teacher emotions

Underhill (2013: 204) argues that teacher expertise comprises 'knowledge of the topic, skill with classroom methods and competence with inter- and intrapersonal relationships and the psychological learning atmosphere of the group'. Thus, on top of having the necessary technical methods and tools, teachers should also attend to the emotional climate of their classes, an effort which requires that they become emotionally engaged in whatever takes place in class and – potentially to a lesser extent – outside of class. In particular, teaching requires that teachers empathize with their learners, consider how best to interact with them and with parents and colleagues, and also reflect on how they themselves feel about their lessons and themselves as professionals. All these processes engage teachers on an emotional level, though they might not always be conscious processes. Although teachers might often be honest about their own emotion experiences, the school cultures in which they work construct 'emotional rules' (Zembylas, 2002: 196) that often determine what they 'should' feel, thus requiring them to control or hide their 'bad' emotions and instead express only the 'desired' ones. Emotional engagement thus requires 'emotional work' (2002: 196) or emotion labour (Benesch, 2012, 2017), where teachers need to edit out their truly felt emotions in order to project the organizationally desired ones.

In its original conceptualization, emotion labour was depicted as negative and as leading to self-estrangement and depersonalization (see Hochschild, 1979, 1983; also Zembylas, 2002, 2003). However, recent theorizing, mainly in light of poststructuralist approaches to emotion research, suggests that emotion labour might not always be imposed but rather, at times, willingly undertaken for the benefit of students and for teachers' own personal and professional well-being (Chang & Davis, 2009; Hargreaves, 2000; Isenbarger & Zembylas, 2006; King, 2016; King & Ng, 2018; see also Burkitt, 2014, for an analysis of emotion labour in nursing). Previous research has shown that language teachers who engage in emotional work position themselves as caring and view their efforts as ethically necessary (see Gkonou & Miller, 2019; Miller

& Gkonou, 2018). Reflecting on good language teaching by drawing on interview data with two experienced language teachers in Austria, Mercer and Gkonou (forthcoming) also discuss the 'dual energy-giving and energy-draining character of teacher–learner relationships'. This inherent paradox is indicative of the teachers' realization of the importance of caring about their students and investing in the process of forming quality relationships with them, whilst at the same time finding this process demanding and a source of emotional stress. In his study with nurses working in the UK National Health Service – nursing being an example of an other-oriented profession much in the same way that teaching is – Burkitt (2014: 129) also departs from Hochschild's view by arguing that her theory of emotion labour implies 'a fundamental split created between what one is or feels inside and the demands of society'. Instead he advocates for a dialogical and relational approach to emotion, which depends on how individuals relate to the situation that has generated the emotion and to the people in it. He goes on to explain that in undertaking emotion work, nurses might seek to adhere to the feeling rules of their work environments, but at the same time they are bound by and personally invest in and identify with the values of their professions. In thinking of professional values among language teachers, we can draw from Burkitt's perspective on caring as 'a core value' for nurses (2014: 139). He notes that caring among nurses 'is not enacted by a "merchant of morality" for dramaturgical effect, but by a practitioner committed to the act of caring as central to nursing practice and the relationship with patients' (2014: 139). We can thus understand how a professional value, such as investment in caring among nurses and teachers, positions emotion as central to professional practice.

Just as learner emotions serve as a powerful vehicle for promoting or inhibiting learning, so too teacher emotions shape teaching and the emotional atmosphere of the class. At the same time, teacher emotions contribute to learner emotions and vice versa, through processes of emotional contagion (Frenzel & Stephens, 2013). Given the intangible and ever-changing 'rollercoaster' nature of emotions during teaching (Gregersen *et al.*, 2014), it is often hard for teachers to articulate them or even consciously understand them. A useful way to delve into the world of emotions during teaching is through teacher self-reflection, which might be handled systematically as part of teacher education programmes or emerge in conversations between teachers and researchers.

Stories of teacher self-reflection and critical incidents

Barkhuizen (2016: 659) argues that 'storytelling contributes to our making sense of the world and our place within it' and discusses the usefulness of 'short stories' produced by research participants as tools for understanding and appreciating their experiences. He defines short stories as excerpts of data from larger narrative sets such as interviews or journals, which narrate past experiences, are reflective, have a temporal dimension and describe action in the same way that stories in general do. In producing, analysing and reflecting on short stories, emphasis is placed on the dimensions of content and context. In other words, the language that is used is often carefully chosen (content) but at the same time these stories happen within specific relational, sociopolitical and historical situations (context). As Riessman (2008: 105) succinctly puts it, 'stories don't fall from the sky'.

With relation to teachers in particular, Johnson and Golombek (2002: 6) argue that teacher narratives tell 'stories of teachers' professional development within their own professional worlds'. Teacher stories are an important component of self-reflection, a process which is both professionally and emotionally driven. In this case, stories can offer teachers 'a safe and non-judgmental support system for sharing the emotional stresses and isolating experiences of the classroom' (Jalongo & Isenberg, 1995: 162). This process of teacher dialogizing through stories 'must also be a learning conversation' which is 'constant, continual, and critical' and 'involves conversations with Self, with texts, and with others on matters related to learning, teaching, and theorising' (Kumaravadivelu, 2012: 94; see also Mann & Walsh, 2017). Thus, short stories often carry professional and emotional significance for teachers, and constitute a learning experience for them both in terms of professional development and emotional self-awareness.

One type of such self-reflective stories that combines professional and emotional learning for teachers are stories that involve critical incidents. Originally proposed by Flanagan (1954) as part of the Aviation Psychology Program of the US Army Air Forces, with a view to identifying effective and ineffective work behaviours, reflection on critical incidents is now used in teaching as a means of developing professional judgment. Tripp (2012: 8) explains that 'incidents *happen* but critical incidents *are produced* by the way we look at a situation' (italics added) and by the value judgments we make once we come across a situation that deviates significantly from what is normally expected (Edvardsson, 1992). From this perspective, critical incidents refer to unanticipated events that are 'vividly remembered' (Brookfield, 1990: 84) in storytelling occasions. Webster and Mertova (2007: 73–74) explain the brain processes that occur during the formation of critical incidents, and we cite them here at length:

> a critical event as told in a story reveals a change of understanding or worldview by the storyteller. [...] It is almost always a change experience, and it can only ever be identified afterwards. [...] The longer the time that passes between the event and recall of the event, the more profound the effect of the event has been and the more warranted is the

> label *critical* event. Such events can then be characterised by time, challenge and change. Over time, the mind refines and discards unnecessary detail and retains those elements that have been of changing and lasting value. [...] The event is likely to have changed their [the participants'] experience and understanding, informing future behaviour and understanding [italics in the original].

Self-reflection through narrating critical incidents also enables teachers to analyse their own personal theories and sets of beliefs that inform their professional judgment and thereby their agency. Tripp (2012: 105) explains how certain critical incidents can elucidate historical dimensions of teaching and can be treated as formative in the sense that they leave teachers 'a quite different teacher in some respects afterwards'. Webster and Mertova (2007: 77) add that critical incidents can restore ideals and commitment in teachers and often serve 'as a coping strategy' against 'assaults that might customarily be made on them'. These 'assaults' could be interpreted as attacks to teachers' professional integrity and idiosyncrasies but also as threats to their emotional well-being in their professional roles.

Within education, critical incidents have been used to provide solutions to teacher ethical dilemmas (Shapira-Lishchinsky, 2011), for programme development (Kosnik, 2001), pre-service teacher training (Farrell, 2008) and transition from teacher education programmes to future workplaces (Kilgour *et al.*, 2015). The focus has overall been on what teachers can learn and how they can benefit from reflective practice through critical incident analysis. For example, teachers were found to be better able to cultivate the habit of engaging in reflective practice (Farrell, 2007), action research (McCabe, 2002) and developing a problem-solving mindset (Farrell & Baecher, 2017). However, as yet, it is not clear how critical incident analysis could shed light onto the vast array of teacher emotions and what implications such analysis might have on our understanding of emotional experiences throughout teachers' careers and trajectories. Kasper and Prior (2015: 228) explain that although the focus of storytelling is understandably more often than not on the storytellers, the role of story recipients should also be considered; they further argue that 'if we are to treat stories as interactional accomplishments, we must investigate how both production and understanding are achieved in and through the telling'.

This chapter will thus address the content and context of stories which are remembered as critical incidents by teachers, though the stories we examine were not deliberately elicited for reflection as in the above studies, but rather they emerged spontaneously as teachers discussed the role of emotions in their past and current teaching practice in the research interviews. The chapter further considers the implications of such spontaneously produced incidents for teaching practice and for research that employs critical incident analysis. The following research questions guided the study:

(1) What emotion-related language do teachers use in their recollection of past critical incident stories?
(2) What meanings and/or outcomes do teachers assign to these critical incidents?
(3) How do their past critical incidents impact on their emotions?

Methodology

Context and participants

The 13 participants in this study are English language teachers who are working in tertiary education programmes in the US and the UK. They are part of a larger study that focused on language teacher emotions and agency (see Miller & Gkonou, 2018). In launching this larger study, we contacted the programme directors of six English language programmes affiliated with universities, three in the US and three in the UK, explaining the nature of our study and asking for permission to contact the teachers in their programmes. Once permission was obtained, we then sent emails to individual teachers. Thirty teachers from these six programmes completed an anonymous online questionnaire. Of these, 25 teachers indicated willingness to participate in follow-up, semi-structured interviews with the researcher who was based in the same country as them. The critical incident stories that we analyse for this study were narrated in the interviews. Table 8.1 includes a summary of the demographic information for the teachers included in this study.

Data collection

The semi-structured interviews with the language teacher participants were conducted either face to face on university premises or via Skype. The 11 open-ended questions in the interview protocol focused on the

Table 8.1 Demographic information of teacher participants

Location	US: 8 UK: 5
Gender	Female: 12 Male: 1 Prefer not to disclose: 0
Full-time/Part-time	Full-time: 10 Part-time: 3
Qualifications	MA: 10 Language teaching certification: 3
Years of teaching experience	Mean: 21.8 (min = 9, max = 45)

following topics: teachers' primary responsibilities in their current positions, aspects of their teaching that they enjoyed the most and those they enjoyed the least, the types of emotions that they experienced most frequently while teaching, the extent to which they found it easy or difficult to manage their emotions and the steps that they took to do so, stress related to their teaching responsibilities, perceived autonomy in their teaching roles and advice on emotion management for colleagues. Though organized around the prepared questions, the interviews adopted a conversational approach, thereby allowing for unexpected topics to be introduced and explored, and for both the interviewer and interviewee to shape the trajectory of the interaction. As a result, some interviews lasted up to an hour, with an average length of 33 minutes. There were no questions that directly elicited teachers' critical incident stories; these emerged unprompted as teachers reflected on their past teaching experiences. We began to notice the recurrence of these stories as we conducted our analysis of the larger corpus of interviews and decided to undertake closer analysis of them for this study.

Data analysis

The interviews were transcribed verbatim and then inserted into the qualitative data management software Atlas.ti for analysis. Each researcher coded the data separately and then consulted together in order to refine and group the codes into meaningful themes (see Miller & Gkonou, 2018, for further discussion). It was at this stage that we began to identify recurrent story types that we later identified as critical incident stories. Approximately half of the interviewees (13 of 25) narrated such stories and produced a total of 28 unsolicited critical incident accounts.

In refining our criteria for selection and analysis of these stories, we drew on Webster and Mertova's (2007) approach to identifying critical incidents as well as Barkhuizen's (2016, 2017) approach to identifying small stories. For this study, a critical incident story needed to meet the following four criteria: (a) it referred to a past event that related to interviewees' teaching experience; (b) it incorporated emotionally charged language; (c) the past event was treated by the teacher as a significant turning point for his or her teaching practice or teacher identity; and (d) the past event was evaluated, explained and/or assigned meaning in terms of its impact on the teacher's ensuing experiences.

We include here one of the critical incident stories to illustrate how the above criteria guided us in making our selections.

(1) Because one of the pieces of advice that was helpful for me is, well it wasn't a piece of advice
(2) but somebody asked me 'Why are you taking this so personally? It's not a personal attack on

(3) you'. And I responded with 'Yes it is. I'm the one spending all this time reading this, I'm the
(4) one that has to do all this and have these conversations over and over again. Like, I spend so
(5) much time planning, you know' and you feel like that – but then over time, I think that is a
(6) question that has been, that I've come back to many times, you know? 'Why are you taking
(7) this personally? Why are you taking this personally?' Um, so I think that that's something
(8) that I tend to bring up with new teachers when I see that they're really getting that frustration
(9) and anger sometimes is ... Do we need to take this personally? What would it look like if you
(10) didn't take it personally? (T1)

In lines 1–3, the narrator's verb tense indicates that the event of being asked 'Why are you taking this so personally?' occurred in the past (Criterion A). In lines 8–9, the narrator uses emotionally charged language in connecting her past experience to new teachers' 'frustration and anger' and also in revoicing the original questioner's language as relating to her perception of students' behaviour as 'personal attacks' (line 2) (Criterion B). In lines 5–6, the teacher treats the event of being asked the question as a significant turning point in noting that 'over time' she has 'come back to [that question] many times' (Criterion C). Finally, she treats this past event as important and meaningful for her ongoing efforts to change how she responds to emotional provocations from students, in part through recalling the words of the original questioner and reissuing them as challenges to the new teachers she interacts with (lines 6–7, 9–10) (Criterion D).

Findings

Emotionally charged discourse in teachers' critical incidents

One of the structural features that we identified in our teacher participants' stories, which urged us to classify them as critical incidents, was the use of highly emotionally charged language. Table 8.2 lists emotionally charged words or phrases which appeared in our teacher interview corpus more than once, and their frequency of occurrence. The remaining cases of emotionally charged words with only a single occurrence in the corpus can be found in the Appendix.

As shown in Table 8.2, there is a mixture of emotion-related words with both positive and negative valence. The same can be noted when looking at the general picture and full list of emotionally charged language included in the Appendix. The language selected by teachers

Table 8.2 Most frequently used emotionally charged words

anger/angry (4)
betrayed/betrayal (3)
blossom (2)
care (2)
cruel (2)
difficult time/situation (7)
emotional (2)
enjoyable/enjoy (2)
exciting (2)
failure (2)
frustration/frustrated/frustrating (5)
happy (2)
hurt (2)
interested/interesting (2)
laughing/laughter (2)
mad (5)
nose to nose with me/nose-to-nose conflict (2)
problem (3)
rapport (3)
respect (2)
scary/scared (2)
struggle (6)
terrible time (3)
value/valuable (2)
vulnerability/vulnerable (2)
yell (4)

to recount these critical incidents indicates that they are mainly cast as emotionally difficult and represent negative moments in their teaching careers. However, in further analysing the way these critical incident stories are narrated in their entirety and not just by focusing on individual words or phrases, it becomes apparent that teachers perceive them as leading to positive outcomes.

From emotionally charged situations to emotional victories

In recollecting past teaching experiences through storying critical incidents, all teachers explained that these highly emotionally charged situations, which they most frequently characterized as problematic or negative experiences, led to emotional rewards. Though the teachers were not consciously recalling 'critical incidents', they treated certain experiences from their past as particularly meaningful in their retrospective storytelling (see also Falout, this volume) in the research interviews. In other words, in narrating their stories, teachers constructed their critical incidents as turning points and treated them as formative, thus assigning positive meaning to them despite their negative valence as shown in the previous section.

Dealing with challenging students

Most of the events recounted by teachers (20 out of 28) which were treated as formative and can thus be classified as critical incidents concerned students from the past whose behaviour in class was described as 'disruptive' or 'difficult' or 'awkward'. In reflecting on how they dealt with those students and situations, teachers indicated very explicitly how they feel positively rewarded at an emotional and professional level now. For example, T3 recounted how she came to realize the need to avoid getting caught up in students' emotional turmoil, what she described as getting 'caught in the same current', so that she can, in fact, be able to help them. She indicates that in keeping herself a bit removed from her students' highly emotional situations, i.e. 'on firm ground', she is better able to help them 'deal with whatever is happening'.

> So what I have to remember is that if I'm caught in the same current, then we're both swept down the river. So if I can stay out of the current, I'm much more likely to throw them a lifeline or help guide them to shore or help them out, than if I get caught up. So, I know that about myself, so when I see something starts happening, I make sure that I'm on firm ground. [...] so there are times when I've had to just take a deep breath and deal with whatever is that is happening. (T3)

Similarly, T9 recounted an experience with a male student who found it difficult to view her, a female teacher, as an authority figure. In describing her efforts to help him become accustomed to and more accepting of egalitarian gender roles in the classroom, she noted that her efforts finally 'worked' and that she 'broke the ice'. She treated this experience in dealing with a former challenging student as helping her to recognize the need to work pre-emptively to avoid the risk of a single student creating a 'negative classroom atmosphere', and, more generally, the need to find 'any positive out of the negative situation' and to work to turn difficult situations with students into 'a valuable tool'.

> And it worked and it broke the ice because I knew that could be a problem and no problem after that. So it's about using, again, finding any positive out of the negative situation and turning it into a valuable tool as far as you can. It doesn't always work, you know, but again that's about managing the students' emotions rather than, because the dynamic of the class is so important, because if one student creates an atmosphere that's negative, all, all the other students get dragged down. It's much easier to get dragged down than to be pulled up. But I just wanna go and pull everybody up, because that's my job. (T9)

Understanding students' behaviours and emotions

Other critical incident stories which were treated as formative showed that language teachers are often so immersed in their teaching practice, prioritizing teaching methods and materials and student assessment, that they do not always take the time to 'read between the lines' in interpreting students' behaviours. Although methods, materials and assessments are fundamental components of good teaching practice, teachers' critical incident stories demonstrate that investing time and effort in understanding students' emotions and finding out about the reasons behind students' disruptive or problematic behaviour was also a key aspect of good practice. T1 recounted a critical incident which helped her come to this realization. She commented that she needs to remind herself that she often has 'no idea' about what is going on with students and that she has learned to 'keep that in the back of [her] mind all the time' when she is dealing with difficult student behaviours.

> I had a student last – I think this happened about a year ago and all semester it was a battle because he wouldn't pay attention to directions. He would disrupt the class a hundred times. He was really immature but very outspoken and it was this struggle with him constantly throughout the whole semester. This was happening to where I would say, yeah, in that semester, managing my emotions looked completely different than normal because it was him [...] And then I found out at the very end of the semester, one of the last, final writing assignments that we did, a timed writing, was about, to write about, they had three or four different topics and one of the topics was to write about a difficult experience for you and he wrote about how he didn't want to come to the US. [...] And he came here and then had to live with an American family and then we had him in class and the whole semester this was going on and so I'm thinking 'Oh, I'm in tune and I know he's just a stubborn personality' and I had no idea [...] so I'm keeping that in the back of my mind all the time. It's that we never really know what the emotions of the students are. (T1)

Similarly, T5 noted that 'probably the times I've been unhappiest as a teacher over the last ten years are when I've badly misread students' emotions'. She then recounted a story about one of her students who was facing a number of family-related issues that she was unaware of and whom she was just seeing as 'a student who is insecure about her grading'. She concluded,

> And then I looked back and it's like, yeah, come on, who comes to your office that often, why didn't you ask? I mean I never asked about her personal life. I just talked to her about writing, and I should have because it was, she was clearly saying 'I need to talk to somebody', and I just wasn't hearing it so those were hard times for me. (T5)

Reinforcing the importance of teachers seeking to understand their students' behaviours and emotions, T6 recounted a critical incident story in which she did recognize that a student was 'really depressed' so she walked with the student to the counselling centre on campus. She then related how this student looked her up some years later to thank her for 'holding out a hand' to her.

> Maybe five years later, and this was just a couple of years ago, she came back and looked me up and she said 'Oh, you were the person who held out a hand to me', and that kind of thing. [...] when students get emotional about something, and it's not necessarily class related but you know, they're dealing with so many things, um, so I mean, those are easy things to read I guess, 'cause that's when working with them one on one, and you're talking about things and you can see that they're troubled by something, um. In the classroom, obviously I can't always know everything. (T6)

T6 treated this success story as reinforcing her awareness of the importance of trying to 'treat the students with respect and show that I really do appreciate and value what they do and the hard task they've taken on'.

Not taking it personally

The recounted stories also provided opportunities for teachers to remind themselves of how particular past events led them to realize the importance of not taking things personally any more. T1, for example, noted that she used to take students' seemingly disrespectful behaviours personally when she first started working with students from diverse cultural backgrounds, but that upon reflection and through constant discussions with significant others outside of her professional network, she learned that 'it's not like a personal attack and so just having, taking a step back, and then having the conversations when they're necessary' has made her emotionally stronger. Relatedly, T8 elaborated on how she felt the first time that she had a student plagiarize and how learning not to take such experiences personally has boosted her emotional self-regulation skills.

> Here's an example from when I first started teaching, the first time that I had a student plagiarize ... I felt that it was about me, like I took it very personally, and I was like 'Why would they do this to me?'. It was like a betrayal of me, and I'm a failure and now I totally don't make it a personal thing, so something like that I'd say, this isn't about you. (T8)

T5 discussed a similar feeling of betrayal when one of her students physically hurt her hand in the process of performing an in-class roleplay activity. Like T8, she commented that this experience and others over time have led her to understand that students are going to 'test you', jokingly noting that 'they're all little devils' and that she has come to not 'take it so personally any more'.

> I remember feeling really betrayed one time because I was teaching students to shake hands properly because they were going to be meeting a bunch of tourists and I think it's important to look someone in the face when you shake their hand. You don't look down at your hand and you don't squeeze too hard because these are elderly people and you don't, you know, give them a dead fish, and so trying to teach, you know. There was an Oral Skills Class and this one guy just crushed my hand and it really hurt and I was like (whimpering sound), but mostly I felt really betrayed, and like, why would you do that? And I remember it being a really difficult time making it to the end of the class, but now I know they're all little devils and they'll test you and they'll do things that maybe they would regret, so I guess I don't take it so personally any more. (T5)

Experiencing emotional rewards

Another group of stories which we classified as critical incidents due to the formative character of the recounted events concerned the emotional rewards that teachers gained after dealing with difficult experiences. For example, T12 commented on how she has 'learnt so much' from her students. In describing her efforts to understand why a particular group of students was struggling so much with reading comprehension, she indicated that she had to learn a little bit about their language and the script that they used (Arabic). She then commented that it 'was so exciting' for her to arrive at some understanding of why her students were struggling and to then 'help them to understand why they are struggling and overcome the difficulties' of learning to read English texts.

> But by exploring that and helping them, I learnt much more about their language. I didn't learn their language, but I learnt about how it works and how it's very different from English and why students use their first language reading strategies to read English and it doesn't work effectively. So **that was so exciting for me**[1] to be able to understand why these students are struggling. And then help them to understand why they are struggling and overcome the difficulties of a script. (T12)

T12 then narrated a related case of how learning how to help students get beyond their struggles with learning English, in this case because of their perceptions of themselves as poor language learners, 'makes [her] feel really happy'. She connected what she has learned about how to lead students to this point of recognizing that they can actually learn English to her own experiences as a student of Maths. She recounted how she used to view herself as a 'terrible' student and as a 'failure' in Maths but two of her teachers helped her to understand that 'it's not just about getting the right answers. It's about understanding the whole process to get to the answer.'

> I was terrible at Maths, and yet have two ... I had two very good Maths teachers and they changed my attitude to the subject completely. I thought 'I can't do it. I am a failure. Just go on and get on with it. Jump the hurdles and probably fail them'. But one teacher in particular, she made me realize that it's not just about getting the right answer. It's about understanding the whole process to get to the answer. And that it can be enjoyable. It can be exciting to a certain degree ... I think it's also true with language. You know people said 'I am not good at language', 'I can't learn language'. But when you take them away, you are able to distract them from that view and give them a purpose in doing something and they get to the stage that 'oh, I am actually doing it', 'I am actually using it', 'maybe not so bad after all', 'maybe I can do this'. **That makes me feel really happy** that I have ... I have just enabled people to move on and achieve. (T12)

Furthermore, several teachers treated some of their past stories or experiences as formative in noting how their encounters with certain students helped them become better teachers and people afterwards – and with positive human qualities. T4's story is illustrative of this point.

> I can think of two different students that I had when I first came back from being overseas and it was my first time ever teaching Saudi students and I had some preconceived notions about how Saudis would be. [...] but my first semester teaching I encountered these two women from Saudi Arabia who were absolutely lovely, extremely intelligent. One of them was a mother of four and she was there in the programme just to learn, and she's somebody I look up to with great respect and there was another girl who was also from Saudi Arabia. [...] she was full of ideas and lots of different interesting experiences. She had travelled quite a bit and she was able to articulate her opinions quite well. She had even been a motivational speaker, so I think my encounters with those two ladies **made me feel like I'm such a richer person for knowing them.** (T4)

A final note comes from three teachers who emphatically stated that if teachers' emotional experiences throughout their careers and the many years of emotional self-regulation have not yet led to emotional rewards, teachers should then seriously consider changing jobs. T7, in fact, advised teachers to 'keep your eye on what your goals are and if you have lots of negative emotions find a new job'.

Discussion

Our analysis of emotion-related experiences in language teaching shows how these emotional rollercoaster moments can be triggers for self-reflection and potential change in practice. In recounting their critical incident stories, all teachers used negative emotion-related words and phrases; and quite understandably, as they described events throughout their careers which were uncomfortable and difficult to deal with (see also Chang & Davis, 2009). These included, among others, ethical dilemmas, difficult students or students whose behaviour it took them a long time to 'decode', issues with gender and power dynamics among themselves and their students, academic offences and difficulties with creating positive and healthy group dynamics in their classes. However, in reflecting upon what they learned from these challenging situations, they made use of positive terms such as feeling like a 'richer person', feeling 'happy' and finding an experience to be 'exciting'. Thus, the emotionally charged and draining situations they had gone through were treated as formative in the sense that teachers treated them as meaningful to their later teaching practices and developing teacher identities (Miller & Gkonou, 2018; Tripp, 2012). Ultimately, these critical incidents are cast as leading them to find something positive out of a negative and emotionally demanding teaching experience. This reflective activity, even though it was unsolicited, has strong implications for understanding the development of teacher resilience, which for the participating teachers in this study came through dealing with difficult experiences and many years of emotion management (see also Kostoulas & Lämmerer, this volume).

Our findings also show that in producing critical incident narratives, teachers referred to behaviours of specific students, which they found difficult to understand and manage. The narratives indicate that those students' behaviours were likely not intended in the way teachers initially perceived them. That is, teachers labelled their students as being 'a stubborn personality' (T1) or 'insecure about her grading' (T5); however, as teachers came to understand these students' situations more clearly, they felt remorseful when they realized that they had misjudged their students' behaviours and had assigned labels to them that were wrong, simply because they had not invested in finding out more about their students and their backgrounds. In the end, they empathized with their students and highlighted the importance of analysing students' behavioural reactions and the need to make an effort to understand their emotions (Gkonou & Mercer, 2017; Frenzel & Stephens, 2013).

A final note concerns our participants' switch from emotional turmoil to emotional rewards. This aspect struck us in the data and we were keen to understand where the participating teachers' positivity came from. Upon closer analysis and as evinced by the data extracts included in the previous section, we see that for these teachers gaining emotional rewards took time and emerged from moments of hardship, required hard work with their own teaching selves, personalities and idiosyncrasies, as well as carefully thought-out changes in their lesson preparation and actual classroom practice. T12 even invested in learning more about the writing conventions in her students' L1 in the hope that she would be better able to understand and analyse her students' difficulties with writing in the L2. Therefore, the recounted and lived critical incidents are cast as enabling the participating teachers to become more effective and successful practitioners (Mann & Walsh, 2017; Webster & Mertova, 2007) and to develop more caring personalities for their students (Gkonou & Miller, 2019; Miller & Gkonou, 2018). In this way, they treated these experiences as formative at a professional as well as ethical and personal level.

Conclusion

Our aim in this study was to show how language teachers can move from emotional turmoil and important ethical dilemmas to emotional rewards. The critical incident stories analysed in the chapter indicate that although these experiences were initially cast as negative, upon reflection teachers framed the experiences as helping them learn how to deal with difficult students, to better understand students' behaviours and emotions, and to not view them as personal attacks. Teachers also treated these critical incidents as leading to positive and meaningful moments related to teaching. Teacher emotions could therefore be seen as being in a state of flux and changing within the same lesson, across lessons or even throughout one's career. Although our study was not longitudinal, useful insights can be drawn about the 'rollercoaster' nature of teachers' emotional experiences, which became particularly salient through their critical incident narratives. We would encourage applied linguistics researchers to engage with this form of narrative and use it with teachers who are at different stages of their teaching journeys. Such narratives also come with a number of participant benefits in that they enable teachers to reach a better understanding of themselves, their practices and their students.

Post-Reading Tasks

(1) What emotion-laden experiences from your own practice could be classed as critical incidents?
(2) In what way/s could teachers make the most of the emotional challenges experienced during their practice?
(3) What are some reasons why it is important for teachers to understand the emotions of their students? How could such understandings be reached?
(4) How could self-reflection through critical incident narratives be incorporated into teacher education?

Note

(1) Emphasis added by authors to indicate positively valenced expressions.

References

Barkhuizen, G. (2016) A short story approach to analyzing teacher (imagined) identities over time. *TESOL Quarterly* 50 (3), 655–683.

Barkhuizen, G. (2017) Investigating language tutor social inclusion identities. *The Modern Language Journal* 101, 61–75.

Benesch, S. (2012) *Considering Emotions in Critical English Language Teaching: Theories and Praxis*. New York: Routledge.

Benesch, S. (2017) *Emotions and English Language Teaching: Exploring Teachers' Emotion Labor.* New York: Routledge.

Brookfield, S. (1990) Using critical incidents to explore learners' assumptions. In J. Mezirow (ed.) *Fostering Critical Reflection in Adulthood: A Guide to Transformative and Emancipatory Learning* (pp. 177–193). San Francisco, CA: Jossey-Bass Inc.

Burkitt, I. (2014) *Emotions and Social Relations.* Thousand Oaks, CA: SAGE.

Chang, M.-L. and Davis, H.A. (2009) Understanding the role of teacher appraisals in shaping the dynamics of their relationships with students: Deconstructing teachers' judgements of disruptive behavior/students. In P.A. Schutz and M. Zembylas (eds) *Advances in Teacher Emotion Research: The Impact on Teachers' Lives* (pp. 95–127). Dordrecht: Springer.

Damasio, A. (2006) *Descartes' Error: Emotion, Reason and the Human Brain.* London: Vintage/Random House.

Edvardsson, B. (1992) Service breakdowns: A study of critical incidents in an airline. *International Journal of Service Industry Management* 3 (4), 17–29.

Farrell, T.S.C. (2007) *Reflective Practice for Language Teachers: From Research to Practice.* London: Continuum Press.

Farrell, T.S.C. (2008) Critical incidents in ELT initial teacher training. *ELT Journal* 62 (1), 3–10.

Farrell, T.S.C. and Baecher, L. (2017) *Reflecting on Critical Incidents in Language Education: 40 Dilemmas for Novice TESOL Professionals.* London: Bloomsbury.

Flanagan, J.C. (1954) The critical incident technique. *Psychological Bulletin* 51 (4), 327–358.

Frenzel, A.C. and Stephens, E.J. (2013) Emotions. In N. Hall and T. Götz (eds) *Emotion, Motivation, and Self-Regulation: A Handbook for Teachers* (pp. 1–56). Bingley: Emerald.

Gkonou, C. and Mercer, S. (2017) *Understanding Emotional and Social Intelligence Among English Language Teachers.* London: British Council.

Gkonou, C. and Miller, E.R. (2019) Caring and emotional labour: Language teachers' engagement with anxious learners in private language school classrooms. *Language Teaching Research* 23 (3), 372–387.

Gregersen, T., MacIntyre, P.D. and Meza, M. (2014) The motion of emotion: Idiodynamic case studies of learners' foreign language anxiety. *The Modern Language Journal* 98 (2), 574–588.

Hargreaves, A. (2000) Mixed emotions: Teachers' perceptions of their interactions with students. *Teaching and Teacher Education* 16 (8), 811–826.

Hochschild, A. (1979) Emotion work, feeling rules, and social structures. *American Journal of Sociology* 85 (3), 551–575.

Hochschild, A. (1983) *The Managed Heart: Commercialization of Human Feelings.* Berkeley, CA: University of California Press.

Isenbarger, L. and Zembylas, M. (2006) The emotional labour of caring in teaching. *Teaching and Teacher Education* 22, 120–134.

Jalongo, M.R. and Isenberg, J.P. (1995) *Teachers' Stories: From Personal Narrative to Professional Insight*. San Francisco, CA: Jossey Bass Publishers.
Johnson, K.E. and Golombek, P. (2002) *Teachers' Narrative Inquiry as Professional Development*. New York: Cambridge University Press.
Kasper, G. and Prior, M.T. (2015) Analyzing storytelling in TESOL interview research. *TESOL Quarterly* 49 (2), 226–255.
Kilgour, P.W., Northcote, M.T. and Herman, W. (2015) Pre-service teachers' reflections on critical incidents in their professional teaching experiences. *Research and Development in Higher Education: Learning for Life and Work in a Complex World* 38, 383–393.
King, J. (2016) 'It's time, put on the smile, it's time!': The emotional labour of second language teaching within a Japanese university. In C. Gkonou, D. Tatzl and S. Mercer (eds) *New Directions in Language Learning Psychology* (pp. 97–112). Cham: Springer.
King, J. and Ng, K.-Y.S. (2018) Teacher emotions and the emotional labour of second language teaching. In S. Mercer and A. Kostoulas (eds) *Language Teacher Psychology* (pp. 141–157). Bristol: Multilingual Matters.
Kosnik, C. (2001) The effects of an inquiry-oriented teacher education program on a faculty member: Some critical incidents and my journey. *Reflective Practice* 2 (1), 65–80.
Kumaravadivelu, B. (2012) *Language Teacher Education for a Global Society: A Modular Model for Knowing, Analyzing, Recognizing, Doing, and Seeing*. New York: Routledge.
Mann, S. and Walsh, S. (2017) *Reflective Practice in English Language Teaching: Research-Based Principles and Practices*. New York: Routledge.
McCabe, A. (2002) A wellspring for development. In J. Edge (ed.) *Continuing Professional Development* (pp. 82–96). Whitstable: IATEFL Publications.
Mercer, S. and Gkonou, C. (forthcoming) Relationships and the good language teacher. In C. Griffiths (ed.) *Lessons from Good Language Teachers*. Cambridge: Cambridge University Press.
Miller, E.R. and Gkonou, C. (2018) Language teacher agency, emotion labor and emotional rewards in tertiary-level English language programs. *System* 79, 49–59.
Riessman, C.K. (2008) *Narrative Methods for the Human Sciences*. Los Angeles, CA: SAGE.
Shapira-Lishchinsky, O. (2011) Teachers' critical incidents: Ethical dilemmas in teaching practice. *Teaching and Teacher Education* 27, 648–656.
Tripp, D. (2012) *Critical Incidents in Teaching: Developing Professional Judgment*. Abingdon: Routledge.
Underhill, A. (2013) The inner workbench: Learning itself as a meaningful activity. In J. Arnold and T. Murphey (eds) *Meaningful Action: Earl Stevick's Influence on Language Teaching* (pp. 202–218). Cambridge: Cambridge University Press.
Webster, L. and Mertova, P. (2007) *Using Narrative Inquiry as a Research Method: An Introduction to Using Critical Event Narrative Analysis in Research on Learning and Teaching*. Abingdon: Routledge.
Zembylas, M. (2002) 'Structures of feeling' in curriculum and teaching: Theorizing the emotional rules. *Educational Theory* 52 (2), 187–208.
Zembylas, M. (2003) Emotions and teacher identity: A poststructural perspective. *Teachers and Teaching: Theory and Practice* 9 (3), 213–238.

Appendix

Table 8.3 Emotionally charged discourse with single occurrence

ah dear!
anti-depressant
awkward
battle
beat them down
beaten
blame
box of Kleenex
broke the ice
broken
burst into tears
concerned
confidence
cope
crushed
crying
depressed
disillusion
disjointed
driving me nuts
elevated
extreme case
feel good
feel like a richer person
fire
flip out
friendly
friendships
fun
get on well
hostile
isolated
loud
love
lovely
manage emotions
my heart would sink
oh my god
personal attack
pressured
sobbing
stressful
stunned
supportive
surprised
tension
the end of her very frayed rope
trick them up
troubled
upset
we had nothing left
wrong

9 'Please Teach Me How to Teach': The Emotional Impact of Educational Change

Simon Humphries

Introduction

Despite the messiness that is often involved in fieldwork (Naveed *et al.*, 2017), published studies tend to contain data that can be categorised and generalised. The unusable data remain unreported. However, we can learn a great deal from when things go wrong. Focusing on interviewing, Prior (2016: 156) says, 'I hope that we fail more often and that we fail in unexpected ways'. He notes that researchers can learn from challenging situations and calls for greater reflexivity into the emotional work that goes into research and the interactions between researcher and participants.

This chapter returns to an earlier study (Humphries, 2014; Humphries & Burns, 2015), where four male Japanese teachers of English (JTEs) struggled to use communicative language teaching (CLT) textbooks in an engineering college. Data from one teacher seemed largely unusable, due to his unpredictable behaviour during interviews and classroom observations. It was difficult to categorise and compare him with other JTEs using the constant comparison framework (Corbin & Strauss, 2008) that underlay the original study. Moreover, my presence in the classroom appeared to provoke some disruption and my interview questions may have stimulated some anxiety for him. In turn, this caused stress for me and I frequently considered halting his part of the study to avoid causing him emotional strain. Therefore, this chapter re-analyses this *intrinsic case* (Stake, 1995) from a post hoc self-reflexive emotional labour perspective. In other words, readers of this 'Emotional Rollercoaster' volume can see how the process of data collection has emotional consequences for both the participant and the researcher.

CLT implementation problems

English language teaching methods are not value-free and CLT carries cultural and social assumptions originating from Western contexts (Canagarajah, 1999). Research and publications tend to diffuse from a *centre* consisting of Britain, Australasia and North America (BANA) to a *periphery* of tertiary, secondary and primary (TESEP) institutions in the rest of the world (Holliday, 1994). Mismatches can occur when CLT carries *interpretation-based* BANA values to *transmission-based* regions (Wedell, 2003). Although cultures continually evolve in the direction of more diversity, East Asia can be regarded traditionally as a transmission-based region, where countries share a Confucian heritage culture (CHC) (Carless, 1999). Broadly speaking, in CHCs, students should show respect to elders and teachers, who are sources of wisdom, which infers a passive style of learning (Carless, 1999).

The Japanese Ministry of Education, Culture, Sports, Science and Technology (MEXT) has tried to improve the communicative competence of secondary school students since the 1980s, through hiring assistant language teachers (ALTs) from English-speaking countries and the implementation of 'Course of Study' policies. Despite these attempts, transmission-based grammar-translation teaching, known as *yakudoku*, has been widely observed (Underwood, 2017).

A recent survey of nearly 4000 secondary school JTEs across Japan by Negishi *et al.* (2016) reflects the continued existence of *yakudoku*. Respondents indicated that students do mechanical English production such as reading aloud and pronunciation practice; moreover, teachers tended to conduct grammar explanations and reading comprehension. Very few respondents indicated that they gave their students creative English production activities such as debates, speeches/presentations or writing about feelings. The main difficulties faced by JTEs included (1) student issues (poor study habits and low motivation), (2) a lack of preparation time due to too many extracurricular responsibilities, (3) difficulty trying to use CLT while preparing students for entrance examinations and (4) inability to find effective teaching methods.

Analytical framework

I analyse the emotions of a JTE from an emotional labour perspective (Hochschild, 1983) in relation to the *demand control support* (DCS) model (Karasek, 1979; Johnson & Hall, 1988), which can predict emotional burnout (Brotheridge & Grandey, 2002; Näring *et al.*, 2006). Moreover, I review my own role in triggering such emotions through a post hoc self-reflexive lens (Prior, 2016).

Emotional labour

The term emotional labour (also known as emotion labour) was first proposed by Hochschild (1983) following her study of flight attendants. She stated that this labour 'requires one to induce or suppress feeling in order to sustain the outward countenance that produces the proper state of mind in others' (Hochschild, 1983: 7). She asserted that there is a greater strain of emotional labour when a worker's inner feelings diverge from the *feeling rules*. Feeling rules are the 'tacit expectations about how employees are supposed to react to particular workplace situations' (Benesch, 2017: 1). When inner feelings diverge from feeling rules, workers may have two strategies. Firstly, they may employ *surface acting*, where they pretend to show a particular emotion. Secondly, people may apply *deep acting* 'by directly exhorting feeling' or 'making indirect use of a trained imagination' (Hochschild, 1983: 38). In contrast, if workers' feelings match the feeling rules, there is *emotional consonance*.

Demand control support and burnout

Näring *et al.* (2006) noted the importance of tying together emotional labour with the DCS model to predict burnout in teachers. Based on the *job strain* model proposed by Karasek (1979), Johnson and Hall (1988) developed the DCS model that includes social support. Studying from a biological perspective, they found that low social support combined with low autonomy could increase the risk of cardiovascular disease even in undemanding jobs. Brotheridge and Grandey (2002: 17) studied how limited autonomy to express emotions could predict burnout from the perspective of three states: 'employees feel emotionally "spent" (emotional exhaustion), display a detached attitude toward others (depersonalization), and experience a low sense of efficacy at work (diminished personal accomplishment)'. Their questionnaire collected responses from 238 full-time Canadian employees from a variety of job titles that included managers, human service workers and physical labourers. Human service workers reported the highest degrees of deep acting, but they had lower levels of depersonalisation and higher levels of personal accomplishment than workers in other occupations. In contrast, surface acting was related to feeling exhausted and detached. In the survey by Näring *et al.* (2006) of 365 maths teachers from the Netherlands, they found similar results. Surface acting and suppressing emotions were significantly related to depersonalisation. Regarding exhaustion, they found that DCS factors were more important than emotional labour, but the third dimension of burnout (personal accomplishment) was strongly related to emotional consonance.

Although large-scale quantitative studies provide useful generalisations, emotions are complex and dynamic; therefore, smaller-scale qualitative studies of language teachers can provide a finer-tuned understanding in relation to the context of my study.

Qualitative studies of emotional labour and burnout in language teachers

Recent qualitative studies seeking to explain language teacher emotions were undertaken by Acheson *et al.* (2016) and King (2016). Both studies used individual exploratory interviews and a grounded theory iterative approach to data analysis. Acheson *et al.* interviewed five language teachers from a rural secondary school in Georgia (USA), while King's five participants were non-Japanese instructors of English in a Japanese university.

Interestingly, both studies had similar results. Firstly, from a DCS perspective, participants felt that they had poor support. The teachers in King's study felt locked out of the decision-making and they worked on five-year limited-term contracts that naturally made them feel expendable and undervalued. The language teachers from Acheson *et al.* perceived disinterest for foreign languages across society in America. Secondly, a feeling rule internalised by teachers in both studies arose from the motivational burden to inspire students who they regarded as having negative attitudes to languages (Acheson *et al.*) or reluctance to participate orally (King). In their attempts to motivate students, teachers used surface acting, which included faking enthusiasm or suppressing negative emotions. Both studies reported burnout from the teachers, but it manifested in different ways. In King's study, while one teacher attempted to care for students like a *third parent*, other participants used depersonalisation strategies to avoid emotional exhaustion by mentally separating between the performance/role in the classroom and life outside. One instructor opted to fabricate a private life. In contrast, Acheson *et al.* noted teachers' feelings of inefficacy through failing to motivate students and one participant felt so emotionally exhausted that she wanted to stay in bed during the daytime.

Self-reflexive analysis

During an interview study into sociolinguistic and language learning experiences of Southeast Asian immigrants in North America, Prior (2016) noted emotionality in his research journal. Therefore, he returned to his transcripts and conducted a post hoc self-reflexive discourse analysis. This approach focused on the researcher and the interview process with emotional interviewees. Prior's approach differed from earlier studies of emotional labour (such as Hoschild, 1983), which tended to be anecdotal and concentrated on *self-regulation*. Instead, he analysed *other-regulation*: 'the ways in which we display our recognition of others' emotions and our work to shape others' emotions' (Prior, 2016: 158). Prior noted two disturbing phenomena for researchers. Firstly, *emotional contagion*, where empathetic listening can lead to researchers becoming *infected* with the interlocutors' emotional states. Secondly, the interviewer can suffer secondary trauma from the exposure to emotionality that he defines as *emotional danger*. In the post hoc analysis of the data, Prior noted that his original attempts to maintain a professional focus on the interview agenda led to emotional labour as he resisted sharing emotions with the interviewee.

As outlined in the introduction, during a study into the use of new communicative textbooks by four JTEs teaching Grade 11, one of the participants behaved unpredictably during the interviews and it was difficult to discern a pattern in his teaching during classroom observations. Therefore, most of the data were unusable from the constant comparison (Corbin & Strauss, 2008) perspective and I felt concerned about the emotional impact on him. Therefore, in this chapter, I re-analyse the data using the following questions:

(1) To what extent did elements of emotional labour (e.g. surface acting, deep acting and feeling rules) and DCS influence the teacher's approach? Was there evidence of burnout?
(2) From a self-reflexive perspective, how did the classroom observations and interview interactions impact the teacher and researcher emotionally? What can we learn from this?

The Study

The CLT attempt at the *Kosen*

I worked at a *Kosen*, which was a five-year Japanese engineering college, containing Grades 10–12 pus two tertiary-level years. In other words, students were aged 15–20. At the secondary level, students had a mixture of regular school courses including five or six 45-minute periods of English per week. As a private institution, the *Kosen* did not need to follow MEXT guidelines. However, during the study, the *Kosen* was applying for membership of the Japan Accreditation Board for Engineering Education (JABEE, n.d.). The JABEE guidelines included a focus on developing communicative competence in both the L1 (for the wider curriculum) and the L2. To satisfy the entry criteria, the English department introduced new textbooks for Grades 11 and 12 but continued to use a MEXT-recommended textbook for Grade 10.

I explored how four teachers used and responded to the Grade 10 textbook known as *Vivid English Course (New Edition) I* (Vivid) (Minamimura *et al.*, 2006) and the new Grade 11 textbook called *On*

Table 9.1 Textbook comparison

Vivid	***On the Go***
Teacher-centred	Learner-centred
Emphasis on reading comprehension	Emphasis on listening and speaking
Overt grammatical usage instruction	Focus on communicative situations
Japanese publisher, aimed at Japanese high schools	British publisher, aimed at a variety of institutions in East Asia
Instructions and explanations in Japanese	Only glossary and 'phrase book' contain Japanese
Low output, highly structured exercises	Meaning-focused exercises, designed to encourage students to creatively share information and opinions

(Note: This table appeared originally in Humphries (2014: 255).

the Go (OTG) (Gershon *et al.*, 2004). Vivid focused on teacher-centred reading comprehension and *yakudoku* activities; whereas OTG followed a learner-centred CLT approach (Table 9.1).

During the study, the teachers tended to use the *yakudoku* approach for both textbooks. They outlined various problems preventing them from using CLT (see Humphries, 2014; Humphries & Burns, 2015). One teacher, Daiki (pseudonym), proved difficult to analyse because his teaching patterns changed frequently and his interview responses contained many contradictions. In return, I worried about the effect of my study on him. As a result, Daiki's part of the study seemed to be an emotional rollercoaster that we both rode, which is valuable for re-analysis through an emotion-focused lens.

The participant: Daiki

Daiki was a part-time 41-year-old male JTE who taught lower-intermediate students in Grades 10 and 11. For 19 years, he had taught part-time at various local schools and had also tutored students privately. At the time of the study, he only taught at the *Kosen*, where he was in his sixth year. Daiki held a BA in American Literature and he had taken extra credits during his undergraduate study to qualify for a teaching licence. As this study takes a self-reflexive perspective, power dynamics and relationships are important, including my connection to Daiki and the *Kosen*. I was 34, full time and the only native speaker of English. I had taught there for seven years and was studying for my PhD. Before the study, I did not know Daiki's opinions about English education and I had not shared my own CLT principles with him. Instead, we had normally socialised at work parties without discussing work. We both had an intermediate level of the other's L1, so we tended to communicate by switching between Japanese and English.

Data collection and analysis

For both grades, I observed four 45-minute periods, which enabled a comparison of how Daiki used Vivid and OTG. The first observation began in June, which was in the middle of the first semester (two months after the first class in April). This timing was deliberate to allow Daiki time to develop a routine with his students using the new textbook, while avoiding the end of semester stress to prepare for tests. During observations, I sat at the back of the classroom taking notes about methods used and questions to pursue in the interviews. The classes were also video-recorded, transcribed and translated by an independent Japanese speaker. By sitting at the back of the classroom quietly with the video camera and by doing extensive observations (total of six hours from eight periods of classes), I hoped to mitigate the observer effect from Daiki and the students (Humphries & Gebhard, 2012). Moreover, I explained before the study that I was not evaluating performance. However, as I will describe in this chapter, some uncomfortable issues emerged.

I interviewed Daiki eight times for a combined total of 154 minutes. The interviews were conducted using a mix of Japanese and English due to our shared lack of fluency in the other person's L2 (miscommunication due to language errors occurred, but it is beyond the scope of this chapter). I used a semi-structured format, based on issues that I wanted to explore such as pedagogical background, textbook opinions, local factors (such as *Kosen* stakeholders and working conditions) and external factors (such as JABEE and MEXT). Also, issues arose from memos taken during Daiki's class observations and interviews with his colleagues. In other words, in the original study, concepts and questions arose through using the constant comparison approach to memo-writing (Corbin & Strauss, 2008), which helped to guide the interviews and ground the analysis.

For this chapter, I re-analyse my memos and transcripts from the interviews and observations with a focus on the episodes that caused emotionality for me and potential emotionality for Daiki.

Findings

During the observations, student issues and Daiki's divergence from the principles of the new textbook indicated potential areas of emotional labour that were pursued in the interviews. Moreover, his demeanour during some classes indicated that he might have suffered some symptoms of burnout. Daiki could not perceive any institutional pressures, but the lack of direction caused some uncertainty. Inadvertently, my interview questions seemed to cause the strongest signs of emotional impact. These five areas are summarised in Table 9.2 and described in the following sections.

Table 9.2 Areas of potential emotional labour

Issue	Sample
Student issues	*School is their sleeping place*
Divergence from the textbook	*Word and word order*
Teacher demeanour	*Looks like he does not have the energy to teach*
Freedom and uncertainty	*No pressure*
Unconventional interview	*Please teach me how to teach*

Student issues

For both grades, during most observations, there were many behavioural issues such as: students arriving late, having private conversations, not using their textbooks, mocking his pronunciation, whistling, singing and sleeping. In the second observation for Grade 11, I noted the following:

> 11:01 (26 students present). 11 students have their heads down on their desks (sleeping). (Note: this tally increases to 13 later in the class.)

During the first observation of Grade 11, one male student (S1) appeared to lead a group of boys in teasing Daiki for changing his teaching style in front of the video. S1 began by saying:

S1: *Sensei! Itsumoto chigaujyanaidesuka~!* [Teacher! Today you are teaching us differently to normal.]

He followed this with comments such as:

S1: *E? Sensei nande wakarun sonnan?* [Eh? Teacher why do you know it?]

T: *E?* [Eh?]

S2: *Itsumo denshijisho mottekitesa shirabetesa.* [Normally, you bring an electronic dictionary to search for words.]

In addition, students also said:

S3: *Sensei yokuitterujyanaidesuka. Hatsuon komakaku oshietekureterujyanaisuka.* [Teacher you are speaking well today aren't you. You're carefully teaching us the pronunciation aren't you.]

S1: *E, sensei hatsuonsuruno mendokusaikara ittsumo rajikaseyan.* [Eh, teacher you normally can't be bothered to pronounce so you always use the audio player.]

S1 also expressed fake surprise that Daiki was in the room to teach them, claiming that he normally left them alone and also joked that he was using a different colour of chalk from normal. The student behaviour during this observation concerned me to the point that I wondered if my presence had led to an adverse reaction and caused anxiety or embarrassment for Daiki. I wrote: 'am I disrupting the class? Should I stop observing this? Hopefully, the novelty will stop'. However, in the subsequent interview, Daiki assured me that it would be fine to continue.

In the third Grade 11 observation, a group of students seemed to openly challenge Daiki's authority by claiming that '*kuzu*' [scum] should sleep rather than speak:

S1: *Sensei, mae, oreramitainakuzuwa netokettsuttayaro.* [Teacher, before, you said that scum like us should sleep in class.]

Ss: *Itta itta.* [He said it he said it.]

T: *Shaberugurainara netokeyutanya.* [I said that if you are about to speak, it is better to sleep.]

S3: *Kuzuwa netokeyuttade.* [You said that scum should sleep.]

This confrontation continued with a challenge for Daiki to wake up all the sleeping students followed by questions about his school and derogatory comments about its baseball team. In addition to the cheekiness/rudeness, the students seemed to struggle academically. Most of them spoke using Japanese (*katakana* syllable) pronunciation, many seemed to be on the wrong textbook page and when asked to answer a question, they tended to stay silent or answer quietly.

Daiki had a pragmatic approach for dealing with students' disinterested attitudes, making such claims as '(they were) good person, but not good students'. By distinguishing between students on a human and an academic level, he could gain some pleasure from the banter and develop a rapport with them. Such a strategy could avoid potential stress or burnout from struggling to motivate them to learn English.

From his university days, Daiki remembered the words from a professor: 'don't make people students who don't like English'. He added that it is important for teachers to enjoy the class: '*dakara yappari senseiga tanoshindenakattara seitowa kanarazu* (pause) [therefore, of course, if teachers don't enjoy teaching, students (don't enjoy the classes either)]'. He also indicated the need for surface acting when he felt tired and stated 'Performance *taisetsudane* [is important isn't it]'.

Despite Daiki's stated appreciation of the students on a human level, he often talked during the interviews about problems he faced if he tried to make them study.

Daiki: I like them.

Interviewer: Yeah, sometimes *haaa* (exhausted sound) or no problem?

Daiki: *U~* sometimes *so~dane ano~ sukoshiwa ano~ mouchotto benkyoudane, benkyou!* [Sometimes, well, they need to study a bit harder.]

Interviewer: (laughing) want them to study

Daiki: *Sou sou. Unto~ hambunkuraiwa hambun rikaishitenaiy-one~* [Yes. Half of the students don't understand.]

Interviewer: *Rikaishinai*? [They don't understand?]

Daiki: *U~n* didn't learn English grammar and word

Interviewer: *A~* (inaudible) All students or just

Daiki: Almost all students.

The extract above summarises how Daiki felt about the students. He felt that they lacked the basic grounding in vocabulary and grammar to understand the textbooks, but they also seemed to lack the motivation to do necessary studying. In other interviews, he mentioned that students did not copy from the blackboard, do homework or practise in pairs.

Even when students demonstrated some ability, Daiki expressed doubt. For example, after a nominated speaker responded directly to a direction, Daiki looked surprised; the student said '*makasero* [I can do it]' and they both laughed. In the subsequent interview, Daiki indicated that the student might have cheated: 'Maybe maybe, third grade [Grade 12], *ano~* their, elder students, handed to them, and he read it'.

In a later interview, after asking Daiki about the students' interests, I wrote the following memo:

> [Like two other teachers interviewed before him], Daiki is stumped when I ask him what the students are interested in for studying. This question is quite amusing now when I ask it, because I can almost predict the reaction. The teachers almost take it for granted that students are not interested in learning.

He explained that it was hard to know how students liked to study, because they tended to sleep:

Daiki: *Ano~ gakuseiga sukinagakushuuhouhouwane, kitto ne~ (pause) kitto, nandarouna~~~* [Erm, students favourite way of studying is surely (pause) surely, what is it?]

Interviewer: Maybe nothing? (laughing)

Daiki: *Omoitsukanai. Mou min na ZZZZZ* [I can't think of anything, because they are all sleeping]

Interviewer: *Ne.* [Right.]

Daiki: School is their sleeping place.

Divergence from the textbook

As described earlier, the new textbook for Grade 11 (OTG) followed a CLT approach within the interpretation-based paradigm. It encourages learners to study independently and with classmates to share meanings and construct their own answers. However, Daiki guided them through the textbook by giving translations and grammatical explanations in Japanese. Sometimes, he asked students to read sections in English or translate meanings.

The third observation of the Grade 11 class provided a good illustration of Daiki's style. He covered pages 22–23 of OTG which contained listening comprehension (Image 9.1), role play (Image 9.2), reading comprehension and personalised pair work questions (Image 9.3). Daiki directed students to the transcript at the back of the textbook and translated the meaning. He then played the CD and supplied the answers.

Therefore, the listening comprehension had been converted into a teacher-led explanation. After completing this listening section, he skipped the role play, reading comprehension questions and personalised pair work in favour of translating the reading passage. Unlike the translation of the listening transcript, where Daiki had given the answers directly, he asked students to read sections of the passage in English and supplied some Japanese translations. Students answered correctly on two occasions (translation of 'think' and dictionary form of 'chose'). However, for most of his questions, Daiki gave the answers himself.

When asked what he would include in his ideal textbook, Daiki stated '*U~nn, yappari, bumpouo meinnisurukana. Motto* more grammatical part, *un.* [I want to put more grammar mainly and more

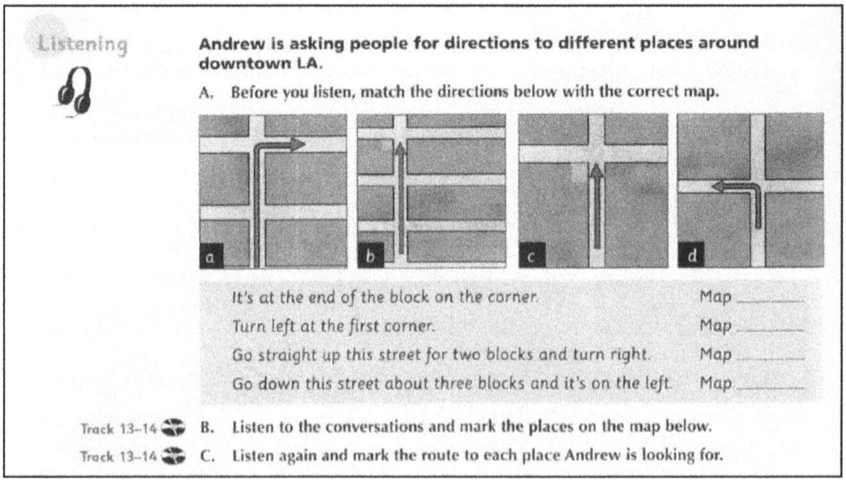

Image 9.1 Listening exercise (*On the Go*: 22)

Frequently, Daiki showed a light-hearted side to the students. He seemed happy to answer many questions even when they were off-topic and he laughed at banter from Grade 11 about changing his class from normal for that first observation.

In contrast, when the same Grade 11 students challenged him during the third observation, Daiki showed signs of anger. Unlike previous classes, where he ignored sleeping students and tolerated those without textbooks, Daiki challenged one boy who claimed to have handed in his notebook by saying '*usostuitemo akanzo* [you mustn't lie to me]' and told students that they would be counted as absent if they forgot their books or slept.

On other occasions, Daiki showed apathy, which became visible from sighing and leaning on equipment or the desk. One example was from the second observation of Grade 11:

> Waiting for students to answer, [Daiki] looks at the book and rests on the CD-player. [There are] often long pauses in this class. He looks around and sometimes sighs. Looks like he does not have the energy to teach.

Therefore, despite Daiki's claim that teachers need to enjoy the class or perform positively, he seemed unable to suppress or manage his emotions. This lack of control could indicate signs of burnout (emotional exhaustion and depersonalisation). It is also likely that the negative emotions were triggered by the study as I will explain later.

Freedom and uncertainty

As outlined earlier, according to Benesch (2017), emotional labour is stronger when the institutional feeling rules clash with a worker's beliefs. During the interviews, Daiki struggled to reconcile his experiences with his current teaching practice. Regarding the workplace, he seemed to feel a great deal of freedom and autonomy, but a lack of support and knowledge caused uncertainty.

Daiki did not seem to experience any feeling rules or any restrictions on his autonomy. He was not conscious of pressure from stakeholders such as parents, students or other teachers.

Interviewer: OK. *Kousende, oshierukotonitsuite hogoshaya gakusei matawa kousenno kyouinniyoru puresshao kanjimasuka*? [Do you feel any pressure to teach in a certain way from parents, students or other teachers?] Do you feel any pressure like (pause)

Daiki: *Zenzen kanjimasen*. [Not at all.]

Interviewer: (Laughing) *Ne*. [Right.]

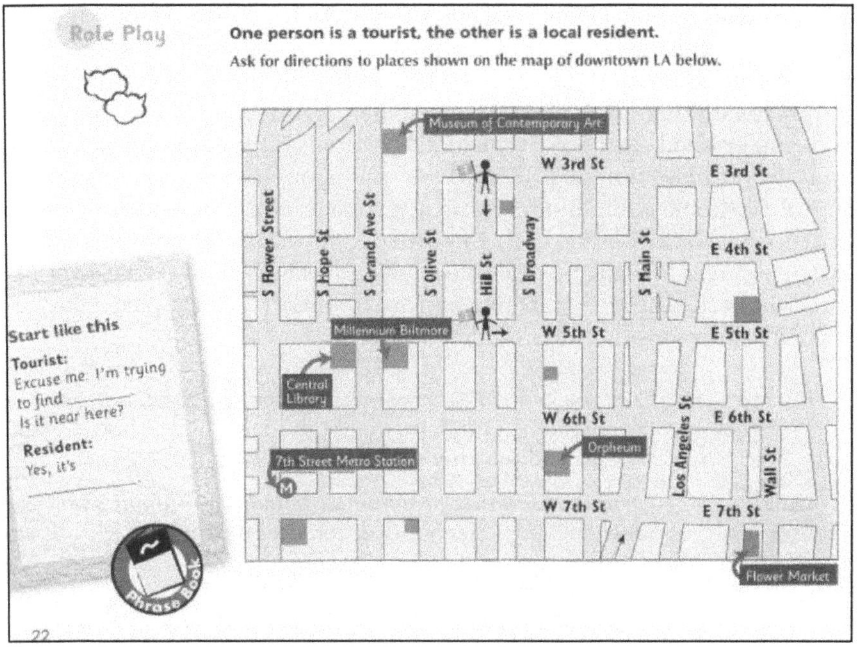

Image 9.2 Role play (*On the Go*: 22)

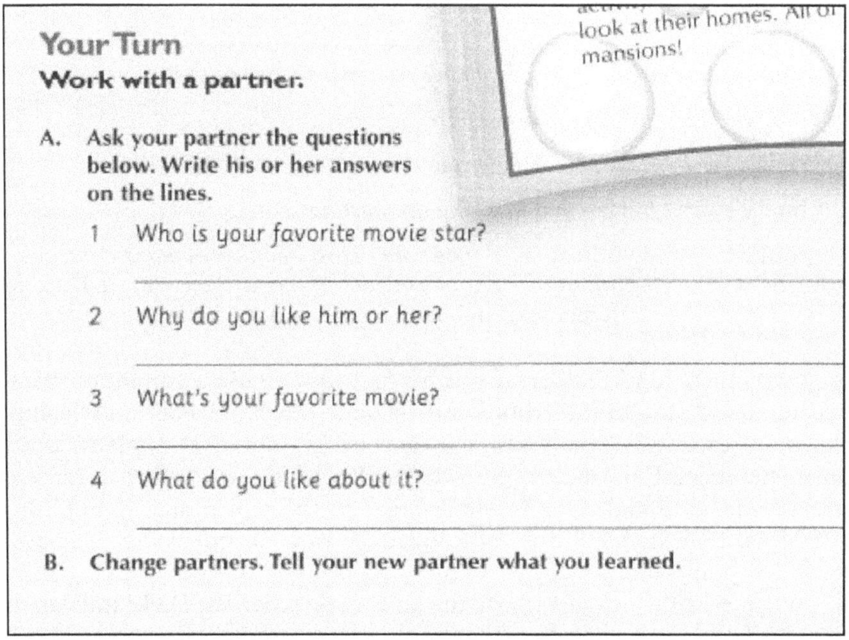

Image 9.3 Personal questions (*On the Go*: 23)

grammatical parts]'. He also felt that it should include 'current English' and defined this as being 'like a newspaper ... contents ... something new'. During Grade 10 observations, Daiki spent most time explaining grammatical points in Japanese from some parts of the reading passages in the main Vivid textbook. When I asked about his method for selecting areas for explanation, he showed me an annotated teacher's version of the textbook containing linguistic explanations above some of the sentences: 'On the blackboard, *kouiutoko kaiterudake.* [I only write this part] ... students want this book (laughing)'. The Vivid textbook fitted the style of teaching that Daiki had used when teaching part time at various institutions, but OTG differed:

Interviewer:	Like you did *chugakkou koukoutoka jukutoka, donoyouni niteimasuka?* [You have taught in junior high schools, high schools and tutoring schools. What is similar?]
Daiki:	*U~nnto, oshieru daitai naiyoutteiunowa sonnani sawanaidesho.* [There aren't any differences in teaching.]
Interviewer:	Ah, *naiyou*, content?
Daiki:	Content. *Dakara kihontekiniwa, bumpouorikaishite hondekara ma, bumpou rikaisuru, tangoto sorekara gojunyawane.* [So, students basically understand grammar and words, and then put words in order.] Word and word order.
Interviewer:	Ah, yeah. Yeah.
Daiki:	*Kurikaeshi, kurikaeshi.* [Keep repeating them.]
Interviewer:	Ah, same same style?
Daiki:	*Sou sou* [That's right.]
Interviewer:	Ok so *matawa chigattemasuka?* Different style?
Daiki:	Different style *tteiunowa kore imaninenseikara chottochigaudeshou? Kyoukashoga.* [What is different ... I use a different textbook now for the Grade 11 class, don't I?]

Daiki then admitted that it was his first time to use a communicative textbook and said 'that textbook is difficult to teach'. His difficulty using the new textbook came from the lack of grammatical explanations: '*ano*, practical English, so, knowledge knowledge *to shitewa taihen iikeredomo* grammar *toka* usage *tokaganai.* [It's got practical English. It is good that students can get knowledge from it, but it doesn't have grammar points and usage]'.

When asked if he tried to use the pair work activities, Daiki indicated that he faced resistance from students. For example, when he tried to make them practise, they would talk or sleep: '*muzukashiine, dakarane~,*

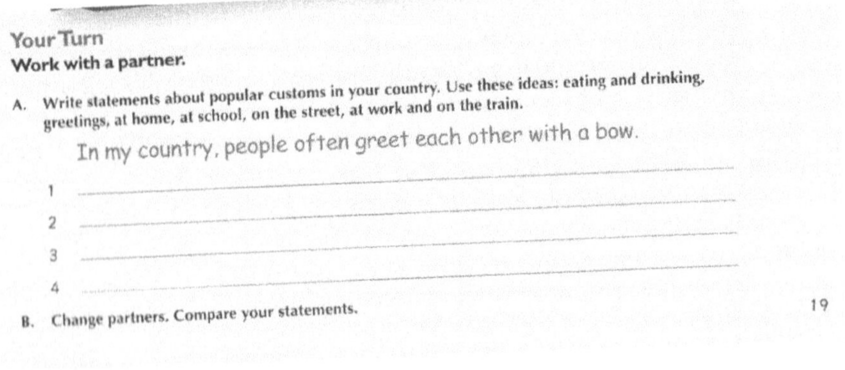

Your Turn

Work with a partner.

A. Write statements about popular customs in your country. Use these ideas: eating and drinking, greetings, at home, at school, on the street, at work and on the train.

In my country, people often greet each other with a bow.

1 ____

2 ____

3 ____

4 ____

B. Change partners. Compare your statements.

19

Image 9.4 Your turn (*On the Go*: 19)

renshuu sase [it is difficult to make the students practise] practice, practice, read, role play *ne* [right] (simulating giving the instruction to the students) but *beraberabera guuuu* [they are talking and then sleeping]'. Therefore, it appears that he avoided the negative emotional consequences of making students work in pairs.

Despite the challenges that Daiki faced from the students, he indicated that he could use his test to encourage them to prepare longer answers. For example, he used an activity from OTG that encouraged students to write about their own country (Image 9.4).

Daiki: This is *ano~ koko tesutoni dasuyo~* (announces to the students) [I will put this part in the test]

Interviewer: (laughing) If it is in the test they study. Ah yeah. Yeah yeah. Okay so students wrote

Daiki: Students say Japanese I write English (laughing).

Daiki's approach differed from the textbook because, rather than working in pairs to create English, it turned into a teacher-centred translation exercise. However, it was a way for Daiki to encourage students to think about what they wanted to say and then memorise the target language.

Teacher demeanour

As shown in the previous two sections, Daiki experienced student and textbook issues. However, during the observations, his demeanour fluctuated between light-heartedness, apathy and anger, which indicates that he did not engage in surface acting or attempt to suppress his emotions.

Daiki: *U~n* [OK]

Interviewer: No pressure *ne.* [right]

Daiki: No pressure *mo* No pressure [No pressure at all!]

Due to the lack of feeling rules, Daiki seemed to feel freedom to teach how he desired. I made the following memo during the observations as I struggled to discern a pattern in his teaching:

> Daiki does not appear very systematic in the way that he decides to work through the exercises. Sometimes he asks the students, but he does not always wait for a correct answer. I wonder if it depends on the perceived difficulty level of the questions or the pace that he wants to progress through the exercises.

When I asked Daiki about his process for selecting students to speak, he replied 'feeling' and when asked about how his methods came from his prior learning, he said 'my own way, no theory'.

His own school experiences seemed to cause regret, because Daiki studied for entrance examinations rather than undertaking wider reading for pleasure:

Daiki: *Shinakattakara ienaindana. Ittemodamenandayo kore~. Adobaisuwa dekirukedone.* [I didn't (read for pleasure), so it's bad for me to say this. I can only give advice.]

When asked about memories from teaching methodology classes during his university days, Daiki said 'I forgot' initially. However, in later interviews, he talked about one of his professors who had written a book that stated that teachers cannot teach clearly without good English proficiency. Recollecting this information seemed to provoke emotional strain during the interviews, because Daiki felt that he had not taken the risks to improve his spoken ability.

Interviewer: So what do you think then in each person is most important (in terms of English proficiency)

Daiki: I think conversation

Interviewer: Ah, conversation? Most important?

Daiki: But but *ano~* reading, I like reading (laughing)

Interviewer: American literature?

Daiki: *Anone dakarane,* Simon-*sensei wakarukana. Shippaishinakya nakanakane shippaishinakya* conversation *nouryokuwa minitsukanaidesho? Anatamo nihonnikite iron nahitotoshabette kou nihongonokaiwanouryokune. Nakanaka kaiwanouryokuo shippai saserudakeno*

> *utsuwaga mouhitotsu* I don't have confident *kana~*. [Simon, I wonder if you understand or not. If you don't make mistakes your conversation ability will not improve. You came to Japan and then you have talked to different people. Your Japanese conversational ability (has improved). I don't have the capacity to take the risk of making mistakes. Maybe I lack confidence.]

As mentioned earlier, Daiki felt 'no pressure' from any stakeholders within the *Kosen*. However, this caused uncertainty too, because he felt there was no clear direction. He did not know the goals from external sources such as JABEE '*Zen zen shirimasen*. (laughing) [I don't know anything]' or MEXT '*Monbushouno shiranai* [I don't know about MEXT]'.

Apart from some translations received from a part-time colleague two years earlier, Daiki said that there was no sharing of materials or information, because everybody made their own separate tests and progressed at different rates through their textbooks. Moreover, Daiki felt that English departmental meetings failed from a lack of information sharing.

> *Kaigika~ kaigiwa amaritameninattemasen. Jyouhoukoukandene, jyouhoukoukan iukoto deshou keredo nanka u~nnn ammari purasuni youmottettenaine*. [Meetings? The meetings are not so useful for me. I suppose the meetings are for exchanging information, but they have not been useful.]

Daiki outlined that the main problem was the lack of goals, which meant that teachers needed to improvise with the new textbooks: '*Sonobashinogidayo. Kyoukashomo ichiou imane,* communication *iukotoninatterudeshou*? (laughing) [We just have to wing it. Now we are supposed to use a communicative textbook aren't we?]'. When asked what kind of target the *Kosen* English department ought to aim for, Daiki had quite a modest ambition: '*saiteigen chuugakude benkyoushitakotoguraiwa saiteigen chantorikai* (laughing) [At least, we should make sure that they understand what they studied at junior high school]'. When I pushed him to think of a communicative target, Daiki aimed even lower: 'three words conversation (laughing). Most student one word or no word (laughing)'.

Rather than the textbooks, students or the institution, my questions may have provoked the strongest negative emotional consequences as Daiki reflected on his need for professional development. The next section shows how Daiki inverted the interview by trying to extract my ideas.

Unconventional interview

Negative emotional reactions seemed to become apparent during discussions about teaching methodology and Daiki's professional development, as he sometimes seemed to contradict himself, scold himself or appeal to me for advice.

The first instance where Daiki seemed to suffer negative emotions occurred while discussing out of class assignments. When I asked if he had given an activity as homework, he answered affirmatively, but then changed his stance later in the interview with the following explanation: '*yattekonaikara un ma isshoniyatterutoiu* [they don't do it by themselves, so we do it together in the class]'. Daiki seemed to worry about my attitude to homework. Before starting the study, I had told the participants that they would not be evaluated, but his apparent evasiveness and requests for my opinion caused me to repeat this information:

Daiki:	*Maa sorewa ikenaindayone hontouwane yokunaine.* [That is not good for students.] Not good. I have to give them homework
Interviewer:	Ah~ no no as you as you
Daiki:	What do you think?
Interviewer:	I don't have any opinion. I just want to know how you use the textbook, I am not saying you are a good teacher or bad teacher. Just how do you use. That's my research. So, it's a *tsukaukotono kenkyuu* [it's research about how you use (textbooks)]

Discussing the homework dilemma seemed to cause negative emotional consequences for both of us. I worried that my line of questioning caused stress for him, but it increased the need to understand whether he really did set homework or not. Daiki may have felt the need to clarify, so we returned to this issue in the next interview.

Interviewer:	Do you give like homework? *Shukudai*? [Homework] Or in class or
Daiki:	*Shukudainiwa shitemasen.* [I don't give them homework.]
Interviewer:	Ah, no homework?
Daiki:	No homework.
Interviewer:	No homework, always class?
Daiki:	Yeah.
Interviewer:	Why not homework?
Daiki:	*U~ tto*, because almost that class students are sports *no kurabu haittetene* [Well, almost all students in that class are in sports clubs]
Interviewer:	Sports club yeah
Daiki:	He got back home until at 8 o'clock

Interviewer: Very late

Daiki: Very late *sou. Ano~ sorekara ofuronihaitte sentakushite osoine.* [Yes, very late. Then, they take a bath and wash their clothes. It is very late.]

Interviewer: Ah~ yeah.

Daiki: *Sore chotto atama izen watakushiwa ano~ yakyubunokomon yattetakotoarune. Sorede chotto chotto* pity *aaa~~ mazui* pity *mazuikeredo haicchatta.* [That's quite painful. I have been involved with a baseball club. Due to that I pity them. Ah it's bad to say that I pity them, but I think that way.]

Like his unease about pitying the students, Daiki seemed to reproach himself when I asked him some questions about his methodology – for example, he forgot to read about a location in the textbook: '*korewa chotto shiraberunowasureta korene. Shirabetokana akankattane. Chanto kichintone~* [I forgot to look up about this. I should have looked it up. I've not been thorough].' However, my questions about how he studied teaching methods seemed to provoke the most unease:

> Ah. Teaching meth, teaching *wane~* teaching *wa~ nai.* Teaching *wa doushitara yappari* teaching *o* improve improve my teaching method *yappa kouiunojanaito damedaroune.* [I don't study teaching methods. Actually it's bad that I don't study to improve my teaching method, isn't it?]

In addition to my questions provoking unintended unease, Daiki also seemed to misinterpret some of them as teaching suggestions. As indicated earlier, this occurred when I asked about homework and about a location in the textbook. On other occasions, I inadvertently seemed to direct him toward teaching in ways that I have no enthusiasm towards, which added to my emotional rollercoaster. This is indicated in my memos below:

> I want to ask how he finds the pronunciation of words (from the textbook) that I consider unnecessary and difficult. However, Daiki reacts in a panic that he has not made the students say them.
>
> ...
>
> I asked him a question about choral repetition, because I had discussed this in a previous interview with (his colleague). Daiki responds by saying 'good idea', although I am not sure that it is.

Interviewer: Do you do much, choral repetition? Like, Daiki-sensei you speak and students repeat after you. Do you do that?

Daiki: *A~ ripito? Ripito wa~ ano~ a, souya, ripitogaiine.* [Repeating, ah that's good isn't it.]

Interviewer: Ah, no I'm not saying you must do, asking do you do (laughing)

Daiki: Good idea, good idea.

Interviewer: Anything.

Daiki: I take your idea.

Interviewer: (laughing)

Daiki: Repeat after me! Repeat after me. Repeat after me. Or repeat after CD

On other occasions, Daiki switched roles from interviewee to interviewer to ask for my help regarding teaching methodology. He often asked how to teach activities requiring creative student output from OTG and at the end of one interview, he made a direct appeal for help.

Interviewer: Any final comment

Daiki: Final comment, final *commento e~ tto* Please teach me how to teach English (laughing)

Discussion

The first research question explored elements of emotional labour and DCS on Daiki's teaching approach and examined evidence of burnout. Regarding the DCS model, Daiki perceived (a) low demands on his emotions (despite behavioural problems from students), (b) high autonomy to teach without controlling his feelings and (c) low support. This perceived lack of support mirrored the findings of other qualitative studies of teacher emotions by King (2016) and Acheson *et al.* (2016), where participants engaged in surface acting due to an internalised feeling rule that they needed to motivate students. However, although Daiki stated his preference for such a 'performance', it was not evident during observations where he showed his irritation and apathy. It is possible that teachers who hold learner-centred interpretation-based values may feel a greater need to motivate, whereas Daiki comes from a transmission-based CHC (Carless, 1999; Wedell, 2003). Like a feudal lord with the classroom as his domain, he could be viewed as holding absolute power to transmit knowledge as it suited him. He was the executive decision-maker in the classroom (Barnard & Nguyen, 2010) who felt little need to adapt.

Despite freedom to express his emotions, Daiki displayed evidence of burnout. During the observations, he showed signs of exhaustion. Moreover, depersonalisation became clear during the interviews because he noted student problems and lack of institutional support. The interviews also seemed to trigger a crisis of confidence. Daiki began to regret that he had not engaged in professional development and criticise himself for not exploring alternative approaches.

The second research question took a self-reflexive perspective to investigate the impact of the study on both researcher and participant and to consider the implications. As noted in my research journal, I considered halting the study during some observations. However, despite my concerns, Daiki claimed that he did not mind the student disruption. As noted above, he did not seem to suppress his emotions or engage in surface acting. In contrast, during the interviews, Daiki began to reflect on his practice and lack of professional development, which caused him some discomfort. In a similar vein to Prior (2016), I attempted to keep a professional distance and stay neutral when Daiki asked for help. Although avoiding emotional contagion or danger (Prior, 2016), I felt emotional strain when Daiki grasped some interview questions believing (incorrectly) that they were my teaching suggestions. In order to mitigate awkward feelings, I laughed with him about areas of shared understanding as a teacher such as student issues while avoiding telling him how to teach. In retrospect, I could have helped Daiki. He had used the same teaching approach in all of his part-time locations and seemed to suffer from fossilisation. While the new textbooks and the study provoked some self-reflection and discomfort, Daiki was reaching out for my advice as an L1 English speaker and teacher-researcher. Such a balance of outside pressure and guidance could have helped him develop. Instead, unfortunately, shortly after this study, the *Kosen* closed down and relocated. Subsequently, Daiki left the profession.

Conclusion

Qualitative researchers tend to report patterns and generalisations from their data that can resonate. However, individuals – participants and researchers – have emotions that change dynamically leading to interactions that influence each other. This chapter reported on an intrinsic case, where problems arose during observations and interviews. As noted by Prior (2016), participants may treat their interviewers like therapists. Daiki seemed to require a mentor rather than a therapist but, as a novice researcher younger than him, I felt unprepared to fill that role. This study reaffirms Prior's assertion that we need to share emotional problems arising from research and I hope that more publications will explore this under-researched area.

Post-Reading Tasks

(1) Think of a previous study where you may have interviewed or observed participants. Did you notice an emotional influence on them? If so,

how did you deal with their emotions? If you were to conduct the study again, what changes would you make to minimise/mitigate the emotional impact?

(2) Think of a time when you may have been observed or interviewed. How did it affect you emotionally? Can you remember using any strategies to control or suppress your emotions? If you were to encounter the same situation again, would you employ different strategies to manage your emotions?

(3) In your workplace, do you or any of your colleagues suffer from symptoms of emotional burnout? What changes could you or your employer instigate to alleviate this problem?

(4) What advantages and disadvantages can you foresee if a researcher provides feedback to participants during a study?

Acknowledgments

This work is financially supported by JSPS KAKENHI grant number 17K02995 and the Kansai University Fund for Domestic and Overseas Research, 2018–2019. I would like to thank Pearson Longman for granting permission to reproduce sections of *On the Go*.

References

Acheson, K., Taylor, J. and Luna, K. (2016) The burnout spiral: The emotion labor of five rural U.S. foreign language teachers. *The Modern Language Journal* 100 (2), 522–537.

Barnard, R. and Nguyen, G.V. (2010) Task-based language teaching (TBLT): A Vietnamese case study using narrative frames to elicit teachers beliefs. *Language Education in Asia* 1 (1), 77–86.

Benesch, S. (2017) *Emotions and English Language Teaching: Exploring Teachers' Emotion Labor*. New York: Routledge.

Brotheridge, C.M. and Grandey, A.A. (2002) Emotional labor and burnout: Comparing two perspectives of 'people work'. *Journal of Vocational Behavior* 60 (1), 17–39.

Canagarajah, A.S. (1999) *Resisting Linguistic Imperialism in English Teaching*. Oxford: Oxford University Press.

Carless, D.R. (1999) Perspectives on the cultural appropriacy of Hong Kong's Target-Oriented Curriculum (TOC) initiative. *Language Culture and Curriculum* 12 (3), 238–254.

Corbin, J. and Strauss, A. (2008) *Basics of Qualitative Research* (3rd edn). London: SAGE.

Gershon, S., Mares, C. and Walker, R. (2004) *On the Go: English Skills for Global Communication*. Hong Kong: Pearson Education Asia Limited.

Hochschild, A.R. (1983) *The Managed Heart: Commercialization of Human Feeling*. Berkeley, CA: University of California Press.

Holliday, A. (1994) The house of TESEP and the communicative approach: The special needs of state English language education. *ELT Journal* 48 (1), 3–11.

Humphries, S. (2014) Factors influencing Japanese teachers' adoption of communication-oriented textbooks. In S. Garton and K. Graves (eds) *International Perspectives on Materials in ELT* (pp. 253–269). New York: Palgrave Macmillan.

Humphries, S. and Burns, A. (2015) 'In reality it's almost impossible': CLT-oriented curriculum change. *ELT Journal* 69 (3), 239–248.

Humphries, S. and Gebhard, J.G. (2012) Observation. In R. Barnard and A. Burns (eds) *Researching Language Teacher Cognition and Practice* (pp. 109–127). Bristol: Multilingual Matters.

JABEE (n.d.) *What's JABEE? Japan Accreditation Board for Engineering Education*. See https://jabee.org/en/ (accessed 9 March 2018).

Johnson, J.V. and Hall, E.M. (1988) Job strain, work place social support, and cardiovascular disease: A cross-sectional study of a random sample of the Swedish working population. *American Journal of Public Health* 78 (10), 1336–1342.

Karasek, R.A. (1979) Job demands, job decision latitude, and mental strain: Implications for job redesign. *Administrative Science Quarterly* 24 (2), 285–308.

King, J. (2016) 'It's time, put on the smile, it's time!': The emotional labour of second language teaching within a Japanese university. In C. Gkonou, D. Tatzl and S. Mercer (eds) *New Directions in Language Learning Psychology* (pp. 97–112). New York: Springer.

Minamimura, T., Asai, M., Ishihara, Y., Itoh, T., Iwamoto, K., Goi, C., Torio, N., Harada, Y., Miyagawa, K., Miyamoto, T., Watanabe, K. and Rockenbach, B. (2006) *Vivid English Course (New Edition) I*. Tokyo: Daiichi Gakushusha.

Näring, G., Briët, M. and Brouwers, A. (2006) Beyond demand–control: Emotional labour and symptoms of burnout in teachers. *Work & Stress* 20 (4), 303–315.

Naveed, A., Sakata, N., Kefallinou, A., Young, S. and Anand, K. (2017) Understanding, embracing and reflecting upon the messiness of doctoral fieldwork. *Compare: A Journal of Comparative and International Education* 47 (5), 773–792.

Negishi, M., Sakai, H., Shigematsu, K., Takagi, A. and Kudo, Y. (2016) *Chuukou no Eigo Shidou ni Kansuru Jittai Chousa 2015 [Survey of Actual English Teaching Situation in Secondary Schools 2015]*. Tokyo: Benesse Educational Research and Development Institute.

Prior, M. (2016) *Emotion and Discourse in L2 Narrative Research*. Bristol: Multilingual Matters.

Stake, R.E. (1995) *The Art of Case Study Research*. London: Sage.

Underwood, P.R. (2017) Challenges and change: Integrating grammar teaching with communicative work in senior high school EFL classes. *SAGE Open* 7 (3), 1–15.

Wedell, M. (2003) Giving TESOL change a chance: Supporting key players in the curriculum change process. *System* 31 (4), 439–456.

10 Investigating Dynamic Changes in Elementary School Teachers' Anxiety when Teaching English[1]

Maiko Ikeda, Osamu Takeuchi and Hiroyuki Imai

Introduction

Ever since the seminal work by Scovel (1978), studies on anxiety in language learning have attracted the attention of second/foreign language (hereafter, L2) researchers and practitioners around the world. A large body of research has emerged since then, and anxiety has become a central learner factor when we talk about individual differences in L2 acquisition, especially in classroom settings. One of the prime periods in L2 anxiety research was the 1990s, when two influential anthologies were compiled (Horwitz & Young, 1991; Young, 1999). The two volumes shaped subsequent research and their influence is still being felt. Recently, however, with the surge of interest in dynamic systems theory (DST) in L2 research in general (Larsen-Freeman & Cameron, 2008) as well as in the classroom (e.g. Larsen-Freeman, 2016), a new research direction concerning L2 learning anxiety has materialized and several important insights are being obtained from the DST perspective (e.g. Gkonou *et al.*, 2017). Within the framework of DST, L2 research 'is situated and process-oriented, which means that learner attributes are neither stable nor context-independent, but interact with the context and vary over time' (Dewaele, 2012: 43). Research on L2 learning anxiety thus needs to highlight the aspect of change (or fluctuations) as well as the influence of the context, along with the types of anxiety adaptations that can lead learners to different outcomes in their L2 learning.

An Emotions Perspective

Another recent development in research concerning L2 anxiety is the introduction of an *emotions* perspective, influenced by the positive psychology movement (e.g. Fredrickson, 2001, 2003; Seligman & Csíkszentmihályi, 2000). Research based on this perspective has emphasized a move away from an exclusive focus on a single negative emotion such as anxiety, to a more holistic analysis of both negative and positive emotions and their interplay in L2 learners (e.g. Dewaele & Alfawzan, 2018; Dewaele & MacIntyre, 2014, 2016; MacIntyre & Mercer, 2014; Piniel & Albert, 2018). Negative emotions here encompass such constructs as *anxiety*, *sadness*, *boredom*, *fear* and *anger*, while positive emotions include, for example, *enjoyment*, *happiness*, *interest* and *satisfaction*. According to a theory in positive psychology (Fredrickson, 2003), negative emotions tend to lead to characteristic thoughts and actions, resulting in focusing and narrowing. By contrast, positive emotions share the ability to broaden learners' thoughts and actions, thereby helping them to build different resources, resulting in the investment of more time and energy into their further L2 learning.

In this line of research, as in the DST framework, learners' emotions are considered to fluctuate over different timescales, ranging from seconds to months. They are also considered to vary according to the degree of the learner's mastery of particular L2 skills, as well as the socio-educational and cultural context of L2 use (Piniel & Albert, 2018). Moreover, emotions, both positive and negative, are deemed to be closely connected to cognition and are assumed to influence each other, and hence to affect L2 learning behaviour extensively (Oxford, 2015; Piniel & Albert, 2018).

Interestingly, researchers and practitioners have operated on the basis that positive and negative emotions in L2 learners are located at either end of a continuum, forming a see-saw relationship. For example, motivation and anxiety were reported to function as a trade-off, or in a see-saw relationship, in which one goes up and the other goes down (e.g. Gardner *et al.*, 1997; Ehrman, 1996; Noels *et al.*, 1999; Tremblay & Gardner, 1995). However, focusing on the relationship between enjoyment and anxiety in L2 learning, Dewaele and MacIntyre (2014) recently demonstrated that enjoyment and anxiety shared only 12.5% of the variance (a small effect size), which suggests that these two emotions (i.e. one positive and one negative) should not be treated as endpoints of the same continuum, but as two different dimensions, each of which has a different function and operates independently of the other under the influence of the context in which learners live and learn the L2. Dewaele and Alfawzan (2018) also reported that enjoyment and anxiety cooperated in L2 learners and that the former was found to have a slightly stronger effect on L2 performance than the latter had.

From the Perspective of L2 Teachers

Still another emerging issue in this field is related to the fact that 'even L2 teachers get the blues' (Horwitz, 1996). L2 anxiety research has had a tendency to focus on the learner and has consequently underestimated teacher anxiety. However, classrooms have both learners and teachers. As both Daubney (2010) and Kunt and Tüm (2010) pointed out, L2 teachers, especially those who are foreign language users (Dewaele, 2018) of the target language, are as susceptible to the influence of anxiety in the classroom as L2 learners are. L2 teacher anxiety affects teachers' use of the target language and pedagogy, which, in turn, has serious implications and consequences for learners and their learning outcomes. This is exactly the situation that is looming for Japanese elementary school teachers who will be obliged to teach English as a required academic subject, effective from April 2020, because of the reforms to the national education policy formally announced in 2017 (MEXT, 2017a). Accordingly, since then, their anxiety has been mounting, and they have been desperately seeking help because most teachers have virtually no formal pre-service training or in-service experience of teaching the language (Ikeda *et al.*, 2019). Furthermore, most of them have relatively low proficiency in the language (Asahi Shimbun, 2017).

In this chapter, we focus on Japanese elementary school teachers who are faced with the daunting challenge of teaching English and investigate how their anxiety (as well as their satisfaction) changes over time in response to a particular in-service training programme. First, to explain the background, both the specific social context surrounding elementary school teachers in Japan and the details of the in-service training programme implemented to help reduce their anxiety in teaching L2 are described. Following this, we introduce the main study and focus on how a teacher training intervention programme affected the longitudinal fluctuation of L2 teacher anxiety and satisfaction. On the basis of the results obtained, the implications for L2 anxiety research and L2 teacher training are then discussed.

Background

Social context

Ikeda *et al.* (2019) report that as part of the newly introduced national curriculum guidelines in Japan, the Ministry of Education, Culture, Sports, Science and Technology (hereafter, MEXT) has announced that English will be introduced into the elementary school curriculum, starting in 2020. One reason for this decision is the nationwide perception that the current English language teaching system in public schools has failed to achieve the government's target of producing Japanese who are fluent enough in English to communicate clearly. In the early 2000s, given the rapid globalization of the economy and the introduction of English into primary school curricula in neighbouring countries, such as China and Korea, MEXT was obliged to cope with the urgent need to improve the country's system of English language teaching. Thus, in 2002, the ministry decided to start English language teaching at an earlier stage and introduced English classes into elementary schools as an optional subject. In 2011, amid fierce opposition from some researchers and practitioners, this optional class was changed to 'Foreign Language Activity', an academic domain taught in every elementary school. Its primary focus was placed on providing chances to become familiar with English in a playful atmosphere for pupils in the fifth and sixth grades. The annual hours of English class were only 35 (once a week) for fifth- and sixth-graders.

The primary school English teaching system has continued to arouse nationwide dissatisfaction, however, which eventually resulted in another major revision in the form of the introduction of English as a required academic subject for fifth- and sixth-graders, effective from 2020. Reading and writing, as well as listening and speaking, will be taught for the first time in elementary schools. Furthermore, the curriculum guidelines require that 'Foreign Language Activity', in which pupils are expected to experiment with English by speaking and listening, be conducted for third- and fourth-graders.[2] The annual number of English class hours will increase to 70 (twice a week) for fifth- and sixth-graders, and 35 hours (once a week) for third- and fourth-graders. As a result, a total of 210 class hours will be devoted to teaching English at elementary schools throughout Japan, beginning in 2020.

Since the government's initial move to introduce English into the nationwide school curriculum, in-service teachers at elementary schools have felt great anxiety about teaching the subject (e.g. Ikeda *et al.*, 2019; Machida, 2016; Machida & Uchida, 2015; Yonezaki *et al.*, 2016). This is mainly because most of them do not have the appropriate pre-service training or in-service experience in teaching English. In fact, the basic knowledge and skills for teaching English have not been mandatory to obtain elementary school teaching credentials from colleges (see Ikeda *et al.*, 2019, for a recent reform). Most teachers are inexperienced in teaching English, having either no or just a few years' experience in 'Foreign Language Activity'. Only 5% of them have a secondary level teaching credential in English (MEXT, 2017b). Furthermore, a very small proportion of them have attained English language proficiency above B1 on the Common European Framework of References for Languages (CEFR) scale (Asahi Shimbun, 2017). It is thus only natural that elementary school teachers feel they are not well qualified or prepared for teaching English.[3]

Intervention programme

As explained above, in the Japanese primary school context, teachers have tended to have high levels of English teaching anxiety due to a lack of appropriate professional preparation, hands-on experience and English ability. Thus, research into alleviating their anxiety is urgently needed. However, relatively little research has been conducted on this issue so far. Ikeda *et al.* (2019) is one of the few studies to have attempted to address this pressing problem. The authors developed a new intervention programme for in-service teacher training readily available at individual schools.

In the intervention programme, a needs analysis was conducted at each school with a focus on reducing teacher anxiety in teaching English. After determining the needs at the school, possible ways of meeting them were discussed and teacher training sessions were implemented accordingly at each school for its specific needs, with the full support of school administrators, academic domain experts from a university, and supervisors from the local Board of Education. For example, if teachers at a particular elementary school were worried about their ability to use English in the classroom, then a series of sessions concerning the use of English in the classroom was planned and implemented. If they had no concrete idea of how to teach English effectively in a lesson due to a lack of hands-on experience and had high anxiety as a result, then in order to reduce their anxiety, workshops were planned and put into practice, in which sound teaching plans and practices from other elementary schools were shared.

Sessions were usually conducted after school for about an hour or an hour and a half, which allowed the busy teachers to attend them without any difficulty. After each session or series of sessions, reflection was conducted among the teachers and further training needs were assessed. One striking feature of this intervention programme is that teachers at individual schools managed all these procedures on their own with the help of academic experts. In addition, graduate/college students of Teaching English as a Foreign Language (TEFL), who were highly proficient in the language and knowledgeable about EFL teaching, were dispatched to each school and helped teachers to plan and implement the training sessions. The dispatched students were in a unique position because no hierarchical consideration by teachers was necessary. Thus, the joint building and implementation of training was possible in a relaxed and non-threatening atmosphere among the participants. Such an atmosphere might not have been possible had school administrators, university experts or supervisors from the local Board of Education been directly involved in the implementation of the programme. This is because working teachers generally regard these people as their managers/mentors (not as equals), and thus they would have felt inhibited when participating in the process. Note that the dispatched students also served as a liaison between teachers and university experts, thereby ensuring relevant and timely advice for teachers from the experts (Ikeda *et al.*, 2019).

All the features explained above were intended to contribute to the reduction of anxiety among elementary school teachers in teaching English. At the end of a programme lasting for two academic terms, during which approximately five sessions were conducted, it was found that the intervention had led to a reduction in teachers' anxiety in teaching English, although some differences were found depending on the school contexts (Ikeda *et al.*, 2019). For example, the relationship between teachers and school administrators at each school, as well as the degree of understanding of the goals of the training sessions among the school staff members, influenced the outcomes of the intervention programme.

An examination of improvement among teachers only at the end of the programme is not considered sufficient, however, because there is the possibility that teacher anxiety fluctuated at any point over the course of the programme, rendering the final measurement an arbitrary figure. In addition, each teacher seems to have had his/her own unique response to the training sessions during the course of the intervention. Accordingly, it is necessary to examine both the general and the unique changes in teacher anxiety over time and possibly to ascertain the specific factors/ events influencing the changes.

The Study

Purposes

The purposes of this study were twofold: (1) to investigate how elementary school teacher anxiety in teaching English fluctuates over time in relation to the in-service intervention programme explained above and (2) to ascertain the factors and events that influence the fluctuation. In addition, fluctuation in the programme satisfaction among the teachers was examined over time in this study.

Participants

The participants were 42 teachers from two public elementary schools in a suburban city of the Osaka Metropolitan Area, which is located in the western part of Japan. As of 2017, the city (with a population of 374,500 as of 2015) has 35 elementary schools of various sizes. Of these, two schools were selected on the basis of their size, location and availability. Most teachers at the schools did not receive any formal instruction at college in teaching English as part of their pre-service training to obtain a primary school teacher credential. Only a small portion of them (7.1%) had a secondary school teaching licence in English. Their English proficiency was relatively low and was estimated to be at A1–B1 on the CEFR scale. Most of them had a strong sense

Table 10.1 Details of the participants

Teachers and schools (R or J)*	Teaching experience at primary school (years)	Homeroom teacher experience (years)	English teaching experience at primary school (years)	Taught demonstration lesson in the year**	English proficiency level (CEFR)	Attitudes towards English
Moji at R	1	1	1	✓	A1	ambivalent
Shika at R	1	1	1		A1	ambivalent
Naka at J	2	2	2	✓	A1	ambivalent
Tana at R	7	7	5	✓	A2	positive
Nami at J	8	8	4	✓	B1	positive
Sasa at J	16	15	1		A1	ambivalent

*Their names are pseudonyms. R and J stand for the initial letter of each school's name.
**'Demonstration lesson in the year' refers to whether the teacher was in charge of an English demonstration lesson in the year we conducted the study. See the qualitative analysis section of the chapter for a detailed explanation of the 'demonstration lessons'.

of their weakness in English and consequently had high anxiety about teaching the language. Their age range varied from young to old (min.: 23; max.: 55), with an English teaching experience of nearly zero to a few years (min.: 0.5; max.: 5; mean: 2.58; at the start of the study). Of the 42 teachers, six (three from each school) were selected on the basis of pre-set criteria[4] for the purpose of follow-up interviews. See Table 10.1 for details of the six participants.

Methods

A questionnaire was used to assess the teachers' overall tendencies in the fluctuation of English teaching anxiety as well as their programme satisfaction. The questionnaire comprised six-point-scale Likert-type items and free-description-type items (see Appendix).[5] The wording of the items was formulated on the basis of our previous study and was piloted in a similar context (Ikeda *et al.*, 2017). It was administered to the participants at the end of each session in Sessions 1 to 4.

In order to investigate further the longitudinal fluctuations in the teachers' anxiety, at the end of the programme, six of the 42 teachers who filled out the questionnaire were selected on the basis of the pre-set criteria and asked to draw an anxiety timeline graph showing their retrospective changes in English teaching anxiety. They were also asked to draw a satisfaction timeline graph showing their retrospective changes in satisfaction with the in-service training programme implemented in this study. Song and Kim (2017) demonstrated the usefulness and high reliability (r = .733, N = 64) of such retrospective graphs in charting high school students' motivational changes from kindergarten to college in South Korea.[6] In the current study, participants were given a graph

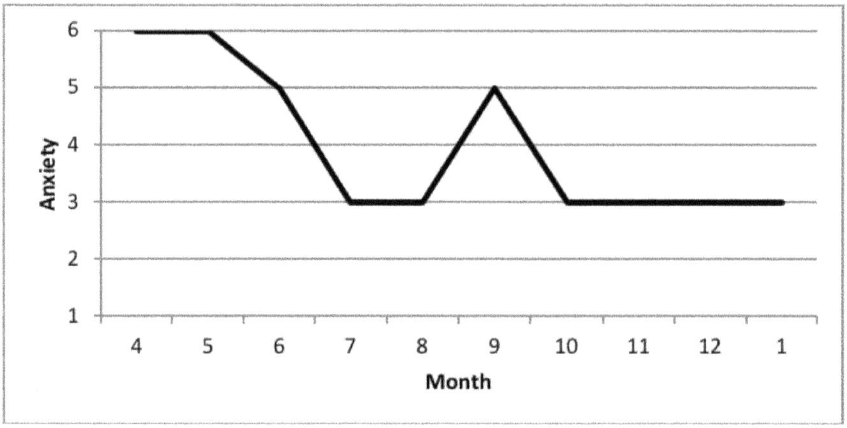

Figure 10.1 A sample graph indicating the fluctuations in anxiety regarding the teaching of English over time

indicating the months (on the horizontal axis) during which they were in the intervention programme. They were then asked to indicate their anxiety (or satisfaction) levels (on the vertical axis) using the scale of one (low) to six (high) for each month until the last month of the programme. Afterwards, they were asked to draw a graph connecting the anxiety (or satisfaction) index for each month. Figure 10.1 above shows a sample anxiety timeline graph based on imaginary data. This was created to help readers understand how to read the graph. The solid line in the figure indicates that this participant regarded the teaching of English as high-anxiety-inducing for the first two months, reporting the highest anxiety level (6). The level then dropped to (5) in June and to (3) in July and remained the same in August. It then rose to (5) in September before dropping to (3) in October and levelling off until the last month of the programme.

A follow-up stimulated recall interview (Gass & Mackey, 2000) was subsequently administered in which each participant was interviewed while looking at his/her own anxiety and satisfaction graphs, along with a school calendar, a brief session summary record, and the materials from each session, as recall stimuli, thereby effectively allowing the authors to confirm the factors and events behind the ups and downs observed in the individual graphs. The interviews were conducted in the teachers' L1, i.e. Japanese, on an individual basis by the first author of this chapter. A positive rapport between the interviewees and the interviewer was confirmed as established because the latter had regularly visited the two schools (R and J) and had given advice and comments to the teachers on their English lessons in a cordial atmosphere. All the interview data were recorded by using a digital voice recorder and transcribed verbatim by the first author with comments on speakers' prosodic features (e.g. small voice, special emphasis). The data were then read many times by the authors and the remarks referring to a similar theme were grouped together, producing categories such as '*ways to deal with anxiety*', '*adverse influence of demonstration lessons*', '*getting used to teaching English*' and so forth. Interview excerpts used in the ensuing section are the authors' translations. To ensure the reliability of the translations, the first and the second authors translated the original remarks separately, and resultant discrepancies, if any, were resolved by discussion.

Results and Discussion

Quantitative analysis

As Table 10.2 and Figure 10.2 show, the overall tendency for the level of English teaching anxiety remained high and showed no significant change across the sessions ($F = 0.26$, $N = 42$, $p = .86$, partial $\eta^2 = .01$). At the same time, Table 10.3 and Figure 10.3 indicate that programme satisfaction level also remained high and that there was no significant

Table 10.2 Means and SDs of English teaching anxiety after training sessions

	Session #1	Session #2	Session #3	Session #4
Mean	4.60	4.46	4.38	4.65
SD	0.81	1.04	1.05	0.89

Note: Rounded off to the second decimal place. Sessions were conducted about 1 to 1.5 months apart.

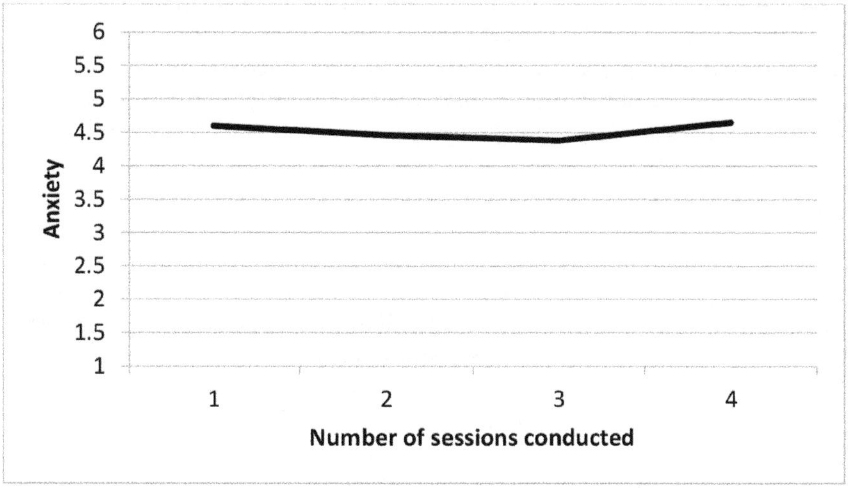

Figure 10.2 Levels of English teaching anxiety among the participants

Table 10.3 Means and SDs of programme satisfaction after training sessions

	Session #1	Session #2	Session #3	Session #4
Mean	5.11	5.16	5.10	5.04
SD	0.85	0.55	0.54	0.53

Note: Rounded off to the second decimal place. Sessions were conducted about 1 to 1.5 months apart.

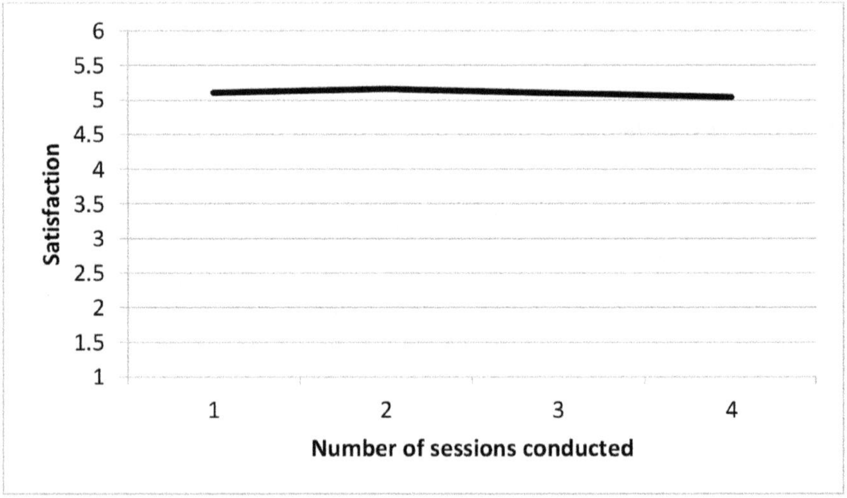

Figure 10.3 Levels of programme satisfaction among the participants

change over the course of the sessions, as confirmed by an ANOVA ($F = 0.45$, $N = 42$, $p = .72$, partial $\eta^2 = .02$). Putting these tables and figures together, our interpretation is that the in-service programme implemented was perceived as satisfactory by teachers in terms of its contents, but did not actually contribute effectively to the reduction of English teaching anxiety overall.

Qualitative analysis

Despite the results of the quantitative analysis, comments from several participants (see Interview excerpts 1 and 2 below for examples) indicate that the reactions of individual teachers differed from the general trends observed in the above-mentioned analysis, suggesting the possibility that the individual differences offset each other and blurred fluctuations that could have been identified. It was therefore deemed necessary to look into each individual change and examine the reasons for the ups and downs of teacher anxiety (as well as programme satisfaction).

Interview excerpt 1
Thanks to the first session of the in-service training, I learned an effective way of using praise in English. I learned how to use praise in context. I then realized that my anxiety of teaching English dropped. It was a kind of euphoria ... But after observing a class in which another teacher used words or phrases of praise very frequently and successfully, I again felt a high level of anxiety, thinking that I would never be able to attain the level that the teacher had achieved. (J-Naka)

Interview excerpt 2
This first in-service training session was useful, but I became more anxious at this point (just after the first training session) because the open demonstration class that I was going to teach was scheduled for two or three weeks from then. So, I think that my anxiety level did not drop easily in the face of the impending challenge of the demonstration class. (Brackets ours: J-Nami)

Analysis of the anxiety timeline graphs drawn by the six teachers selected confirms that each teacher's level of anxiety fluctuated uniquely, sometimes in relation to the implemented sessions of the in-service training programme, but at other times in response to the contextual factors other than those related to the intervention. A closer look at the graphs, along with the comments obtained in the follow-up interviews, suggests that the length of teaching experience at elementary school might be a factor moderating the effect of the in-service training sessions aimed at reducing teacher anxiety.

As Figure 10.4 shows, Shika, a junior teacher with only one year's experience, responded well to the training sessions. Accordingly, his English teaching anxiety dropped after the first few sessions and remained relatively low until January. This trend was corroborated by

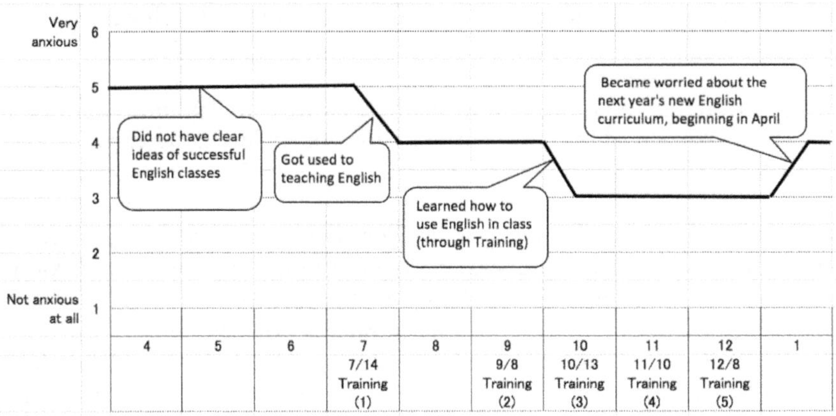

Figure 10.4 Fluctuation of English teaching anxiety of Shika, a junior teacher[7]

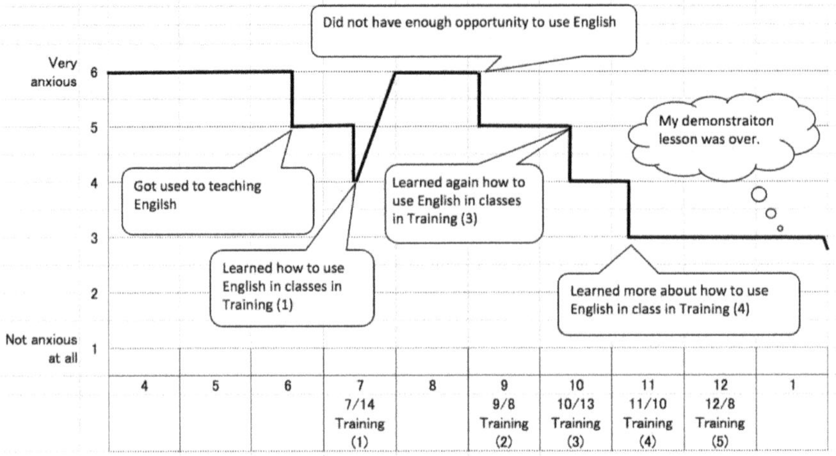

Figure 10.5 Fluctuation of English teaching anxiety of Moji, a junior teacher

his remarks in Interview excerpt 3. Likewise, as Figure 10.5 indicates, the English teaching anxiety of Moji, who was also a junior teacher with one year's experience, decreased each time training was conducted. His comments in Interview excerpt 4 provided a possible reason for this decrease. These two figures, as well as their comments, suggest that junior teachers were readily amenable to the influence of in-service intervention and that they had a lower level of English teaching anxiety as a result.

Interview excerpt 3

Thanks to the training sessions, I managed to gain a concrete idea of successful English lessons. Correspondingly, my English teaching anxiety dropped, especially after the first and second sessions. (R-Shika)

Interview excerpt 4

Each training session reminded me how to use English in classes. This may be one reason for the decrease in my anxiety level after each session. (R-Moji)

On the other hand, Nami, a teacher in school J with eight years' experience, did not respond well to the training sessions. Her anxiety level fluctuated but with little relation to the intervention (Figure 10.6). This anomaly may be due to the influence of the burden of the administrative roles that she had assumed at school. As in Interview excerpt 5, she admitted that the training sessions were meaningful in reducing fellow teachers' anxiety. However, she said that since she was in charge of managing the sessions, her focus was mainly on the

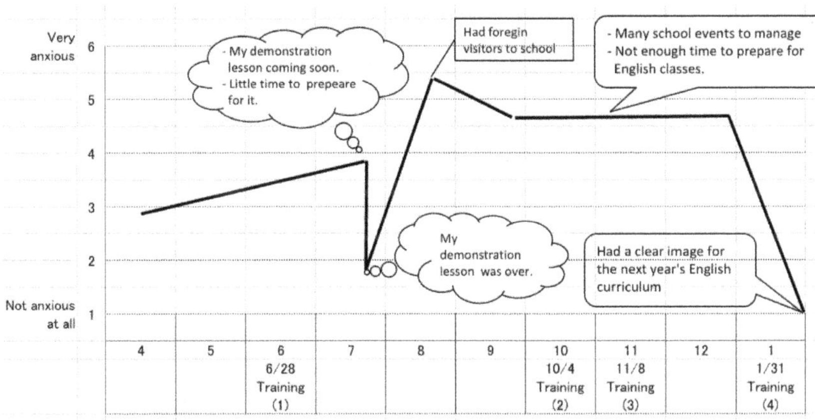

Figure 10.6 Fluctuation of English teaching anxiety of Nami, a teacher with eight years' teaching experience

administrative side, not on the pedagogical one. Furthermore, her mind seemed to be preoccupied by other school events, such as a visit by foreign guests to the school and a school excursion to a popular tourist site where pupils were encouraged to talk to foreign visitors in English. Presumably, the burden of managing these school events led to her having less time to spend on the preparations for teaching English, thereby causing her a higher level of anxiety in October and November. Since these administrative roles tend to be assigned to relatively experienced teachers in schools, it is assumed that the length of teaching experience was found to moderate the effect of the training sessions.

Interview excerpt 5

The training sessions were certainly meaningful in reducing the anxiety levels of my colleagues, but since I was on the managing side of the sessions, I was always worried about the reactions of fellow teachers to them. For example, 'How many teachers attended the sessions?' or 'Did they enjoy the sessions?' and so forth. In addition, I had many school events to take care of. I was so busy that I had little time to prepare well for teaching English in the classroom. I think that's why my anxiety level did not drop easily in relation to the training sessions. (J-Nami)

In this study, the 'English demonstration lesson' was identified as another possible factor influencing changes in English teaching anxiety. In a demonstration lesson, the class is officially open to teachers and school administrators not only from the school with which the teacher is affiliated but also from other schools in and outside of the region. It is also open to supervisors from the local Board of Education as well as university experts. After the demonstration lesson, a reflection session

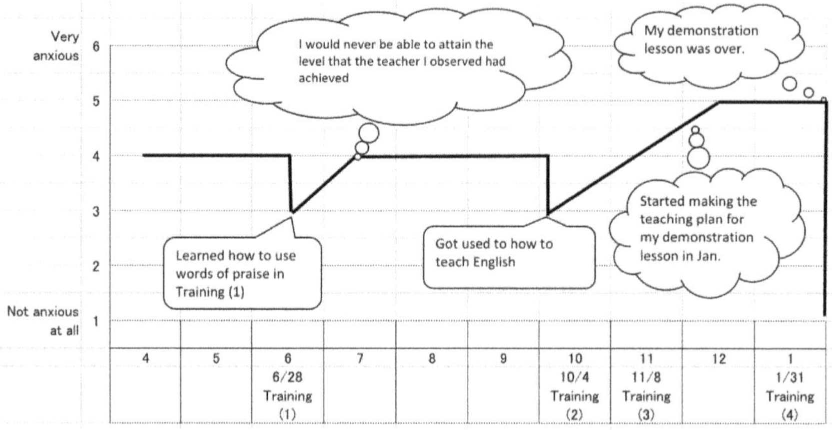

Figure 10.7 Fluctuation of English teaching anxiety of Naka, a junior teacher

is usually conducted, and critical comments are sometimes made by the observers of the lesson. Teachers are supposed to improve their teaching techniques on the basis of the comments. Due to the formal nature of 'English demonstration lesson', the teachers in charge usually spend a lot of time and energy on its preparation and receive feedback for improvement from their colleagues in a rehearsal run. Demonstration lessons are thus generally considered to be challenging experiences that can raise the level of teaching anxiety situationally.

As can be seen in Figures 10.6 and 10.7, the demonstration lesson was always on the minds of the teachers, whether they were relatively experienced or not. Nami, with eight years' teaching experience at elementary school, felt that the scheduled demonstration lesson was quite a challenge, and after it was over, her anxiety level dropped sharply from 4 to 2, as seen in Figure 10.6. Naka, a junior teacher with two years' experience, felt the same way as Nami, and after the demonstration lesson was finished, her anxiety level plummeted from 5 to 1 (see Figure 10.7). Naka's comment in Interview excerpt 6 also shows how the demonstration class, vis-à-vis the intervention programme implemented, was influential for her in determining her level of English teaching anxiety. These two examples are therefore good indicators that the 'demonstration lesson' is a strong determinant of the level of English teaching anxiety at elementary schools.

Interview excerpt 6

In January, I was scheduled to give the demonstration class. I was required to speak in English in front of the other teachers and administrators present. Thinking about the teaching plan for it more seriously <though I had been thinking about the plan since April> (remarks in the angular bracket made in a quiet voice) and wondering how I should use

> English in it in a more concrete manner, my anxiety level jumped up in December ... However, it fell sharply after the demonstration class was over. You know, the pupils really enjoyed the class. At the same time, they showed a serious attitude towards learning English. Comments from other teachers were favourable in general ... It is true that the training sessions were good, but I was obsessed by the approaching demonstration class and thus my English teaching anxiety did not dissipate easily in response to the sessions. (Brackets ours: J-Naka)

Turning to the satisfaction graphs, another interesting observation can be made. Among the junior teachers, the fluctuation of English teaching anxiety was roughly in inverse proportion to that of their satisfaction level with the in-service training programme. For example, comparing the fluctuations in the anxiety level (a solid line) with those in the satisfaction level (a dotted line) in Figure 10.8, both of which were drawn by the same junior teacher, Moji, an approximate inverse relationship between them can be confirmed, implying that the intervention programme worked effectively in reducing anxiety, assuming that the satisfaction level is a sign of success.

By contrast, among the relatively experienced teachers, the fluctuation in English teaching anxiety was in proportion to that of their satisfaction level with the intervention programme. For instance, comparing the fluctuations in the anxiety level (a solid line) with those in the satisfaction level (a dotted line) in Figure 10.9, both of which were drawn by the same teacher, Tana, with seven years' experience, a roughly proportional relationship can be observed. This relationship indicates that although they were satisfied with the intervention programme, their anxiety level was affected more by other contextual factors, such as

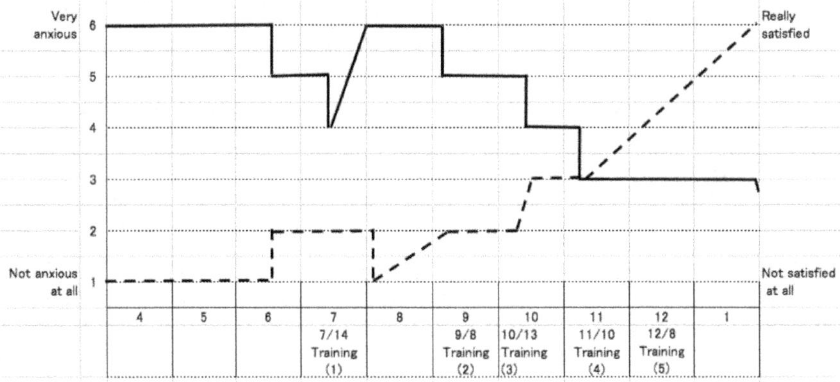

Figure 10.8 Fluctuation of Moji's English teaching anxiety and satisfaction levels with the intervention programme (the former is the same as that shown in Figure 10.5 above, cited again here for the purpose of comparison). A solid line (—) represents the anxiety level, while a dotted line (- - -) stands for the satisfaction level.

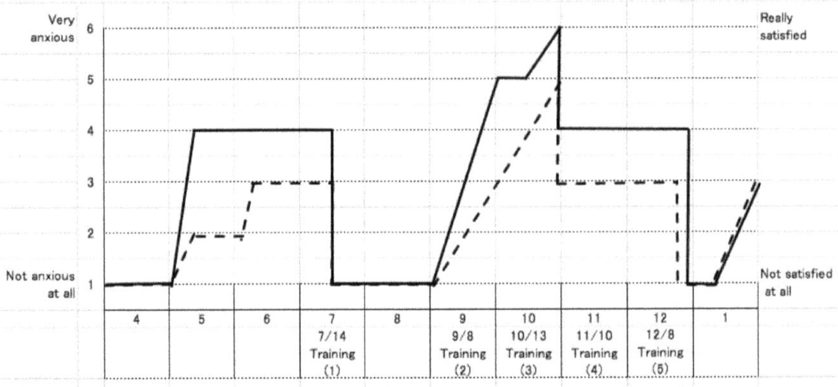

Figure 10.9 Fluctuation of Tana's English teaching anxiety and satisfaction levels with the intervention programme. A solid line (—) represents her anxiety level, while a dotted line (- - -) stands for her satisfaction level

(1) their administrative roles, which may be associated with their length of experience at elementary school, and (2) the demonstration class that they were scheduled to teach. Consequently, their English teaching anxiety did not decline easily in response to the training sessions.

Conclusion

After examining elementary school teachers as a group, no major change in English teaching anxiety over the two terms was confirmed in this study. It remained high and the intervention programme implemented did not seem to work effectively. However, looking at individual teachers, their English teaching anxiety levels fluctuated dynamically, sometimes in response to the training sessions given, at other times in relation to such contextual factors as the administrative roles assigned to them and the demonstration classes scheduled. These findings clearly corroborate Dewaele's remark for L2 learners (2012: 43) cited in the introductory section of this chapter: *learner* (in the current study, teacher) *attributes are neither stable nor context independent, but interact with the context and vary over time.*

Several implications can be drawn from the results of this study. First, in-service training programmes aimed at reducing English teaching anxiety can be meaningful, especially for junior teachers, who were found in our sample to be quite susceptible to the intervention. Second, with regard to relatively experienced teachers, cutting down as much as possible their administrative roles and letting them focus on what they teach, in this case English, might be helpful. Once they have enough time for preparation, the intervention may work effectively for them, too. Third, the 'demonstration lesson' is a strong factor affecting teachers. Since conducting demonstration lessons is considered to be good practice in the teaching profession, getting rid of them altogether might not be a wise decision. Instead, providing teachers with ample scaffolding and helping them to reduce their teaching anxiety associated with the practice might be a practical solution that would be welcomed by teachers in Japanese public elementary schools.

As is the case with L2 learners, L2 teachers are complex entities individually. Their attributes are not stable even within a limited time period. Furthermore, teachers are not independent of the context surrounding them. Thus, it is not advisable to look at teachers cross-sectionally as a group without thinking about the context in which they find themselves. A closer look at the data obtained over time from each individual teacher, along with the contextual factors affecting him/her, as was attempted in this study, is definitely needed in future studies to elucidate the 'emotional rollercoaster' involved in language teaching.

Post-Reading Tasks

(1) This chapter highlights the challenges facing primary school teachers in Japan as curriculum reforms require them to teach English despite having had little or no L2 teacher training. What do you think are some possible solutions to the predicaments that Japanese primary school teachers currently face in teaching English? You might like to think about this in terms of what solutions education policymakers could provide or in terms of what individual teachers and their schools could do to deal with this situation.

(2) Anxious people tend to modify their behaviour in order to mitigate feelings of anxiety or avoid anxiety-inducing situations. Can you think of some ways in which anxiety might affect teachers' pedagogical approaches and use of the target language?

(3) We know that environmental factors can dynamically interact with people's feelings of anxiety. With the participants in this study in mind, what are some contextual factors (e.g. at classroom, institutional and societal levels) which could affect L2 teachers' anxiety levels?

Notes

(1) A part of this study was supported by the Grants-in-Aid for Scientific Research (No. 16K02989) provided by the Japan Society for the Promotion of Science (JSPS). We are grateful for the support and cooperation of the teachers, school administrators, the local Board of Education and graduate/college students of EFL involved in this project.

(2) It is true that 'Foreign Language Activity' includes the possibility of teaching languages other than English. However, the newly introduced Elementary School Course of Study suggests that the English language be taught in principle in elementary schools nationwide (MEXT, 2017a: 145).

(3) To help ease this situation, a variety of in-service training sessions, ranging from those sponsored by MEXT to those conducted by local (prefectural or municipal) Boards of Education, have been implemented (Ikeda *et al.*, 2019). For example, at a national level,

MEXT has commissioned the British Council, a UK-based educational institution, to train motivated teachers to be the leaders in English language teaching. The Leaders of English Education Project (LEEP), launched in 2014, is a five-year project aimed at upgrading English language teaching across Japan. By 2019, about 1,000 elementary school teachers will be trained. Although in-service training such as LEEP has been producing future leaders in the field, its effects so far have been limited. This is partly due to the sheer number involved. In Japan, as of August 2017, there were 19,929 elementary schools (with 4,319,595 third- to sixth-grade classes), and a total of 418,776 teachers are working in them (MEXT, 2017c).

(4) The pre-set criteria were (1) the length of general teaching experience at elementary school, (2) the length of English teaching experience at elementary school and (3) whether the teacher was in charge of a demonstration class during the year in which the current study was conducted.

(5) Test-retest (with one-day interval) reliabilities for Items 1 and 3 were $r =. 792$ (teacher anxiety) and $r =. 853$ (programme satisfaction) respectively. The population we used for confirming reliabilities comprised 17 elementary school teachers who worked for a different school in the same city in which the present study was conducted.

(6) Timeline graphs have also been used in small-scale qualitative studies. Miura (2011), for example, used a timeline graph showing the retrospective changes in learning motivation of six successful foreign language learners in Japan.

(7) Generally speaking, in primary and secondary schools, the academic year in Japan begins in April and ends in March of the next year. The first (Spring) academic term starts in April and ends in July, while the second (Autumn) begins in September and concludes in December. January is the beginning month of the third (Winter) academic term, which ends in March. Summer recess is usually in August.

References

Asahi Shimbun (2017) Shogakko eigo wo oshieru chikaratte? [What kind of abilities are required in teaching English at elementary school?]. See https://www.asahi.com/articles/DA3S13062944.html (accessed 30 July 2017).

Daubney, M. (2010) Language anxiety in English teachers during their teaching practice. Unpublished PhD dissertation, University of Averio, Portugal. See https://ria.ua.pt/bitstream/10773/3720/1/240596.pdf (accessed 28 February 2018).

Dewaele, J.-M. (2012) Personality: Personality traits as independent and dependent variables. In S. Mercer, S. Ryan and M. Williams (eds) *Psychology for Language Learning: Insights from Research, Theory and Practice* (pp. 42–57). New York: Palgrave Macmillan.

Dewaele, J.-M. (2018) Why the dichotomy 'L1 Versus LX User' is better than 'Native Versus Non-native Speaker'. *Applied Linguistics* 39, 236–240.

Dewaele, J.-M. and Alfawzan, M. (2018) Does the effect of enjoyment outweigh that of anxiety in foreign language performance? *Studies in Second Language Learning and Teaching* 8, 21–45.

Dewaele, J.-M. and MacIntyre, P.D. (2014) The two faces of Janus? Anxiety and enjoyment in the foreign language classroom. *Studies in Second Language Learning and Teaching* 4, 237–274.

Dewaele, J.-M. and MacIntyre, P.D. (2016) Foreign language enjoyment and foreign language classroom anxiety: The right and left feet of FL learning? In P.D. MacIntyre, T. Gregersen and S. Mercer (eds) *Positive Psychology in SLA* (pp. 215–236). Bristol: Multilingual Matters.

Ehrman, M.E. (1996) An exploration of adult language learning motivation, self-efficacy and anxiety. In R.L. Oxford (ed.) *Language Learning Motivation: Pathways to the New Century* (pp. 81–99). Honolulu, HI: University of Hawai'i SLTCCS.

Fredrickson, B.L. (2001) The role of positive emotions in positive psychology: The broaden-and-build theory of positive emotions. *American Psychologist* 56, 218–226.

Fredrickson, B.L. (2003) The value of positive emotions. *American Scientist* 91, 330–335.

Gardner, R.C., Tremblay, P.F. and Masgoret, A. (1997) Towards a full model of second language learning: An empirical investigation. *The Modern Language Journal* 81, 344–362.

Gass, S. and Mackey, A. (2000) *Stimulated Recall Methodology in Second Language Research*. New Jersey: Lawrence Erlbaum.

Gkonou, C., Daubney, M. and Dewaele, J.-M. (eds) (2017) *New Insights into Language Anxiety: Theory, Research and Educational Implications*. Bristol: Multilingual Matters.

Horwitz, E. (1996) Even teachers get the blues: Recognizing and alleviating language teachers' feelings of foreign language anxiety. *Foreign Language Annals* 29, 365–372.

Horwitz, E. and Young, D.J. (eds) (1991) *Language Anxiety from Theory and Research to Classroom Implications*. Englewood Cliffs, NJ: Prentice-Hall.

Ikeda, M., Imai, H. and Takeuchi, O. (2017) Jizokukanona kyoinkenshu shisutemno kochiku: Shougakkoeigo (gaiokugo) katsudoniokeru fuannokeigenni shotenwoatete [Development of a sustainable system of in-service teacher training: Focusing on the reduction of teacher anxiety for teaching English at primary schools]. *JES Journal* 17, 4–19.

Ikeda, M., Imai, H. and Takeuchi, O. (2019) An innovative approach to in-service teacher training for teaching English at Japanese public elementary schools. In H. Reinders, S. Ryan and S. Nakamura (eds) *Innovation in Language Learning and Teaching: The Case of Japan* (pp. 42–57). New York: Palgrave Macmillan.

Kunt, N. and Tüm, D.O. (2010) Non-native student teachers' feelings of foreign language anxiety. *Procedia: Social and Behavioral Sciences* 2, 4672–4676. doi: 10.1016/j.sbspro.2012.06.948.

Larsen-Freeman, D. (2016) Classroom-oriented research from a complex systems perspective. *Studies in Second Language Learning and Teaching* 6, 377–393.

Larsen-Freeman, D. and Cameron, L. (2008) *Complex Systems and Applied Linguistics*. New York: Oxford University Press.

Machida, T. (2016) Japanese elementary school teachers and English language anxiety. *TESOL Journal* 7, 40–66.

Machida, T. and Uchida, H. (2015) Kyoshino gaikokugofuanno keigenwo mezashita kyouinkenshu no kaihatsu [Development of in-service teacher training aimed at reducing the anxiety of teachers in teaching English at elementary schools]. *JES Journal* 15, 34–49.

MacIntyre, P.D. and Mercer, S. (2014) Introducing positive psychology to SLA. *Studies in Second Language Learning and Teaching* 4, 153–172.

MEXT (2017a) Shogatsuko gakushshido yoryo [The Elementary School Course of Study Effective from 2020.] See http://www.mext.go.jp/component/a_menu/education/micro_detail/__icsFiles/afieldfile/2018/05/07/1384661_4_3_2.pdf (accessed 30 May 2018).

MEXT (2017b) *Heisei28nenndo eigokyoiku jitsushijyoukyou chosa* [The 2016 Fiscal Year Survey on English Language Education in Japan]. See http://www.mext.go.jp/a_menu/kokusai/gaikokugo/1384230.htm (accessed 28 February 2018).

MEXT (2017c) *Gakko kihon chosa* [Fundamental Statistics Regarding Schools in Japan]. See http://www.e-stat.go.jp/SG1/estat/NewList.do?tid=000001011 (accessed 28 May 2018).

Miura, T. (2011) Motivational trajectories of successful foreign language learners: Six biographical case studies. Unpublished PhD dissertation, Temple University, Japan.

Noels, K.A., Clément, R. and Pelletier, L.G. (1999) Perceptions of teacher communicative style and students' intrinsic and extrinsic motivation. *The Modern Language Journal* 83, 23–34.

Oxford, R.L. (2015) Emotion as the amplifier and the primary motive: Some theories of emotion with relevance to language learning. *Studies in Second Language Learning and Teaching* 5, 371–393.
Piniel, K. and Albert, Á. (2018) Advanced learners' foreign language-related emotions across the four skills. *Studies in Second Language Learning and Teaching* 8, 127–147.
Scovel, T. (1978) The effect of affect on foreign language learning: A review of the anxiety research. *Language Learning* 28, 129–142.
Seligman, M.E.P. and Csíkszentmihályi, M. (2000) Positive psychology: An introduction. *American Psychologist* 55, 5–14.
Song, B. and Kim, T.-Y. (2017) The dynamics of demotivation and remotivation among Korean high school EFL students. *System* 65, 90–103.
Tremblay, P.F. and Gardner, R.C. (1995) Expanding the motivation construct in language learning. *The Modern Language Journal* 79, 505–518.
Yonezaki, M., Tara, S. and Tsukuda, Y. (2016) Shougakko gaiokkugokatudo no kyoukaka teigakunenka nitaisuru shougakkokyouin no fuan. [Primary schoolteachers' anxiety about teaching English as a compulsory subject and teaching English to middle-grade students: Structuring and transition]. *JES Journal* 16, 132–146.
Young, D.J. (ed.) (1999) *Affect in Foreign Language and Second Language Learning: A Practical Guide to Creating A Low-Anxiety Classroom Atmosphere.* Boston, MA: McGraw-Hill.

Appendix: Questionnaire Items Used in the Present Study (originally written in Japanese)

(1) *Are you anxious about teaching English?*

Not at all anxious — Highly anxious
1--------------------2---------------------3---------------------4--------------------5---------------------6

(2) *Please provide reasons for your perception above.*

(3) *Are you satisfied with the training session?*

Quite unsatisfied — Quite satisfied
1--------------------2---------------------3---------------------4--------------------5---------------------6

(4) *Please provide reasons for your perception above.*

Thank you for your cooperation.

11 Emotion Regulation among University EFL Teachers in Japan: The Dynamic Interplay between Context and Emotional Behaviour

Sam Morris and Jim King

Introduction

If we are to fully recognise the importance of emotions in a language teacher's work, then it is crucial to understand how and why they might choose to influence the course of their emotions, be that the quality of the emotion, when it is experienced, its intensity, its length or how it is displayed. Such behaviour is known as emotion regulation (Gross, 2015), and its prevalence in language classrooms cannot be understated: we constantly regulate our emotions in some fashion (Koole, 2009), with Goleman (1995: 57) claiming the activity is a 'full-time job'. Situated and ecologically valid studies of emotion regulation are rare, particularly within language education, but there is increasing agreement that emotions (and consequently emotion regulation behaviours) function on multi-dynamic levels (King & Ng, 2018; Fried *et al.*, 2015). In light of this, emotions should not only be considered as intrapersonal phenomena, but also as being continually shaped by contexts; from the micro-level of a teacher's personal experiences and history, through their relationships with their students, peers and administrators, to the surrounding political, cultural and social systems within which they lie (Boiger & Mesquita, 2012). Endorsing the positions that (1) contexts are not 'monolithic external variables' (Mercer, 2016a: 25) but are subjectively interpreted by individuals, and (2) that the shaping of emotions by context is dynamic, non-linear and best served by the tenets of complexity science (e.g. Larsen-Freeman & Cameron, 2008), this chapter reports on an exploratory project into the emotion regulation behaviour of EFL teachers based at a university in Japan. We demonstrate that experienced teachers skilfully regulate their emotions in diverse ways to achieve a range of goals relating to their perceived responsibilities, their pedagogy and their well-being, and argue that the efficacy of their behaviour must be interpreted in relation to the internal and surrounding contexts that shape it. Given the important mediating role that emotion regulation can play in promoting psychological health (see Gross & John, 2003; Haeussler, 2013), we give special attention to some of the ways that the participants use emotion regulation to manage their well-being.

Emotion Regulation

Emotion regulation is contingent upon *goals*, higher-order motivations of regulation behaviour, and Tamir (2016) suggests that such goals pertain not only to performance and social aims (instrumental goals), but also to an individual's sense of self (epistemic goals), and their psychological health (hedonic goals). Research in general educational contexts shows that teachers apply emotion regulation in aid of each of these goals, including instrumental goals relating to classroom management (Hosotani & Imai-Matsumura, 2011; Sutton, 2004; Yin & Lee, 2012), epistemic goals relating to the perceived responsibilities of teaching (Hagenauer & Volet, 2014; Hosotani & Imai-Matsumura, 2011; Sutton, 2004; Yin & Lee, 2012) and hedonic goals relating to well-being (Haeussler, 2013). Thus, when a teacher wishes to hide their anger from their students it may be because they do not wish to impact on the class atmosphere (instrumental), because they feel it is their tacit responsibility (epistemic) or because they do not wish to feel negative emotions (hedonic).

Of course, teachers need a way of achieving such goals, and in the field of emotion regulation the term *strategies* is used to represent the tangible behavioural routines that modify the courses of emotions. There exists a large number of such strategies, and thus various heuristic frameworks have been proposed to taxonomise them. The most widely utilised framework, and the one that we adopt herein, is Gross's *process model of emotion regulation* (Gross, 2015), which has previously been employed in a range of studies within general education (e.g. Haeussler, 2013; Jiang *et al.*, 2016; Sutton, 2004). While reductionist (see Quoidbach *et al.*, 2015 for a full discussion of its temporal limitations), the model's virtue is its cohesiveness: it accounts for multiple ways that individuals might manipulate their external environments, as well as their own internal cognitions and behaviours, to regulate emotion.

The process model of emotion regulation posits that emotions unfold along a timeline. When an emotional situation is encountered, attention will be drawn to the event and it will be appraised. Should the event be deemed significant, an emotion will be triggered along with behavioural and physiological responses. Five opportunities for emotion regulation are afforded across this situation-attention-appraisal-response timeline. In advance of an emotion taking place individuals may apply *situation* strategies to the external world. These are actions modifying the external environment to manage emotions. *Situation selection* refers to when individuals choose to experience or avoid emotional stimuli – for example, when a teacher avoids teaching a particular class because it is stressful – whilst *situation modification* refers to individuals making changes to an ongoing situation, such as when a teacher stops dead an activity that is causing them frustration (see Morris & King, 2018). Once attention has been drawn to the emotional event *attention deployment* strategies may be employed. These strategies involve moving attention away from the source of an unwanted emotion or towards the source of a desired emotion – for instance, when a teacher ignores a student who is off-task to reduce anger. *Cognitive change* strategies influence the moment of appraisal itself and involve cognitive adjustments to how one evaluates the emotional event in question. A teacher here might excuse bad behaviour because of a student's troubled background. Finally, *response modulation* strategies, which occur towards the end of an emotional episode, target the symptoms of emotions. They are considered to be the only strategy which occurs after the emotion has formed, when teachers may choose to hide or display an emotional expression to the class, such as when a teacher hides their anger from the students.

One of the most exciting consequences of emotion regulation theory is that it affords teachers agency over their emotions, helping them to achieve a wide range of instrumental, epistemic and social goals, as well as playing a mediating role in their well-being (see Brackett *et al.*, 2010; Haeussler, 2013; Hagenauer & Volet, 2014; Hosotani & Imai-Matsumura, 2011; King, 2016b; Sutton, 2004; Yin & Lee, 2012); thus, emotion regulation can be considered an important teaching proficiency influencing a myriad of classroom outcomes. Although some qualitative investigations have been conducted within general education (e.g. Haeussler, 2013; Hagenauer & Volet, 2014; Hosotani & Imai-Matsumura, 2011; Sutton, 2004), little attention has been paid to the role of emotion regulation in language teaching. As we shall see later in the chapter, this is unfortunate since the unique emotional and social responsibilities of language teaching (Gkonou & Mercer, 2017), coupled with the fact that emotion experience and display is culturally informed (Mesquita *et al.*, 2016), means that language teachers who are working in unfamiliar emotional climates are likely to experience subject-specific tensions and stress.

Although emotion regulation behaviour as an action in itself is not unhealthy, it has been suggested that certain strategies are more adaptive than others. Laboratory research, for example, has highlighted the benefits of trait cognitive change behaviours over trait response modulation behaviours (Gross & John, 2003), and studies in general education (particularly quantitative studies) have tended to adopt this rather linear approach (e.g. Chang, 2013; Kafetsios *et al.*, 2012; Tsouloupas *et al.*, 2010). However, there is some evidence to suggest that the relationship between emotion regulation strategies and well-being is more complexly aligned with an individual's sense of emotional dissonance, particularly with regard to their higher-order emotion regulation goals and their identity (Humphrey *et al.*, 2015); thus, the performative nature of teaching means that it may not be maladaptive to use response modulation to achieve instrumental or epistemic goals (Hagenauer & Volet, 2014; Humphrey *et al.*, 2015; Tamir, 2016). For these reasons in particular, we adopt the perspective that emotion regulation should be investigated through a contextually valid methodology that attempts to uncover both the motivating factors and outcomes of event-specific behaviour.

Data Collection and Analysis

The research project discussed herein was designed as an exploration of three general areas of emotion regulation behaviour: the goals that language teachers report, the strategies they use to achieve these goals, and the contextual factors that underlie their behaviours. Data was collected over a six-week period during the second half of the final semester of the academic year, and analysed iteratively from one participant to the next in line with the principles of a grounded theory-based approach (Hadley, 2017).

The research was conducted at Matsugawa University (a pseudonym), a private institution located in a metropolitan area on Honshu, the main island of Japan. Matsugawa University has a significant foreign language department staffed by more than 50 full-time non-Japanese faculty members, who primarily teach skills-based courses to first- and second-year students. Given the aforementioned focus on the temporal, social and cultural components which shape individuals' displayed and experienced emotions, we employed a purposive sampling technique (Dörnyei, 2007) to recruit medium- and long-length career teachers that had taught for a significant amount of time within Japan. The seven teachers (three female, four male) who agreed to take part in the research originated from the USA, the UK and New Zealand, and all had master's degrees in topics related to TESOL, applied linguistics or international culture. They had been teaching EFL for 6–17 years (mean = 12 years), and had all taught in Japan for more than

5 years (mean = 7 years), with the exception of Kenneth (3.5 years). Each participant agreed to take part in an initial interview, a class observation and a subsequent stimulated recall session (Gass & Mackey, 2017). Prior to this, orientation meetings with individual teacher participants were arranged to discuss the goals of the study and gain informed consent. Classroom observations only proceeded once consent was obtained from students.

The interviews with participants were semi-structured in nature, and like other studies focusing on emotion regulation (e.g. Gross & Richards, 2006; Sutton, 2004), began with participants being asked to recall a time in the recent past when they had altered their emotions as part of their work. The proceeding classroom observations and stimulated recall sessions afforded independent observations of emotion regulation behaviour, contextualised the initial interviews and provided highly detailed accounts of event-specific incidents of emotion regulation. During classes, the observer took semi-structured notes on incidents of potential emotion, which were defined to be moments in the class when the observer (himself an experienced language teacher) reasonably considered that the teacher may have been experiencing an emotion. Recorded details included the participants' facial expressions, their movements within the classroom (including where they were looking) and their vocal transactions with interlocutors. In line with best practice (Gass & Mackey, 2017), stimulated recall sessions took place within 24 hours of the classroom observation to ensure that the details of the class remained fresh in the minds of both the participants and the interviewer. Given the short time span between the classroom events and these sessions, it was possible to walk the participant through the lesson from start to end in a form of mental time travel, with the participant commenting on their emotional behaviour throughout, and the audio-recording of the class being used to supplement moments of significant interest. All interviews and stimulated recall sessions took place in a quiet meeting room at the research site, were audio recorded and lasted up to an hour. A research journal was kept for the duration of the study and supported the analytical process.

Formal data analysis was conducted using the data analysis software QDA Miner. To begin, descriptive and structural coding (Saldaña, 2016) of the emotion regulation strategies and higher-order goals was conducted to situate the data within the agreed framework. This was followed by multiple further initial and axial coding cycles. Although generally speaking, individuals employ more than one strategy at a time when regulating their emotions (Heiy & Cheavens, 2014), the coding revealed salient themes that coordinated well with the varying stages of the process model of emotion regulation. Consequently, we took the decision to organise our discussion of the data around four main points: (1) situation strategies, combining both situation selection and situation modification strategies with the focus placed on behaviours that make external world changes to regulate emotions, (2) attention deployment strategies, (3) cognitive reappraisal strategies, and (4) response modulation strategies.

Results and Discussion

Situation strategies and pre-emptive emotional control

All of the teachers consciously used situation strategies for creative control of their work and to maintain their well-being. Control was certainly at the heart of Roger's testimony regarding his omnipresent anxieties at perceived negative opinions of his teaching, feelings which stemmed from a mixture of internal and external sources: Roger reported being a generally anxious person in social situations, he was a relatively new teacher at Matsugawa University having worked there for less than two years, and he had been having problems with a particular student recently which had caused him significant distress. On top of these factors, he continued to feel anxiety from his formative teaching experiences working in an *eikaiwa* (private language school) where he reported that the discordant power dynamic established through the fiscally motivated teacher–client relationship had had a powerful effect on the teacher he has become: 'I had customers who had wielded quite a lot of power over you know, my living, and um yeah, sometimes when students get upset or they're just roll their eyes. I panic.' While consistent feelings of anxiety over a 12-year career may have led some to emotional burnout, Roger has learned a variety of situation selection strategies to maximise his control of classroom variables: he is highly communicative with students, making a sincere effort to engage with them outside of class; he ensures that negative experiences with students are followed up quickly with positive ones, perhaps by taking them aside to talk, or by simply making eye contact and smiling towards them; he eschews technology in favour of paper, claiming that 'it cuts down on chaos'; he employs his own set of class rules in accordance with his own beliefs on say, the use of L1, that go against the institutional status quo; and he frequently arrives in excess of 30 minutes early to class, despite occasional cynicism from colleagues.

Roger's behaviour, when considered as a whole, represents an effective form of emotion regulation known as *proactive coping*, whereby an individual builds skills and resources to predict and prevent future emotional events (Aspinwall & Taylor, 1997). Proactive coping is potent in reducing the long-term effects of negative emotions (Quoidbach *et al.*, 2015), which is particularly important considering that even experienced teachers can be overloaded by the demands of the profession (Hagenauer & Volet, 2014). Although on the surface it may seem that it was relatively easy for Roger to craft such a set of anxiety-reducing strategies, he reported that he was not always so secure, and it is important to remember that proactive coping does not simply arise within a vacuum. Indeed, Roger acknowledged that the high level of autonomy he was provided by institutions such as Matsugawa University and the diverse experiences he had gained through a range of settings had been critical for him to come to grips with his past stressful experiences within the profession:

> I moved to a context where I was allowed to be a better teacher ... (In my first school) the system was too tight. Like you know you could get a trained chimp in there to teach a lesson ... (The job) took its toll. But then when I went to the other *eikaiwa*, it had its problems, but I could do whatever I want. And I you know, I dealt with it better.

Autonomy and control were at the heart of Hannah's use of situation selection strategies too. With six years in teaching, Hannah was one of the least experienced teachers interviewed. She noted that coming into the profession, she had held a strong vision and desire to be 'a great teacher ... to change people's lives', but she reported feelings of frustration and disappointment, particularly in the early years of her career, that she wasn't always 'being who I want to be'. One of the ways that Hannah had dealt with these negative feelings was through situation selection: she had chosen to teach an extra elective which afforded her a substantial deal more control over content than her contractually obliged classes, and the impact of this control was revealed through her testimony:

> I like smile more ... I have more energy ... When (students are) like 'this was really interesting' and 'I can– I've changed this in my life because of what we learned' ... It's really motivating I think to me.

Dörnyei and Kubanyiova (2014) have drawn on the notion that constraints on teacher autonomy are a demotivator, as well as on ideal and possible selves theories, to suggest that teachers make efforts to maintain their vision of their ideal teaching image even when expected to follow extrinsic protocols. Hannah's use of situation selection here certainly appears to be an interpretation of this solution. It is clear that for Hannah, positive reactions to her work feed her ideal teacher self; therefore, when actively taking the opportunity to teach a class where she can forge her own learning goals, she is rewarded with a greater sense of well-being. From an emotion regulation perspective, the situation selection that Hannah is engaging in here is a form of *job crafting*: actions taken which help provide more meaningfulness to one's regular work (Wrzesniewski & Dutton, 2001), and which can help to sustain positivity across careers (Falout & Murphey, 2018). Hannah is becoming what Falout and Murphey (2018: 225) call a 'transformer', one who in the creation of her own course has redefined her role to teach more than just language, and her students' comments echo the way she describes her ideal teaching self, whether she believes she has yet attained such an ideal or not.

Attention deployment and the social responsibilities of language teaching

In contrast to the pre-emptive use of situation strategies, attention deployment strategies were applied for more immediate emotional gratification. For the teachers at Matsugawa University, their use highlighted the complex and dynamic relationships between a teacher's attempts to maintain their hedonic well-being whilst accomplishing their epistemic responsibilities, particularly within the confines of teacher–student relationships.

For four of the participants, their application of *distraction*, the movement of cognitive attention away from a source of emotion, was habitually applied to offset the negative emotions experienced when interacting with problematic students. Frank was particularly cognisant of this strategy: 'I have dead zones in my classrooms … Areas that I will avoid, often consciously.' Such a dead zone became readily apparent during his observed class, where it was noted that he rarely made eye contact with a particular student on the left side of the room. Frank revealed that his relationship with this student had recently soured following a reprimand for sleeping in class. Thus, when Frank was observed to be distracting his attention, he recognised that it was because he 'didn't want to engage … I don't quite know what to do with (her) … I don't want to have to go back and re- and revisit that memory.'

The first thing to note is that Frank's comments highlight the emotional complexities of maintaining positive working relationships with students in the face of behavioural transgressions. It is unfortunately true that fractured group cohesion can lead to an arduous school year; a thought to which Abigail, who sees some of her students at Matsugawa University four times a week, was well attuned: 'when you see students that often, you wanna be on the right side of them.' Language teaching relies on social interaction, perhaps even more so than other subjects due to its communicative methodologies and intercultural foundations (Gkonou & Mercer, 2017), and some have noted that the responsibility for imparting enthusiasm and positive emotions to students is in itself a stressful act: 'a motivational burden' (Acheson *et al.*, 2016; King, 2016b). This is heightened within the Japanese university context where it has been reported that non-Japanese lecturers like Frank are tacitly expected to be welcoming, energetic and positive (King, 2016b; McVeigh, 2002). We contend from Frank's testimony that a potential reason for the stress of the motivational burden is his emotion regulation goal conflict. When faced with the intractable student, Frank was in the uncomfortable position of negotiating his desire for a productive social relationship against his epistemic notion of teacher responsibility. He eventually fell on to the side of the latter, perhaps in response to the very real consequences that ignoring the behaviour might cause for his relationship with the rest of the class: 'I need to send the message that this is not okay.' Unfortunately, Frank's chosen resolution came at a price, and a week after the reprimand he still referred to the incident as a 'trauma'. From the perspective of well-being, Frank's distraction should be viewed as a short-term solution. Frank is performing emotional distancing, a potential symptom of burnout when used habitually (Maslach *et al.*, 2001). Such behaviour could also be considered short-sighted, in that it may lead to further degradation of his relationship with the student, though since the semester was drawing to a close at Matsugawa University, there is also the sense that Frank could perhaps simply wait out the end of term.

Equally common were the participants' uses of a similar, though opposing, attention deployment strategy: that of *concentration*. Rather than being repelled by strained relationships, four participants reported being drawn towards, or lingering around, students whose level of engagement with the class was high. Abigail, for example, spoke enthusiastically about a group of students she frequently engages with: 'the richness of the interactions I have with them, it makes them enjoyable. Yeah, I might linger a little bit longer talking to them than I do with other students'. She reported that the group were of a high level, were studious, asked questions from 'a place of real curiosity', and self-selected to sit geographically close to her desk at the front of the class. It was clear from her interview that Abigail recalled these interactions fondly, and this makes sense when we consider that attending to positive events (both at the time, and later in our minds) brings benefits to overall well-being (Quoidbach *et al.*, 2015). Indeed there is a sense in the way that the participants applied concentration of a form of positive emotional labour (Humphrey *et al.*, 2015): that perhaps by attending to 'good' students, teachers are able to find some emotional congruence, and offset their negative emotions.

Such behaviour was not without its own emotion regulation goal tension, however, particularly for Dennis and Abigail, who reported conflicts over the ethics of preferential student attention. This delicate balance of negotiating hedonic emotion regulation goals against epistemic responsibility has recently been highlighted by Gkonou and Mercer (2017: 35) in what they have called 'the teacher paradox'. The authors therein suggest that there is a difference between treating students 'fairly' and 'equally', an idea that is worthy of further discussion, particularly on what such behaviour might resemble in practice. For now, however, it seems that for some of the teachers at Matsugawa University, the emotional difficulty of balancing students who they would class as brilliant, or problematic, against the class group as a whole, remains a stressor tied to their emotion regulation goals which are themselves in a dynamic state of contention.

Cognitive change and the temporal dimensions of emotional behaviour

Emotion regulation, of course, can take place over a range of timescales, from the micro-scales of our mental processes, to the ontogenetic scales of our lifetimes, and it has been shown that it is routine for emotional responses to mature across careers as a result of experience (Mevarech & Maskit, 2015). It became apparent, however, throughout the data analysis, that *cognitive reappraisal* was applied even more dynamically by the participants, and this was most clearly illustrated in a series of incidents described by Dennis. During his initial interview Dennis described the following incident from a recent class in which a student shared some offensive stereotypical beliefs:

> One of the students was going on about how dirty Chinese people are and um, and he meant it … I was just just a short shortest period of disappointment, but then again caught myself and I thought actually no this is good, because this is the environment I want to create where we can share our thoughts.

Dennis here is describing prototypical cognitive reappraisal: in the milliseconds before an emotion took hold, he was able to reassess whether the unfolding emotion was constructive in light of his instrumental goals and modify the course of the emotion into something more productive. Of course, a complexity view suggests a series of underlying influences on this behaviour, and upon further exploration, it was revealed that a much deeper change had occurred in Dennis during the two years post-MA, when he worked as an assistant language teacher (ALT) in a Japanese junior high school:

> In the English class, the– it's all rote learning and the *ichinensei* (first year) kids would stand up … (the teacher) would just go 'No. Again. No. Again. No. Again.' And you could see all the– see them wilting in the spotlight.

Dennis spoke despairingly of this incident and others during his time as an ALT, describing what he saw as the crippling pedantry of the Japanese education system playing a causal role in the students' inability to engage orally in the language classroom, an issue that has been shown to be pervasive in the Japanese university EFL context (King, 2013). He reported that these critical incidents, coming at a time when Dennis himself was becoming a parent and reflecting on what education should be and do, when mediated through cognitive reappraisal, led to a stark downshift in the optimism that he had for students' success. These experiences have led him to conclude that issues such as silence lie 'at the feet of the education system', helping him to feel empathy for the students. Such empathy, Mercer (2016b: 91) argues, is 'vital' to language education given its 'centrality of relationships, social interaction, communication and intercultural competence', and it is hard to argue with such a stance, at least from the perspective of teacher well-being, given the positive outcomes of Dennis's reappraisals, which have led to reduced frustration over time.

Five participants also suggested that applications of cognitive reappraisal functioned in more local timelines, most commonly across the school year. Again, we exemplify with Dennis, for whom such behaviour was vividly reported in his descriptions of ongoing interactions with a particularly difficult student. Dennis described his student as the 'alpha male', who had 'excellent English' and 'so much potential', but he also felt continually let down by him, and his emotions had fluctuated across the academic year. He reported three major changes:

> Explicitly in my mind I was like 'no I'm not having this. I can't start this way.' So called him up and gave him a bit of a dressing down, um in front of everybody, in the hopes of sort of putting him in his place a little bit. (Beginning of the academic year)

> Okay now, now I'm going to be his best buddy ... I'm going to reward him by being more social and friendly. (Midpoint of first semester)

> I'm back to tough cop you know. Bad cop routine. I um, quite frosty ... There's a sense of resignation about it. (Midpoint of final semester)

Dennis begins the year by adopting strict control methods as a way to cement his identity as the leader of the class, serving epistemic and instrumental higher-order goals. He then transitions through cognitive reappraisal into emotional warmth, serving social goals, before transitioning again into resignation and emotional distance by the year's end (hedonic goals). Dennis's behaviour is a clear example of how individuals and their contexts are inseparable: that they are joined in a dynamic reciprocal relationship (King, 2016a); thus, through emotion regulation behaviour, teachers can shape and be shaped by their contexts over time. Dennis's regulation and resulting emotional displays directly influence the student's behaviour, and thus all proceeding interactions with the student. These in turn reflect back, affecting Dennis's future emotion regulation behaviour. Dennis referred to his changes throughout this relationship as 'exhausting his emotional repertoire' and it was surprising to the researchers just how common such an experience was: four participants spoke of their negative feelings of frustration and anger at student behaviour having been reappraised into what they deemed resignation as the academic year progressed. Since the data was collected at a late stage of the academic year, again there was a strong sense that these four teachers were in a kind of holding pattern until their stressful situations disappear of their own accord. Dennis's emotional journey, however, is indicative of the way that priorities in emotion goal conflict may be reorganised and resolved by teachers over time as contexts dynamically fluctuate. It suggests that while many teachers move into the school year with a sense of optimism, under sustained difficult circumstances they are liable to prioritise their well-being over other more instrumental goals, particularly if students do not respond well to their teaching.

Response modulation and the epistemic responsibility of emotional honesty

Emotional regulation, of course, can refer to an individual choosing to *genuinely express* an emotion or to *suppress* it, and both strategies are encapsulated by our final heuristic category of response modulation behaviours. As in previous studies (Hagenauer & Volet, 2014; King, 2016b; Sutton, 2004) the teachers at Matsugawa University generally accepted that it was their responsibility to suppress their negative emotions, particularly when they originated outside of the classroom. They were also cognisant of the power of exaggerated positive emotions in the generation of enthusiasm (Dörnyei & Kubanyiova, 2014; Hatfield *et al.*, 1994). Reminiscent to participants in King's (2016b) study who described their behaviour using performative terminology, the teachers at Matsugawa University used indicative language to suggest that their response modulation behaviours had become automatised, with Roger noting that he simply 'switches it on', and Frank referring to his behaviour as 'showtime!'

Interestingly, however, the participants seemed to wear different masks for different age groups, with the five participants who taught both freshman and sophomore students reporting stark differences in their behaviour between the two cohorts. With freshmen, teachers reported wanting to display 'warmth' and 'compassion' (Roger), be more 'lenient' (Abigail), or more 'solicitous' (Dennis), but they also reported controlling their emotions more: 'I'm much more aware of what I need to be expressing' (Dennis). In contrast, with sophomores the participants reported to show 'more frustration' (Abigail), to not be 'quite so animated' (Emma) and they reported being more emotionally honest: 'I am more relaxed about my emotions and managing them and um, just let come what comes' (Dennis). The participants lent diverse voices to the reasons why such a change in emotional behaviour occurred. There was a sense throughout the interviews that the students at Matsugawa University should be performing at a higher level after one year's university experience: 'they should be a bit more responsible' (Abigail). In addition, Roger noted that sophomore classes contained the word 'academic' in their titles, which he felt as an institutional pressure to treat them more seriously. Dennis felt that the power disparity had changed: 'with the freshman students I feel like, you know, the quintessential teacher with the – all powerful that needs to coax these people towards where I want them to be. Uh in sophomore there's much less of that'. No matter the reason, four of the five teachers reported that sophomore students generally did not meet their classroom expectations leading to a greater degree of overall stress than in freshmen classes.

Kenneth observed that since 20 is the age of adulthood in Japan, the mostly 19-year-old sophomore students may be undergoing emotional identity changes themselves. This sense that the teachers were dealing with young people on the cusp of adulthood was a particularly important issue for Emma, who reported a strong epistemic responsibility to provide emotional honesty to the sophomore students. This became clear through discussions of her observed class, the focus of which was a video introducing a series of sensitive topics such as female genital mutilation, gender inequality and pornography. Emma commented that when she had taught this lesson to a different group the previous week (unfortunately not observed) she found herself displaying very honest emotions:

> They wanted to know what X-rated was and you know we were talking about the sexualised images of women, and pornography ... And I said it just makes me crawl when I see it ... Even now you can feel, I'm like agghh! So I got that in class and and they – I let them know.

Even a week later in the interview, it was noted that Emma displayed strong emotions at the memory of this incident, but importantly, perhaps in response to the pronounced Japanese cultural tendency towards emotional suppression (Matsumoto *et al.*, 2008), or the tacit feeling rules prohibiting the display of powerful emotions within distal social relationships in Japanese society (Safdar *et al.*, 2009), Emma saw her conscious decision to display genuine emotion as a teaching point for her 'quiet' class:

> I got passionate, but I wanted them to see that ... to get some reaction ... To be able to show that I can get passionate but I can – I can regulate my

> emotions as well like. I'm reacting to these and this is how we react … I don't expect them to need to go and follow up on any of this or, but I do expect them to react even somewhere in there as a human.

Emma's testimony reflects what Cowie (2011) and Loh and Liew (2016) have described as the 'moral' dimensions of language education: that content invariably moves beyond a focus on the simple nuts and bolts of sentence construction, towards a skill set for articulating complex opinions on emotive issues. In this instance, there is the sense that Emma is modelling an emotional morality: that she is demonstrating the emotional responses she feels it is important for the students to display and acknowledge when dealing with sensitive issues. Though engaging with these topics has the potential to be overtly distressing for teachers, Emma did not report this experience as being pervasively stressful. On the contrary, she appeared to feel a sense of congruence that her epistemic 'responsibility of an adult with these topics to young impressionable people' had been achieved; exemplifying the notion that emotion regulation cannot be defined as maladaptive when considered outside of its context (Hagenauer & Volet, 2014; Humphrey *et al.*, 2015; Tamir, 2016).

This moral dimension (or what Emma calls her 'human response') could also extend into the duty of care discourse, which purports that teachers in Japan have a prominent care-giving role to play in the lives of their students (King, 2016b). An incident described later by Emma suggested that she felt her role in this capacity also calls for genuine emotional responses, and on occasion physical displays of support in the form of a hug. The incident in question was a highly sensitive conversation with a male student who had come to ask for permission to miss class since he would be accompanying his partner to receive an abortion: 'he needed to tell me about how he was feeling and his disappointment and his confusion, and we were talking for almost an hour … I gave this student a hug because tap, tap on the shoulder didn't suffice.' Emma was aware that affection of this kind could be considered inappropriate, and recalled that during her pre-service training in her home country she had been strongly warned away from physical contact with students. Yet this attitude is not universal, and Emma cited a pivotal experience in a Korean elementary school where she was critiqued for not being physical enough with the students as informing a more contextually nuanced approach to her interactions. While she still had 'mixed' feelings on the use of touch and affection, in light of the seriousness of the incident at Matsugawa University, and the contextually appropriate duty of care, the use of Emma's hug becomes readily understandable. Emma's role as caregiver here was undoubtedly intensely emotional, and Emma reported to feeling the ramifications for an extended period. As a highly experienced teacher of more than

15 years, it was her support network of family and mentors that she could call upon to deal with issues such as these, but Emma questioned whether that might not always be the case:

> Does anyone have that kind of appropriate training to deal with teacher burnout? Teacher stress? Teacher frustration? Um depression? ... What if people are getting depressed as a result of working here? How do we deal with that? Or any institution for that matter like, what is your mental health policy for your teachers?

We agree with Emma's sentiments, and support Haeussler's (2013) conclusions that institutional support can play a salient role in reducing negative emotions and informing healthy emotion regulation strategies by, for example, implementing formal support procedures, which have the added secondary benefits of increasing staff loyalty and commitment, and reducing levels of burnout.

Conclusions and Recommendations

This study has demonstrated that language teachers employ emotion regulation in skilfully diverse ways to achieve higher-order goals pertaining to their perceptions of responsibility, their classroom instruction and their well-being, and that such behaviour is contingent on dynamic interpretations of their internal and external contexts. Through the use of interviews, class observations and stimulated recall sessions with a group of EFL teachers employed in a Japanese university context it has been shown that teachers apply *situational strategies* in proactive attempts to maintain control over the positivity of their emotional experiences, *attention deployment strategies* to afford immediate, though short-sighted emotional gratification in correspondence with the quality of the student–teacher relationship, *cognitive reappraisal* in diverse temporal timescales to adapt to classroom stressors, and *response modulation* to support their teaching goals and relationships. It has become clear throughout that the efficacy of behaviours and emotion regulation strategies cannot be removed from the contextual factors that they emerged within, and that with regards to well-being, incidents of emotion regulation goal conflict frequently contribute to negative teacher emotions and stress. Training and professional development programmes can benefit from reflecting on the diverse ways in which teachers use their emotions to achieve classroom goals and their efficacy within context; raising awareness of the negative emotions that may occur during goal conflict, and how these may be resolved; and considering more apt long-term solutions to classroom behavioural concerns. The issues we raise in this study suggest that it is the institutions themselves which have a leading role to play in affording teachers skills that they may use to manage their emotions effectively. Considering that emotion regulation behaviours remain underexplored, we believe emotion regulation to be fertile research ground for delineating the emotional skills of teachers and finding effective solutions to support them in the management of their classrooms and their psychological health.

Post-Reading Tasks

(1) This chapter discusses situational strategies of emotion regulation. Think about something frustrating or stressful that you have been experiencing in your current teaching or working context. What situational strategies could you employ to take charge of the situation?
(2) We considered how teachers might deploy their attention in order to regulate their emotions. Try to think of a time in your current working context when you have employed the distraction strategy. Why did you use it and was it effective? How about a time when you have employed the concentration strategy?
(3) Cognitive change is another emotion regulation strategy considered in this chapter. How have your emotions evolved as you have become more experienced in your current working context?
(4) The chapter also focuses on response modulation strategies. When do you think it is (or would be) appropriate to be emotionally honest with students, and when do you think it is (or would be) appropriate to suppress your emotions? Why?

References

Acheson, K., Taylor, J. and Luna, K. (2016) The burnout spiral: The emotion labor of five rural U.S. foreign language teachers. *The Modern Language Journal* 100 (2), 522–537.
Aspinwall, L.G. and Taylor, S.E. (1997) A stitch in time: Self-regulation and proactive coping. *Psychological Bulletin* 121 (3), 417–436.
Boiger, M. and Mesquita, B. (2012) The construction of emotion in interactions, relationships, and cultures. *Emotion Review* 4 (3), 221–229.
Brackett, M.A., Palomera, R., Mojsa-Kaja, J., Reyes, M.R. and Salovey, P. (2010) Emotion-regulation ability, burnout, and job satisfaction among British secondary-school teachers. *Psychology in the Schools* 47 (4), 406–417.
Chang, M.-L. (2013) Toward a theoretical model to understand teacher emotions and teacher burnout in the context of student misbehavior: Appraisal, regulation and coping. *Motivation and Emotion* 37 (4), 799–817.
Cowie, N. (2011) Emotions that experienced English as a Foreign Language (EFL) teachers feel about their students, their colleagues and their work. *Teaching and Teacher Education* 27 (1), 235–242.
Dörnyei, Z. (2007) *Research Methods in Applied Linguistics*. Oxford: Oxford University Press.
Dörnyei, Z. and Kubanyiova, M. (2014) *Motivating Learners, Motivating Teachers: Building Vision in the Language Classroom*. Cambridge: Cambridge University Press.
Falout, J. and Murphey, T. (2018) Teachers crafting job crafting. In S. Mercer and A. Kostoulas (eds) *Language Teacher Psychology* (pp. 211–230). Bristol: Multilingual Matters.

Fried, L., Mansfield, C. and Dobozy, E. (2015) Teacher emotion research: Introducing a conceptual model to guide future research. *Issues in Educational Research* 25 (4), 415–441.

Gass, S.M. and Mackey, A. (2017) *Stimulated Recall Methodology in Applied Linguistics and L2 Research* (2nd edn). New York: Routledge.

Gkonou, C. and Mercer, S. (2017) Understanding emotional and social intelligence among English language teachers. *ELT Research Papers* 17 (03). London: British Council.

Goleman, D. (1995) *Emotional Intelligence: Why It Can Matter More Than IQ*. New York: Bantam Books.

Gross, J.J. (2015) Emotion regulation: Current status and future prospects. *Psychological Inquiry* 26 (1), 1–26.

Gross, J.J. and John, O.P. (2003) Individual differences in two emotion regulation processes: Implications for affect, relationships, and well-being. *Journal of Personality and Social Psychology* 85 (2), 348–362.

Gross, J.J. and Richards, J.M. (2006) Emotion regulation in everyday life. In D.K. Snyder, J. Simpson and J.N. Hughes (eds) *Emotion Regulation in Couples and Families: Pathways to Dysfunction and Health* (vol. 2006). Washington, DC: American Psychological Association.

Hadley, G. (2017) *Grounded Theory in Applied Linguistics Research*. New York: Routledge.

Haeussler, S. (2013) Emotional regulation and resilience in educational organisations: A case of German school teachers. PhD thesis, Northumbria University.

Hagenauer, G. and Volet, S.E. (2014) 'I don't hide my feelings, even though I try to': Insight into teacher educator emotion display. *The Australian Educational Researcher* 41 (3), 261–281.

Hatfield, E., Cacioppo, J.T. and Rapson, R.L. (1994) *Emotional Contagion*. Cambridge: Cambridge University Press.

Heiy, J.E. and Cheavens, J.S. (2014) Back to basics: A naturalistic assessment of the experience and regulation of emotion. *Emotion* 14 (5), 878–891.

Hosotani, R. and Imai-Matsumura, K. (2011) Emotional experience, expression, and regulation of high-quality Japanese elementary school teachers. *Teaching and Teacher Education* 27 (6), 1039–1048.

Humphrey, R.H., Ashforth, B.E. and Diefendorff, J.M. (2015) The bright side of emotional labor. *Journal of Organizational Behavior* 36 (6), 749–769.

Jiang, J., Vaura, M., Volet, S. and Wang, Y. (2016) Teachers' emotions and emotion regulation strategies: Self and students' perceptions. *Teaching and Teacher Education* 54, 22–31.

Kafetsios, K., Nezlek, J.B. and Vassilakou, T. (2012) Relationships between leaders' and subordinates' emotion regulation and satisfaction and affect at work. *The Journal of Social Psychology* 152 (4), 436–457.

King, J. (2013) *Silence in the Second Language Classroom*. Basingstoke: Palgrave Macmillan.

King, J. (2016a) Introduction to the dynamic interplay between context and the language learner. In J. King (ed.) *The Dynamic Interplay Between Context and the Language Learner* (pp. 1–10). Basingstoke: Palgrave Macmillan.

King, J. (2016b) 'It's time, put on the smile, it's time!': The emotional labour of second language teaching within a Japanese university. In C. Gkonou, D. Tatzl and S. Mercer (eds) *New Directions in Language Learning Psychology* (pp. 97–112). Dordrecht: Springer.

King, J. and Ng, K.-Y.S. (2018) Teacher emotions and the emotional labour of second language teaching. In S. Mercer and A. Kostoulas (eds) *Language Teacher Psychology* (pp. 141–157). Bristol: Multilingual Matters.

Koole, S.L. (2009) The psychology of emotion regulation: An integrative review. *Cognition and Emotion* 23 (1), 4–41.

Larsen-Freeman, D. and Cameron, L. (2008) *Complex Systems and Applied Linguistics*. Oxford: Oxford University Press.

Loh, C.E. and Liew, W.M. (2016) Voices from the ground: The emotional labour of English teachers' work. *Teaching and Teacher Education* 55, 267–278.

Maslach, C., Schaufeli, W.B. and Leiter, M.P. (2001) Job burnout. *Annual Review of Psychology* 52, 397–422.

Matsumoto, D., Yoo, S.H., Nakagawa, S. and Multinational Study of Cultural Display Rules (2008) Culture, emotion regulation, and adjustment. *Journal of Personality and Social Psychology* 94 (6), 925–937.

McVeigh, B.J. (2002) *Japanese Higher Education as Myth*. New York: M.E. Sharpe.

Mercer, S. (2016a) The contexts within me: L2 self as a complex dynamic system. In J. King (ed.) *The Dynamic Interplay Between Context and the Language Learner* (pp. 11–28). Basingstoke: Palgrave Macmillan.

Mercer, S. (2016b) Seeing the world through your eyes: Empathy in language learning and teaching. In P.D. MacIntyre, T. Gregerson and S. Mercer (eds) *Positive Psychology in SLA* (pp. 91–111). Bristol: Multilingual Matters.

Mesquita, B., De Leersnyder, J. and Boiger, M. (2016) The cultural psychology of emotions. In L. Feldmann Barrett, M. Lewis and J.M. Haviland-Jones (eds) *Handbook of Emotions* (4th edn) (pp. 393–411). New York: The Guilford Press.

Mevarech, Z.R. and Maskit, D. (2015) The teaching experience and the emotions it evokes. *Social Psychology of Education* 18 (2), 241–253.

Morris, S. and King, J. (2018) Teacher frustration and emotion regulation in university language teaching. *Chinese Journal of Applied Linguistics* 41 (4), 433–452.

Quoidbach, J., Mikolajczak, M. and Gross, J.J. (2015) Positive interventions: An emotion regulation perspective. *Psychological Bulletin* 141 (3), 655–693.

Safdar, S., Friedlmeier, W., Matsumoto, D., Yoo, S.H., Kwantes, C.T., Kakai, H. and Shigemasu, E. (2009) Variations of emotional display rules within and across cultures: A comparison between Canada, USA, and Japan. *Canadian Journal of Behavioural Science / Revue canadienne des sciences du comportement* 41 (1), 1–10.

Saldaña, J. (2016) *The Coding Manual for Qualitative Researchers* (3rd edn). London: SAGE.

Sutton, R.E. (2004) Emotional regulation goals and strategies of teachers. *Social Psychology of Education* 7 (4), 379–398.

Tamir, M. (2016) Why do people regulate their emotions? A taxonomy of motives in emotion regulation. *Personality and Social Psychology Review* 20 (3), 199–222.

Tsouloupas, C.N., Carson, R.L., Matthews, R., Grawitch, M.J. and Barber, L.K. (2010) Exploring the association between teachers' perceived student misbehaviour and emotional exhaustion: The importance of teacher efficacy beliefs and emotion regulation. *Educational Psychology* 30 (2), 173–189.

Wrzesniewski, A. and Dutton, J.E. (2001) Crafting a job: Revisioning employees as active crafters of their work. *The Academy of Management Review* 26 (2), 179–201.

Yin, H. and Lee, J.C.-K. (2012) Be passionate, but be rational as well: Emotional rules for Chinese teachers' work. *Teaching and Teacher Education* 28 (1), 56–65.

12 Should I Stay or Leave? Exploring L2 Teachers' Profession from an Emotionally Inflected Framework

Peter De Costa, Wendy Li and Hima Rawal

Introduction

The field of applied linguistics has increasingly recognized that emotions play an important role in shaping teachers' pedagogical practices in the classroom, professional identity construction and teachers' well-being in general. In addition, research on language teacher emotions has evolved beyond cognitive approaches (Gkonou & Mercer, 2017) to include sociocultural and political perspectives (Benesch, 2017; Loh & Liew, 2016). For example, language teacher emotions are now examined in terms of how emotions are discursively constructed (Golombek, 2015) at personal, institutional and societal levels (Wolff & De Costa, 2017). Despite the growing interest in language teacher emotions, there is a paucity of research in documenting language teachers' emotional experiences in the Nepali context. Against a backdrop characterized by globalization and English as a lingua franca (Erling & Seargeant, 2013; Tsou & Kao, 2017), there has been an emergent emphasis on enhancing citizens' competitiveness in the global economy. Such an emphasis is noticeably manifested in educational systems that have adopted English as a medium of instruction (Toh, 2016), with developing countries, in particular Nepal (Sah & Li, 2018), not having been spared from such a phenomenon.

In 2010, the Ministry of Education (MoE) in Nepal implemented the Education Act (Government of Nepal, 2010), which made both Nepali and English the legitimate instruction languages in public schools. As a result, a large number of public schools in Nepal have geared towards English as a medium of instruction (EMI), regardless of their 'low socioeconomic status and limited resources' (Sah & Li, 2018: 110). Problems have been reported, however. Specifically, these problems, which are associated with EMI adaptation, include the lack of educational infrastructure for effective implementation, linguistically qualified teachers and professional training courses for in-service teachers (Phyak, 2016; Sah & Li, 2018). Managing the conflicts between societal expectations on English language education and classroom realities (i.e. large classes, high labour demands on grading, teaching for examination purposes and limited professional support and guidance) has resulted in teacher emotional exhaustion and emotional burnout, which ultimately has led to attrition within the profession (De Costa *et al.*, 2018).

In this chapter, we seek to give voice to the English teachers whose emotional experiences and feelings have remained invisible within the broader EMI trend in Nepal. Viewing emotions as being discursively constructed, we adopted Benesch's (2017) conceptualization of emotion labour in order to explore how two Nepali English teachers negotiated the emotional demands and labour of work as we seek to illuminate the professional challenges and realities these English teachers encountered.

Literature Review

Conceptualizing emotion labour

The construct of emotional labour was first coined by Hochschild and described as 'the management of feeling to create a publicly observable facial and bodily display' (1983: 7). Hochschild (1979, 1983) further argued that humans monitor and manipulate their external emotion display and also consciously negotiate the 'inner feelings' (1979: 562) which are considered normative or socially appropriate in particular social contexts or situations. These 'inner feelings', though tacit, are deemed as emotional conventions or 'feeling rules' that allow people to evaluate whether their emotion displays are appropriate in particular social situations or contexts. Individual management of emotions in response to the feeling rules in daily life are thus framed as *emotional management* (Hochschild, 1979). Relatedly, emotional labour refers to how individuals deploy emotional management in the workplace to display emotions and feelings deemed desirable and appropriate in that context. Thus, individuals' performance of emotions and feelings become part of the job as individuals learn to also navigate tacit institutional feeling rules at their respective places of work.

Hochschild's notion of emotional labour was later adopted in applied linguistics to explore its application to language teaching (e.g. Ho & Tsang, 2008; King, 2016). Benesch (2012, 2017), in particular, has contributed much to the establishment of emotion labour as a central concern in language teacher education research. Benesch (2017) proposed to replace 'emotional labour' used in Hochschild's original conceptualization with 'emotion labour'. According to Benesch, the juxtaposition of 'emotion' and 'labour' indicates the departure from a cognitive perspective that considers emotions as personal traits, and instead proposes to understand emotions as discursively constructed and shaped by external environments and social norms that they need to adhere to. Therefore, by adopting a poststructural perspective, Benesch defined emotion labour as the efforts by which 'humans actively negotiate the relationship between how they feel in particular work situations and how they are supposed to feel, according to social expectations' (Benesch, 2017: 37–38). In this study, we used Benesch's conceptualization of 'emotion labour' to guide our understanding of how Nepali teachers negotiated an EMI policy implemented at their schools.

Benesch's (2017) conceptualization of emotion labour and that of several other teacher emotion researchers enlarges Hochschild's (1979, 1983) understanding of emotion labour in several ways. First, instead of investigating emotion labour through the dichotomy of performing individuals' fake selves and authentic selves at the workplace, Benesch argues that one's self is constructed historically and also in everyday interactions. Second, as Zembylas (2005) pointed out, emotion labour is manifested in the everyday dynamics of teaching and is thus considered as routine practices, such as managing the classroom, grading student essays, etc. However, this everyday routine facet of emotion labour warrants close scrutiny in order to expose the sociopolitical and unequal power relations in which teaching is embedded (Benesch, 2017; Miller & Gkonou, 2018; Zembylas, 2005). A contemporary understanding of emotion labour within applied linguistics, therefore, enables researchers to examine how language teachers' exercise of emotion labour is shaped by the feeling rules at the workplace that are often politicized by normative ideologies about the teaching profession.

Researching emotion labour in language teacher education

As a result of professional norms, teachers are expected to manage their emotional states in classroom or school settings and be sensitive to the emotional needs of learners by encouraging and motivating them through appropriate displays of emotions, such as showing care and love, warmth, affection and concern (Gkonou & Miller, 2017; King, 2016; Loh & Liew, 2016; Miller & Gkonou, 2018; Yin *et al.*, 2017). This discourse of an *ethics of care* (Gilligan, 1982; Gkonou & Miller, 2017; Miller & Gkonou, 2018) accounts for most of the emotion labour in language teaching. While the emotion labour of teaching is mainly discussed in the interaction between teachers and students, Yin *et al.* (2017) also examined the emotion labour in the interaction between teachers and their colleagues in the Hong Kong context where teachers were engaged in much collaborative work outside the classroom (Pang *et al.*, 2016). In addition, recent studies on language teacher emotions have examined teacher emotion labour in relation to other constructs, such as *teacher agency* (Miller & Gkonou, 2018), *teacher burnout* (Acheson *et al.*, 2016) and *teacher identity* (Wolff & De Costa, 2017), thus illustrating how it can be a useful construct in expanding our understanding of language teacher education.

Within English language education, Benesch (2017) explored the emotion labour of ESL teachers in relation to high-stakes literacy tests by theorizing emotion labour as discursively constructed. Her findings revealed that the conflict between teaching to improve students' academic literacy in general and teaching for passing the tests not only constrained their exercise of agency in teaching, but also elicited the discourse of shame. Similarly, Loh and Liew (2016) adopted a discursive approach in their investigation of the emotion labour of secondary English language teachers in Singapore. Due to government demands to improve English language literacy and the culture of testing, the Singaporean English teachers in their study experienced emotional conflicts between teaching English in accordance with their teaching beliefs and teaching English to prepare students for the high-stakes tests. The emotion labour of teaching, according to Acheson *et al.* (2016), might unveil more serious issues such as emotional exhaustion or attrition. Acheson *et al.* (2016) studied the emotion labour of five foreign language teachers in rural US high schools. They found that having internalized the ideology of English as a lingua franca, students were demotivated to learn other foreign languages. Thus, the emotion labour of having to motivate students created an excessive burden for their focal teachers. Moreover, due to the lack of foreign language assessment in the test system, the institution and community in which their teacher participants worked did not provide sufficient support to help ease the burden. The performance of emotion labour and lack of emotional resources eventually affected the teachers' willingness to stay in the profession.

While most studies have explored language teachers' negative emotions derived from performing emotion labour in school, Miller and Gkonou (2018) examined language teachers' positive emotions in relation to emotion labour in US and British tertiary settings. Drawing on Benesch's (2017) poststructuralist view, they investigated language teachers' common emotional experiences through administering a questionnaire and conducting semi-structured interviews. Their findings demonstrated that while discourses of a *teaching-as-caring ethic* at school led to positive emotions in teachers' work lives, this ethic was not part of teachers' 'natural' feelings of caring (Miller & Gkonou, 2018: 8); instead, such an ethic was constructed and subsequently fostered socially and politically at the workplace. To raise the awareness of this latent feeling rules at work, Miller and Gkonou underscore how teachers' reflexive practices 'intersect with their emotion experiences and choices to exercise agency through emotion labour' (2018: 9). Relatedly, other teacher emotion researchers such as Wolff and De Costa (2017) have emphasized the need to explore teacher emotions from an ecological stance, by taking into consideration how social, institutional and personal forces influence teacher emotions. Specifically, they have called for a longitudinal investigation of how teacher emotions are impacted by events that occur at the macro-national policy level, and meso-institutional and micro-individual teacher levels. In short, teacher emotions are multi-dimensional and permeate across a range of social contexts.

Investigating the emotion labour of Nepalese teachers

Sharing many of the school culture realities with the above-mentioned studies, our study takes a discursive approach in the analysis of the emotion labour of secondary English language teachers in public schools in Nepal. As Acheson *et al.* (2016) observed, emotion labour is institutionally imposed on teachers in the hope of complying to latent feeling rules about the teaching profession that give reference to what feelings or emotion expressions are appropriate for teachers. These tacit rules are shaped by overarching ideologies about language and also the teaching profession (Benesch, 2017). Drawing on insights from Benesch's (2017) conceptualization of emotion labour and from Wolff and De Costa's (2017) ecological framework of investigating emotion from multi-dimensions, this study explores how the tacit feeling rules at the macro- (societal) and meso- (school and community) levels shaped the English teachers' emotion labour and how the performance of different types of emotion labour led to their emotional burnout.

Methodology

Focal participants

Our two participants, Chhabi and Sunil (pseudonyms), were interviewed by the third author (Hima). Hima actively sought to ensure that Chhabi and Sunil were comfortable sharing their emotions related to their teaching experiences. The interviews were guided by some open-ended interview questions, which were adopted from the interview questions for English language teachers in Benesch's book (2017: 111) (see Appendix). Benesch combined Zembylas's (2005) list of teacher emotions and sample questions from his Meta-Emotion Questionnaire. Each participant was interviewed for two hours (during two one-hour interviews). Although most of the interviews were conducted in English, the participants switched to the use of Nepali quite often, especially when they adopted some sayings and proverbs in Nepali. Because the analysis drew largely from the content of the interviews, author Hima transcribed the interviews verbatim, without going into details on the paralinguistic features such as tone, pitch of voice, gestures or pauses. When transcribing the interviews, Hima also checked with participants about a few audio segments where the recordings were not clear. Then, she translated into English the parts of interviews where Nepali was used, which were later reviewed by a colleague of Hima's who worked in the English education department in Nepal.

Chhabi

Chhabi is a 25-year-old English teacher at a K-10 public school in the western part of Nepal. He became an English teacher in a non-tenure position immediately after graduating with a master's degree in English Education from a large public university in Nepal. At the time of our study, Chhabi had not taken the permanent teacher recruitment exam conducted by the Ministry of Education. Chhabi teaches high school English and each of his classes comprises 80 to 100 students. Although he encountered several emotion labour-related issues, these issues emerged because of his ambition to be a teacher.

Chhabi had always wanted to be a teacher despite the fact that many children would dream of going into other professions. His aspiration stemmed from his observation of the respect his own teachers would receive from their students. On the one hand, it was his personal desire to join the teaching profession. On the other hand, the perceived lack of professionalism in teaching from the societal point of view made him question if he should stay in the job or quit.

Sunil

Sunil is a 30-year-old former English teacher at a public high school in the eastern part of Nepal. He taught for six and a half years before he quit his job in 2017. He had started teaching English at the school after his graduation from a large public university, having specialized in English Education. His classes often consisted of over 100 students, which according to him, was normal in many public schools in his area. He is currently working as a programme coordinator in a non-governmental organization that is committed to improving infant health in Nepal. Initially, he wanted to be a good teacher and his inspiration came from some of the good teachers who had left positive imprints in his mind. However, his desire eroded when he exited the teaching profession.

Despite the early enthusiasm shown by both teachers regarding their decision to pursue an English language teaching career, Chhabi and Sunil experienced emotional highs and lows, which will be examined in greater detail in subsequent sections, during their teaching careers.

Study context

The number of private schools in Nepal has been increasing at an accelerated speed and the main reason for such rapid change has been the English-medium instruction in such private schools. The ideologies of English-as-a-global language and English-as-social-capital have had a strong influence on how society views the role English plays in the Nepalese educational context (Phyak, 2016). Irrespective of whether students attend public or private schools, they all are required to take the same national level exam to exit from their high schools, which is administered by the Ministry of Education. While the textbooks are produced and distributed by the national level curriculum development centre, private schools generally introduce and expose the students to extra and international standard textbooks and various other resources. Not surprisingly, teachers are often under intense pressure to prepare their students for the school leaving exam, a phenomenon that has resulted in limited teacher agency and autonomy (De Costa *et al.*, 2018).

Data analysis

To guide our data analyses, we adopted Braun and Clarke's (2006) six-phase thematic analysis framework.[1] First, we familiarized ourselves with the data and generated initial codes, which was followed by the examination of themes that emerged from the data. The themes that recurred throughout the data from both participants were as follows: (1) emotion labour and the pressure of English-medium instruction, (2) emotion labour and lack of teacher agency, (3) emotion labour and lack of mentoring and (4) emotion labour and emotional burnout. We then extracted the related excerpts from the data that would support the common themes found across data from both participants. By examining and analyzing each of these themes, this study addresses the following research questions:

(1) What factors at the macro- (societal) and meso- (school and community) levels shaped the English teachers' emotion labour?
(2) How did the performance of different types of emotion labour lead to our focal participants' emotional burnout?

Findings and Discussion

Emotion labour and the pressure of English-medium instruction

One of the recurring themes from both participants' data was their emotion labour related to the growing demand for English-medium instruction (EMI) in Nepalese schools. Having to choose between complying with the mandate to use English only in the classroom and the need for the use of the first language (Nepali) in specific teaching contexts to facilitate students' learning caused great pressure and frustration among two English teachers. Both participants attributed the emotional low they encountered to the pressure of using English as the medium of instruction in their teaching.

> *Excerpt 1: I need to use translation (Chhabi)*
> I use English most of the time in my classes because I want my students to practise as much English as they can. The parents and the school also desire that but there are many situations in my classes when I need to use translation during the teaching. There are some students whose first language is not Nepali but still they can understand Nepali because it is the national language. Another English teacher who teaches in my school is a graduate from a private English medium college and he only uses English in his classes … at least he claims [laughs]. This pressure to use only English in English classes from the school administration frustrates me sometimes but I think it is okay to use Nepali sometimes when the students struggle to understand.

As revealed in Excerpt 1, Chhabi pointed out that the pressure from the administration level to use only English in English classes caused an emotional burden, as this leaves him in a contested space to make choices between what is required of him and what makes the teaching-learning process easy. In addition, Chhabi's statement exhibits that using only English was not practical when it came to communicating with students with varying proficiencies in English. Likewise, Sunil asserted:

> *Excerpt 2: EMI has made many lives miserable (Sunil)*
> I was able to use only English in my classes. I could do that but some students specially with low English background would lag behind others … so I switched to Nepali sometimes … and the principal said '*sir tapaai ta angrezi teacher ho ni math science teacher ho ra bich bichma Nepali bolnalaai*' [sir, you are an English teacher and not a science or math teacher to use Nepali in between]. That was embarrassing to me. I did not use to do that because I could not use English throughout my classes but just to help my students to understand. *Yo angreziko bhoot le kati dherai teacher laai dukhi aatma banayeko chha.* [The ghost of this English language has made many teachers' lives miserable].

Although Sunil is no longer in the teaching profession, he explicitly expressed his dissatisfaction with the English-only policy that many

Nepalese schools are trying to adopt, describing its presence as a ghost that haunts teachers. Although the teachers sought to make judicious use of the first language to navigate the meaning making process, the English-only policy suppressed their agentive power to do so. The pressure was not only being imposed by the school administration but also by the students' parents. Thus, the administrative pressure and the parents' desire to make the students proficient in English placed an additional burden on teachers, which in turn contributed to their emotion labour and exhaustion. Despite the dissatisfaction evidenced in the above excerpts, both participants stated that they generally tried to comply with the idea of using English as a lingua franca in their respective classrooms. Chhabi stated, 'I know I do not teach content courses but I teach a language course. The language is English, not other languages which are less commonly used. So, using English to teach English is reasonable, but the use of the mother tongue to ease the learning process for students should be allowed'. Similarly, Sunil noted that he did not like the idea of teaching content courses through English as that might add 'more burden on both teacher and the students'. However, he also acknowledges that 'using English in English classes is not a bad idea if some use of mother tongue is permitted'. In short, the contested views of both participants exhibited that their management of emotion labour was associated with their perceptions of English as an international lingua franca as they attempted to negotiate the emotional burden and pressure imposed on them due to the EMI policy.

Emotion labour and lack of teacher agency

According to Grandey (2000), personal and organizational factors influence individuals' emotion regulation processes. Organizational factors include job autonomy and social support from supervisors and co-workers. In the context of this study, it was not only the exhaustion of emotion labour at the physical and mental level that prompted one participant to question his decision to choose the teaching profession and the other participant to quit his job. Rather, it was also the lack of teacher autonomy in relation to their pedagogical practices that led them to dissociate with their profession.

Excerpt 3: I feel very helpless (Chhabi)

I have learnt so many theories of language teaching and learning in my English Education and English Language Teaching courses. I was so excited with the feeling of using them in my classes, but I do not have control over what I do. I might be able to do some tasks and activities sometimes, but I have to finish the course in a time frame and then revise the whole course to prepare my students for the exams. After all, it is the students' scores and pass percentage that determine my success as well as the school's success. I feel very helpless and my every action becomes less energetic.

Excerpt 4: I had no control over anything (Sunil)
One of my dissatisfactions in the teaching job was that I had no control over anything. I wanted to bring interesting tasks, videos, etc. in the English classes, but I was advised to use the textbook produced by the government because the students' scores in the exams mattered the most, to the parents and schools and perhaps the society also evaluated a particular school in terms of the pass percentage. The school's pamphlets and brochures would then have the pass percentage printed on them. No one would care about the volcano of mixed feelings inside a teacher. I never felt having any type of authority.

Excerpts 3 and 4 demonstrate that the pressure of preparing the students for the high-stakes exams and the expectation of using English only in the classes imposed upon them by the administration, parents and society as a whole impeded their free use of teaching methods. This, in turn, constricted their exercise of teacher agency and autonomy. This scenario is similar to the 'performance culture' experienced by Singaporean teachers in Loh and Liew's (2016) study who were also pressured to deliver strong student exam results. This whole scenario would have resulted in the draining of teacher efforts. However, despite the lack of teacher agency and the pressure to target their teaching to the high-stakes exams, both Chhabi and Sunil remained resilient in their teaching and successfully managed their emotion labour. Putting aside their frustration and relative helplessness to exercise their agency, they attempted to navigate the complexities and dynamics of their respective teaching situations.

Emotion labour and lack of mentoring

Both participants disclosed that they experienced a lack of mentoring from the teacher educators in their teaching contexts. Chhabi, for example, lamented the lack of mentoring during his teacher induction period:

Excerpt 5: Should I stay or leave? (Chhabi)
I had expected that I would be provided a lot of support during the early years of my teaching. I though the senior teachers would guide me, help me … do you get what I mean? I thought they would hold my hand and show me the way … instead they just gave me the entire responsibility over the subject I was assigned to teach without much resource and support … one senior teacher once told me to teach his class and he never restarted … there was not much course left to teach but still I felt he was so irresponsible … I just feel a lack of guidance and direction for my teaching and for my further progress in the profession … I feel should I stay or leave the job to find some other job?

Whereas Chhabi experienced a lack of professional guidance during his initial years of teaching, Sunil experienced this gap even in the later years of his teaching.

> *Excerpt 6: Feedback … nothing related to ELT (Sunil)*
> Sometimes the local teacher educators used to come to the schools to observe our teaching, but they were not very helpful. The feedback used to be very personal rather than professional. Once I attended a teacher training in the headquarters of my district. I liked the tips given by the educator, but they were all general tips … nothing related to English language teaching. Then, the same educator came to observe my class after a few days … said that I did not seem interested in teaching … actually it was a day when I was revising what I had already taught so there were not any activities … later, I came to know that his expertise lay in mathematics education … how could his feedback help me in improving my teaching of language … that was very awkward.

Yin *et al.* (2017) found that teachers' perception of trust in colleagues helps them to cope with the perceived challenges caused by emotion labour. Thus, they suggested that schools should facilitate an atmosphere of trust. By contrast, Excerpt 6 shows that before Sunil quit his job, he expected specific guidance regarding ELT from the teacher educators assigned to observe his teaching. Sunil stated that he was not experiencing any professional growth while he was in the teaching profession.

Despite the lack of mentoring, guidance and professional support, both teachers attempted to be engaged in some sort of professional development opportunities on their own.

> *Excerpt 7: I want to keep growing (Chhabi)*
> I attend the conference organized by Nepal English Language Teachers' Association and [I] like to join teacher trainings … read tips in teaching effectively in the internet … I want to keep growing and find as many opportunities to learn as possible although I fail to use all the techniques I learn due to time pressure and large number of students to handle.

These resourceful efforts illustrate how Chhabi's willingness to grow professionally led him to try to overcome the negative emotions that resulted from a lack of expected support and mentoring. In other words, Chhabi sought to take matters into his own hands and manage his emotions as he found creative ways to sustain his professional development. On the other hand, Sunil explained that although he had been willing to grow professionally, he felt that he was 'like rotten … doing the same thing like robots every year same content and same methods every year … like stagnated food'. He conceded that he 'did not feel [like he was] progressing at all'. Hence, Sunil's resistance to learning from the experts of other subjects and his feeling of job stagnation exemplifies how it is not always possible for teachers to constructively manage emotions that may be dampened because of a lack of professional support.

Emotion labour and emotional burnout/exhaustion

Apart from our participants' lack of mentoring support from teacher educators, one of the major issues related to the emotion labour they engaged in was their exhaustion. This exhaustion was manifested in terms of physical labour and perceived emotional fatigue.

> *Excerpt 8: Tiring: emotionally, physically and mentally (Chhabi)*
> I teach for about 10 hours in a day ... six hours at the school and four hours of tuition outside of school ... I have to prepare lesson plans for each of my class at the school which takes much of my time ... the students' English proficiency is not very high and so I have to use translation a lot of times ... I rarely achieve my goals set in the lesson plans. The lesson plans are never checked well by anyone but the principal of the school has made it mandatory ... it's just a burden to add in the fatigue. I feel exhausted at the end of the day ... feel like taking the voice rest for some time but the next day the same routine continues ... I have to speak loudly in the class as I teach large classes of about eighty to a hundred students. Most of the time I am standing and moving around the class. It is really emotionally tiring ... also physically and mentally.

Chhabi's exhaustion took on physical, mental and emotional dimensions, with each dimension being interrelated to the others. Importantly, he made explicit reference to these varied dimensions, even though the distinction between mental and emotional exhaustion was somewhat blurred. Despite all these challenges, Chhabi sought professional sustenance. He conceded, 'I think no job is free of challenges. Teaching is not an easy job and after all I chose this myself. Although my family and relatives tell me to find a decent job, I think all the hard work is worth [it] when it comes to educating so many lives ... to leave an impact on people's lives'. His resistance to giving up despite his exhaustion further illustrated the emotion labour he had to endure. In a similar vein, Sunil disclosed that he had become tired of the demands of his job.

> *Excerpt 9: I was waning ... drained (Sunil)*
> I was a different person when I started teaching. I had so much energy and positivity ... [but] after about four years, it was too much. I was investing a lot of my time and effort, but I had to conduct some before and after school tuition classes to supplement my low teaching salary

> in order to support my family. However, teaching so many classes in a day started making me exhausted. I was waning inside and it was only seven years of the job ... my life was like a very busy routine without any benefit ... then I got a chance to volunteer in a sports and health event near my village ... people liked my work ... I had put equal amount of effort or even less ... [and] it prompted me to change my profession ... However, I did not give up teaching immediately ... I tried to find out reasons to stay, but I was really drained of my internal energy and will power to continue. I miss teaching and sometimes teach the children in the sports project, but I do it voluntarily and just for my happiness. I wish I did not have to leave.

The above excerpt shows that Sunil's burnout is related to multiple issues. First, although he worked hard to cope with his teaching responsibilities, he was drained by the excessive amount of work on his part. This predicament was exacerbated by his socioeconomic situation: teachers in Nepal are paid less relative to other professions. Thus, they take on additional work outside of school for supplementary income to support their families. Next, despite his internal desire to stay in the profession, Sunil found it hard holding on to his teaching job. His indecisiveness shows how he strove to manage his emotional exhaustion despite the challenges. He sought to find ways to stay in the job even though he had been facing several challenges such as the pressure to use English only in the classes and the pressure to gear his teaching towards test preparation, while grappling with other socioeconomic issues. However, the unfortunate situation of his quitting the job signals how the commodification of emotions could take different forms: while it might give strength to someone to stay in the job despite challenges (e.g. Chhabi), it could also cause someone to give it up (e.g. Sunil). Crucially, our findings are in line with those of Acheson *et al.* (2016) who found that emotional exhaustion and burnout affect teachers' willingness to stay within the teaching profession.

Conclusion and Implications

This study sought to investigate how our participants' emotion labour was related to various factors that led to their emotional exhaustion. To summarize, the four major themes that were found to be connected to their emotion labour were: (1) their perceived pressure related to the use of EMI in their multilingual classes, (2) the lack of mentoring for their professional growth, (3) their inability to exercise agency and autonomy in targeting the test-oriented teaching and (4) emotional exhaustion as a whole. While one participant is still striving to remain in the profession despite all the challenges, the other has already quit his job, thereby illustrating how the intricacies of emotion management can exist at different levels.

As stated, teachers' emotional exhaustion can be examined from three different levels: the micro-, meso- and macro-level. At the micro-personal level, although the two participants showed their interest in becoming English teachers, their interest suffered from limited teacher agency in choosing the appropriate teaching methods and having to comply with the imposed institutional policy of using English only in the classroom. Consequently, they had to wrestle with emotion labour in order to sustain themselves professionally at work, despite the causes that led to emotional burnout. At the meso-school level, their emotion labour was enhanced due to the lack of interaction with colleagues and support from the administrators. At the macro-societal level, the ideology of English as the lingua franca and a powerful language had been widely accepted and internalized by the government, schools, parents and even teachers themselves. The prevalence of this ideology has contributed to Chhabi and Sunil's perceived lack of autonomy in their teaching practices and overall professional growth.

Zembylas (2005) suggested that an examination of teachers' emotions and emotion labour can thwart the unfavourable conditions in which students and teachers are situated by opening up discussions on how to challenge and transform these demanding conditions in productive ways. In our study, Sunil's decision to leave the profession is the result of having to negotiate the emotion labour at his school. By giving voice to Sunil's emotional experience, this study revealed that teacher attrition is closely related to the negotiation of emotion labour in the workplace. At the macro-level, English is considered as an international lingua franca, supported by the Education Act policy (Government of Nepal, 2010) and the government's promotion of using English as the medium for instruction. This educational stance is advocated even though many schools do not have appropriate linguistic resources or enough qualified teachers. Therefore, teachers like the participants in this study were left on their own to navigate the parents' and administration's expectations of them without receiving any mentoring and sufficient professional guidance.

Given these conditions and in light of the findings of our study, we call for the incorporation of the affective dimensions of teaching in English language teacher education to better prepare teachers for emotion labour in the workplace. As suggested in King (2016), this could be achieved by making teachers aware of different types of emotion labour they might experience or anticipate at individual, institutional and societal levels. Then, informing them about different strategies to cope with those emotions would equip them to navigate the layers, dynamics and complexities of emotion that might affect them as teachers and their teaching profession. In addition, we hope the stories of our two focal teachers, Chhabi and Sunil, will provoke much-needed discussion on bringing teachers' emotions into the public discourse as they find new ways to address the different types of emotion labour at school.

Post-Reading Tasks

(1) Based on the two focal participants' experiences in this study, how would you negotiate emotion labour at your own workplace? How would emotion labour influence your decisions to stay in or leave the teaching profession?
(2) One of the reasons Sunil dropped out of the teaching profession was his perceived pressure of EMI policy. If he had agentive power to freely choose the medium of instruction in his classes, how do you think he would exercise his teacher agency to negotiate the emotional burden he encountered?
(3) As presented in the chapter, both participants expressed the lack of institutional support and opportunities for professional growth. What could the school administration do to help teachers grow professionally?
(4) Based on the experiences of the two teachers in this study, what should the teacher education programmes do to equip teachers in managing emotion labour associated with their profession? What strategies could be included in teacher education programmes to promote awareness of teacher well-being?

Note

(1) Braun and Clark's (2006) six phases of thematic analysis are as follows:
   a. Familiarizing yourself with your data
   b. Generating initial codes
   c. Searching for themes
   d. Reviewing themes
   e. Defining and naming themes
   f. Producing the report

References

Acheson, K., Taylor, J. and Luna, K. (2016) The burnout spiral: The emotion labour of five rural U.S. foreign language teachers. *The Modern Language Journal* 100 (2), 522–537.

Benesch, S. (2012) *Considering Emotions in Critical English Language Teaching: Theories and Praxis*. New York: Routledge.

Benesch, S. (2017) *Emotions and English Language Teaching: Exploring Teachers' Emotion Labor*. New York: Routledge.

Braun, V. and Clarke, V. (2006) Using thematic analysis in psychology. *Qualitative Research in Psychology* 3 (2), 77–101.

De Costa, P.I., Rawal, H. and Li, W. (2018) L2 teachers' emotions: A sociopolitical and ideological perspective. In J.D.M. Agudo (ed.) *Emotions in Second Language Teaching: Theory, Research and Teacher Education* (pp. 91–106). New York: Springer.

Erling, E.J. and Seargeant, P. (eds) (2013) *English and Development: Policy, Pedagogy and Globalization*. Bristol: Multilingual Matters.

Gilligan, C. (1982) *In a Different Voice*. Cambridge, MA: Harvard University Press.
Gkonou, C. and Mercer, S. (2017) *Understanding Emotional and Social Intelligence among English Language Teachers*. London: British Council.
Gkonou, C. and Miller, E.R. (2019) Caring and emotional labour: Language teachers' engagement with anxious learners in private language school classrooms. *Language Teaching Research* 23 (3), 372–387. doi: 10.1177/1362168817728739.
Golombek, P.R. (2015) Redrawing the boundaries of language teacher cognition: Language teacher educators' emotion, cognition, and activity. *The Modern Language Journal* 99 (3), 470–484.
Government of Nepal (2010) Education Act. http://www.nnfsp.gov.np/PublicationFiles/076a5c79-1d15-4747-98b8-523901d95a4a.pdf (accessed 3 February 2019).
Grandey, A.A. (2000) Emotional regulation in the workplace: A new way to conceptualize emotional labour. *Journal of Occupational Health Psychology* 5 (1), 95–110.
Hochschild, A. (1979) Emotion work, feeling rules, and social structures. *American Journal of Sociology* 85 (3), 551–575.
Hochschild, A. (1983) *The Managed Heart: Commercialization of Human Feelings*. Berkeley: University of California Press.
Ho, Y.F. and Tsang, W.K. (2008) The besieged teaching profession and the corroded teachers' selves in the context of education reforms in Hong Kong SAR. In Z. Li, J.C.K. Lee and L. Shiu (eds) *Developing Teachers and Developing Schools in Changing Contexts* (pp. 155–176). Hong Kong: Chinese University Press.
King, J. (2016) 'It's time, put on the smile, it's time!': The emotional labour of second language teaching within a Japanese university. In C. Gkonou, D. Tatzl and S. Mercer (eds) *New Directions in Language Learning Psychology* (pp. 97–112). Dordrecht: Springer.
Loh, C.E. and Liew, W.M. (2016) Voices from the ground: The emotional labor of English teachers' work. *Teaching and Teacher Education* 55, 267–278.
Miller, E.R. and Gkonou, C. (2018) Language teacher agency, emotion labor and emotional rewards in tertiary-level English language programs. *System* 79, 49–59. doi: 10.1016/j.system.2018.03.002.
Pang, N.S.K., Wang, T. and Leung, Z.L.M. (2016) Educational reforms and the practices of professional learning communities in Hong Kong primary schools. *Asia Pacific Journal of Education* 36, 231–247.
Phyak, P. (2016) Local-global tension in the ideological construction of English language education policy in Nepal. In R. Kirkpatrick (ed.) *English Language Education Policy in Asia* (pp. 199–217). New York: Springer.
Sah, P.K. and Li, G. (2018) English Medium Instruction (EMI) as linguistic capital in Nepal: Promises and realities. *International Multilingual Research Journal* 12 (2), 109–123.
Toh, G. (2016) *English as Medium of Instruction in Japanese Higher Education: Presumption, Mirage or Bluff?* London: Palgrave.
Tsou, W. and Kao, S.M. (eds) (2017) *English as a Medium of Instruction in Higher Education: Implementations and Classroom Practices in Taiwan* (vol. 8). New York: Springer.
Wolff, D. and De Costa, P.I. (2017) Expanding the language teacher identity landscape: An investigation of the emotions and strategies of a NNEST. *The Modern Language Journal* 101 (S1), 76–90.
Yin, H., Huang, S. and Lee, J.C.K. (2017) Choose your strategy wisely: Examining the relationships between emotional labour in teaching and teacher efficacy in Hong Kong primary schools. *Teaching and Teacher Education* 66, 127–136.
Zembylas, M. (2005) *Teaching with Emotion: A Postmodern Enactment*. Greenwich, CT: Information Age Publishing.

Appendix: Interview questions (adopted from Benesch, 2017: 111)

(1) Which of these emotions do you feel most commonly when teaching:

Happiness/joy	Frustration
Sadness/grief	Disappointment
Anger/irritation	Disillusion
Fear/anxiety	Guilt
Disgust	Despair
Fascination	Caring
Pride	Love
Wonder	Intimacy
Enthusiasm	Loss
Boredom	Powerlessness
Awe	Compassion

The following questions will be repeated for each emotion identified by the respondent in question 1:

(2) What are your reactions to being (name of emotion)? What do these reactions have to do with your ESL teaching?
(3) Does the way you feel about (name of emotion) have a history in your teaching career?
(4) Can you tell if your students feel (name of emotion)? How? What do you do when a student feels (name of emotion)? What are you trying to teach your student about (name of emotion)?
(5) Are there things you do regularly during your teaching to make sure you feel (name of emotion)? Are there things you do regularly during your teaching to make sure you don't feel (name of emotion)?

13 Dealing with the Emotions of Teaching Abroad: Searching for Silver Linings in a Difficult Context

Tammy Gregersen, Peter D. MacIntyre and Nicole Macmillan

Introduction

Language teachers often experience significant amounts of stress in their workplace, especially when teaching internationally. In the present research we adopt a case study approach to examine an intervention from the literature on positive psychology called *Finding Silver Linings*, a cognitive reappraisal strategy that is proposed to alleviate some of the negative emotional effects of stress. The participant (whom we will call Elizabeth) enacted the intervention daily for a week in a stressful context. Results show complex effects that suggest the types of stressors faced by Elizabeth were not especially conducive to the Finding Silver Linings intervention, which yielded only temporary effects in the moment, and not long-lasting change. We conclude that the relationships among the individual, context and specific positive interventions interact to determine their efficacy. The implications of these results suggest that specific interventions should be evaluated at the individual level.

Teachers' well-being is important, both for teachers themselves and for their pupils. According to Hiver and Dörnyei (2015), knowledge is propagated through the teaching profession, and even with this status, it is a vocation in crisis – including language education. Even though teachers comprise the most valuable facet of education (Leiter & Maslach, 1999), they receive little attention relative to learners. The classroom teacher is the conduit through which group relations and communication pass, an influential social role with responsibility for providing an affectively healthy atmosphere (Frenzel & Stephens, 2013). Positivity is cyclical: teachers can constructively affect learners as individuals and as a collective, which encourages enhanced engagement; likewise, engaged learners promote greater teacher well-being and positive emotions (Mercer & Kostoulas, 2018). In sum, teachers' professional well-being has repercussions in their quality of instruction and learner success (Woolfolk-Hoy, 2008). The present research uses a case study approach to investigate a specific intervention designed to ameliorate a teacher's stress; we will call her Elizabeth. The results, however, turned out to be almost as complex as the international teaching context in which she works.

Increasing evidence suggests that teachers in general experience significant amounts of stress, exerting an impact on their physical and psychological health (Brown, 2012). Teaching is a relatively high-stress, social profession requiring constant interaction with other people. Stressors may range from interpersonal conflicts with parents and other staff to conflicting messages from administration (Skaalvik & Skaalvik, 2007). Teachers are also expected to make important decisions quickly, with personal, economic, social and other impacts (Kyriacou, 2001 cited in Papastylianou *et al.*, 2009). Language teachers in particular may be especially susceptible to stress due to the unique elements of their teaching roles, including insecurities about their own proficiency when using the foreign language orally in class and dealing with diverse learner cultures and proficiency levels. Some language educators find themselves advocating for immigrant learners who are linguistic minorities, helping newcomers make a smooth transition into an unfamiliar culture. Additionally, language teachers in foreign language environments may feel the added stressors that accompany their own adaptation to a new culture and institutions. The intercultural nature of language learning often results in added responsibilities being placed on teachers' emotional well-being and brings additional psychological loads.

Stress occurs 'when there is a mismatch between perceived pressures of the work situation and the individual's ability to cope with it' (Education Service Advisory Committee, 1990 cited in Eyre, 2017: 12). Individual emotions that contribute to feelings of stress are often neglected in the literature, thus creating a significant gap in understanding the role emotions play. Perhaps the most basic distinction is between positive and negative emotions. Fredrickson's (2001, 2008, 2013) broaden-and-build theory suggests that positive emotions (such as joy, happiness and excitement) broaden an individual's awareness and stimulate exploratory thoughts and actions. As time passes, individuals' expanded awareness allows them to build up skills and personal and social resources for future use. This process contrasts with the effects of negative emotions (such as contemptuousness, anger and sadness) which narrow thinking and can lead to fight-or-flight responses for survival, and negatively impact an individual's well-being.

Although teacher stress has been well documented, there is relatively little research on how to intervene. Positive psychology is a relatively new subfield of psychology devoted to the scientific study of how people thrive (Peterson, 2006). Its primary aim, put simply, is to help people live happier, more fulfilling lives by focusing on developing what goes well in life. In the positive psychology literature, there is evidence that positive psychology interventions (PPIs) can be effective in ameliorating emotional distress (Seligman *et al.*, 2005). More specifically, PPIs have been proposed as one way of facilitating growth and development among language learners (Gregersen *et al.*, 2016); applications for language teachers certainly are possible as well. Cultivating resilience in the face of adversity appears to be a precondition to becoming a capable, emotionally and psychologically healthy teacher (Bullough, 2005; Kelchtermans, 2011). According to a review of PPIs by Sin and Lyubomirsky (2009), 'PPIs may be an option for treating a variety of mental disorders, they can be particularly useful for addressing a paucity of positive affect, engagement, and life meaning' (2009: 468). Further, the efficacy of PPIs was found to be moderated by four factors: the PPIs were most effective for persons experiencing some form of stress (e.g. depression); self-selected participants (volunteers) found the PPIs more effective than non-volunteers; older participants benefited more than younger ones; and the treatments were most effective when tailored to individuals (as opposed to applied in groups or with self-administered treatments).

The literature on the effectiveness of PPIs and ways in which they are employed is developing rapidly and generating mostly positive findings (Mongrain & Anselmo-Matthews, 2012; Seligman *et al.*, 2005; Sin & Lyubomirsky, 2009). Although evidence from studies of large samples with a focus on comparing averages between treatment and control groups generally is supportive of PPIs, group-level data analysis can obscure the variability among individual reactions to the PPIs and make it difficult to identify the various processes that account for change (or no change) as experienced by an individual. In general, it is rarely possible to apply group-level results to individuals (Molenaar & Campbell, 2009), generating an enduring, and as yet largely unmet, need to conduct in-depth research with individuals (Eid & Diener, 1999; Lazarus, 2003). Recently a call to employ qualitative methods, made in the flagship *Journal of Positive Psychology*, outlined ways in which interpretive methods can lead to better understandings of the variability and complexity of personal strivings (Hefferon *et al.*, 2017). The present study is in part a response to the call for in-depth study of how individuals employ PPIs, with the present focus on a case study of a notably resilient language teacher who was asked to reappraise stressful situations by finding their so-called 'silver linings'.

Individuals differ in their adjustment to stressful life events; some exhibit impaired functioning while others demonstrate impressive resilience. The present study begins with the premise that the ability to deploy a particularly adaptive type of emotion regulation – cognitive reappraisal – may be a protective factor for language teachers, as successful reappraisal influences many aspects of emotional responding, including self-reported negative affect (Gross, 1998).

Emotion regulation is an important strategy to achieve well-being (Gross & John, 2003) and adjustment to stress (Garnefski *et al.*, 2001), employing behavioral and cognitive strategies to modify both how long and how deeply an emotion is felt (Gross & Thompson, 2007) and an individual's adjustment to it (Garnefski *et al.*, 2001). A variety of strategies to regulate emotions are available (Parkinson & Totterdell, 1999), so it is imperative that we recognize which emotion regulation strategies are effective, and for whom. Emotion appraisal theories propose that it is not simply an event itself that causes a specific emotional reaction, but rather it is a person's subjective appraisal of it, including what it means and its significance (Lazarus, 2003; Ortony *et al.*, 1988; Scherer, 1988). In fact, previous research on appraisals and stress discovered that individuals respond quite differently to similar life events depending on how they appraise the event (Folkman & Lazarus, 1985; Scherer & Ceschi, 1997; Smith & Ellsworth, 1987). Furthermore, learning to change the appraisals one makes in emotional situations is thought to be a key ingredient of many psychological interventions. Because appraisals appear to play an important role in the generation of emotional states, emotion regulation strategies that target appraisals should be particularly effective (Troy *et al.*, 2010).

Although investigators have found the reframing of events through finding a silver lining (i.e. reappraisals) to be useful in many situations, research also suggests that it might actually backfire when applied indiscriminately or in poorly chosen situations; the technique can actually increase negative emotions when used in situations that are *within* one's control (Troy *et al.*, 2013). For example, language teachers stressed by the prevalence of standardized testing may have little or no control over broad systemic requirements. In such a case, reappraising might be a useful strategy because modifying one's emotions may be one of few options available to facilitate coping. On the other hand, for a teacher facing distress at school due to her own chronic lateness – something within her locus of control – finding a silver lining may be a less appropriate strategy because the optimal solution is to be more punctual. The larger point is that any specific emotion regulation strategy will not necessarily be appropriate in all contexts nor be an appropriate remedy in all stressful circumstances. Troy *et al.* (2013) suggest that effective emotion regulation likely implicates the application of an array of coping strategies that are dependent upon context.

The nature of the stressor in question, and its intensity, will influence the efficacy of emotion regulation strategies. Overall, research suggests that finding a silver lining in an adverse situation is more difficult in instances where the stressor is demonstrably more severe. The feasibility and appropriateness of a positive coping strategy may be contingent on the nature and intensity of the stressor in question (Tugade & Fredrickson, 2004; Tugade *et al.*, 2004).

The Present Study

Given the importance of language teachers in today's globalizing world, it is imperative that we pay more attention to their well-being, especially in dealing with the inherently stressful conditions of the profession. With this in mind, we recruited an in-service teacher to participate in a week-long intervention called Finding Silver Linings. She began by taking a battery of established measures that allowed us to take her 'emotional pulse' before the interventions began – including what she perceived her role as a teacher to be and why she wanted to be a language teacher in the first place. During the week-long positive psychology intervention in building resiliency, she was asked to write journal entries about the stressors in her daily life and upon encountering one, to reframe it in a positive way and share her silver linings with those around her. With these narratives, we were able to address the following two questions:

(1) What stressors arise in the language teacher's life?
(2) What is the nature of the silver linings the teacher might create to re-frame stressful events?

Upon completion of the week-long intervention, our participant was asked to answer three Likert-type questions and an open-ended interview question that permitted an evaluative judgment resulting in the answers to the following two questions:

(3) How effective are cognitive reappraisals perceived to be in mediating negative emotion in the face of adverse situations?
(4) In retrospect, did the teacher find value in the Silver Linings intervention a month after it was completed?

Participant

To examine how the silver linings PPI works on the individual level, we contacted a language teacher (a previous student of one of the authors) via the messaging function on Facebook and asked her to participate in the case study portion of our research. Elizabeth (pseudonym) was born in the US and teaches English as a foreign language in West Africa. She has taught internationally for six years, with no prior full-time teaching experience at home in the United States.

Procedures

After giving informed consent to participate, Elizabeth completed the following measures to provide a sense of some key aspects of her psychological context at the beginning of the study:

(1) The 10-item **Life Orientation Test-Revised** (LOT-R) which measures dispositional optimism or one's expectations about the future based on the notion that optimists usually maintain favorable expectations.
(2) The 10-item **Perceived Stress Scale** (Cohen *et al.*, 1983) which measures the degree to which circumstances in one's life are perceived as stressful via items that tap into how unpredictable, overwhelming and burdened respondents consider their lives.
(3) The 10-item **Generic Job Satisfaction Questionnaire** (Macdonald & MacIntyre, 1997) which assesses respondents' overall workplace morale.
(4) The 20-item **Modified Differential Emotions Scale (mDes)** (Fredrickson, 2013) which ascertains the presence of 10 positive and 10 negative emotions.
(5) Demographic survey.
(6) Two open-ended interview questions concerning the participant's: (1) perceptions of the role of a language teacher; and (2) initial motives for becoming one.

After providing this preliminary information, Elizabeth began the Silver Linings intervention which consisted of paying particular attention to problems – big and small – that arose in her classes or her life outside of school during the following week. The purported 'active ingredient' in the intervention is to engage in the process of finding the bright side of a bad situation, making a habit of reframing situations to include consciously noting their beneficial outcomes. This process does not deny the negative aspects of any situation, but allows for a realistic, participant-generated mix of negative and positive in a situation that might be perceived otherwise as monolithically negative. Our participant language teacher was asked to verbalize the 'silver lining' of the situation to her students, colleagues or others, and to document each episode in writing as soon as possible.

A month later, we contacted Elizabeth again and provided her with a table with a summary of her responses. We asked her to reply to three, five-point Likert-type questions about her self-perceived degree of control over the adverse circumstance, the intensity of the stress caused by the negative occurrence, and the level of success she felt each reappraisal had on relieving the stress produced by the difficult occurrence. She was also asked an open-ended question that addressed the immediate as well as lasting effects of finding silver linings, the value of the intervention over time and her sustained use of reappraisals.

The final step in the procedure was a member check (Maxwell, 2013). The present manuscript was sent to Elizabeth with a request to review it for accuracy of interpretation, especially with respect to our discussion of the efficacy of the Silver Linings intervention. Elizabeth agreed that the manuscript reflects her views and asked that we not name the country in which she was working during the study.

Analysis

The first part of our analysis focuses on the narratives describing the reframing of a negative event in a positive way. We set the context by providing information about emotional/psychological backdrop that consists of her descriptions concerning what she perceived the role of a language teacher to be; her reasons for initially becoming a language teacher; and a brief overview of specific items on each of the surveys that we found relevant to her emotional and psychological profile. It was not our intention to use the surveys for any kind of psychometrics, to calculate total scores or to make generalizations. Subsequently, we provide evidence from her narratives to answer the research questions about the specific stressors that surfaced and the way in which she reframed them. After this section, we address the evaluative part of our results and address the second set of two research questions.

Elizabeth

Elizabeth is an unmarried North American teacher who teaches EFL at an international school in West Africa, a culture very different from her home. Elizabeth embodies all four of Sin and Lyubomirsky's (2009) criteria for a potentially successful PPI: she is mature, has volunteered to try the intervention, participates as an individual, and perhaps most importantly, experiences significant stress in her job as a teacher.

Elizabeth sees her teacher role as 'coordinating curriculum and communicating reporting procedures while also developing adult English classes'. Becoming a language teacher allowed her to fulfill her desire to live and travel abroad, but also aligned with her gender role:

> In high school, while applying for university I was not sure what else to study. My mother was a teacher, and I reflected later in life that I did not see a variety of females in various career fields. Women in my small agricultural community growing up were teachers, nurses, secretaries or housewives. It wasn't until I went to college that I was exposed to women in science or technical fields.

Although Elizabeth's endorsement of nine out of the ten optimism items on the Life Orientation survey demonstrate a high degree of optimism, her answers on the Perceived Stress Scale reveal that Elizabeth is under rather severe stress. She subscribed to items reporting nervousness and an inability to control irritations. Beyond this, she also felt that she is not always on top of things, angered by out-of-control life events and that her difficulties sometimes seem insurmountable. Emotionally, Elizabeth's balance on the mDES scale of positive and negative emotions was tipped in favor of the negative. She endorsed items reflecting distrust, anger, contemptuousness, sadness and stress. Positive emotions – amazement, interest and trust – were reported as rarely present in the 24 hours before Elizabeth took the survey. Elizabeth's job satisfaction survey presents a mixed impression. She does not feel good about working for her school, her wages, or how her talents and skills as a teacher are being used. However, Elizabeth 'agreed' with items that indicate she is recognized for a job well done, feels close to colleagues, gets along with supervisors, her job is secure and she feels good about the job she is doing. In sum, Elizabeth's answers on the pre-tests identified her as optimistic and high-stressed, tending toward negative more than positive emotion and showing a conflicted sense of job satisfaction.

Elizabeth's silver linings (RQ1 & RQ2)

In reading Elizabeth's silver linings narratives, it becomes clear that the 'international' part of her teaching milieu has considerable impact on the types and intensity of the stressors Elizabeth faces. She is a North American living and teaching in West Africa with associated professional and personal stressors. Elizabeth became a teacher in order to travel and live abroad, but on the first day of the intervention Elizabeth writes about being caught in a street riot and needing to flee the scene in a taxi. Yet she successfully found silver linings in an unquestionably stressful situation; she 'had coffee ... used the fast Wi-Fi to do some personal business ... had lunch with a colleague and went home in a safe car during a tumultuous time in the city'. Analysis of Elizabeth's word choices in her narrative for this incident reveal sociopolitical differences. She reports:

> The government had a local election which was not held on time. It has been delayed for quite some time, years. It's rumored the current president's party didn't win local elections and the current president is also rumored to be preparing to run for a 3rd, unconstitutional term. So his party not winning local elections would upset his 2020 plan. All that means protests, and increased fear in the streets, limited WiFi as the oppositional voices are shut out and a general low morale in country.

Elizabeth uses words like 'unconstitutional' to describe some of the current president's political activities and words like 'protests', 'increased fear' and 'low morale' to describe a situation where she sees 'oppositional voices' being 'shut out'. Bochner, Furnham and Ward (2001) emphasize that sojourners often learn ways of doing things in the new culture so as not to draw undue attention to themselves. An international teacher's political conscience can be seriously tested when local events create situations that conflict with her core beliefs. Such incidents remind teacher sojourners of their guest status in a country where there are risks in becoming politically active.

In this same post, Elizabeth transitions from the political turmoil of the country to the issue of leadership in the school. She explains:

> School was closed today for violent protests. We had 2 teachers leave this week, breaking contract [...] It's a hardship post and it's affected our school as well. Hardship tailored with weak admin has resulted in 5 [teachers] leaving since August of 2017. We're a small school of 77 students so 5 teachers is near half our staff. There's silver lining and survival. I'm in the later stage now.

Many teachers experience differences with administrators and colleagues, but it seems clear that Elizabeth also experiences a cultural dimension to her struggles, noticed as different from the experiences to which she is accustomed (Halicioglu, 2015). In Elizabeth's case, the school leadership style of her current teaching position conflicts with her expectations:

> I'm in [West Africa] until June if I don't get the axe. We have a Director who is a hot mess and whose sense of direction (i.e. none) is not aligned with my need to create systems and organize the chaos that comes with living in a developing nation ... My current Director is a woman and fits the negative stereotypes of a poor leader who just happens to be a woman. She's doing the same as the overconfident guy in [...] that said, 'I'm great at this, but this place doesn't allow me to show you how good I am ...', people are leaving this year and the Director blames [...], but the reality is that her version of [the country] and why we can't have nice things is to blame on the country, rather than her weak leadership and lack of systems.

Elizabeth also perceives cross-cultural leadership as an issue for the international teaching milieu in West Africa. In fact, she calls into question the cultural competence of her current and past administrators and recommends that to help themselves they should participate in silver linings interventions:

> In my two experiences, I see these directors come for the power position, but I can say in both cases the individuals aren't 'Africa Smart' a concept

> we use here to identify people who can't figure out how to navigate the culture. I can say, I haven't been robbed, taken advantage of, rather I can walk down the street, hold my head high, speak some but not all the language, enjoy myself, get most basic needs and do my job. These directors, however, blame all the ills of the school on the country and what they don't have. So a 'silver lining activity' would benefit them.

Conflicting cultural expectations of leadership by international teachers and administrators may create challenges that rupture contractual ties. In Elizabeth's case, her disgruntlement is great enough for her to take the initiative to change employers, and in a previous case, the dissatisfaction was so deep that the school board fired the school administrator:

> 'Divide and conquer' was the motto of my previous Director in [...], I stayed in [the country] long enough to see him dismissed and feel vindicated. He told the School Board and parents that he was good at hiring, but the teachers didn't like [the country] and left because of the country. In my exit interview I could [say] I wasn't leaving the school to leave the country, rather I had the chance to stay in the country, but felt compelled to leave the school due to his weak leadership.

Broken contractual ties between the administration and teachers are not the only triggers of stress resulting from conflictive cultural expectations. According to Elizabeth, relationships among teachers in the school environment are also affected:

> What's helped or the silver lining: I've adopted the concept of 'casualties of mismanagement'. I've said to all my colleagues, I will at some point in time have a problem with you and you will have a problem with me, not because we are bad people, or not competent, but because we are in a leaderless environment where we have to act with the best interest and apologize as we do our jobs. So far I've kept my colleagues as friends.

Such struggles are also mentioned as catalysts for job dissatisfaction in the research of Odland and Ruzicka (2009) who investigated reasons that teachers leave international schools after only a short tenure. Their evidence suggested that the top reasons are all related to frustration with school leadership.

Although the above stressors are peripherally related to being a language teacher in that Elizabeth teaches English in a cross-cultural setting, there is one particular excerpt from her narrative that speaks profoundly to a stressor that arises because of the nature of foreign language instruction: the complex and diverse learner population. She comments that her initial goal was to teach in West Africa for five years, and now after only four, she will be taking a position elsewhere (in Turkey):

> When it comes to teaching ELL it's all fine and well to teach a heterogeneous population, but it's much more difficult to serve a wide array of learners. I'm going back to an environment similar to that which I joined out of Grad school when I went to [...] and taught in a 7–12 domestic populated college prep program.

We have focused thus far on the *stressors* found in Elizabeth's narratives, but her ability to reframe them says volumes about her ongoing resiliency. According to Cushner and Brislin (1996), a familiar struggle, particularly for unmarried people living abroad, is the capacity and occasions for nurturing true friendships, not merely superficial acquaintances. For Elizabeth, her close relationships most often generate positivity in her life. On the day of the street riots, Elizabeth communicated the following: 'Another silver lining was that I had lunch with a colleague and went home in a safe car during a tumultuous time in the city.' On Day 3 of the interventions, Elizabeth confronted the following scenario: 'Today, a conversation with a colleague went more down the way of an argument. Conflict at work bubbling over into social life.' Rather than shying away from social contact, Elizabeth sought it out: 'The silver lining is that the friend I spoke to on the phone also struggles with her work and shares frustrations with the country, so I hope in a way to build our relationship by sharing our struggles living in the same community.'

On the penultimate day of the PPI, Elizabeth's students arrived late. Elizabeth not only found a silver lining in the experience, but also incorporated an opportunity to use authentic language to address the issue. She found a creative way to reframe an undesirable event. Finally, on the last day of interventions, Elizabeth spent time away from her own obligations to initiate three new teachers into the curriculum in three different areas and said that 'the silver lining of this is that I was able to build relationships and offer support to three new and fresh individuals to our school. This allowed me to spend time productively and not involve myself in conversations about the internal conflict at school.'

The efficacy of Elizabeth's reappraisals (RQ3 & RQ4)

Having described the types of Elizabeth's stressors and reappraisals, we now examine their effectiveness, which presents a more complex portrait of the Silver Linings intervention. The Likert-type survey responses ranged from 1 (none) to 5 (completely) and asked about Elizabeth's degree of control over the stressor, the level of severity of the stressor, and the efficacy of the specific reappraisal in question. A complete list of Elizabeth's stressors and silver linings, along with the Likert ratings of each, is presented in Table 13.1.

Table 13.1 Elizabeth's stressors, silver linings and appraisal scores

UNDESIRABLE EVENT	SILVER LINING	Degree of control	Severity of stressor	Reappraisal efficacy
Ex-pat friend backed out of dinner due to father's illness	Used the time to clean cupboards and bake	1	4	4
Students in physical altercation; missed lunch	Was present to break up the fight	1	2	4
Students arrived late	Explaining classroom policy provided opportunity for authentic communication	1	2	4
Missed private English class due to street riots	Used driver to get to a safe place and got work done	2	4	4
Added a new adult English student to an already over-booked schedule	Class will be interesting and a change from other students	2	5	4
New teachers needed guidance	Used opportunity to build relationships and offer support to three new colleagues	3	3	5
Too busy to celebrate her own birthday	Stayed active and busy, rather than bemoaning the entire day was not free	4	2	3
'Conflict at work bubbling over into social life'	Realization she needs to reflect on thoughts quietly rather than discuss with colleagues	5	5	4
Continued ruminating over work conflict	Called a friend who she discovered also has work conflicts	5	3	3
Teachers received email about cyber-bullying; she responded negatively via email to Director	Opportunity to tell Director about failed school policies	5	5	1

Note: All Likert ratings are on a scale that ranged from 1–5.

The table is ordered by the degree of control over each stressor. In general, reappraisal efficacy is heightened when the stressor is within one's control, is not too intense and aligns with the type of stressor experienced (Tugade & Fredrickson, 2004; Tugade *et al.*, 2004; Troy *et al.*, 2013). Consistent with previous research, we see that among Elizabeth's 10 stressors, three of them were seen as *outside* her control (friend backing out of dinner, students participating in a physical altercation and students arriving late) and three were *within* her control (conflict at work, continued rumination over said conflict and her negative email addressed to the director of school). In all three of the stressors *outside* Elizabeth's control, she ranked the efficacy of her reappraisal as 4 out of 5, or 'somewhat effective'. On the other hand, for those reappraisals that corresponded to stressors completely *within* her control, she rated two of them (calling a friend with a similar conflict and using the opportunity to address problems with the director) as less successful (3 and 1, respectively) than she did those outside her control.

In terms of the severity of the stressor, a similar tendency was found. For those experiences Elizabeth ranked as not at all stressful (1 out of 5), she consistently ranked the efficacy of the reappraisal as somewhat effective (4 out of 5), but for those she ranked as highly stressful (5 out of 5), she ranked two of them below 4 and even suggested that the reappraisal for the conversation with the director was completely ineffective. When viewing reappraisals in light of the stressor's severity, Elizabeth's ranking again tended to align with previous investigations that suggest that reappraisals generated from less stressful conditions tend to be more productive.

Elizabeth's open-ended response to the interview question a month after she completed the intervention sheds additional light on the way she thinks about herself and her situation, and helps to clarify the mixture of efficacy ratings assigned to the individual occasions wherein she applied the reappraisal process.

> As for the Silver Lining, I've found out I generally imagine the worst case scenario and then build my thoughts up from there, rather than starting with the silver lining. What I can focus on doing is taking time to think rather than acting, or sending emails or opening my mouth until I've worked through the scenarios in my head. I could imagine the silver lining when explicitly told to do so. It may have reduced my stress level when expressly instructed to do so. But as I'm not practicing it automatically, then I am just kicking myself for not doing something I should know may be useful for me and could reduce my stress. I can find a silver lining when I feel good, but when times are tough, like difficulties at work, or not being able to secure a visa, I am not looking to the silver lining, but rather thinking what the worse possible scenario could be from that point on.

This pattern of thinking is highly consistent with a cognitive strategy, defensive pessimism, which can be healthy if applied in anxiety-provoking situations (Norem & Cantor, 1986). Defensive pessimism is an active, preparatory strategy whereby a person lowers expectations for a future stressful situation and plans for possible negative events, as a way to manage anxiety and uncertainty. In contrast, chronic dispositional pessimism is an internal, global and stable tendency to expect the worst without doing much about it, typically a demotivating and self-defeating way of thinking (del Valle & Mateos, 2008). Elizabeth exhibits defensive pessimism by thinking about possible negative events in advance, planning for them, and guiding her behavior toward more favorable possible outcomes. She does not 'sit back and take it' as a dispositional pessimist might, but she said she imagines the worst possible scenario and plans how to deal with it.

In light of such a defensive cognitive strategy, Elizabeth finished with a comment challenging the overall efficacy of the Silver Linings intervention.

> The intervention, independent of reminders to explicitly consider the silver lining didn't work for me. Perhaps when I am in a different country, or as my level of professionalism increases then I can focus on silver lining thinking.

This final comment is especially instructive when considered in conjunction with the results of Silver Linings. When explicitly reminded to report a negative event and identify a silver lining, Elizabeth clearly was able to do so, and the intervention was perceived to be effective on more than half of the occasions (rated 4 or 5 out of 5). However, this is not her typical way of thinking and a week's worth of the intervention did not create a different habit of mind. The complex, overwhelming stress of the situation, coupled with Elizabeth's preference for proactive planning, seems to be a factor in triggering defensive pessimism, which may be a more appropriate long-term strategy under the circumstances. In the face of a street riot it seems far better to plan for trouble, think about avoidance and escape strategies, and protect oneself from harm rather than finding a good internet hotspot. Whereas good Wi-Fi most often is genuinely appreciated, it should not be top of mind in a situation requiring immediate escape, and emerged as a silver lining when one had to be found to meet our request.

Discussion

The case study reported here is instructive on a number of issues, but two are of particular concern. The first is the process of cognitive reappraisal that lies at the center of the Silver Linings intervention. The second issue is the need to consider individual-level data in conjunction with group-level data, as highlighted in the present case study.

Elizabeth's comments remind us that PPIs are enacted by fully formed individuals; the intervention is not written *de novo* on a blank slate. Considering the dynamics of the educational, cultural and political systems in which a person functions, as well as the dynamic systems that make up our motivations and emotions, the effectiveness of any given PPI will depend on any number of interactions. For this reason, it behooves researchers to evaluate the effectiveness of a PPI on emotional processes on the individual level, and examine intraindividual variation. Layous and Lyubomirsky (2014) emphasize several factors influencing the efficacy of PPIs, including the need to find a fit between the person and the specific PPI. Elizabeth's engagement with the Silver Linings PPI is quite instructive in this regard. She encountered stressors in both her professional and personal life. As noted by Sin and Lyubomirsky (2009), PPIs are not designed to remedy an illness or heal pathology, but rather to break out of a languishing 'rut' to facilitate flourishing. Therefore, the nature of the stressors is not at issue but rather the individual's capacity to deal with them by altering one's line of thinking. Elizabeth engaged successfully, even admirably, in finding silver linings in extraordinary circumstances. We did not employ tests for depression, anxiety, trauma or similar conditions with Elizabeth so a definitive claim about those factors is not possible. However, the narratives show no evidence of such disorders in her particular case. Based on Elizabeth's case study, there appears to be evidence that finding silver linings can be employed effectively under stressful teaching conditions to temporarily ameliorate the negative effects of those stressors on the teacher's well-being, especially when the stressors are outside her control, are manageable and the strategy matches the nature of the stressor. This almost certainly was aided by Elizabeth's dispositional optimism which coincides with, and likely facilitates, the process of employing the silver linings intervention.

Overall, however, the results are mixed and warrant caution moving forward in research on PPIs in SLA. The strategic caution emerging from this case study lies in Elizabeth's comments a month after the week-long intervention was complete. She did not dismiss Silver Linings as ineffective; indeed she had previously rated them as 4 out of 5 and 5 out of 5 on specific occasions. Further, she later proposed conditions under which the intervention might have worked better (more experience, a different teaching context); it appears that she experienced some positive emotions in the moment of finding silver linings. However, her summary comment was clear: 'The intervention, independent of reminders to explicitly consider the silver lining didn't work for me.' The negative conclusion was preceded by an explanation of her active cognitive strategies for dealing with stressful situations in her teaching context, which we identified as defensive pessimism. For Elizabeth, perhaps it is ironic that her dispositional optimism is so closely associated with defensive pessimism in the face of significant stressors. Elizabeth's answers on the pre-tests suggest that she is generally optimistic but high-stressed, tending to experience more negative than positive emotions, and only moderate job satisfaction at best. As Elizabeth suggests, if we can imagine the stress being lessened by moving to another context (as she did), we can imagine persistent negative emotions subsiding, and both positive emotion and job satisfaction increasing. Under different conditions, the Silver Linings intervention likely would have worked very differently and might have provided more than a temporary burst of positive emotion.

The second major issue for discussion emphasizes methodological concerns. A founding principle of positive psychology is that its activities be critically evaluated and evidence-based (Seligman &

Csíkszentmihályi, 2000). For most of its history as a discipline, psychological research methods have focused on means and variability between groups, evaluating theory in light of statistical relationships obtained in empirical data (Lazarus, 2003). However, applying findings from group-based statistics directly to a specific individual often is not appropriate, for a variety of reasons (Molenaar & Campbell, 2009). This is a noteworthy caution when it comes to interpreting the results of a PPI. Most research using PPIs is based on between-group comparisons, but we chose to avoid group-level data for two reasons. First, we wanted to describe the individual reactions to finding silver linings. Second, group data are not necessarily sensitive to all relevant aspects of individual contexts that might modify the effects of a PPI such as Silver Linings (Woodsworth *et al.*, 2015).

Previous studies in positive psychology focused on increasing subjective well-being are not designed to document the potential for each participant to respond differently to an intervention strategy. In order to evaluate how individuals employ the PPIs, it is highly advisable to add individual-level data in order to evaluate PPIs and their effectiveness. According to Eid and Diener (1999), it is necessary to take into account intraindividual differences in understanding affective experiences such as those described in PPIs. They also argue that intraindividual variability is a key consideration in examining the ways in which PPIs operate. In observing Elizabeth's experiences, we see interactions among the characteristics of the individual teacher, the context in which she works and the specifics of the PPI. Furthermore, Molenaar and Campbell (2009) argue that in studies looking at emotions and their processes, such as the current study, it is important to remember that emotions occur in real time at the level of individual persons. Despite solid arguments in favor of the methodological approach, very few studies of PPIs have focused on individuals.

Conclusions

Since the publication of Seligman *et al.*'s (2005) study on PPIs, there is growing interest in positive psychology's ability to increase happiness and subjective well-being. That said, very rarely are PPIs studied in terms of perceived stress literature, especially among language teachers. The present study sought to test the process of implementing a PPI in order to evaluate its effects. Elizabeth reported personal and professional stressors. Specifically, the cultural milieu in which Elizabeth was inserted had a tremendous impact. The specific types of stressors the language teacher experienced were challenging, and in retrospect, using Silver Linings to reframe undesirable events might not have been the optimal approach for this individual. However, the larger methodological point is that the individual-level case study approach taken here better accounts for the personal life occurrences and the manner in which PPIs interact with language teachers' lives. Studying emotions is complex, and since emotions occur in real time on an individual level, using individual-level approaches in emotion research may be a promising direction for future studies.

To conclude, Elizabeth mentioned the concept of 'Inshallah', reporting that it is a common way of thinking for people in West Africa. She defined it as '"(G)god willing" something will happen today, and if it's willed we'll just wait for it.' Through this study, we have come to understand that finding silver linings can be an effective way of reframing events over which we have little control – something that might benefit language teachers the world over. Its effects, however, were not long lasting in the present study. The overriding message is to consider carefully the fit between the person and the intervention. In particular, PPI research and practice can evaluate how the effects of an intervention such as Silver Linings might be interpreted over various timescales, taking into account brief bursts of positive emotion as well as longer-term cognitive and emotional processes that effectively deal with stress and promote teacher well-being.

Post-Reading Tasks

(1) List two stressors you have experienced in the past day or two and try to find at least one silver lining for each. After doing so, how difficult was the process of cognitive reappraising for you, does it come easily or only with effort?

(2) Reflect for a moment on how you typically, proactively deal with anticipated stressful events in your life as a language teacher. Why do you think such actions are more effective than others?

(3) Discussion question: is there a potential danger in searching for and finding silver linings, is there a risk in 'overdoing' it? How does one retain an optimal approach to balancing silver linings in negative events, and what are the potential roles for defensive pessimism and learned optimism?

References

Bochner, S., Furnham, A. and Ward, C. (2001) *The Psychology of Culture Shock*. East Sussex: Routledge.

Brown, C.G. (2012) A systematic review of the relationship between self-efficacy and burnout in teachers. *Educational and Child Psychology* 29 (4), 47–63.

Bullough, R. (2005) Teacher vulnerability and teachability: A case study of a mentor and two interns. *Teacher Education Quarterly* 32 (2), 23–40.

Cohen, S., Kamarck, T. and Mermelstein, R. (1983) A global measure of perceived stress. *Journal of Health and Social Behavior* 24, 386–396.

Cushner, K. and Brislin, R. (1996) *Intercultural Interactions: A Practical Guide* (2nd edn). Thousand Oaks, CA: SAGE.

del Valle, C.H. and Mateos, P.M. (2008) Dispositional pessimism, defensive pessimism and optimism: The effect of induced mood on prefactual and counterfactual thinking and performance. *Cognition and Emotion* 22, 1600–1612.

Eid, M. and Diener, E. (1999) Intraindividual variability in affect: Reliability, validity, and personality correlates. *Journal of Personality and Social Psychology* 76 (4), 662–676.

Eyre, C. (2017) *The Elephant in the Staffroom: How to Reduce Stress and Improve Teacher Wellbeing.* New York: Routledge.

Folkman, S. and Lazarus, R.S. (1985) If it changes it must be a process: Study of emotion and coping during three stages of a college examination. *Journal of Personality and Social Psychology* 48, 150–170.

Fredrickson, B.L. (2001) The role of positive emotions in positive psychology: The broaden-and-build theory of positive emotions. *American Psychologist* 56, 218–226.

Fredrickson, B.L. (2008) Promoting positive affect. In M. Eid and R.J. Larsen (eds) *The Science of Subjective Well-Being* (pp. 449–468). New York: Guilford Press.

Fredrickson, B.L. (2013) Positive emotions broad and build. *Advances in Experimental Social Psychology* 47, 1–53.

Frenzel, A.C. and Stephens, E.J. (2013) Emotions. In C. Hall and T. Goetz (eds) *Emotion, Motivation, and Self-Regulation: A Handbook for Teachers* (pp. 1–56). Bingley: Emerald Group Publishing.

Garnefski, N., Kraaij, V. and Spinhoven, P. (2001) Negative life events, cognitive emotion regulation and emotional problems. *Personality and Individual Differences* 30, 1311–1327.

Gregersen, T., MacIntyre, P.D. and Meza, M. (2016) Positive psychology exercises build social capital for language learners: Preliminary evidence. In P.D. MacIntyre, T. Gregersen and S. Mercer (eds) *Positive Psychology in SLA* (pp. 147–167). Bristol: Multilingual Matters.

Gross, J. (1998) Antecedent and response-focused emotion regulation: Divergent consequences for experience, expression, and physiology. *Journal of Personality and Social Psychology* 74, 224–237.

Gross, J. and John, P. (2003) Individual differences in two emotion regulation processes: Implications for affect, relationships, and well-being. *Journal of Personality and Social Psychology* 85, 348–362.

Gross, J. and Thompson, R.A. (2007) Emotion regulation: Conceptual foundations. In J. Gross (ed.) *Handbook of Emotion Regulation.* New York: Guilford Press.

Halicioglu, M. (2015) Challenges facing teachers new to working in schools overseas. *Working Papers Series International and Global Issues for Research*, 2015/5, University of Bath, Bath, UK.

Hefferon, K., Ashfield, A., Waters, L. and Synard, J. (2017) Understanding optimal human functioning – The 'call for qual' in exploring human flourishing and well-being. *The Journal of Positive Psychology* 12 (3), 211–219.

Hiver, P. and Dörnyei, Z. (2015) Language teacher immunity: A double-edged sword. *Applied Linguistics* 38 (3), 405–423.

Kelchtermans, G. (2011) Vulnerability in teaching: The moral and political roots of a structural condition. In C. Day and J.C.-K. Lee (eds) *New Understandings of Teacher's Work: Emotions and Educational Change* (pp. 65–82). New York: Springer.

Layous, K. and Lyubomirsky, S. (2014) The how, why, what, when, and who of happiness: Mechanisms underlying the success of positive interventions. In J. Gruber and J. Moscowitz (eds) *Positive Emotion: Integrating the Light Sides and Dark Sides* (pp. 473–495). New York: Oxford University Press.

Lazarus, R.S. (2003) The Lazarus manifesto for positive psychology and psychology in general. *Psychological Inquiry* 14 (2), 173–189.

Leiter, M.P. and Maslach, C. (1999) Six areas of worklife: A model of the organizational context of burnout. *Journal of Health and Human Resources Administration* 21, 472–489.

Macdonald, S. and MacIntyre, P. (1997) The generic job satisfaction scale: Scale development and its correlates. *Employee Assistance Quarterly* 13 (2), 1–16.

Maxwell, J. (2013) *Qualitative research design: An interactive approach* (3rd edn). Thousand Oaks, CA: SAGE.

Mercer, S. and Kostoulas, A. (2018) *Language Teacher Psychology*. Bristol: Multilingual Matters.

Molenaar, P.C.M. and Campbell, C.G. (2009) The new person-specific paradigm in psychology. *Current Directions in Psychological Science* 18 (2), 112–117.

Mongrain, M. and Anselmo-Matthews, T. (2012) Do positive psychology exercises work? A replication of Seligman *et al.* (2005) *Journal of Clinical Psychology* 68 (4), 382–389.

Norem, J.K. and Cantor, N. (1986) Defensive pessimism. Harnessing anxiety as motivation. *Journal of Personality and Social Psychology* 51, 1208–1217.

Odland, G. and Ruzicka, M. (2009) An investigation into teacher turnover in international schools. *Journal of Research in International Education* 8 (1), 5–29.

Ortony, A., Clore, G.L. and Collins, A. (1988) *The Cognitive Structure of Emotions*. New York: Cambridge University Press.

Papastylianou, A., Kaila, M. and Polychronopoulos, M. (2009) Teachers' burnout, depression, role ambiguity and conflict. *Social Psychology of Education* 12 (3), 295–314.

Parkinson, B. and Totterdell, P. (1999) Classifying affect-regulation strategies. *Cognition and Emotion* 13, 277–303.

Peterson, C. (2006) *A Primer in Positive Psychology*. New York: Oxford University Press.

Scherer, K.R. (1988) Criteria for emotion-antecedent appraisal: A review. In V. Hamilton, G.H. Bower and N.H. Frijda (eds) *Cognitive Perspectives on Emotion and Motivation* (pp. 89–126). New York: Kluwer Academic/Plenum Press Publishers.

Scherer, K.R. and Ceschi, G. (1997) Lost luggage: A field study of emotion antecedent appraisal. *Motivation and Emotion* 21, 211–235.

Seligman, M.E.P. and Csíkszentmihályi, M. (2000) Positive psychology: An introduction. *American Psychologist* 55 (1), 5–14.

Seligman, M.P., Steen, T.A., Park, N. and Peterson, C. (2005) Positive psychology progress: Empirical validation of interventions. *Tidsskrift for Norsk Psykologforening* 42 (10), 874–884.

Sin, N.L. and Lyubomirsky, S. (2009) Enhancing well-being and alleviating depressive symptoms with positive psychology interventions: A practice-friendly meta-analysis. *Journal of Clinical Psychology* 65 (5), 467–487.

Skaalvik, E.M. and Skaalvik, S. (2007) Dimensions of teacher self-efficacy and relations with strain factors, perceived collective teacher efficacy, and teacher burnout. *Journal of Educational Psychology* 99 (3), 611–625.

Smith, C.A. and Ellsworth, P.C. (1987) Patterns of appraisal and emotion related to taking an exam. *Journal of Personality and Social Psychology* 52, 475–488.

Troy, A.S., Wilhelm, F.H., Shallcross, A.J. and Mauss, I.B. (2010) Seeing the silver lining: Cognitive reappraisal ability moderates the relationship between stress and depressive symptoms. *Emotion* 10, 783–795.

Troy, A.S., Shallcross, A.J. and Mauss, I.B. (2013) A person-by-situation approach to emotion regulation: Cognitive reappraisal can either help or hurt, depending on the context. *Psychological Science* 24 (12), 2505–2514.

Tugade, M.M. and Fredrickson, B.L. (2004) Resilient individuals use positive emotions to bounce back from negative emotional experiences. *Journal of Personality and Social Psychology* 86 (2), 320.

Tugade, M.M., Fredrickson, B.L. and Feldman Barrett, L. (2004) Psychological resilience and positive emotional granularity: Examining the benefits of positive emotions on coping and health. *Journal of Personality* 72 (6), 1161–1190.

Woodsworth, R.J., O'Brien-Malone, A., Diamond, M.R. and Schuz, B. (2015) Happy days: Positive psychology interventions effects on affect in an N-of-1 trial. *International Journal of Clinical and Health Psychology* 16, 21–29.

Woolfolk-Hoy, A. (2008) Commentary: What motivates teachers? Important work on a complex question. *Learning and Instruction* 18, 492–498.

14 The Well of Language Teachers' Emotional Well-Being

Rebecca L. Oxford

> The Tao is like a well: used but never used up[,] ...
> filled with infinite possibilities.
> – Lao-Tzu, 2006: 4

Introduction

The well of language teachers' emotional well-being (see Image 14.1) is this chapter's motif. In the epigraph, ancient sage Lao-Tzu[1] (2006) likened the primordial energy field known as the Tao to a well, filled with possibilities. In a related sense, wells are healing places. The Sisters of Mercy (2018) beckon travellers to stop and drink from the well of emotional and spiritual healing in their gracious retreat centre. Irish poet Seamus Heaney (1991: 77) enjoined us to 'Believe in miracles/And cures and healing wells'. This chapter discloses new meanings for emotional well-being for everyone, with a special focus on language teachers and language teacher educators, whom I collectively call 'teachers' for the sake of simplicity. (An exception occurs in one section, where I present authentic cases of the fluctuating emotions of specific teachers and teacher educators.)

Emotions within the well of well-being[2] are complex. Emotion (affect) is never separate from attitudes and belief (Dörnyei, 2009; Kalaja *et al.*, 2016; Ostrom, 1969; Oxford, 2020). Whenever we speak of affect, cognitive elements are necessarily implied. Affective-cognitive bubbles swirl, some smoothly and others agitatedly, inside each person's internal well of emotional well-being, and the dynamics often shift without notice.

Emotion has countless forms, strengths and shadings. Emotions vary in duration (fleeting emotional states, longer moods and much more consistent personality traits that influence emotions; Dörnyei, 2009).

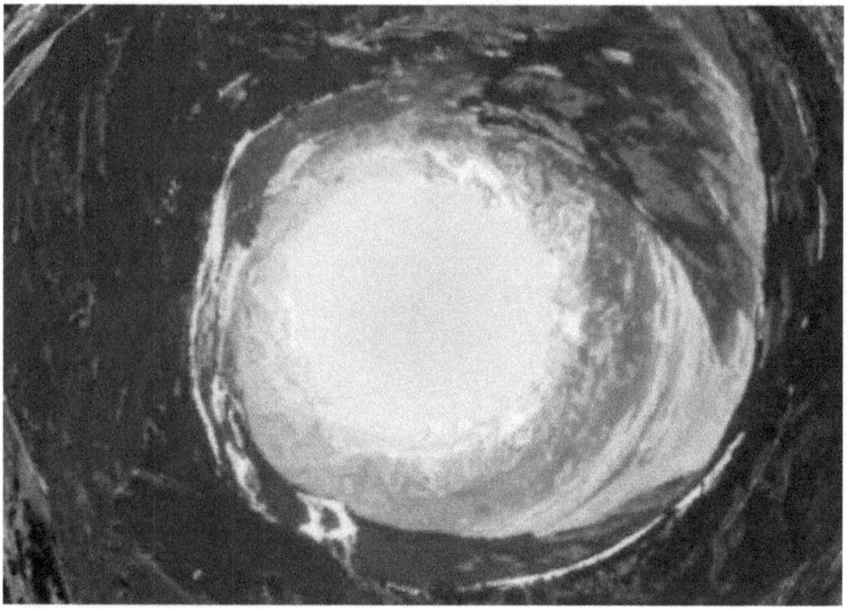

Image 14.1 Inside the well of emotional well-being
Source: Photo by Daniel Frank (2017), Pexels. Creative Commons License. https://www.pexels.com/photo/blue-bubble-calamity-clean-287229/

For a given person at a particular time, an emotion can be conscious or below consciousness. The bubbles in the well of emotional well-being also merge in various ways. Emotions are often mixed (like sorrow/rage and happiness/relief) and not felt as separate emotions. Ambivalent emotions, such as excitement co-occurring with fear, are common (MacIntyre & Mercer, 2014).

In the perspective of positive psychologists such as Fredrickson (2004) and Seligman (2011), there are positive emotions, such as happiness, joy, curiosity, interest, pleasure, contentment, satisfaction and love, and negative emotions, such as fear, anger, sadness, jealousy and shame. I prefer to use descriptive terms such as painful, challenging, difficult or uncomfortable emotions and pleasant, enjoyable, easy or comfortable emotions instead of the more judgmental terms 'negative emotions' and 'positive emotions'. There is positivity in gaining insight from both sets of emotions, as explained later. Nevertheless, when necessary in this chapter (especially in the discussion of positive psychology), I will speak in terms of negative and positive emotions. The well of emotional well-being includes all these emotions. Emotions of any kind offer crucial information, which, when discerned, can contribute to well-being.

Emotion amplifies (MacIntyre, 2002; Oxford, 2015a), bringing urgency, intensity and energy to behavior. Physiologically speaking, emotions involve alterations in blood pressure, heart rate, body temperature and stomach sensations and are accompanied by feelings, i.e. conscious, subjective interpretations. Berry, Poortinga, Segall and Dasen (2002) spoke of emotions in terms of antecedent events, situation appraisal, subjective feelings, physiological reaction patterns, action readiness, behavioral expression and emotion regulation, while Lewis (2005) described emotions as involving arousal, action tendencies, attentional orientation and affective feeling. Emotion has two subsystems: a primitive, subcortical, automatic subsystem including joy, sadness, anger and other basic emotions, centralized in the amygdala of the limbic system and helping to shape perception, attention and cognition; and the second, more regulatory subsystem in the cerebral cortex.

Two edited books (Martínez Agudo, 2018; Mercer & Kostoulas, 2018) in the field of applied linguistics and language education examine a plethora of angles on teachers' emotions. Compared to the past, articles are now being published in greater numbers on teachers' emotions. The rest of this chapter offers important perspectives on teachers' emotional well-being. Some of these perspectives have not been discussed in print within our field. For example, van Deurzen's (2012) 'compass of emotion', little known in TESOL and applied linguistics, is the subject of the next section. Following a discussion of empathy, emotional intelligence, emotion regulation and emotional labour, I present the perhaps surprising benefits of difficult emotions and thereby pose a challenge to certain ideas in positive psychology. Then I set out five short case studies of teachers' dynamic emotions and offer an analysis.

The 'Compass of Emotion'

This section introduces the 'compass of emotion', a system created by the acknowledged leader of existential psychotherapy, Emmy van Deurzen (2012; see also Oxford, 2015b). Her work, which can shed light on what is meant by the well of emotional well-being, discusses emotions with the intention of helping people 'gain insight into the unavoidable paradoxes that life presents' (van Deurzen, 2012: xiii). A large array of emotions is organized in a highly structured fashion in the 'compass of emotion' (Figure 14.1).

A compass is normally a navigational tool that guides decisions about direction, just as emotions help shape human actions. Exhilaration and happiness are at the high-tension apex of the compass of emotion, while despondency, depression and sadness are at the low-tension, release-based, agency-less nadir. The four small rectangles (or clusters of emotions) circularly arranged between the two poles are framed in relation to a 'value', understood in the model to be something important that we want. A value might be a success in teaching, a good relationship, a car, physical beauty or something else, tangible or intangible.

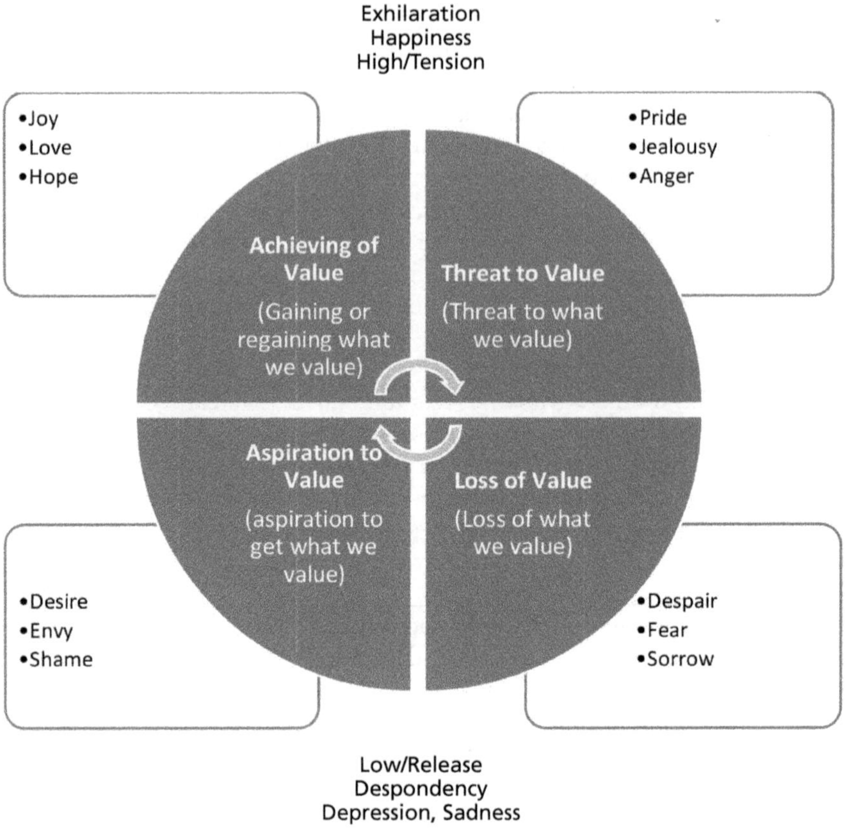

Figure 14.1 The compass of emotion
Note: This figure was compiled from Figures 5.1 through 5.7 in van Deurzen (2012: 151–155). A somewhat different version was published in Oxford (2015b) and is further clarified here. Anxiety is not shown in Figure 14.1 because it is 'a more general and basic experience' and influences many parts of the compass of emotion (van Deurzen, 2012: 153).

- In the upper right rectangle are pride, jealousy and anger, which reflect perceived threats to something we want. Pride occurs when we still feel control of what we value but are perhaps too eager to show it off, suspecting that it might be under threat. Jealousy arises when what we value is being threatened and we feel that it might be taken away. Anger emerges when what we value is deeply threatened, and we are making a desperate effort to get it back or to hold on tightly to it.
- The emotions of despair, fear and sorrow are in the lower right rectangle. These signify steps in the loss of what we want. Despair emerges when we recognize we might have to give up this important thing. Fear in this model is a severe apprehension that what we want is about to be stolen and that we might be letting go. Sorrow arises when we realize that the

threat became real and has actually taken what we value, and we had no choice but to let go.

- The bottom left rectangle contains shame, envy and desire, which together signify aspiring to what we value when we do not have it. Shame emerges because we feel we are unable to accomplish what we want. Envy happens when we see what we want being gained by others; we feel we cannot be the same as they are, so we covet what they have. Desire occurs when we start reaching out once more towards what we value.
- The upper left rectangle involves hope, love and joy, which together indicate the gaining or regaining of what we want. Hope springs forth when we have a sense that we might actually gain what we want. (Note: Some theorists do not consider hope an emotion but instead contend that it is a complex of emotion and cognition.) Through love, we participate in committing to what we value and in working towards attaining it. Joy arises when we feel we are finally integrating with what we value, taking it (in)to ourselves.

These elements of the compass of emotion are helpful for understanding the well of well-being inside teachers. For instance, a teacher might feel a twinge of shame when perceiving an inability to 'get through' to a group of students. Great sorrow might occur when a teacher realizes a student has been in a car accident and the teacher could do nothing to prevent it. Envy might be a teacher's emotion when he or she has been rejected for a major academic opportunity and then hears that a close colleague receives a summer fellowship in Italy or is accepted to present research at an important conference in a desirable city. Joy might emerge during a wonderful lesson or when a student texts words of gratitude, and this might bring a novice teacher hope for his or her own future as an educator. Fear might occur when a teacher realizes that the calmness and cultural sameness of the community is being ripped away by the arrival of new immigrants about whose culture the teacher knows little (see Case 2 in the Appendix).

Using the compass of emotion, teachers can understand that their painful emotions, like their pleasant emotions, are normal. The compass of emotion implies that teachers who experience the pain of despair or fear can hope to experience more pleasant emotions, which are part of the same cycle. There is a 'potential for transformation of destructive emotional experience to constructive emotional experience' (van Deurzen, 2012: 153). Van Deurzen cautioned that loss and gain are not the same as failure and success, and that letting go is as important as building up. She criticized positive psychology's tools, which she considered to be one-sided solutions and overly simplistic techniques. I will discuss positive psychology later.

Now let us turn to teacher's empathy, emotional intelligence, emotion regulation and emotional labour. These are crucial for understanding the well of teachers' emotional well-being.

Teachers' Empathy, Emotional Intelligence, Emotion Regulation and Emotional Labour

Empathy, emotional intelligence, emotion regulation and emotional labour overlap in the well of well-being, as this section will reveal. At the same time, these phenomena offer their own particular contributions to teachers' well-being.

Empathy

Palmer (2009) stated that a broken heart can become a truly open heart. 'Imagine that small, clenched fist of a heart "broken open" into largeness of life, into greater capacity to hold one's own and the world's pain and joy' (Palmer 2009: 6). For a teacher to embrace another person's pain and joy requires empathy. Empathy is not really an emotion; it is a complex emotional response, comprised of caring about the perceived well-being of another person, feeling what that other person feels, sensing his or her needs, and sometimes nonjudgmentally comprehending the person's strengths and weaknesses. To have empathy with others, teachers need, on some level, to recognize their own emotions, needs, strengths and weaknesses.

The constellation of emotions in empathy includes 'sympathy, compassion, soft-heartedness tenderness, and the like' (Batson *et al.*, 2011: 418). This is *emotional (affective) empathy*, which involves feeling an emotion, such as sadness or happiness, that we observe in another (Ghaemi, 2011). This type of empathy has sometimes been called 'fellow feeling' or 'inner sympathy' (Harper, 2018). Other types of empathy are *cognitive empathy*, or thinking someone else's thoughts (or successfully trying to understand that person's thoughts); *motor empathy*, or moving the way another person is moving, as in facial expression or posture; and *sensory empathy*, or experiencing a sensation, such as pain or burning, that the other person experiences. I believe that all these forms of empathy – affective, cognitive, motor and sensory – might be understood in terms of imagination and intensity of feeling: imagining how various people or people in general might feel in a specific situation, imagining a specific person's feelings in that situation, projecting oneself into another person's situation, and actually feeling that person's feeling. (Additionally, see Gordon, 2009; Krznaric, 2014; Lanzoni, 2015.)

Serious, scientific works on empathy are of rather recent vintage (Ghaemi, 2011). The German word (*Einfühlung*, or feeling into), which in the 19th century concerned aesthetic feeling, was translated into English as 'empathy' (*em* + *pathos*, or into + suffering) in 1903. The word comes from the Greek *empatheia* (passion, emotion), which was based on an ancient Proto-Indo-European root word meaning 'to suffer' (Harper, 2018).

Thus, in the early 20th century, empathy became a psychological, psychiatric and neurological issue, no longer a purely aesthetic one (Ghaemi, 2011). Researchers discovered that monkeys' brains mirrored the activity (e.g. arm movements) or feeling (e.g. pain) of other monkeys. 'Coining the term "mirror neuron system," researchers found that 10 percent of the human brain is wired to turn on as if it is *doing* what is only *observing* ... [The human] brain is wired for empathy' (Ghaemi, 2011: 82). Why is that?

> We can't understand each other through words alone; we need to touch, to feel, to stroke each other emotionally and even physically. It is generally estimated that at least one-half of human communication is nonverbal ... Without empathy, we can barely communicate with each other. Empathy is, it seems, central to the human (and rodent and primate) experience. (Ghaemi, 2011: 83)

As noted, the etymology of the term *empathy* (into suffering) strongly suggests 'feeling into' another person's suffering or pain, but Ghaemi makes clear that empathy can also involve experiencing another's good feelings. The following poetic comment reflects this more expansive version of empathy: 'And every time we're touched by another, whether by the contagion of their joy or the opening of their pain, every time the song of life moves from them through us, we carry their note, and add our own, ... [to move] our way into harmony' (Nepo, 2015a).

Emotional intelligence

Empathy can be deepened when the individual has developed emotional intelligence (EI). EI, like empathy, is related to an open heart. EI is the cognitive capability to use reason to comprehend and deal effectively with emotions. It is the 'ability to understand feelings in the self and others and to use these feelings as informational guides for thinking and action' (Salovey *et al.*, 2011: 238). Research shows that EI can reduce anxiety and conflict, improve relationships, and increase harmony, achievement and motivation (Goleman, 2005). In an applied linguistics study (though not a study of teachers), adult multilinguals with higher EI perceived themselves as more self-confident, more capable of controlling stress, and better able to understand others' emotions (Dewaele *et al.*, 2008).

In another study with English language teachers in the UK and Austria, Gkonou and Mercer (2017) examined how six highly emotionally and socially intelligent teachers managed their classrooms and made the effort to understand the emotions of themselves and their students. Through lesson observations and stimulated recall interviews, the authors concluded that the teachers with higher levels of EI delivered lessons with humour, welcomed their students' humour, empathized with their emotions and attended to the emotional needs of individual students as well as of the group as a whole.

A series of research findings (Dewaele & Mercer, 2018; Dewaele *et al.*, 2018; Dewaele, this volume) based on feedback from 513 EFL teachers revealed that high levels of Trait Emotional Intelligence (TEI) were linked to more positive attitudes towards students, more creativity, better classroom management and stronger pedagogical skills. Moreover, high levels of global TEI, and more specifically high levels of the TEI dimensions well-being, self-control, emotionality and sociability, corresponded with high levels of teacher motivation.

Interestingly, Mayer, Caruso and Salovey (2016) described EI as a 'hot' intelligence, i.e. an intelligence that combines reasoning with personally significant information. This contrasts with cool intelligences, which relate to less personal knowledge (e.g. math, visual-spatial).

Emotion regulation

Emotion regulation, like EI, uses reason and logic. According to Gross (2014), the core features of emotion regulation are: (a) activating a *goal*, either intrinsic (regulating one's own emotions), or extrinsic (regulating someone else's emotions); (b) choosing and employing relevant *strategies*, or processes, from explicit to unconscious/automatic, that can alter the emotion trajectory and thus fulfill the goal (regulation of one's or someone else's emotions); and (c) identifying the *outcome* (the emotion dynamics, as well as the emotion modulation or change caused by activating the goal and using the strategies). Gross noted that emotion regulation is part of affective regulation, which also includes mood regulation and coping. (See also Boekaerts, 2011.)

Emotional labour

The term 'emotional labour' (sometimes called 'emotional work'; Oplatka, 2007) is very pertinent to EI and emotion regulation. Winograd (2003) served as an elementary school teacher during a sabbatical from his role as an education professor. He kept a journal and studied functional and dysfunctional aspects of his emotional experiences and the strategies he used for 'emotional labour'. Winograd discovered that discussions with other teachers enabled a much greater understanding of emotions. He found that collective naming and exploration of emotions helped him and other teachers to learn to use emotions like disgust and anger in helpful ways as catalysts for social activism and change.

The following subject, paradoxical benefits of difficult emotions, needs to become better known in relation to teacher emotions. I offer some insights on this subject from key theorists.

Paradoxical Benefits of Difficult Emotions

Positive psychology has recently become well known in applied linguistics (see MacIntyre *et al.*, 2016). Positive psychologist Martin Seligman (2011) used the term 'well-being' to operationalize the more general concept of 'flourishing'. With a history that goes back to the ancient Greek 'virtues philosophies', positive psychology was officially named by Seligman in 2000 and identified as a means of focusing on the strengths of human existence and promoting well-being (Lopez & Gallagher, 2011). Positive psychologists emphasize the value of positive emotions, which they believe broaden learners' response options and build up new skills (Fredrickson, 2004). According to Frederickson, negative emotions serve only to narrow the individual's response options to survival behaviours (fight-or-flight) and fail to build skills for the future.

Gaining wisdom from difficult emotions

Contrary to Frederickson's arguments, under some circumstances (for example, see the stories included in this chapter) difficult emotions can offer helpful learning experiences that strengthen dedication and prepare the way for greater skills. The change can be a major emotional shift, known as *metanoia* (change of the spirit), or it can be a less major but still crucial stroke of insight, a lessening of a burden, a relief, a release or even a 'strange grace', as Weller (2015: 31) put it. Stimulation and sharper focus are potential benefits of anxiety that occurs in anticipation of an event (Marcos-Llinas & Juan Garau, 2009; for other discussions of anxiety, see Gkonou *et al.*, 2017 and Horwitz, 2001). Singer (2007) and Jamison (1993) noted that artists, poets and musicians often distilled their painful emotions into beauty. Further benefits of painful emotions occur in spiritual-philosophical therapy and exploration (Fox, 2000; Frankl, 1984; Oxford, 2015b). It seems appropriate that Nepo's (2015b) poem revealed that hardships contain jewels and that painful and pleasurable emotions are dark and light, curled up together.

Positive psychologist Sonja Lyubomirsky (2007), in contrast with Frederickson and Seligman, presented a more nuanced and more hopeful view of difficult emotions. She emphasized that emotional trauma, which consists of multiple painful emotions, can have benefits, such as a new life perspective, greater maturity, a sense of personal growth, and an overall feeling of transformation potentially leading to happiness. This does not happen automatically; it takes reflection and forgiveness of others and of oneself. Psychiatrist Bessel van der Kolk (2014) provided another rich understanding of emotions and cognitions in trauma. He encouraged writing as a powerful way for traumatized people to discover and understand their emotions.

Political leaders Winston Churchill and Abraham Lincoln were often depressed. They experienced a range of painful emotions, but they managed to live heroically with their various sufferings. These two individuals' painful emotional experiences might have actually *helped them* develop characteristics that made them heroic: sudden insight, empathy, patience, leadership and resilience (Ghaemi, 2011). Emotions of all types, including enjoyable and searing emotions, can be viewed as messengers of the soul (Dirkx, 2002), offering wisdom that contributes to well-being. Buddhist nun Pema Chödrön (2016: 57) noted that when a person experiences difficult emotions, 'a golden opportunity' arises. Rather than panicking, the person can relax 'in the moment of sadness and longing … [and] touch the limitless space of the human heart' (Chödrön, 2016: 57). Chödrön (1991: 81) also encouraged all of us to reconnect to our emotions: 'reconnect with the weather that is ourselves', whether windy, raining, snowing, hailing or calm. Chödrön's books offer reminders that teachers would find extremely helpful.

Happiness is something much greater than just an enjoyable emotion. Matthieu Ricard (2003), a biochemist turned Buddhist monk who wrote *Happiness: A Guide to Developing Life's Most Important Skill*, declared that we often confuse actual happiness with merely seeking pleasant emotions. For Ricard, happiness is about acceptance. Consider this excerpt from Leonard Cohen's (1992) 'Anthem', a song of emotional self-awareness, acceptance and personal enlightenment: 'Ring the bells that still can ring/Forget your perfect offering/There is a crack, a crack in everything/That's how the light gets in'. Recognition of emotional pain and impermanence ('the crack in everything') does not have to stop teachers in their tracks; it can allow them to be more open ('Ring the bells that still can ring') about what is good and joyous.

I am certainly not suggesting that teachers should try to experience difficult emotions in order to develop wisdom or other benefits. The fact is, painful emotions arise without prodding. The question is what teachers should do with those emotions. I support a more balanced perspective than that of Seligman and Frederickson, who incorrectly dismiss painful emotions (which they call negative) as useless or, in the sense of preventing the growth of future skills, destructive. I believe that unenjoyable emotions, like enjoyable ones, are in the well of well-being and ready to offer information if teachers pay attention. Wisdom and compassion come from reflecting on all kinds of emotions in oneself and from understanding such emotions in others. There are a few other necessary steps as well, discussed next.

Experiencing emotional pain and then letting it go

Letting go is a key step not yet discussed above. Singer (2007) explained that becoming familiar with pain is part of our development, but we cannot stay there, holding on tight to pain. 'If you maintain your center, you can learn to *appreciate and respect* even the most difficult [emotional] experiences ... You can experience these very human states without getting lost in them or resisting them' (Singer, 2007: 86). Thus, teachers can experience difficult emotions, learn from them and then let them go.

Chopra (2004: 65) addressed suffering, which is 'pain that we hold on to'. He explained that suffering comes from getting lost in pain, overlooking facts, adopting an unhelpful perspective and obsessing about it, and comparing oneself with others. Chopra argued in favor of detachment, i.e. not making suffering the dominant reality. This is similar to Singer's suggestion of experiencing/accepting difficult emotions but making sure to let them go. Many experts (e.g. Culham *et al.*, 2018; Hutcherson *et al.*, 2008; Zajonc, 2009) suggest meditation, mindfulness and reaching out to others in loving-kindness as ways to handle painful emotions, including in the classroom.

The cases in the next section are stories of specific teachers and teacher educators as they experience the well of emotional well-being for themselves. Not all of the emotions experienced by these individuals were pleasant, but they all contributed to growth and development.

Brief Case Studies of Real Teachers and Teacher Educators Experiencing the Well of Emotional Well-Being

All stories 'identify, unify, give meaning to. Just as music is noise that makes sense, a painting is color that makes sense, so a story is life that makes sense' (Martel, 2011: 15; see also Barkhuizen, 2011, 2013). Storytelling shows how '[p]ersonal identities are ... continually constructed and revised' (Moen, 2006: 5), as well as negotiated and transformed (Bell, 1997; Llovich, 1997), through the help of experience, thought and emotion.

In my prior narrative research (e.g. Cuéllar & Oxford, 2018; Oxford & Bolaños, 2016; Oxford & Cuéllar, 2014; Oxford *et al.*, 2015), I used grounded theory to help discover these meanings (for principles and procedures, see Corbin & Strauss, 2007; Hadley, 2017). Grounded theory keeps researchers from simply overlaying their own ideas and concepts in trying to understand a narrative. Interpretations, or theories, are grounded in the text itself and arise through multiple rounds of analysis. In the right column beside each story I list the emotions next to the place in the text where they occur. At the end of each story, I provide a short interpretation. Following the five stories, I point out themes that tie the stories together and aspects that distinguish each story from the others.

The cases

Case 1. Kathryn

This story was written by an advanced master's student, Kathryn (a pseudonym), reflecting on her teaching experience in a community ESL program.	**The teacher's emotions mentioned or clearly implied**
All students are expected to teach in the CEC while earning our MA-TESOL degree. This was a painful learning experience, but it was also the most 'growing' learning experience for reasons I will explain. I was assigned to teach the highest level (4) of CEC students, who range from high intermediate to advanced proficiency level. I was nervous from the beginning, because I did not know what I could offer to these students in order to challenge them.	Anxiety
While I was teaching these students, I was in a graduate class that was focusing on the instruction and assessment of speaking and listening skills. For this class, I began an exploratory project on fostering fluency through storytelling. I remember being excited to implement this project in my Level 4 CEC, and I was excited and hopeful as I told students how we were going to work on our fluency through storytelling.	Excitement Hope
I started by having students share stories of how they came to the United States. The night that we asked students to come prepared to share their stories, I was so disappointed.	Disappointment
Almost half of the class did not show up, and the students that did show up did not seem to fully understand the task. I left that night feeling defeated. My grand plan of incorporating storytelling into this class seemed pointless.	Feeling of defeat
This was one of the many nights that semester that I left the classroom feeling like a failure of a teacher. I could never seem to adequately challenge my students enough, and I felt like I was in way over my head.	Feeling of failure, inadequacy 'Over my head'
Through writing lesson reflections and lesson reports, I began to narrow down where I was making mistakes in class. Throughout the time I was teaching this course, I was also very transparent with my students. I told them that I was learning and that they needed to help me. This collaboration that we started in the classroom really brought our class together as a community of learners, teacher included.	Transparency (openness, honesty)
I left that semester feeling like I had really grown as a teacher. I walked away from that classroom knowing that I had given my all for the students, but also for myself. I know that I am a better teacher because of the challenges presented to me by that semester.	Satisfaction in accomplishment
Brief interpretation: Kathryn, anxious about not knowing how to teach adults in the community English program and caring deeply about her students, came up with a grand idea: student storytelling. Her hopes crashed, leaving her with a powerful sense of being defeated and over her head. She started figuring out what went wrong, asked for students' help, and ended the semester satisfied that she had given her all for her students and for herself.	

Case 2. Mark

This story was told to me in an interview by Mark (a pseudonym), a first-grade teacher in a rural southern town in the US. Some details were changed for anonymity's sake.	**The teacher's emotions mentioned or clearly implied**
I am a first-grade teacher in a rural town in the southeastern part of the US. The state ESL coordinator offered me full tuition to earn master's level certification in teaching ESL. I accepted because I was eager to earn an extra certification, which would increase my salary.	Eagerness (for salary)
However, I had never met a Mexican kid. I distrusted their parents, who were called 'undocumented workers' and 'aliens' and who had recently come to work at the new chicken processing plant.	Distrust
Like my neighbors, I feared that these newcomers were taking the jobs of local people and would hurt our town's economy.	Fear
When the Mexican immigrants arrived, I was studying at night for my ESL certification and knew I would eventually teach the children of these undocumented workers, but I was very conflicted.	Confusion
I felt hostile toward the kids' parents for breaking the law, being here without papers, and invading our town socially and economically.	Hostility
I felt scared to have them in the community.	Fear
I looked down on these Mexicans; I saw them as shifty for not making eye contact with me and crude for living ten to twelve people together, for dressing poorly, and (because they didn't know English) for being stupid.	Disdain ('looked down on')
Also, I was worried about how I could teach these Spanish-speaking kids without knowing Spanish myself.	Fear, worry
However, in graduate school discussions, I reflected on my own emotions, attitudes, and stereotypes toward the immigrants. I felt ashamed that I had considered them crude, stupid, and dangerous.	Ashamed
I realized that they were courageous for making the long and dangerous trip, often with the purpose of escaping greater danger from gang warfare back home.	Respect for courage
This empathy led me to want to help. Before finishing the ESL certification program, I started tutoring some of the older kids. I gathered up clothing and food for the families. I started learning Spanish.	Empathy (→ positive action)
All this made me feel more confident and more capable of improving the situation.	Confidence
I finished the ESL certification program and began to teach many Mexican kids in my first-grade class. I helped them become friends with the local kids through games, sports, and class activities.	Kindness (help, encouragement)
I encouraged my fellow church members to get committed to social justice, a new stance in our almost lily-white town.	Commitment/ dedication
I kept reminding everyone what the Bible said about sharing freely with poor people and about loving the stranger. The church gradually remembered that being Christian meant being generous and loving to the new people, even though we didn't expect or want them at first. More church members started tutoring, leading after-school soccer that included the new kids, and giving Mexican mothers rides to the grocery store. Many prejudices fell away, not just in me but in my long-time neighbors.	Love
We care about the newcomers. It was a transformation from the time when they had just arrived – the time when no one wanted them here. They did not come to take our jobs after all.	Care
None of our locals wanted a chicken-plucking job, which is difficult, dirty, and underpaid. These immigrants work hard, so we will keep working to integrate, educate, and help those who arrive.	Respect for hard work
By living here they are teaching us about another culture and helping us to practice their language. And their presence reminds us about what charity and friendship mean.	Friendship
Brief interpretation: Mark, a first-grade teacher, was motivated by money to get his ESL teaching certification. When the first Mexican immigrants showed up in his town, he was simultaneously fearful of and disdainful towards the new arrivals. In his graduate coursework towards ESL certification, he felt ashamed when realizing that he had stereotyped the immigrants. Experiencing a tremendous change (metanoia), he became committed to helping the newcomers. His confidence grew along with his caring and respect for the immigrants, who are teaching the town about culture, charity and friendship.	

Case 3. Ellen

This story was written by a language teacher, Ellen (a pseudonym), who was shocked by the treatment of a troubled student.	**The teacher's emotions mentioned or clearly implied**
I loved teaching the high school language classes and adored the kids, who mostly worked hard and well. Our classes were lively and unorthodox and full of learning. I confidently gathered up all sorts of extra material (like magazines and pictures) to bring to class. I brought in records and a tiny record player. All this was fine, but I had no room of my own and had to lug all the stuff from room to room. The happiness was worth every effort. *Once we had a 'field trip' to the city hospital. I had been invited to translate for a young Russian steamship cook (her ship was in our city harbor) who had just had surgery for an ectopic pregnancy. I was anxious about translating, but it all worked out because the students were so eager to meet the patient, and she was pleased, too. It was wonderful for the students to be part of this odd, exciting event.* *However, one student, Peter, sorely struggled in school. He had family problems, including fights with his father. I was worried about this, but I did not yet know that Peter had started using drugs and that he was actively trying to get his Russian class friends involved. When I heard about this from another student, I was angry and anxious. The harmony of the Russian program was being shaken. I felt guilty for not having been aware of the situation. When I went to see Mr. Hardwicke, the assistant principal, I cried real tears from frustration. He said it was not my fault and that no teacher could have prevented Peter's problems. He reminded me that I had been doing a 'very good job' with the children and that the school was glad that I had organized the district's first and only Russian language program. As I was calming down, Mr. Hardwicke told me the terrible news that he had expelled Peter from school for the rest of the academic year and that the boy would receive failing grades in every class. Teachers were not allowed to contact Peter, take him study assignments, or get involved with his family. However, he was allowed to say goodbye to me. When he came to see me, he was angry at the school for not giving him another chance. I, too, was outraged at the school and very sad for him.* *Somehow the Russian program continued and thrived. The students and I continued to experience moments of great joy in Russian classes, but we all remembered Peter, who, despite his great flaws, had been a class jokester and a friend to many. As I discovered the complexity of teaching in high school and the sorrow of not being able to help Peter, I became distrustful of and less hopeful about an educational institution that merely punished troubled children without creating a way for them to grow and become more responsible. There was a hole in my heart for Peter, a confused, wayward young man who had been thrown off the education tribe, perhaps forever. I never saw him again.*	Love of teaching and students Confidence Happiness Anxiety Eagerness Pleasure Worry Anger Worry Guilt Frustration (Slight calm) Outrage Sadness Joy Sorrow Decreased trust and hope
Brief interpretation: Ellen, a new teacher, was overjoyed with her experience of Russian language teaching and loved her students. However, one student's drug problems incited the wrath of the administration, which ejected the boy from the education 'tribe' with no support. Though still experiencing moments of joy with her Russian classes after that, she felt continuing sorrow for the lost student and experienced decreased trust and hope concerning the school.	

Case 4. Al

The following story, composed of prose and poetry, was written by Al (a pseudonym), a retired ESL teacher.	**The teacher's emotions mentioned or clearly implied**
With teaching certification in both mathematics and ESL, I taught algebra in self-contained high school classes in the outskirts of Washington, DC. I taught 150 immigrant ESL students per day. Most of them came from Mexico and Central America without legal identity papers. A very large percentage of students had experienced violence and deprivation, and some of their relatives had been killed by gangs in the home countries. Only a few of my ESL students were from middle-class homes. I felt great compassion for all the students and wanted them to learn.	Compassion
The most frustrating thing was not dealing with immigrant teenagers, who were mostly good kids. What caused me the most grief was constantly having to fight with the school administrative staff to get them to pay attention to the academic and social needs of ESL students. Some of the students could not read in any language but were immediately assigned to algebra classes with textbooks in English and repeatedly forced to take (and fail) half-day standardized tests several times a year, sometimes just after arriving. I often felt angry, frustrated, and impotent when dealing with an uncaring, disorganized administrative staff. I could understand why the wonderful math department chair had left after getting nowhere in championing ESL students' rights with the school administrators. After fighting and losing the battle with the school administrators over many years, I finally retired with a sense of grief and futility. I tried to forget the situation.	Frustration Grief Anger Frustration Impotence (helplessness) Grief Sense of futility
Ironically, I heard that the year after I left, the administration had finally started implementing some of my suggestions, such as creating classes for students who could not yet handle the language demands of algebra. I felt a tiny bit vindicated, but mostly relieved that something, even a little thing, was being done to help ESL students in math.	Vindication Relief
Years later, I felt calmer and more serene. Here is a poem I wrote recently.	Calmness Serenity
Step out, move slowly. *Flow into the next step, and the next,* *Smoothly sliding along.* *Each glide is a poem.* *The journey is an endless flow.*	
Yet some frightening things are happening to disturb my calmness and that of the whole country. Our president refers to undocumented Mexican and Central American immigrants as thieves, murderers, rapists, and animals. This angers me. He instituted a new policy to separate the undocumented parents from their children at the southwestern border of the US. His minions sent the children all over the country without tracking them effectively. There is still no real plan for bringing all of the separated families back together, though some have been unified. The turbulence spurred me to write these anguished lines:	Fear Anger Anguish
The storm is raging. *It comes at us from all sides.* *Scared children cry.*	
Let's hope that the storm stops and that calmness returns to the hearts and minds in our country. As a retired teacher, I can hope and pray for the federal government to cease using cruelty as a political strategy. I can also send money to support family reunification.	Calmness
Brief interpretation: Al, a compassionate ESL-math teacher, was frustrated and angry when the school administration constantly ignored his students' needs. He finally gave up and retired, eventually experiencing calmness and serenity. Then new events shattered the calm. Just as he had objected to a school administration that was uncaring to undocumented immigrant children, he was anguished and angry to discover the federal government's punitive separation of undocumented immigrant families.	

Case 5. Rebecca

Rebecca (the author of this chapter) wrote this brief intellectual-emotional history of her life of teaching and teacher education. She looked back at her peak experiences in these roles.	**The teacher's emotions mentioned or clearly implied**
Among the highest of my peak experiences in language teaching were the everyday instructional interactions with high school students and later on with college students. Most of the time I felt we were treading special ground, sacred ground. We were in a loving space of cooperative learning. Gusts of laughter, gratitude, acceptance, enjoyment, and lowered anxiety permeated the air. *Some years after I taught foreign languages in a high school and a university, I became a language teacher educator and again had memorable peak experiences. I taught future teachers about cooperative learning and about invitational teaching, in which teachers welcome and honor their students and provide inviting, stimulating education. Decades later, I learned about and shared with future teachers 'deep education' and the 'epistemology of love'. I discovered in my fifties that deep education calls on both sides of the brain, aims at wisdom, and involves loving collaboration, compassion, creative imagination, engagement, and radical amazement. The epistemology of love, I learned, is much the same as deep education; it accepts vulnerability and fear (in me and in the learners) but transmutes them into insight, love, and peace. Long ago, when I was a novice teacher in my twenties, I had intuited, felt, and enacted many of these ideas, although at the time I had no words for them and although I had been simultaneously struggling with decisions about marriage and my early career.* *In my role as a language teacher educator in a large TESOL master's program, I have not only been helping prospective teachers to hone their teaching skills but have also been emphasizing the epistemology of love. All the master's students understood the ideas, and a number of them incorporated the concepts into their lives and their language teaching. Two of them allowed me to use their statements, which I will share here (with pseudonyms). Martin wrote, 'Students are not breathing robots that will produce output if you give them enough input. The human soul needs to be fed as much as the brain. Teachers need to create caring environments.' Jessica stated, 'Emotions are from the mind and felt in the body, which is experienced in the spirit. The most powerful part of teaching and learning occurs when love is involved.'* *Martin and Jessica performed passionately and well in their long-term practice-teaching at the university, where they employed the epistemology of love, along with their instructional talents, to establish positive classroom environments, discover students' needs, and engage students. Each then went on to teach EFL, one as a Peace Corps volunteer in Costa Rica and the other as a university teacher in China. They planned to implement their understandings of the epistemology of love into their teaching overseas. I imagined the loving-kindness of Jessica, Martin, and other effective teachers, now and in the past, as a golden aura encircling the planet. With all the difficulties in the world, I was grateful for all teachers who possessed the combination of instructional skills, sensitivity, caring, and love.*	Love Gratitude Acceptance Joy (enjoyment) Lowered anxiety Love Compassion Creativity Amazement Transformation of vulnerability and fear Love Peacefulness Love (Students' comments on caring and love) Love Love Loving-kindness Gratitude Care Love
Brief interpretation: In Rebecca's experiences in language teaching and teacher education, love, joy and gratitude often emerged in her and her students. As a teacher educator, she discovered the meaning of 'deep education' and the 'epistemology of love' and realized that she had experienced aspects of these phenomena as a young teacher. When teaching future ESL/EFL teachers about the epistemology of love, some intentionally used the concepts in their instruction. Rebecca was grateful for the continued spreading of love through language teaching.	

Themes and comments

One theme in the stories is emotions and attitudes regarding immigrants. Mark and Al had strong feelings about immigrants who arrived in the country illegally (without papers). Mark was initially biased against the new, undocumented Mexican immigrants in his town, but his graduate studies awakened him to his stereotypical thinking. He experienced a metanoia – a massive change toward the better in his beliefs, emotions and behaviors as he prepared to become an ESL teacher. In contrast, Al, a teacher of ESL math, always deeply cared about undocumented immigrants, including those in his classes.

Another theme is emotions involved in clashes between caring teachers and uncaring, hostile or immovable administrations. Ellen, a teacher of Russian, was outraged when the assistant principal threw a troubled teenager out of the education 'tribe' with no support and no clear possibility for re-entry. She remained happy in her teaching, but her trust in the school as an institution plummeted. Al was distraught when the administrators dealt miserably with the undocumented immigrant students in the high school where he taught. He eventually retired and lived a calm existence, but his serenity collapsed when the nation's president did far worse things to illegal immigrants than the school administration had done.

Kathryn, who was at the beginning of her teaching career, and Rebecca, who was toward the end of hers, bookended the series of stories. The relevant theme is beginnings and endings, with caring and love throughout. Caring Kathryn was a young teacher-in-training who thought up a creative instructional activity, which flopped completely in the adult ESL classroom. She felt defeated, but her collaborative recovery strategies were perfect, and when the term ended, she felt satisfied that she had given everything she could. Rebecca, after a few years as a foreign language teacher and then many years as a language teacher educator, looked back on peak experiences in those roles. She recognized that love was the subtle song in all the peak experiences. She was grateful that the concepts she shared concerning the epistemology of love were understood and actively implemented.

Conclusion

This chapter discussed the well of language teachers' emotional well-being. I shared Emmy van Deurzen's quite germane 'compass of emotion', followed by brief explorations of empathy, emotional intelligence, emotion regulation and emotional labour as applied to teachers. I also contended that contributions to teachers' emotional well-being come not only from pleasant emotions but also from painful ones. When difficult emotions – the ever-moving bubbles in the well that are brackish-seeming and unappealing – are felt as catalysts for growth and are then let go, they can be immensely valuable to well-being. The five case studies emphasize the value of pleasant and unpleasant emotions in the lives of real teachers and teacher educators.

Post-Reading Tasks

(1) Why does the chapter use the visual metaphor of a well? What other visual metaphors might also be useful for this chapter or other chapters in the book?
(2) In which ways does this chapter support ideas from positive psychology? Why is it important to learn from difficult emotions, even though positive psychology does not emphasize this? How can a teacher learn from difficult emotions without being swallowed up by them?
(3) Please name five new things you learned from Van Deurzen's compass of emotion. How might you suggest adding to or adapting the compass of emotion to make it optimally useful to language teachers or language teacher educators?
(4) Reread the brief case studies at the end of the chapter. Why are case studies helpful for understanding emotions? Write a brief case study or story revealing the emotions you experienced in a recent situation involving language teaching, language learning or language teacher education. What did you learn from this case study or story?

Acknowledgments

I wholeheartedly thank Christina Gkonou and Jean-Marc Dewaele for inviting me to write this chapter and for their outstanding support and ideas. At times I have worked with wonderful, well-informed, intelligent, kind, generous and exciting editors. Christina and Jean-Marc, along with their co-editor Jim King, are among this small and special coterie. I am deeply grateful.

Notes

(1) Lao-Tzu was a spiritual teacher who lived in the 6th century BCE and who reputedly authored the sacred work *Tao Te Ching* (The Book of the Way).The Tao is the absolute principle of the universe; the unity of yin and yang; the combination of spirit, information and matter. It also embodies emotion (Culham *et al.*, 2018). Taoism has much in common with some ideas in this chapter but not others, so I do not use it as a master framework here; yet the image of the Tao as a well is unforgettable and highly relevant.
(2) Well-being has many definitions and descriptions in multiple disciplines, such as health, mindfulness, spirituality, positive psychology and self psychology (e.g. Chopra, 2004; Fredrickson, 2004; Lifton, 1993; Lopez & Gallagher, 2011; Mischke-Reeds, 2015; Mercer & Williams, 2014; Seligman, 2011).

References

Barkhuizen, G. (2011) Narrative knowledging in TESOL. *TESOL Quarterly* 45 (3), 391–444.

Barkhuizen, G. (ed.) (2013) *Narrative Research in Applied Linguistics.* Cambridge: Cambridge University Press.

Batson, C.D., Ahmad, N. and Lishner, D.A. (2011) Empathy and altruism. In S.J. Lopez and C.R. Snyder (eds) *The Oxford Handbook of Positive Psychology* (pp. 417–426). New York: Oxford University Press.

Bell, J.S. (1997) *Literacy, Culture, and Identity.* New York: Peter Lang.

Berry, J.W., Poortinga, Y.H., Segall, M.H. and Dasen, P.R. (2002) *Cross-Cultural Psychology: Research and Applications* (2nd edn). Cambridge: Cambridge University Press.

Boekaerts, M. (2011) Emotions, emotion regulation, and self-regulation of learning. In B.J. Zimmerman and D.H. Schunk (eds) *Handbook of Self-Regulation of Learning and Performance* (pp. 408–425). New York: Routledge.

Chödrön, P. (1991) *The Wisdom of No Escape and The Path of Loving-Kindness.* Boulder, CO: Shambala.

Chödrön, P. (2016) *When Things Fall Apart: Advice for Difficult Times.* Boulder, CO: Shambala.

Chopra, D. (2004) *The Book of Secrets: Unlocking the Hidden Dimensions of Your Life.* New York: Three Rivers Press/Random House.

Cohen, L. (1992) Anthem [song]. *The Future* [album]. New York: Columbia Records.

Corbin, J. and Strauss, A. (2007) *Basics of Qualitative Research* (3rd edn). Thousand Oaks, CA: SAGE.

Cuéllar, L. and Oxford, R.L. (2018) Language teachers' emotions: Emerging from the shadows. In J. de D. Martínez Agudo (ed.) *Emotions in Second Language Teaching.* Cham, Switzerland: Springer International.

Culham, T., Oxford, R. and Lin, J. (2018) Cultivating the abilities of the heart: Educating through the pedagogy of love. In J. Miller (ed.) *International Handbook in Holistic Education.* New York: Routledge.

Dewaele, J.-M. and Mercer, S. (2018) Variation in ESL/EFL teachers' attitudes towards their students. In S. Mercer and A. Kostoulas (eds) *Language Teacher Psychology* (pp. 178–195). Bristol: Multilingual Matters.

Dewaele, J-M., Petrides, K.V. and Furnham, A. (2008) The effects of trait emotional intelligence and sociobiographical variables on communicative anxiety and foreign language anxiety among adult multilinguals: A review and empirical investigation. *Language Learning* 58, 911-960.

Dewaele, J.-M., Gkonou, C. and Mercer, S. (2018) Do ESL/EFL teachers' emotional intelligence, teaching experience, proficiency and gender, affect their classroom practice? In J. de Dios Martínez Agudo (ed.) *Emotions in Second Language Teaching: Theory, Research and Teacher Education* (pp. 125–141). Berlin: Springer.

Dirkx, J.M. (2002) The power of feelings: Emotion, imagination, and the construction of meaning in adult learning. In S. Merriam (guest ed.) *The New Update on Adult Learning Theory.* Special issue, *New Directions for Adult and Continuing Education* 2001 (89): 63–72. doi: 10.1002/ace.9.

Dörnyei, Z. (2009) *The Psychology of Second Language Acquisition.* Oxford: Oxford University Press.

Fox, M. (2000) *Original Blessing: A Primer in Creation Spirituality Presented in Four Paths, Twenty-Six Themes, and Two Questions.* San Francisco: Tarcher/Putnam.

Frank, D. (2017) Photograph. Copyright free use. Creative Commons License. Pexels. See https://www.pexels.com/photo/blue-bubble-calamity-clean-287229/ (accessed 12 January 2018).

Frankl, V.E. (1984) *Man's Search for Meaning: An Introduction to Logotherapy*, trans. I. Lasch. Boston: Beacon.

Frederickson, B.L. (2004) The broaden-and-build theory of positive emotions. *Philosophical Transactions of the Royal Society of London (Biological Sciences)* 359, 1367–1377.

Ghaemi, N. (2011) *A First-Rate Madness: Uncovering the Links between Leadership and Mental Illness.* New York: Penguin.

Gkonou, C. and Mercer, S. (2017) *Understanding Emotional and Social Intelligence Among English Language Teachers*. London: British Council.

Gkonou, C., Daubney, M. and Dewaele, J.-M. (eds) (2017) *New Insights into Language Anxiety: Theory, Research, and Educational Implications*. Bristol: Multilingual Matters.

Goleman, D. (2005) *Emotional Intelligence: Why It Can Matter More Than IQ* (2nd edn). New York: Bantam Books.

Gordon, M. (2009) *Roots of Empathy: Changing the World Child by Child*. New York: The Experiment Publishing.

Gross, J.J. (2014) Emotion regulation: Conceptual and empirical foundations. In J.J. Gross (ed.) *Handbook of Emotion Regulation* (2nd edn) (pp. 3–20). New York: Guilford.

Hadley, G. (2017) *Grounded Theory in Applied Linguistics Research*. New York: Routledge.

Harper, D. (2018) Empathy. *Etymology Online*. See https://www.etymonline.com/word/empathy (accessed 3 February 2020).

Heaney, S. (1991) Doubletake. *The Cure at Troy: A Version of Sophocles' Philoctetes* (p. 77). New York: Farrar, Straus & Giroux.

Horwitz, E. (2001) Language anxiety and achievement. *Annual Review of Applied Linguistics* 21, 112–126.

Hutcherson, C.A., Seppala, E.M. and Gross, J.J. (2008) Loving-kindness meditation increases social connectedness. *Emotion* 8, 720–724.

Jamison, K.R. (1993) *Touched by Fire: Manic-Depressive Illness and the Artistic Temperament*. New York: Free Press.

Kalaja, P., Barcelos, A.M.F., Aro, M. and Ruohotie-Lyhty, M. (2016) *Beliefs, Agency and Identity in Foreign Language Learning and Teaching*. Basingstoke, Hampshire: Palgrave Macmillan.

Krznaric, R. (2014) *Empathy: Why It Matters, and How to Get It*. New York: Rider / Random House.

Lanzoni, S. (2015) A short history of empathy. *Atlantic Magazine*, 15 October. See https://www.theatlantic.com/health/archive/2015/10/a-short-history-of-empathy/409912/ (accessed 2 March 2018).

Lao-Tzu (2006) *Tao Te Ching: A New English Version*, trans. S. Mitchell. New York: Harper Perennial Modern Classics.

Lewis, M. (2005) Bridging emotion theory and neurobiology through dynamic systems modeling. *Behavior and Brain Science* 28 (2), 169–245.

Lifton, R.J. (1993) *The Protean Self: Human Resilience in an Age of Fragmentation*. Chicago: University of Chicago Press.

Llovich, N. (1997) *The Multilingual Self: An Inquiry into Language Learning*. Hillsdale, NJ: Erlbaum.

Lopez, S.J. and Gallagher, M.W. (2011) A case for positive psychology. In S.J. Lopez and C.R. Snyder (eds) *The Oxford Handbook of Positive Psychology* (pp. 3–6). New York: Oxford University Press.

Lyubomirsky, S. (2007) *The How of Happiness: New Approach to Getting the Life You Want*. London: Penguin.

MacIntyre, P.D. (2002) Motivation, anxiety, and emotion in second language acquisition. In P. Robinson (ed.) *Individual Differences and Instructed Language Learning* (pp. 45–68). Amsterdam: John Benjamins.

MacIntyre, P.D. and Mercer, S. (2014) Introducing positive psychology to SLA. *Studies in Second Language Learning and Teaching* 4, 153–172.

MacIntyre, P.D., Gregersen, T. and Mercer, S. (2016) *Positive Psychology in SLA*. Bristol: Multilingual Matters.

Marcos-Llinas, M. and Juan Garau, M. (2009) Effects of language anxiety on three proficiency-level courses of Spanish as a foreign language. *Foreign Language Annals* 42 (1), 94–111.

Martel, Y. (2011) *Beatrice and Virgil: A Novel*. New York: Spiegel & Grau.

Martínez Agudo, J. de D. (ed.) (2018) *Emotions in Second Language Teaching*. Cham, Switzerland: Springer International.

Mayer, J.D., Caruso, D.R. and Salovey, P. (2016) The ability model of emotional intelligence: Principles and updates. *Emotion Review* 8 (4), 290–300.

Mercer, S. and Kostoulas, A. (2018) *Language Teacher Psychology*. Bristol: Multilingual Matters.

Mercer, S. and Williams, M. (eds) (2014) *Multiple Perspectives on the Self in SLA* (pp. 160–176). Bristol: Multilingual Matters.

Mischke-Reeds, M. (2015) *8 Keys to Practicing Mindfulness: Practical Strategies for Emotional Health and Well Being*. New York: W.W. Norton.

Moen, T. (2006) Reflections on the narrative research approach. *International Journal of Qualitative Methodology* 5 (4), Article 5. See http://www.ualberta.ca/~iiqm/backissues/5_4/html/moen.htm (accessed 2 March 2018).

Nepo, M. (2015a) And every time we're touched by another ... Beyond the telling, para. 7. *Field Notes on Living*. Blog.See http://www.patheos.com/blogs/fieldnotesonliving/2015/04/07/beyond-the-telling/#1R0ALQVp0yCEdMSZ.99 (accessed 13 March 2018).

Nepo, M. (2015b) A few turns of the moon. *Huffington Post*, 27 January, updated 29 March.

Oplatka, I. (2007) Managing emotions in teaching: Toward an understanding of emotion displays and caring as nonprescribed role elements. *Teachers College Record* 109 (6), 1374–1400. See http://www.tcrecord.org ID Number: 13099 (accessed 27 March 2018).

Ostrom, T.M. (1969) The relationship between the affective, behavioral, and cognitive components of attitude. *Journal of Experimental Social Psychology* 5 (1), 12–30. doi: 10.1016/0022-1031(69)90003-1.

Oxford, R.L. (2015a) Emotion as the amplifier and the primary motive: Some theories of emotion with relevance to language learning. *Studies in Second Language Learning and Teaching* 5 (3), 371–393. doi: 10.14746/ssllt.2015.5.3.2.

Oxford, R.L. (2015b) How language learners can improve their emotional functioning: Important psychological and psychospiritual theories. *Applied Language Learning* 25 (1&2), 1–15.

Oxford, R.L. (2020) Snapshots in time: Time in Gardner's theory and Gardner's theory across time. In A. Al-Hoorie and P.D. MacIntyre (eds) *Contemporary Language Motivation Theory: 60 Years since Gardner and Lambert (1959)* (pp. 171–193). Bristol: Multilingual Matters.

Oxford, R.L. and Bolaños, D. (2016) A tale of two learners: Discovering motivation, emotions, engagement, perseverance, and mentoring. In C. Gkonou, D. Tatzl and S. Mercer (eds) *New Directions in Language Learning Psychology* (pp. 113–134). Cham, Switzerland: Springer.

Oxford, R.L. and Cuéllar, L. (2014) Positive psychology in cross-cultural narratives: Mexican students discover themselves while learning. *Studies in Second Language Learning and Teaching* 4 (2), 173–203. doi: 10.14746/ssllt.2014.4.2.3.

Oxford, R.L., Pacheco Acuña, G., Solís Hernández, M. and Smith, A.L. (2015) A language is a mentality: A narrative, positive-psychological view of six learners' development of bilingualism. *System* 55, 100–110. doi: 10.1016/j.system.2015.08.005.

Palmer, P.J. (2009) The broken-open heart: Living with faith and hope in the tragic gap. Reprinted from *Weavings: A Journal of the Christian Spiritual Life*, 24 (2). See www.couragerenewal.org/PDFs/PJP-WeavingsArticle-Broken-OpenHeart.pdf (accessed 6 December 2018).

Ricard, M. (2003) *Happiness: A Guide to Developing Life's Most Important Skill*, trans. J. Browner. New York: Little, Brown.

Salovey, P., Mayer, J.D., Caruso, D.E. and Yoo, S.H. (2011) The positive psychology of emotional intelligence. In S.J. Lopez and C.R. Snyder (eds) *The Oxford Handbook of Positive Psychology* (pp. 237–248). New York: Oxford University Press.

Seligman, M.E.P. (2011) *Flourish: A Visionary New Understanding of Happiness and Well-Being*. New York: Atria/Simon & Schuster.

Singer, M.A. (2007) *The Untethered Soul: The Journey Beyond Yourself*. Oakland, CA: Noetic Books.

Sisters of Mercy (2018) Welcome. *Well of Mercy*. See http://www.wellofmercy.org/ (accessed 13 March 2018).

van der Kolk, B.A. (2014) *The Body Keeps the Score: Brain, Mind, and Body in the Healing of Trauma*. New York: Viking Penguin.

van Deurzen, E. (2012) *Existential Counselling and Psychotherapy in Practice* (3rd edn). London: SAGE.

Weller, F. (2015) *The Wild Edge of Sorrow: Rituals of Renewal and the Sacred Work of Grief*. Berkeley, CA: North Atlantic Books.

Winograd, K. (2003) The functions of teacher emotions: the good, the bad, and the ugly. *Teachers College Record* 105 (9), 1641–1673. See http://www.tcrecord.org (accessed 27 March 2018).

Zajonc, A. (2009) *Meditation as Contemplative Inquiry: When Knowing Becomes Love*. Aurora, CO: Lindisfarne.

15 What Psychological, Linguistic and Sociobiographical Variables Power EFL/ESL Teachers' Motivation?

Jean-Marc Dewaele

Introduction

Teachers stand in the middle of a whirlpool of learners' emotions. Rather than standing there as an unmovable rock, they might benefit from being like a flexible reed, or antenna, receptive to the mood and needs of the students, aware of their own emotions and motivations, and able to emit the verbal and nonverbal stream that creates a positive emotional classroom climate focused on attaining the learning objectives. Dewaele, Gkonou and Mercer (2018a) described the qualities of a good teacher as follows:

> Essentially, a good language teacher needs to be in a position to manage the emotional tenor of the classroom. This means not only should they be able to harness the emotions of their learners, but they should also be able to regulate their own emotions to ensure they are in the right frame of mind to create positive rapport with learners, generate enjoyment and manage any anxieties. (2018a: 126)

We are witnessing a growing interest in the psychology of foreign language (FL) teachers in the field of applied linguistics (Mercer, 2016; Mercer & Kostoulas, 2018; Mercer *et al.*, 2016; Talbot & Mercer, 2018) in the wake of the wave of interest in the psychology of the FL learners (Dewaele, 2005, 2012, 2015, 2017, Dewaele *et al.*, 2019; Dörnyei & Ryan, 2015). The focus on FL teachers is of crucial importance as teachers are the guides for FL learners, and without their guidance, many learners would stumble in the dark. As De Costa, Rawal and Li (2018) pointed out, 'there has also been energetic increase in attention to language teacher emotions, making it the proverbial newest kid on the SLTE block' (2018: 401).

The current study contributes to this field by expanding earlier work (Dewaele *et al.*, 2018a; Dewaele & Mercer, 2018) on sources of individual differences in teachers' self-reported classroom behaviour. In these earlier studies EFL and ESL teachers' self-reported classroom practices were connected with their global trait emotional intelligence (Trait EI), their English proficiency, the length of their teaching experience and their gender. In the current study we focus on FL teachers' motivation (Fernet *et al.*, 2008), considering the relationship with previously mentioned independent variables, as well as teachers' age and the status of their English (first or foreign language). By not just considering global Trait EI but also the four facets that constitute it, namely well-being, emotionality, self-control and sociability (Petrides & Furnham, 2000, 2001), we aim for more granularity in the understanding of the complex relationships between these personality dimensions and motivation.

Literature Review

Fernet *et al.* (2008) pointed out that teachers' motivation is associated with students' motivation but that teachers' motivation is particularly complex, given the multiple tasks that they have to perform and the impact these have on their psychological functioning. Indeed, 'motivational processes are not necessarily uniform and may vary across the different work tasks carried out by teachers' (2008: 257). The authors adopted self-determination theory as a theoretical framework to understand teachers' motivation because they like the fact that it considers both quantity and quality of motivation. They developed the Work Tasks Motivation Scale for Teachers (WTMST) based on the feedback of 609 Canadian teachers in Quebec City in order 'to assess the constructs of intrinsic motivation, identified, introjected, and external regulations, and amotivation toward six work tasks (i.e., class preparation, teaching, evaluation of students, class management, administrative tasks, and complementary tasks)' (2008: 274). The WTMST has been used to investigate the link between teacher motivation and effective teaching of pre-service teachers (Perlman, 2013), as well as burnout in teachers (Fernet *et al.*, 2012) and intentions to teach an innovative subject and participate in training (Gorozidis & Papaioannou, 2014).

Fernet *et al.* (2008) distinguished five dimensions: **intrinsically motivated** behaviours that teachers 'are engaged in for the pleasure or the satisfaction derived from performing them' (Fernet *et al.*, 2008: 258). They stand in contrast with **extrinsically motivated** behaviours which are instrumental in nature: **identified regulation** 'is defined as behaviour that individuals choose to perform because it is congruent with their own values and goals' (2008: 258). **Introjected regulation** 'corresponds to the process whereby an external demand becomes an internal representation' (2008: 258). **External regulation** 'occurs when behaviours are regulated to obtain a reward or to avoid a constraint'. Finally, there is **amotivation**, which 'refers to being neither intrinsically nor extrinsically motivated' (2008: 258).

Petrides (2017) explained that Trait EI is a personality trait that is linked to nature rather than nurture:

> Trait EI is currently the only definition that recognizes the inherent subjectivity of emotional experience. That the trait EI facets are personality traits, as opposed to mental abilities or competencies, is also corroborated by research revealing that the same genes that are implicated in the development of individual differences in the Big Five personality traits are also implicated in the development of individual differences in trait EI. (2017: 2)

Trait EI essentially concerns people's self-perceptions of their emotional abilities and their inner world. An alternative label for the same construct is trait emotional self-efficacy. Trait EI consists of 15 facets organised under four main factors: well-being, emotionality, self-control and sociability (Petrides & Furnham, 2001). The factor well-being is characterised by the ability to feel cheerful and satisfied with life (happiness), to be self-confident (self-esteem) and to look at the bright side of life (optimism). The emotionality factor is related to the ability of taking someone else's perspective (empathy), of being clear about people's feelings (emotional perception), of communicating feelings to others (emotional expression) and of maintaining fulfilling personal relationships (relationships). The self-control factor refers to the abilities to control emotions (emotional regulation), not to give in to urges (impulsiveness) and to withstand pressure and regulate stress (stress management). The final factor is sociability, and it refers to the ability to influence other people's feelings (emotional management), to stand up for one's rights (assertiveness) and to establish networks thanks to social skills (social awareness).

Research in general education has revealed that Trait EI is a crucial personality trait for teachers. Those who score highly on Trait EI are better equipped to deal with the challenges of working with diverse heterogeneous classes, managing group dynamics and resisting teacher stress and burnout (see e.g. Brackett *et al.*, 2010; Chan, 2006; Corcoran & Tormey, 2012a, 2012b, 2013; Jennings & Greenberg, 2009). Such teachers are better able to create engaging lessons that boost learners' motivation (Elias & Arnold, 2006; Graziano *et al.*, 2007; Nizielski *et al.*, 2012).

High levels of Trait EI among FL teachers have been found to be linked to stronger teacher self-efficacy (Moafian & Ghanizadeh, 2009) and better emotion regulation skills during teaching (Gregersen *et al.*, 2014). Gregersen *et al.* (2014) focused on one learner and one teacher, extracted from a group of 10 learners and nine pre-service teachers. The analysis of the qualitative data revealed that the two participants 'exercise EI to understand ways in which a wide range of emotional experiences, inside and outside the classroom, affect the language learning and teaching process' (2014: 347–348). Strategic ordering of classroom activities led to a reflection upon daily events that could be transformed into springboards for learning optimism. The authors concluded that 'the process of self-development is facilitated by using EI in effective ways' (2014: 349).

Teachers' gender and length of teaching experience has been linked to their levels of Trait EI (Gkonou & Mercer, 2017, 2018). Qualitative data showed that highly emotionally intelligent English teachers were able to draw on their rich teaching experience to interpret and respond to classroom challenges and to manage the class effectively. The combination of expertise gained through their teaching career and their intuitive knowledge shaped their Trait EI and allowed them to be sure-footed in taking emotion-related decisions in class.

In a study based on data collected from the same 513 participants as in the present study, Dewaele and Mercer (2018) considered variation in teachers' self-reported attitudes towards their students. The authors found that high levels of global Trait EI corresponded with more positive attitudes towards students and higher enjoyment of lively students. The authors pointed out that the teaching profession might be unsuited to people with low levels of EI. More experienced teachers were also found to have significantly more positive attitudes towards their students although they did not explicitly enjoy working with lively students more. The authors speculated that longer teaching experience may boost emotional intelligence over time but acknowledged that a more neutral interpretation of the finding could be that teachers with lower levels of emotional intelligence are more likely to abandon the profession. Teachers with lower levels of English proficiency were found to have significantly less positive attitudes towards their students and enjoyed their lively students less. The authors speculated that this could be linked to teachers' linguistic insecurity, which could have generated a lack of confidence and a certain degree of defensiveness. Finally, the female teachers had significantly more positive attitudes towards their students but no such difference emerged for the enjoyment of lively students. This finding was linked to earlier studies where female teachers were found to have closer, less conflictual and less dependent relationships with students than male peers.

In a second study on the same database, Dewaele *et al.* (2018a) focused on teachers' self-reported classroom behaviour (creativity, predictability, classroom management and pedagogical skills). A statistically significant positive relationship emerged between Trait EI and creativity, classroom management, pedagogical skills – and a marginal negative effect on predictability in the classroom. In other words, emotionally intelligent teachers reported being more creative, better at managing the class, having superior pedagogical skills and being slightly less predictable in class. Length of teaching experience had effects that mirrored those of Trait EI. Teachers with longer experience reported more creativity in their classrooms, better management of classroom activities and stronger pedagogical skills. They were also marginally less likely to be predictable in the classroom. As in the previous study, a word of caution is needed as longer teaching experience might boost Trait EI but, alternatively, it is also possible that teachers with lower levels of Trait EI dropped out of the profession earlier.

In a third study on the same database, Dewaele (2018c) focused on the link between the four factors that constitute Trait EI (well-being, emotionality, self-control and sociability) and 11 dependent variables, including teachers' love of English, attitudes towards their students, their institution, their self-reported classroom practices, their enjoyment, their unpredictability and their creativity. Sociability was found to be significantly positively correlated with nine dependent variables, well-being and self-control with eight variables, and emotionality with six dependent variables. Emotionality was significantly positively linked to the English proficiency of English LX users but not to that of the English L1 users.

The influence of other factors in the teachers' profiles have been hotly debated in the field of TESOL, such as the status of the teacher as a non-native speaker (NNEST) or native speaker (NEST). While a large majority of English language teachers worldwide are NNESTs, they are often victims of unfounded ideas, false beliefs and discrimination (Medgyes, 2017; Selvi, 2014). NNESTS are often considered *outsiders* while NESTs are '*insiders* with absolute authority' and are considered to be better teachers. Selvi (2014) presents a list of the advantages of NESTs and NNESTs compiled from the literature of the subject. Interestingly, there is no mention of teacher motivation. The only psychological factor is empathy which NNESTs have more of because of their experience as FL learners, and a willingness to work hard. Dewaele (2018a) argued that the dichotomy between native and non-native speaker is flawed because it assumes the eternal superiority of the former and the lasting inferiority of the latter in a FL. As both are users of language(s) (and not just 'speakers'), it is preferable to speak about L1 users and LX users. All are legitimate users of their language(s) and their proficiency could vary from minimal to maximal. In the present paper we will refer to English L1 teachers and English LX teachers who all work as EFL/ESL teachers.

This short literature overview shows that teachers' Trait EI has been positively linked to various aspects of their teaching practices, their attitudes and their relationships with students. It has also revealed potentially indirect effects, as teachers' Trait EI has been linked to other independent variables such as length of experience in the teaching profession. A more granular view of Trait EI might throw new light on the effect of specific facets of Trait EI. Also, research into FL teacher psychology has unearthed complex and dynamic interrelationships between psychological dimensions, linguistic and sociobiographical variables and teaching practices. The relations between all these independent variables and teacher motivation remain underexplored. This is the gap that the present study will attempt to fill.

After introducing the research questions, we will present the methodology for the study before reporting the statistical analyses. The results will be discussed in the following section before drawing some tentative conclusions.

Research Questions

The present study aims to address the following research questions:

(1a) What is the relationship between teachers' global Trait EI and their scores on the motivation dimensions?
(1b) What is the relationship between teachers' four Trait EI factors (well-being, emotionality, self-control and sociability) and their scores on the motivation dimensions?
(2) What is the relationship between teachers' years of teaching experience and scores on the motivation dimensions?
(3) What is the relationship between teachers' English proficiency and their scores on the motivation dimensions?
(4) What is the relationship between teachers' age and gender and their scores on the motivation dimensions?
(5) Do English L1 teachers score differently on the motivation dimensions than teachers who have English as an LX?

Methodology

Data were collected through snowball sampling, which is a form of non-probability sampling (Ness Evans & Rooney, 2013). An open-access anonymous online questionnaire was used. Calls for participation were sent through emails to teachers, students and informal contacts asking them to forward the link to colleagues. The questionnaire remained online from April to September 2016 and attracted 513 valid responses from mono- and multilingual ESL/EFL teachers across the world. Online questionnaires are ideal for collecting large amounts of data from participants from different parts of the world belonging to various age groups and language profiles (Dewaele, 2018b; Wilson & Dewaele,

2010). The geographical diversity boosts the ecological validity of the results, as the effects of local educational practices are averaged out. Finally, the psychometric properties of online versions of traditional questionnaires are very similar to the pen-and-paper versions (Denissen *et al.*, 2010).

The research design and questionnaires received ethical clearance from the author's research institution. Participants started by completing a short sociobiographical questionnaire with questions about gender, age, nationality, country of residence, language history and number of years in the teaching profession.

Participants also filled out the short version of the Trait EI Questionnaire (Short Form; Petrides, 2009), which contains a total of 30 items and yielded a global Trait EI score (mean = 4.56, *SD* = .60, with scores ranging from 2.7 to 5.9 [absolute minimum = 1, absolute maximum = 7]). The Cronbach alpha was .88. The Trait EI questionnaire also allowed us to calculate scores on the four main EI factors: well-being, emotionality, self-control and sociability.

Well-being includes items such as 'On the whole, I have a gloomy perspective on most things' (reverse) and 'Given my circumstances, I feel good about myself'. The mean score was 5.63 (*SD* = 1.0), with scores ranging from 1.2 to 7 (absolute min. = 1, absolute max. = 7). The Cronbach alpha score was .84.

Emotionality includes items such as 'I'm normally able to "get into someone's shoes" and experience their emotions' and 'Expressing my emotions with words is not a problem for me'. The mean score was 5.53 (*SD* = .79), with scores ranging from 2.6 to 7 (absolute min. = 1, absolute max. = 7). The Cronbach alpha was .71.

Self-control is measured through items such as 'I usually find it difficult to regulate my emotions' (reverse) and 'I tend to get involved in things I later wish I could get out of' (reverse). The mean score was 4.83 (*SD* = .87), with scores ranging from 1.8 to 7 (absolute min. = 1, absolute max. = 7). The Cronbach alpha was .65.

Sociability consists of items such as 'I can deal effectively with people' and 'I don't seem to have any powers at all over other people's feelings' (reverse). The mean score was 4.95 (*SD* = .90), with scores ranging from 1.3 to 7 (absolute min. = 1, absolute max. = 7). The Cronbach alpha was .70.

In order to identify potential confounding variables, we checked whether there were any gender differences on the EI factors. A Mann-Whitney test revealed that the only significant difference existed for emotionality, where the female teachers scored slightly higher (mean rank females = 263, mean rank males = 229; Mann-Whitney U = 21386, $z = -2.3$, $p < .022$). Number of years in the teaching profession was found to be unrelated to well-being and emotionality but was positively linked to self-control and sociability ($Rho = .17$, $p < .0001$ and

Rho = .12, $p < .0001$ respectively).[1] Age was also linked to self-control and sociability (*Rho* = .20, $p < .0001$ and *Rho* = .11, $p < .0001$ respectively). The effect size is small for these independent variables (less than 4% shared variance). English L1 teachers did only differ from English LX teachers for sociability (mean rank L1: 279, mean rank LX: 249; Mann-Whitney $U = 22722$, $z = -2.0$, $p < .041$).

The next part of the survey consisted of the English version of the LEXTALE, a 60-item lexical test developed by Lemhöfer and Broersma (2012). The authors describe LEXTALE as a 'quick and practically feasible test of vocabulary knowledge for medium to highly proficient speakers of English as a second language. It consists of a simple un-speeded visual lexical decision task', which takes 'on average 3.5 minutes to complete' (Lemhöfer & Broersma, 2012). Participants are asked whether an item is an existing English word or not (items include 'scornful', 'platery', 'stoutly', 'unkempt'). The test gives a good indication of overall English proficiency. LEXTALE scores have been found to correlate highly with TOEIC test results, an established test of English proficiency (Lemhöfer & Broersma, 2012). Thus, even though LEXTALE was not designed to capture general English proficiency fully, it is nevertheless a useful indicator of it (Lemhöfer & Broersma, 2012). For L1 users the LEXTALE scores are probably less an indication of general proficiency and more one of L1 vocabulary knowledge. Scores ranged from a minimum of 15 to the maximum possible score of 100.

A Mann-Whitney test revealed that female teachers scored lower on proficiency than their male colleagues (mean rank females: 244, mean rank males: 285; Mann-Whitney $U = 20672$, $z = -2.8$, $p < .005$). Number of years in the teaching profession was found to be positively linked with proficiency (*Rho* = .18, $p < .0001$). The effect size is small (3.2% shared variance). Age was also linked with higher proficiency (*Rho* = .25, $p < .0001$). The effect size is also small (6.2% shared variance). The English L1 teachers scored higher on proficiency than their LX colleagues: (mean rank L1 teachers: 372, mean rank LX teachers: 215; Mann-Whitney $U = 9983$, $z = -10.6$, $p < .0001$).

Participants

A total of 513 participants (377 females, 131 males) filled out the questionnaire. All were EFL/ESL teachers and their experience in the profession ranged from one month to 52 years. On average, participants had been teaching for 15 years ($SD = 10$). The mean age was 40 years ($SD = 10$). The majority of female participants is typical in web-based language questionnaires (Dewaele, 2018b; Wilson & Dewaele, 2010). The largest group were British ($n = 71$), then American ($n = 40$), followed by Ukrainian ($n = 37$), Greek ($n = 30$), Azerbaijani ($n = 30$), Argentinian ($n = 30$), Chinese ($n = 30$), Indian ($n = 30$), Spanish

(n = 30), Turkish (n = 30), Macedonian (n = 30), Canadian (n = 30), and smaller groups of participants with another 64 nationalities. The sample of participants consisted of 15 monolinguals, 113 bilinguals, 174 trilinguals, 104 quadrilinguals, 81 pentalinguals, 22 sextalinguals, and 4 septalinguals. English was the most frequent L1 (n = 136), and the remaining 376 participants had English as an FL. A majority of participants were teaching English at university (n = 290), with smaller numbers teaching in secondary schools (n = 154), primary schools (n = 63) and nursery schools (n = 6). The largest group of participants were working in Ukraine (n = 37), Greece (n = 32), Spain (n = 30), Azerbaijan (n = 25), Japan (n = 25), the UK (n = 17) and the USA (n = 17). The remaining participants worked in 103 different countries.

Dependent variables

The original WTMST deals with motivation for task completion with items tapping into five different dimensions. The items were reformulated in order to focus on the motivation to teach English. This includes three items per dimension with five-point Likert scales. The section started with the following paragraph:

> Indicate your degree of dis/agreement with the following items concerning the reasons you teach English. Possible answers: not especially, so-so, quite a lot, a lot, very much.

The first dimension is **Intrinsic Motivation**: (1) Because teaching English is pleasant. (2) Because teaching English is interesting. (3) Because I like teaching English. Mean score was 4.3 (SD = .67). A Kolmogorov-Smirnov test revealed that the distribution was not normal (KS = .167, $p < .0001$). The Cronbach alpha value was .83, suggesting very good internal consistency.

The second dimension is **Identified Regulation**: (1) Because it is important for me to teach English. (2) Because I believe teaching English is important for the academic success of my students. Mean score was 4.11 (SD = .74). A Kolmogorov-Smirnov test revealed that the distribution was not normal (KS = .182, $p < .0001$). The Cronbach alpha value was .63, which is rather low but still acceptable.

The third dimension is **Introjected Regulation**: (1) Because if I don't teach, I will feel bad. (2) Because I would feel guilty not doing it. (3) I would feel bad doing something different. Mean score was 2.73 (SD = .97). A Kolmogorov-Smirnov test revealed that the distribution was not normal (KS = .085, $p < .0001$). The Cronbach alpha value was .83.

The fourth dimension is **External Regulation**: (1) Because it is my chosen profession. (2) I teach English because I'm paid to do it. Mean score was 3.48 (SD = .75). A Kolmogorov-Smirnov test revealed that the distribution was not normal ($KS = .157, p < .0001$). The Cronbach alpha value was extremely low: .065. As a consequence, this dimension was excluded from further analyses.

The fifth and final dimension is **Amotivation**: (1) I don't know why because I don't always see the relevance of teaching English. (2) I used to know why I was teaching English, but I don't see the reason any more. (3) I don't know why as sometimes I don't see the purpose of teaching English. Mean score was 1.72 ($SD = .74$). A Kolmogorov-Smirnov test revealed that the distribution was not normal ($KS = .183, p < .0001$). The Cronbach alpha value was .84.

Because our dependent variables are not normally distributed, we opted for general use of non-parametric statistics, namely Spearman rank correlation analyses and Mann-Whitney tests. A Bonferroni correction was applied to avoid Type 1 errors in the second correlation analysis. As a consequence, only *p* values below .007 (.05 / 7) will be considered significant in the second analysis.

Results

To answer the first part of the first research question, we ran a Spearman rank correlation analysis between teachers' global Trait EI and their scores on the motivation dimensions. It is important to point out that since almost three quarters of participants had English as an LX, their influence on results is greater than that of English L1 teachers. A highly significant positive relationship emerged with intrinsic motivation ($Rho = .25, p < .0001$) and with identified regulation ($Rho = .21, p < .0001$). No relationship was found with introjected regulation ($Rho = .06, p =$ ns) and a highly significant negative relationship emerged with amotivation ($Rho = -.34, p < .0001$). This suggests that high Trait EI teachers are more intrinsically motivated, have stronger identified regulation and are less amotivated. According to Plonsky and Oswald (2014: 889), these correlation coefficients are situated between small and medium (.25 and .40).

To answer the second part of the first research question, we replaced global Trait EI with the four trait EI facets. A Spearman rank correlation analysis with Bonferroni correction (see Table 15.1) showed statistically significant positive relationships between motivation dimensions and intrinsic motivation and identified regulation. Well-being and sociability had the biggest effect sizes, with 7.8% and 5.2% of shared variance respectively. Statistically significant negative relationships emerged between the four trait EI facets and amotivation. Emotionality and well-being had the biggest effect sizes, with 10.3% and 9% of shared variance respectively. This finding suggests that teachers with higher levels of well-being, emotionality, self-control and sociability were more likely to be strongly intrinsically motivated and committed to their students and they

Table 15.1 Correlation analysis between motivation dimensions, TEI factors, experience, proficiency and age

Dependent variables		Well-being	Self-control	Emotionality	Sociability	Experience	Proficiency	Age
Intrinsic motivation	*Rho*	.280	.156	.157	.227	.084	–.032	.053
	p	.000	.000	.000	.000	*.056*	*ns*	*.ns*
Identified regulation	*Rho*	.225	.161	.126	.157	.064	–.132	.046
	p	.000	.000	.004	.000	*Ns*	.003	*ns*
Introjected regulation	*Rho*	.057	.040	–.013	.104	.087	–.217	.043
	p	*ns*	*ns*	*ns*	.019	.048	.000	*ns*
Amotivation	*Rho*	–.300	–.236	–.321	–.209	–.092	–.126	–.091
	p	.000	.000	.000	.000	.037	.004	.040

were less likely to suffer from Amotivation. The positive relationship between introjected regulation and sociability failed to reach statistical significance.

The answer to the second research question is brief, as Spearman rank correlation analyses between length of teachers' experience and the scores on the motivation dimensions failed to reach statistical significance. In other words, teachers who have been in the profession for longer are not necessarily more motivated.

The third research question focused on the link between English proficiency and the motivation dimensions. Spearman rank correlation analyses revealed significant negative relationships between English proficiency, identified regulation, introjected regulation and amotivation. In other words, the more teachers were proficient in English, the less likely they were to suffer from amotivation and their behaviours were less extrinsically motivated.

The fourth research question on the effect of age and gender showed that while participants' age was unrelated with the motivation dimensions, the female teachers were more motivated than their male peers but did not differ for amotivation (Table 15.2).

A series of Mann-Whitney tests revealed that the 377 female teachers scored significantly higher than the 131 male teachers on intrinsic

Table 15.2 The effect of gender on the motivation dimensions (mean ranks)

Gender	Intrinsic motivation	Identified regulation	Introjected regulation	Amotivation
Female	267	264	265	2530
Male	219	226	224	2258
Mann-Whitney U	20045	20951	20692	24257
Z	–3.3	–2.7	–2.8	–.31
p	.001	.008	.005	Ns
d Cohen	.288	.231	.247	.027

Table 15.3 The effect of the status of English (L1/LX) on the motivation dimensions (mean ranks)

English	Intrinsic motivation	Identified regulation	Introjected regulation	Amotivation
L1	229	207	195	252
LX	267	275	280	259
Mann-Whitney U	21857	18904	17197	25050
Z	−2.7	−4.7	−5.8	−.50
p	.007	.0001	.0001	ns
d Cohen	.233	.416	.526	.042

motivation, identified regulation and introjected regulation but no difference existed for amotivation (see Table 15.2). According to Cohen (1992) the effect sizes are small (the threshold being d = .20); for Plonsky and Oswald (2014) they do not reach the threshold for L2 research, which is d = .40.

To answer the final research question, a series of Mann-Whitney tests revealed that the 137 English L1 teachers scored significantly lower than the 376 English LX teachers on intrinsic motivation, identified regulation and introjected regulation but no difference existed for amotivation. According to Cohen (1992) the effect sizes are small to medium for identified regulation and introjected regulation (the threshold for medium being d = .50). According to Plonsky and Oswald (2014), these are small effect sizes.

Discussion

Motivation levels of EFL/ESL teachers in the present study were found to be linked to a range of psychological, sociobiographical and linguistic variables.

Teachers with high levels of Trait EI, and more specifically with high levels of well-being, self-control, emotionality and sociability, were more likely to report high levels of motivation. However, the effect size was typically small. This finding extends previous observations on the positive relationships between Trait EI and other dependent variables reflecting teachers' classroom behaviour and attitudes in the same sample of participants (Dewaele *et al.*, 2018a; Dewaele & Mercer, 2018).

A closer look at the relationship between the motivation dimensions and the four facets of Trait EI revealed that the crucial dimension of intrinsic motivation was most strongly correlated with well-being, followed by sociability, and finally with emotionality and self-control. It suggests that the most happy, optimistic, positive, empathic participants who enjoy social interactions and who are able to control their emotions and are sufficiently assertive were most likely to be highly motivated teachers. These participants were also most strongly convinced of their duty towards their students and about their mission as teachers. These psychological characteristics could be read as the profile of natural teachers. It further underlines the importance for teachers to have a sufficient degree of Trait EI before entering the profession (Dewaele *et al.*, 2018a; Vesely *et al.*, 2014). This is crucial not only for their own happiness and ability to cope with the stress in the profession and in-class frustration (Brackett *et al.*, 2010; Chan, 2006; Morris & King, 2018), but also for the classroom atmosphere, learners' emotional well-being, and the teaching outcomes (Gregersen *et al.*, 2014; Jennings & Greenberg, 2009). The effect size is too small to draw a wide-ranging conclusion but a possible implication is that the teaching profession might benefit from discouraging candidates with very low levels of Trait EI to join teacher training programmes. Just like fear of heights precludes one from becoming a window cleaner and fainting at the sight of blood precludes one from entering the nursing profession, a lack of emotional intelligence is a serious obstacle in becoming a teacher. Further research would be needed about teachers' minimal threshold in Trait EI. It is possible, of course, that training (Brackett & Katulak, 2006; Nelis *et al.*, 2009; Vesely *et al.*, 2014) might help candidates with low Trait EI to tackle this problem. Further research is also needed based on actual teacher behaviour rather than self-reported behaviour before any policy implications can be considered.

The answer to the second research question was slightly surprising, namely the fact that length in the teaching profession was unrelated to motivation levels on the various dimensions. Only a long-term longitudinal study could shed light on the possible fluctuations in teachers' motivation. The fact that average motivation levels do not change does not mean that nothing happens beneath the surface (Dewaele & Jiang, 2015). It is reasonable to expect that younger teachers may be more idealistic and highly motivated. While some might maintain or strengthen their motivation, others may suffer from burnout which would certainly dampen their motivation and increase the probability of them leaving the profession early (Brackett *et al.*, 2010). As a consequence, only the most resilient and motivated teachers would remain in the profession until their retirement.

The third research question focused on the relationship between English proficiency and the motivation dimensions. Level of proficiency turned out to be unrelated to intrinsic motivation but negative relationships emerged between proficiency, identified regulation, introjected regulation and amotivation. In other words, high English proficiency was linked to lower levels of amotivation but also lower levels of extrinsic motivation. Having the necessary linguistic capital to teach English meant the teachers tended not to experience amotivation. The difference in the relationship between proficiency and intrinsic motivation on the one hand and proficiency and the other motivation dimensions on the other hand shows that they really reflect different aspects of motivation. It is possible that those who had chosen the profession because of external factors, rather than a burning intrinsic motivation, might invest less overall in English. Having lower levels of non-intrinsic motivation could be both the cause and consequence of lower levels of proficiency in English. Considering the fact that the English L1 teachers had significantly higher proficiency levels than their LX peers, it is worth repeating the correlation analyses for the L1 and LX groups separately. Proficiency turned out to be unrelated to motivation for the English L1 participants, while the negative relationships were stronger for the LX group – with the exception of intrinsic motivation which remained unrelated to proficiency. This suggests that the effort that LX teachers had made to gain proficiency in English had carried over in their identified regulation and introjected regulation, and had lowered their amotivation.

The fourth research question dealt with the link between sociobiographical variables and the motivation dimensions. Age was found to have no relationship with the motivation dimensions but older teachers suffered less from amotivation. This could be linked to the fact that amotivated teachers probably leave the profession early, meaning that teachers with longer experience probably had a stronger motivation from a young age. Gender had a slightly stronger effect, with female teachers scoring higher on both intrinsic and extrinsic motivation than their male peers (a small effect size). This is not surprising, given the finding that the same female teachers had significantly more positive attitudes towards their students than male teachers (Dewaele & Mercer, 2018). However, the same female teachers' self-reported classroom behaviour did not differ from that of their male colleagues (Dewaele *et al.*, 2018b).

The fifth and final question considered the effect of the status of teachers' English, having it either as an L1 or as an LX, on their motivation. Surprisingly, English L1 teachers reported significantly lower levels of motivation (but not amotivation) than LX teachers. The effect size was small to medium depending on the frame of reference. This pattern is very different from the one for proficiency. So English L1 teachers, despite having higher levels of proficiency than LX teachers, are less motivated. Could it be that having had to make less effort to acquire the language, having made less emotional investment in the learning of their L1, they may not value it as much, maybe because they take it for granted? A quick additional Mann-Whitney test confirms this hypothesis: LX teachers scored significantly higher than L1 teachers in response to the item 'How do you feel about the English language?'

with the following range of responses: (1) Hate it, (2) Don't like it much, (3) Neutral, (4) Like it, (5) Love it. The mean rank of LX teachers was 271 versus 219 for L1 teachers (Mann-Whitney $U = 20564$, $z = -4.4$, $p < .0001$).

Might the LX teachers have the faith of the more recently converted? Might they feel more strongly that investing in English is a worthy pursuit, boosting their motivation to master the language as learners and as teachers? This adds an interesting twist to the ongoing debate about the place of LX teachers in foreign language education (Selvi, 2014). It certainly adds fresh evidence for those defending NNESTs in TESOL. Would the benefit of having an L1 teacher with superior proficiency but lower motivation outweigh the LX teacher with lower proficiency but superior motivation?

The main limitation of the present study is the one that applies to all research using non-random sampling, namely the fact that self-selected participants are more likely to be interested in the topic and more likely to score above average on various positive aspects of EFL/ESL teaching. In other words, lowly motivated EFL/ESL teachers were less likely to participate in the research. Therefore, the findings need to be interpreted with this limitation in mind. The current study was also exclusively quantitative in orientation. Much research in this area has been qualitative, based on relatively small samples (Gkonou & Mercer, 2018; Gregersen *et al.*, 2014). The strength of the current approach is its unusually large sample from a wide and diverse population of EFL/ESL teachers, which allowed solid statistical analyses, and the identification of general patterns. Further research is also needed, based on observation of teaching behaviour, in order to find out whether teachers with (very) low Trait EI are really poor teachers. Only then can proper implications for the profession be developed.

Conclusion

The present correlational study found strong relationships between teachers' global Trait EI, as well as the four dimensions that constitute Trait EI (well-being, emotionality, self-control and sociability) and their scores on the motivation dimensions of intrinsic motivation, identified regulation, introjected regulation, external regulation and amotivation (Fernet *et al.*, 2008). English LX teachers turned out to be more motivated than English L1 teachers. High proficiency in English was linked to stronger motivation among the LX teachers. Female participants also scored higher on the motivation dimensions. Only length in the teaching profession was unrelated to motivation.

The main pedagogical implication of this study is that (trainee) teachers who have the right psychological profile, i.e. sufficiently high

Trait EI, are more likely to be good teachers and more likely to be motivated to do their job well. It also means that candidates for the teaching profession with very low levels of Trait EI may have to be discouraged from becoming teachers, for their own sake and that of their future students. Of course, the effect sizes were small and there is no clear cut-off point on what constitutes 'sufficient' Trait EI for teachers. It is also unclear to what extent Trait EI could be boosted by training. To conclude, more experimental research is needed on the topic, based on actual teaching performance.

Post-Reading Tasks

(1) What can individual teachers do to boost their Trait EI and motivation?
(2) What can institutions do to boost their teachers' Trait EI and motivation?
(3) Should the teaching profession be closed to teachers with low levels of Trait EI and motivation? If yes, what should be the threshold? How should this be implemented?

Note

(1) This finding suggests that these two facets of Trait EI may benefit from training.

References

Brackett, M.A. and Katulak, N.A. (2006) Emotional intelligence in the classroom: Skill-based training for teachers and students. In J. Ciarrochi and J.D. Mayer (eds) *Applying Emotional Intelligence: A Practitioner's Guide* (pp. 1–27). New York: Psychology Press/ Taylor & Francis.

Brackett, M.A., Palomera, R., Mojsa-Kaja, J., Reyes, M.R. and Salovey, P. (2010) Emotion-regulation ability, burnout, and job satisfaction among British secondary-school teachers. *Psychology in the Schools* 47 (4), 406–417.

Chan, D.W. (2006) Emotional intelligence and components of burnout among Chinese secondary school teachers in Hong Kong. *Teaching and Teacher Education* 22 (8), 1042–1054.

Cohen, J. (1992) *Statistical Power Analysis for the Behavioral Sciences*. New York: John Wiley.

Corcoran, R.P. and Tormey, R. (2012a) How emotionally intelligent are pre-service teachers? *Teaching and Teacher Education* 28 (5), 750–759.

Corcoran, R.P. and Tormey, R. (2012b) Assessing emotional intelligence and its impact in caring professions: The value of a mixed-methods approach in emotional intelligence work with teachers. In A. Di Fabio (ed.) *Emotional Intelligence: New Perspectives and Applications* (pp. 215–238). Croatia: InTech.

Corcoran, R.P. and Tormey, R. (2013) Does emotional intelligence predict student teachers' performance? *Teaching and Teacher Education* 35, 34–42.

De Costa, P., Rawal, H. and Li, W. (2018) Teacher education agenda: International perspectives on teacher emotions. In H. Rawal, P. De Costa and W. Li (guest eds) Special issue, *Emotions in Second Language Teaching: Theory, Research and Teacher Education. Chinese Journal of Applied Linguistics* 41 (4), 401–409.

Denissen, J.J.A., Neumann, L. and van Zalk, M. (2010) How the internet is changing the implementation of traditional research methods, people's daily lives, and the way in which developmental scientists conduct research. *International Journal of Behavioral Development* 34 (6), 564–575.

Dewaele, J.-M. (2005) Investigating the psychological and the emotional dimensions in instructed language learning: Obstacles and possibilities. *The Modern Language Journal* 89 (3), 367–380.

Dewaele, J.-M. (2012) Personality. Personality traits as independent and dependent variables. In S. Mercer, S. Ryan and M. Williams (eds) *Psychology for Language Learning: Insights from Research, Theory and Practice* (pp. 42–58). Basingstoke: Palgrave Macmillan.

Dewaele, J.-M. (2015) On emotions in foreign language learning and use. *The Language Teacher* 39 (3), 13–15.

Dewaele, J.-M. (2017) Psychological dimensions and foreign language anxiety. In S. Loewen and M. Sato (eds) *The Routledge Handbook of Instructed Second Language Acquisition* (pp. 433–450). London: Routledge.

Dewaele, J.-M. (2018a) Why the dichotomy 'L1 Versus LX User' is better than 'Native Versus Non-native Speaker'. *Applied Linguistics* 39 (2), 236–240.

Dewaele, J.-M. (2018b) Online questionnaires in applied linguistics research. In A. Phakiti, P. De Costa, L. Plonsky and S. Starfield (eds) *Palgrave Handbook of Applied Linguistics Research Methodology* (pp. 269–286). Basingstoke: Palgrave Macmillan.

Dewaele, J.-M. (2018c) The relationship between trait emotional intelligence and experienced ESL/EFL teachers' love of English, attitudes towards their students and institution, self-reported classroom practices, enjoyment and creativity. In H. Rawal, P. De Costa & W. Li (guest eds) Special issue, *Emotions in Second Language Teaching: Theory, Research and Teacher Education. Chinese Journal of Applied Linguistics* 41 (4), 468–487.

Dewaele, J.-M., Chen, X., Padilla, A.M. and Lake, J. (2019) The flowering of positive psychology in foreign language teaching and acquisition research. *Frontiers in Psychology. Language Sciences* 10, 2128. Doi: 10.3389/fpsyg.2019.02128.

Dewaele, J.-M. and Mercer, S. (2018) Variation in ESL/EFL teachers' attitudes towards their students. In S. Mercer and A. Kostoulas (eds) *Language Teacher Psychology* (pp. 178–195). Bristol: Multilingual Matters.

Dewaele, J.-M. and Jiang, Y. (2015) What lies bubbling beneath the surface? A longitudinal perspective on fluctuations of ideal and ought-to L2 self among learners of English in Chinese universities. *International Review of Applied Linguistics* 53 (3), 331–354.

Dewaele, J.-M., Gkonou, C. and Mercer, S. (2018a) Do ESL/EFL teachers' emotional intelligence, teaching experience, proficiency and gender, affect their classroom practice? In J. de Dios Martínez Agudo (ed.) *Emotions in Second Language Teaching* (pp. 125–141). Berlin: Springer.

Dewaele, J.-M., Witney, J., Saito, K. and Dewaele, L. (2018b) Foreign language enjoyment and anxiety in the FL classroom: The effect of teacher and learner variables. *Language Teaching Research* 22 (6), 676–697.

Dörnyei, Z. and Ryan, S. (2015) *The Psychology of the Second Language Learner Revisited.* New York: Routledge.

Elias, M.J. and Arnold, H. (eds) (2006) *The Educator's Guide to Intelligence and Academic Achievement: Social-Emotional Learning in the Classroom.* Thousand Oaks: Corwin.

Fernet, C., Senécal, C., Guay, F., Marsh, H. and Dowson, M. (2008) The Work Tasks Motivation Scale for Teachers (WTMST). *Journal of Career Assessment* 16 (2), 256–279.

Fernet, C., Senécal, C., Guay, F. and Austin, S. (2012) Predicting intraindividual changes in teacher burnout: The role of perceived school environment and motivational factors. *Teaching and Teacher Education* 28 (4), 514–525.

Gkonou, C. and Mercer, S. (2017) *Understanding Emotional and Social Intelligence among English Language Teachers.* London: British Council.

Gkonou, C. and Mercer, S. (2018) The beliefs and practices of highly socio-emotionally competent language teachers. In S. Mercer and A. Kostoulas (eds) *Language Teacher Psychology* (pp. 158–177). Bristol: Multilingual Matters.

Gorozidis, G. and Papaioannou, A.G. (2014) Teachers' motivation to participate in training and to implement innovations. *Teaching and Teacher Education* 39, 1–11.

Graziano, P.A., Reavis, R.D., Keane, S.P. and Calkins, S.D. (2007) The role of emotion regulation and children's early academic success. *Journal of School Psychology* 45 (1), 3–19.

Gregersen, T., MacIntyre, P.D., Finegan, K.H., Talbot, K.R. and Claman, S.L. (2014) Examining emotional intelligence within the context of positive psychology interventions. *Studies in Second Language Learning and Teaching* 4 (2), 327–353.

Jennings, P.A. and Greenberg, M.T. (2009) The prosocial classroom: Teacher social and emotional competence in relation to student and classroom outcomes. *Review of Educational Research* 79 (1), 491–525.

Lemhöfer, K. and Broersma, M. (2012) Introducing LexTALE: A quick and valid lexical test for advanced learners of English. *Behavior Research Methods* 44 (2), 325–343.

Medgyes, P. (2017) *The Non-Native Teacher: Updated and Revised Third Edition.* Callander: Swan Communication.

Mercer, S. (2016) Seeing the world through your eyes: Empathy in language learning and teaching. In P.D. MacIntyre, T. Gregersen and S. Mercer (eds) *Positive Psychology in SLA* (pp. 91–111). Bristol: Multilingual Matters.

Mercer, S. and Kostoulas, A. (eds) (2018) *Language Teacher Psychology.* Bristol: Multilingual Matters.

Mercer, S., Oberdorfer, P. and Saleem, M. (2016) Helping language teachers to thrive: Using positive psychology to promote teachers' professional well-being. In D. Gabryś-Barker and D. Gałajda (eds) *Positive Psychology Perspectives on Foreign Language Learning and Teaching* (pp. 213–229). Cham: Springer.

Moafian, F. and Ghanizadeh, A. (2009) The relationship between Iranian EFL teachers' emotional intelligence and their self-efficacy in language institutes. *System* 37 (4), 708–718.

Morris, S. and King, J. (2018) Teacher frustration and emotion regulation in university language teaching. In H. Rawal, P. De Costa and W. Li (guest eds) Special issue, *Emotions in Second Language Teaching: Theory, Research and Teacher Education. Chinese Journal of Applied Linguistics* 41 (4), 433–452.

Nelis, D., Quoidbach, J., Mikolajczak, M. and Hansenne, M. (2009) Increasing emotional intelligence: (How) is it possible? *Personality and Individual Differences* 47 (1), 36–41.

Ness Evans, A. and Rooney, B.J. (2013) *Methods in Psychological Research* (3rd edn). New York: SAGE.

Nizielski, S., Hallum, S., Lopes, P.N. and Schutz, A. (2012) Attention to student needs mediates the relationship between teacher emotional intelligence and student misconduct in the classroom. *Journal of Psychoeducational Assessment* 30 (4), 320–329.

Perlman, D.J. (2013) Effective teaching and motivation: Application of self-determination theory. *Journal of Research, Policy & Practice of Teachers & Teacher Education* 3 (2), 31–37.

Petrides, K.V. (2009) Psychometric properties of the Trait Emotional Intelligence Questionnaire. In C. Stough, D.H. Saklofske and J.D. Parker (eds) *Advances in the Assessment of Emotional Intelligence* (pp. 85–101). New York: Springer.

Petrides, K.V. (2017) Intelligence, emotional. *Reference Module in Neuroscience and Biobehavioral Psychology* 1, 1–16.

Petrides, K.V. and Furnham, A. (2000) On the dimensional structure of emotional intelligence. *Personality and Individual Differences* 29 (2), 313–320.

Petrides, K.V. and Furnham, A. (2001) Trait emotional intelligence: Psychometric investigation with reference to established trait taxonomies. *European Journal of Personality* 15 (6), 425–448.

Plonsky, L. and Oswald, F.L. (2014) How big is 'big'? Interpreting effect sizes in L2 research. *Language Learning* 64, 878–912.

Selvi, A.F. (2014) Myths and misconceptions about nonnative English speakers in the TESOL (NNEST) movement. *TESOL Journal* 5 (3), 573–611.

Talbot, K. and Mercer, S. (2018) Exploring university ESL/EFL teachers' emotional well-being and emotional regulation in the United States, Japan and Austria. In H. Rawal, P. De Costa and W. Li (guest eds) Special issue, *Emotions in Second Language Teaching: Theory, Research and Teacher Education. Chinese Journal of Applied Linguistics* 41 (4), 410–432.

Vesely, A.K., Saklofske, D.H. and Nordstokk, D.W. (2014) EI training and pre-service teacher wellbeing. *Personality and Individual Differences* 65, 81–85.

Wilson, R. and Dewaele, J.-M. (2010) The use of web questionnaires in second language acquisition and bilingualism research. *Second Language Research* 26 (1), 103–123.

16 Concluding Thoughts on the Emotional Rollercoaster of Language Teaching

Jim King, Jean-Marc Dewaele and Christina Gkonou

This book has presented studies from a variety of scholars whose interest in teacher emotions encompasses a very diverse array of language teaching and teacher training contexts. Taken together, the findings from investigations focusing on language teachers working in or training to teach in elementary, secondary, state and private schools, colleges and universities in countries such as Japan, Austria, the United States, Australia, Nepal and the United Kingdom illustrate the crucial role that emotions play in teachers' professional lives and help contribute to the ongoing quest to enhance teacher effectiveness and well-being. Building upon a very recent surge of interest in the emotional aspects of language teaching (see Martínez Agudo, 2018; Rawal *et al.*, 2018), the state-of-the-art investigations reported on here draw attention to the fluctuating and shifting range of emotions that educators experience on a daily basis in their work. Mercer and Kostoulas (2018) issued a plea in their recent book on language teacher psychology for more educator-focused research, arguing that although teachers are key stakeholders in the learning process, they are relatively neglected in favour of projects which put learners at their centre. The current volume responds to this call, thus building upon the idea that by gaining a better understanding of teacher psychology, we can learn much about learner psychology and ultimately improve classroom life. From joy to frustration, enthusiasm to boredom, fear to anger, teachers' emotional experiences shape not only their professional identities and classroom practices, but also ultimately help to determine their length of service, being as they are intimately linked to teacher stress, burnout and attrition.

Researching language teacher emotions is a far from straightforward proposition. Firstly, individual emotions can be difficult to define and tease apart because their components may overlap or seem similar, hence making the language used to describe them indistinct, or as Scherer (2005) terms it, 'fuzzy'. Another challenge is that emotions are simultaneously intrapersonal (occurring subjectively within the individual's mind) and interpersonal (socio-dynamically constrained and afforded by context) (for a language teacher-related model of this, see King & Ng, 2018: 145). Indeed, as Schutz and DeCuir rightly state, 'emotional experiences and their meaning to the individuals involved do not occur in a vacuum' (2002: 130). To meet the challenge of investigating phenomena which are hard to pin down, difficult to observe and have both intra- and interpersonal aspects, researchers need to be methodologically fleet of foot and innovative in how they collect and analyse data. This book provides examples of a diverse range of approaches for investigating language teacher emotions and illustrates research designs made up of quantitative (Acheson & Nelson, Chapter 3; Dewaele, Chapter 15), qualitative (Hofstadler *et al.*, Chapter 2; Benesch, Chapter 4; Edwards & Burns, Chapter 5; Gkonou & Miller, Chapter 8) and, most notably, mixed methodologies (Kostoulas & Lämmerer, Chapter 6; Humphries, Chapter 9; Ikeda *et al.*, Chapter 10; Morris & King, Chapter 11; Gregersen *et al.*, Chapter 13). Our contributors have employed methods such as classroom observations, structured and semi-structured interviews, stimulated recalls, questionnaires, materials analyses, narrative research and written self-reflections to generate rich and contextually valid accounts of language teachers' emotional experiences. Research into language teacher emotions is still very much in its infancy in applied linguistics but we hope the diverse range of studies presented in this volume provides a stimulus for further, novel investigations encompassing a range of emotionally related constructs. One of the key challenges for future inquiries will be the creation of innovative research designs which reflect emotion as a dynamic state consisting of both cognitive and physical events, while at the same time acknowledging the social dimension of teacher emotions. For example, situated, contextually valid investigations looking at the relationship between emotions and physiological responses, such as changes in heart rate, facial expressions, nonverbal cues and so on, could prove fruitful in gaining a better understanding of the emotional implications of specific classroom scenarios which language teachers encounter. Certainly, if we are to link teacher emotions to the issues of workplace stress and well-being, more research is needed which takes into account the ways in which teachers' thoughts, behaviours, bodily sensations and emotions dynamically interact either in the moment during classroom interactions or over much longer periods of time. Findings on the emotion-specific experiences of teachers during and after particular classroom scenarios could then usefully feed into pre- and in-service training programmes and help in the ongoing battle against teacher attrition.

The works presented in this volume illustrate well that emotions play a crucial and dynamic role in the professional daily lives of language teachers working across a variety of settings. The studies showcased reinforce arguments made in general education literature (see Hargreaves, 1998; Zembylas, 2005) that teaching is a fundamentally emotional endeavour in which effective teachers interact and emotionally connect with their students. With language teaching representing a unique social practice (Gkonou & Mercer, 2017) that relies more heavily on teacher–student interaction than perhaps many other subjects, there exists a strong case that language teachers in particular need to be emotionally competent within their classrooms if they are to achieve pedagogical goals and maintain their well-being. Echoing a number of contributors to this volume (see e.g. Hofstadler *et al.*, Chapter 2; Ikeda *et al.*, Chapter 10; Morris & King, Chapter 11 and De Costa *et al.*, Chapter 12), we believe that pre-service teacher training programmes and in-house professional development programmes need not only to raise greater awareness of the emotional dimensions of teaching foreign languages, but should also develop teachers' emotional skills to enable them to cope with or even thrive in emotionally challenging circumstances. It is critical that such training goes hand in hand with support at an institutional level (and, indeed, within the wider education system) which acknowledges the dynamic interplay between context in the form of working conditions, workload levels and so on, and teachers' emotional experiences. To help prepare individuals for the emotional rollercoaster involved in teaching languages, as a first step we suggest that training programmes focus on two concepts in particular which have been discussed at length in this book: namely, emotional intelligence and emotion regulation.

Emotional intelligence refers to a person's capacity to recognise and deal with one's own and others' emotions in an effective manner, to handle interpersonal relationships empathetically using emotional information to guide thinking and behaviour. In Chapter 15, Dewaele draws our attention to the fact that language teachers who possess high levels of emotional intelligence tend to be more positive and optimistic about their professional role, taking pleasure from interactions with students and enjoying a level of well-being that less emotionally aware teachers might struggle to reach (see also Dewaele, 2018; Dewaele *et al.*, 2018). This of course has implications for teachers' classroom practice and the learning outcomes of students. There has been some debate about whether emotional intelligence is a fixed personality trait or whether it can be developed with appropriate training but evidence from intervention studies in general education (e.g. Brackett & Katulak, 2006; Dolev & Leshem, 2017; Hen & Sharabi-Nov, 2014) does suggest it is malleable and that positive shifts in emotional intelligence are indeed possible. Because early-career instructors are especially vulnerable to the multitude of stressors that accompany teaching, we recommend that training programmes for pre-service language teachers focus on theory-based practical training of emotional intelligence skills (see Kornacki & Caruso, 2007) in order to enhance novice teachers' professional performance, facilitate positive relationships with learners and promote well-being. Strong emotional intelligence skills appear to make language anxiety less likely (Dewaele *et al.*, 2008) and so these types of professional development activities could well go some way in helping highly anxious language teachers, such as those described by Ikeda and her colleagues in Chapter 10. Teacher education programmes which combine input on the technical aspects of teaching and focused instruction on emotional intelligence could lead to improved teaching performance but also to higher levels of teacher resilience. In Chapter 6, Kostoulas and Lämmerer discuss teacher resilience extensively and also introduce the concept of resilient adaptation, which can assist teachers with the regulation of their own emotions and encourage them to constantly look for additional emotion regulation strategies to continue to function effectively in their professional roles. Thus, looking at how teachers can flourish in their professional roles should be a goal of teacher education. As Dewaele cautions in Chapter 15, more research and the implementation of specific interventions are necessary before we embark on investing in emotional intelligence training for language teachers.

As Oxford points out in her discussion of the 'well of emotional well-being' in Chapter 14, intimately related to emotional intelligence is the concept of emotion regulation. At its most basic, emotion regulation is the ability to control how emotions are experienced and how they are displayed to others (Gross, 2002, 2015). Rather than being something specific only to professional settings, individuals constantly engage in emotion regulation either consciously or unconsciously as they move through their day (Koole, 2009). This pervasiveness means that through personal reflection activities and the like, the construct becomes easily relatable for language practitioners who may have had little or no previous psychological education. Emotion regulation presents the possibility for teachers to gain agency over their emotions, helping them to achieve instrumental and social goals within their professional contexts, in addition to hedonic goals related to psychological well-being. In Chapter 12, De Costa *et al.* clearly show that the inability to manage one's own emotions induces a lower sense and exercise of agency, especially within the focal context of their study where the recent trend of English as medium of instruction in Nepalese state schools caused frustration and insecurity amongst their teacher participants. From the surface and deep acting associated with emotional labour through to the up-regulation of positive emotions and the down-regulation of negative ones, there is a dizzying array of processes available to teachers for regulating their emotions. As this book helps to illustrate, though, teachers are individuals whose subjective interpretations of and emotional responses to classroom events show great diversity. Hence, we agree with Gkonou and Mercer (2017) that training programmes which focus on emotional competence should be non-prescriptive, allowing teachers to try out a range of different strategies and affording them the opportunity to reflect upon which strategies are most suitable for both themselves personally and for the different learner groups they engage with. In Chapter 11, Morris and King suggest Gross's well-known *process model of emotion regulation* (Gross, 2015) as being one useful framework for getting teachers to think about how they can better modify the course of their emotions. Presented along a situation-attention-appraisal-response timeline, the model is useful for teacher trainers because it illustrates various ways that teachers can make changes to their external environments and redirect their own thought patterns in order to manage their emotions before, during and after in-class emotional episodes take place.

The one key theme that emerges from all the book's chapters is that teaching is an emotional rollercoaster. The highs are euphoric, the lows can be dispiriting and they can occur within a very short time span. How teachers feel is linked to a combination of interacting micro-, meso- and macro-level factors. At the micro-level are individual students who can be difficult to deal with, at meso-level are issues on how to deal with the group of students or how to implement the curriculum within a particular institution, and finally at macro-level are systemic issues to do with how the teaching is organised, how teachers are trained and how much support they receive from their institution. The metaphorical flapping of the wings of a butterfly in New Mexico that causes a hurricane in China is to be replaced with the angry buzzing of a wasp in the classroom that can cause the teacher to collapse on the spot or months later. While a negative event at any level is unlikely to cause permanent negative emotions, it creates the conditions where the likelihood of something bad happening increases. If negative events at various levels align, it may have dangerous implications for the teacher. A trivial trigger could cause the dam of negative emotions to burst. Teachers thus need to be actively involved in socioemotional engineering of their own and their students' emotions (cf. Falout, Chapter 7). All authors in this volume agree that teachers can be trained to become more emotionally resilient by developing awareness of their own emotions and by developing short-term and long-term strategies to avoid burnout and stress. Regulating one's emotions is a central concept in mindfulness and martial arts. Holders of a black belt have been judged by their teachers to have gained sufficient control of body and mind, and sufficient physical and mental resilience. The practice of martial arts instils physical and spiritual skills which allow practitioners to be confident in their ability to face challenges, to defend themselves if needed, and to remain humble about their skills and achievements. It means that in combat they will not feel anger because it would mean that they cannot control their emotions. The aim of training in potentially deadly fighting techniques is to cultivate a strong character that prevents any attack in the first place. Experienced teachers are linguistic artists that share some of the skill set of black belts. They need the knowledge about language and culture, the skills to teach it, the confidence in their abilities, the emotional thermostat to sense what their students are feeling while simultaneously keeping their own emotions in check. They will be on the rollercoaster but at least they will not be blindfolded. Their ability to see ahead will allow them to tense their core when it is necessary and deflect or absorb strikes without buckling.

Final Thoughts

The chapters contributed by authors in this anthology highlight the ubiquitous nature of language teacher emotions and their impact on classroom practice and teacher professionalisation. This impact is not momentary or one-off; additionally, it does not concern just the teachers. The different chapters have shown that a range of emotions appear throughout teachers' career trajectories, most of which teachers can regulate through their own sets of strategies or even through emotional labour, thus helping towards cultivating resilience, experiencing emotional rewards and improving their professional performance. Yet others are likely to threaten their professional longevity, if teachers cannot manage them effectively and in a timely manner. Additionally, given that the emotions teachers experience influence their teaching, we can safely say that they also influence their students through processes of emotional contagion (Frenzel & Stephens, 2013).

It is therefore imperative to address teacher emotions in ways that work for individual teachers and which also take into account the specificities of their own settings, job roles and aspirations as well as their students' learning goals. We cannot confidently suggest a single way for dealing with the practical and emotional difficulties that teachers may face in their daily practice. But what we can confidently conclude is that the role of workplace emotions needs to be better understood by researchers, practitioners and teacher educators, if we are to offer a higher quality of teaching. Thus, to reach more nuanced understandings of language teacher emotions, future research could concentrate on the relationship between specific emotions and actual teaching performance. This would entail that researchers find ways to measure performance. Also, conversing with and observing the lessons of experienced language teachers could offer useful insights into how emotions work in practice and how they could be potentially managed on the spot. A final note concerns teacher education, both pre-service and in-service, in which specific interventions could be trialled, again with a view to testing their effectiveness and the extent to which they are likely to inform classroom practice. Such interventions could include training on socioemotional skills, emotion regulation strategies, shifts into teacher identities and reflection which directly addresses felt emotions. Researchers may also consider exploring why emotions are not explicitly discussed in well-known teacher education programmes and why they are perceived as less important 'soft skills' despite their influential role, as attested in this volume.

References

Brackett, M.A. and Katulak, N.A. (2006) Emotional intelligence in the classroom: Skill-based training for teachers and students. In J. Ciarrochi and J.D. Mayer (eds) *Applying Emotional Intelligence: A Practitioner's Guide* (pp. 1–27). New York: Psychology Press/ Taylor & Francis.

Dewaele, J.-M. (2018) The relationship between trait emotional intelligence and experienced ESL/EFL teachers' love of English, attitudes towards their students and institution, self-reported classroom practices, enjoyment and creativity. In H. Rawal, P. De Costa and W. Li (eds) Special issue, *Emotions in Second Language Teaching: Theory, Research and Teacher Education. Chinese Journal of Applied Linguistics* 41 (4), 468–487.

Dewaele, J.-M., Petrides, K.V. and Furnham, A. (2008) Effects of trait emotional intelligence and sociobiographical variables on communicative anxiety and foreign language anxiety among adult multilinguals: A review and empirical investigation. *Language Learning* 58 (4), 911–960.

Dewaele, J.-M., Gkonou, C. and Mercer, S. (2018) Do ESL/EFL teachers' emotional intelligence, teaching experience, proficiency and gender, affect their classroom practice? In J. de Dios Martínez Agudo (ed.) *Emotions in Second Language Teaching* (pp. 125–141). Berlin: Springer.

Dolev, N. and Leshem, S. (2017) Developing emotional intelligence competence among teachers. *Teacher Development* 21 (1), 21–39.

Frenzel, A.C. and Stephens, E.J. (2013) Emotions. In N.C. Hall and T. Goetz (eds) *Emotion, Motivation, and Self-Regulation: A Handbook For Teachers* (pp. 1–56). Bingley: Emerald.

Gkonou, C. and Mercer, S. (2017) Understanding emotional and social intelligence among English language teachers. *ELT Research Papers* 17.03. London: British Council.

Gross, J.J. (2002) Emotion regulation: Affective, cognitive, and social consequences. *Psychophysiology* 39 (3), 281–291.

Gross, J.J. (2015) Emotion regulation: Current status and future prospects. *Psychological Inquiry* 26 (1), 1–26.

Hargreaves, A. (1998) The emotional practice of teaching. *Teaching and Teacher Education* 14, 835–854.

Hen, M. and Sharabi-Nov, A. (2014) Teaching the teachers: Emotional intelligence training for teachers. *Teaching Education* 25 (4), 375–390.

King, J. and Ng, K.-Y.S. (2018) Teacher emotions and the emotional labour of second language teaching. In S. Mercer and A. Kostoulas (eds) *Language Teacher Psychology* (pp. 141–157). Bristol: Multilingual Matters.

Koole, S.L. (2009) The psychology of emotion regulation: An integrative review. *Cognition and Emotion* 23 (1), 4–41.

Kornacki, S.A. and Caruso, D.R. (2007) A theory-based, practical approach to emotional intelligence training: Ten ways to increase emotional skills. In J. Ciarrochi and J.D. Mayer (eds) *Applying Emotional Intelligence: A Practitioner's Guide* (pp. 53–88). New York: Psychology Press.

Martínez Agudo, J.D.D. (ed.) (2018) *Emotions in Second Language Teaching: Theory, Research and Teacher Education*. Berlin: Springer.

Mercer, S. and Kostoulas, A. (eds) (2018) *Language Teacher Psychology*. Bristol: Multilingual Matters.

Rawal, H., De Costa, P. and Li, W. (eds) (2018) Special issue, *Emotions in Second Language Teaching: Theory, Research and Teacher Education. Chinese Journal of Applied Linguistics* 41 (4). Berlin: De Gruyter.

Scherer, K.R. (2005) What are emotions? And how can they be measured? *Social Science Information* 44 (4), 695–729.

Schutz, P.A. and DeCuir, J.T. (2002) Inquiry on emotions in education. *Educational Psychologist* 37 (2), 125–134.

Zembylas, M. (2005) *Teaching with Emotion: A Postmodern Enactment*. Greenwich, CT: Information Age Publishing.

Index